# Ribbons and Medals

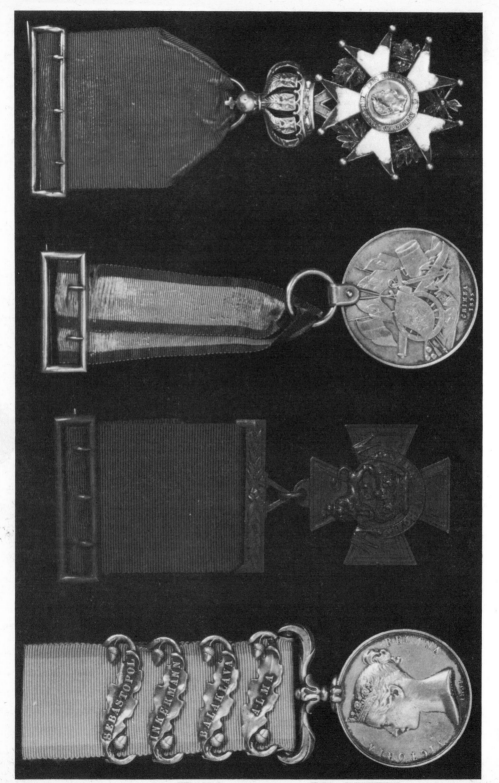

The unique group won by Colour Sergeant (later Major) John Simpson Knox (30–9–1828 to 8–1–1897), Scots Fusilier Guards, later Rifle Brigade, shown as worn. Left to right: The Crimea Medal with all four Army Bars ('ALMA', 'BALAKLAVA', 'INKERMANN' and 'SEBASTOPOL'); The Victoria Cross (inscribed with two dates on the reverse; Knox received his Cross from Queen Victoria at the first investiture on 26 June 1857 in Hyde Park, London); The Turkish Medal for the Crimea (this is the relatively rare 'British' version of the medal); Chevalier de l'Ordre Impérial de la Légion d'honneur (French nomination dated 21 June 1856). Sergeant Knox was commissioned in the field on 2nd March 1855 by H.R.H. Prince Albert in recognition of the gallantry of the Brigade of Guards at the Battle of Inkermann.

# Ribbons and Medals

## The World's Military and Civil Awards

---

By the late

### Captain H. Taprell Dorling, D.S.O., R.N.

("Taffrail")

---

In association with the late

### L. F. Guill

---

This Edition revised under the Editorship of

### Francis K. Mason

F.R.Hist.S., A.R.Ae.S., R.A.F. (Retd.)

---

### George Philip

London

**Publishing History**

| | |
|---|---|
| First published . . . . . . . | 1916 |
| New Editions . . . .1919–26, 1940, 1941, 1944, | 1946 |
| New Enlarged Edition . . . . . | 1956 |
| New Edition with Supplement . . . . | 1960 |
| Second Impression with Enlarged Supplement . . | 1963 |
| Third Impression . . . . . . | 1970 |
| New Enlarged Edition © . . . . . | 1974 |

(This Edition designed by Alban Book Services Limited)

© 1974
**GEORGE PHILIP & SON LTD.**
**SBN 0 540 07120 X**

Set in 9pt. French Old Style on 92 gsm MCC cartridge
Printed in England by
W. S. Cowell Limited, the Butter Market,
Ipswich, Suffolk

Published in Great Britain by
George Philip & Son Limited, 12–14 Long Acre,
London W.C.2, England

# List of Contents

The Publishers wish to express their gratitude
to Spink & Son Limited,
designers and manufacturers of fine insignia
for many countries of the world.
Their fine collectors stock has also been of
considerable assistance.

# Preface to the 1956 Edition

This small book, originally written in 1915 and published a year later, ran into many editions before the end of the First World War. There were further editions between 1919 and 1939, and others in 1940, 1941, 1944 and 1946.

As I have earlier explained, *Ribbons and Medals* does not pretend to give a full, authoritative, or complete account of all the Orders, Decorations and Medals which have ever been bestowed upon British subjects, or of those of every country in the world. Neither is it intended for the expert collector. It aims principally at providing a means whereby the ordinary person may recognize most of the ribbons or medals he sees worn by any sailor, soldier or airman, British or foreign, for which purpose actual pieces of the different ribbons have been reproduced in colour. Their collection has not been easy.

Since the book appeared thirty-seven years ago it has brought me masses of correspondence from all over the British Commonwealth and the world. All of it has been co-operative and helpful, and has resulted in corrections, alterations and additions being made in each successive printing. For this new edition the book has been entirely recast to include medals instituted during the Second World War and since, with alterations made in the regulations affecting various British Orders.

The Forces of all the nations of the British Commonwealth, as well as all Colonial Forces, qualified for the Orders, decorations, campaign stars and medals awarded to the strictly British Forces during the Second World War. In addition, India, Canada, Australia, New Zealand, the Union of South Africa, and Southern Rhodesia struck their own special war medals, all of which have been described.

During or since that war the Governments of Canada and the Union of South Africa also instituted their own decorations and medals which are now permanent awards, and have wholly or in part superseded former British awards. These have all been described, as have decorations and medals instituted in Eire, India, Pakistan and Burma since they attained complete independence.

However, in this new edition I have gone a good deal further than before, and, so far as the exigencies of space permit, have dealt with the awards of various other countries – the United States of America, Belgium, Brazil, Czechoslovakia, Denmark, Egypt, France, Germany, Greece, the Hashemite Kingdom of the Jordan, Luxemburg, the former state of Montenegro, the Netherlands, Norway, the Philippine Republic, Poland, Portugal, Russia (before 1917), the former state of Serbia, Spain, Sweden, Turkey, the Union of Socialist Soviet Republics, and Yugoslavia.

The collection, compilation and arrangement of a great mass of new material has been a difficult task involving considerable research and further correspondence. Selection – what to retain, and what to exclude – has been the main embarrassment; in other words, it is hoped the choice made has been a fair one.

In this and the earlier editions of the book I have to thank many people for practical help, suggestions and encouragement, and must mention the following:

Sir Robert U. E. Knox, K.C.V.O., D.S.O., Secretary of the Political Honours Committee since 1939, and Maj.-Gen. Sir Ivan De la Bere, K.C.V.O., C.B.E., Secretary of the Central Chancery of the Orders of Knighthood, whose knowledge of all British awards is unrivalled, and who have gone out of their way to answer my many questions and give me their wise counsel.

Mr. L. F. Guille, the Hon. Secretary and Treasurer of the Orders, Decorations and Medals Research

Society of Great Britain, who has been responsible for revising and bringing various sections of the book up to date, and without whose ready help and knowledge the work could not have been completed; the late Sir Arnold Wilson, M.P., who was most generous in allowing me to make use of his book *Gallantry*, written in collaboration with Captain Sir J. H. F. McEwen, Bart.; the late Mr. D. Hastings Irwin, who, many years ago, gave me permission to make use of his valuable book *War Medals and Decorations*.

Those well-known firms Messrs. A. H. Baldwin & Sons, Messrs. J. R. Gaunt & Son, and Messrs. Spink & Son, to mention them in alphabetical order, have given their unstinted and most willing assistance in many matters. Without them it would have been impossible to collect the many ribbons newly reproduced in colour for this edition. Mr. R. E. Atkinson and Mr. D. Hall, of Messrs. Baldwin; Mr. L. R. Brandham, of Messrs. Gaunt; and Mr. E. C. Joslin, of Messrs. Spink, have been most kind and patient in answering my persistent enquiries.

I am greatly indebted to Mr. J. McDonell Morgan, of Glendale, California, for permission to make use of his article on United States decorations and medals published in *Our Navy* in August 1940; and am grateful, indeed, to Mr. Morry Luxenberg, of 485 Madison Avenue, New York City, for his great kindness in sending me United States ribbons unobtainable in England, and for much useful information.

Monsieur H. Quinot, of Chaussée de Gand 772, Brussels 8, Belgium, himself the author of an authoritative book on Belgian awards, has been most helpful in conning over our Belgian section, and in providing ribbons for reproduction. Messrs. M. W. Morch & Sons, Eftf, Pederskramsgade 3, Copenhagen, have kindly done the same for Denmark. Mr. A. F. Flatow, 45 Berrylands, Surbiton, Surrey, an expert on French decorations and medals, has advised on our French section, while Mr. A. Purves, Heron's Hill, The Street, Brundall, Norwich, Norfolk, has done the same for the Netherlands.

My thanks are also greatly due to Lieut.-Colonel Howard N. Cole, O.B.E., T.D., F.R.Hist.S., for information on the varieties of the Jubilee and Coronation Medals. Colonel Cole's book on this specialized subject has lately been published by Messrs. Gale and Polden, of Aldershot.

At one time or another further material has been obtained from the Officials of the Lord Chamberlain's Department; His Excellency the Belgian Minister; the Officials of the Yugoslav Legation in London; the Secretaries of the Royal Humane Society, the Royal National Life Boat Institution and the Society for the Protection of Life from Fire; the Secretary of Lloyd's; the Secretary, Shipwrecked Fishermen and Mariners' Royal Benevolent Society; the Secretary, Liverpool Shipwreck and Humane Society; the Secretary, British North Borneo Company; Lieutenant G. B. Stockton, United States Navy; Major John Tombs; Major H. W. Channer, Royal Marines; the Chief Officer, London Fire Brigade; the Chief Officer, London Salvage Corps; G. Drummond Lovell, Esq., Cairo; and M. Kretly, of Paris, who originally supplied many of the French ribbons.

I am indebted to Major D. C. Anderson and Mr. R. D. Hogg, and to the Secretary of the Society for Cultural Relations, for details of certain of the U.S.S.R. Orders and decorations, as well as to the following:

U.S. Army Headquarters in London.
The French Embassy.
The Polish Embassy.
The Portuguese Embassy.
Lieut-Commander Moolenburgh, Royal Netherlands Navy.
The Norwegian Naval Attaché.
The Greek Naval Attaché.
The Chargé d'Affaires, the Czechoslovak Legation.
The Chargé d'Affaires, the Greek Legation.
Major H. Sharon of the Embassy of Israel in London.
Messrs. Garrard & Co. Ltd., Crown Jewellers.
The Publishers of *L'Illustration*, 13 Rue Saint Georges, Paris, for pictures and descriptions of various French medals.
Messrs. Arthus Bertrand et Cie, 46 Rue de Rennes, Paris, who supplied specimens of numerous French ribbons and medals.
The Secretary, The Order of St. John of Jerusalem.

To keep this book within sizeable limits we have had to abbreviate and to exercise a rigid selection in the letterpress. Nor have we been able to reproduce in colour ribbons of the decorations of each and every country in the world. To have done so would have meant producing a book many times the size of this volume.

TAPRELL DORLING.
*Captain, Royal Navy.*

## EDITOR'S NOTE, THIS EDITION

Following the death of Captain Dorling (and that of Mr. Guille, who died during the preparation of an Edition in 1963), *Ribbons and Medals* has been reprinted several times, but has not undergone any material revision since. The past dozen years have witnessed the coming of independence to numerous nations and the last editions of this book were seen to be somewhat dated both in content and presentation. The Publishers therefore decided to embark on a revision of the book and have taken this opportunity to benefit from the improvements recently offered by litho printing.

Broadly, this has taken the form of replacing as many as possible of the old line drawings of medals by photographs, and a re-setting of the entire text. At the same time a wholly new collection of the medal ribbons has had to be undertaken as it was found that most of the original pieces had faded; as before, this was not easy and has entailed the contacting of many hundreds of sources in Great Britain and overseas.

Despite the enlargement of the book, space has still been the limiting factor in deciding what material to include and what to omit. Nevertheless, the guidelines adopted by Captain Dorling have been retained in reaching this decision, namely to include the insignia of such awards that may reasonably be expected to be worn by the subjects of European and North American countries, and awards made by nations in circumstances involving these subjects.

Thus it is that all insignia previously covered by previous editions have been retained and, where possible, brought up to date. Next, the principal awards instituted by the 'emergent' nations have been added, including those which have gained their independence during the past fifteen years. These include Botswana, Ghana, Kenya, Malawi, Guyana, Nigeria, Sierra Leone and Uganda, as well as the Trucial States and Abu Dhabi. The opportunity has also been taken to include the Kingdom of Hawaii, whose nineteenth century awards have hitherto always presented something of an enigma owing to their great rarity.

As the subject of this book is constantly advancing, it has obviously been impossible to achieve completeness on any specific date and it is proposed to continue the process of revision and addition for future editions. To these ends the Publishers will welcome any contributing advice, information and photographs from readers who are specialists in the many varied areas of medal collecting.

I would like to express my sincere gratitude to Mr. E. C. Joslin of Spink and Son Ltd., who once again has generously given his time in the preparation of this book, and whose Company so kindly provided facilities to photograph many of the orders, decorations and medals, as well as making available information about the awards instituted by the emergent nations. My thanks are also due to Michael Dyer Associates, who undertook most of the photography and did so with such meticulous care, and to Ross McWhirter, who kindly gave me the benefit of his knowledge of and notes on certain British awards.

I would also like to record my thanks for all the advice and assistance afforded me by the Printers, W. S. Cowell Ltd., of Ipswich, and especially to Jim Lomax and his staff whose patience and experience have contributed so much in the preparation and production of this book.

It would be quite impracticable to record the names of all the hundreds of individuals and small concerns who have contributed to the collection of medal ribbons but I hope they will accept my thanks nevertheless and derive some satisfaction from the knowledge that together they made possible the preparation of this book. Finally, I should mention the following Embassies and High Commissions

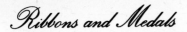

through which I was able to make contact with individuals for advice on the awards instituted by their countries:

The Embassy of the Austrian Republic
The Belgian Embassy
The Botswana High Commission
The Embassy of the Federal Republic of Germany
The Finnish Embassy
The Office of the High Commission of Ghana
The Royal Swedish Embassy

and to Novosti Press Agency for providing material on the awards instituted in the U.S.S.R.

F.K.M.
St. Albans, 1973

'To encourage all valorous hearts and to show them honourable examples.'

FROISSART: *Chronicles: XIV Century.*


'Why are young men told to look in ancient history for examples of heroism when their own countrymen furnish such lessons?'

WILLIAM NAPIER.

**1 – VICTORIA CROSS**

**2 – ORIGINAL NAVAL VICTORIA CROSS**

**3 – GEORGE CROSS**

**4 – ORDER OF THE GARTER**

**5 – ORDER OF THE THISTLE**

**6 – ORDER OF ST. PATRICK**

**7 – ROYAL ORDER OF VICTORIA AND ALBERT**

**8 – IMPERIAL ORDER OF THE CROWN OF INDIA**

**9 – ORDER OF THE BATH**

**10 – ORDER OF MERIT**

**11 – ORDER OF THE STAR OF INDIA**

**12 – ORDER OF ST. MICHAEL AND ST. GEORGE**

**13 – ROYAL GUELPHIC ORDER**

**14 – ORDER OF THE INDIAN EMPIRE**

**15 – ROYAL VICTORIAN ORDER**

**ORDER OF THE BRITISH EMPIRE (FORMER RIBBON)**
**16 – MILITARY**

**17 – CIVIL**

**ORDER OF THE BRITISH EMPIRE (CURRENT)**

**18 – MILITARY**

**19 – CIVIL**

**20 – ORDER OF THE COMPANIONS OF HONOUR**

**21 – DISTINGUISHED SERVICE ORDER**

**22 – IMPERIAL SERVICE ORDER AND MEDAL**

**23 – BARONET'S BADGE**

**24 – ROYAL RED CROSS**

**25 DISTINGUISHED SERVICE CROSS**

**26 – MILITARY CROSS**

**27 – DISTINGUISHED FLYING CROSS (CURRENT RIBBON)**

**27A – DISTINGUISHED FLYING CROSS (FORMER RIBBON)**

**28 – AIR FORCE CROSS (CURRENT RIBBON)**

**28A – AIR FORCE CROSS (FORMER RIBBON)**

**29 – ORDER OF BRITISH INDIA (2nd CLASS)**

**INDIAN ORDER OF MERIT**

**30 – MILITARY**

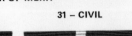

**31 – CIVIL**

**32 – KAISER-I-HIND MEDAL**

**33 – ORDER OF BURMA**

**34 – ORDER OF ST. JOHN OF JERUSALEM**

**34A – RIBBON FOR ASSOCIATES AND DONATS**

**35 – ST. JOHN LIFE SAVING MEDAL**

**36 – ALBERT MEDAL IN GOLD (SEA)**

**37 – ALBERT MEDAL (SEA)**

**38 – ALBERT MEDAL IN GOLD (LAND)**

**39 – ALBERT MEDAL (LAND)**

**40 – UNION OF SOUTH AFRICA QUEEN'S MEDAL FOR BRAVERY**

**41 – DISTINGUISHED CONDUCT MEDAL**

**CONSPICUOUS GALLANTRY MEDAL 42 – NAVY**

**CONSPICUOUS GALLANTRY MEDAL 43 – R.A.F.**

**44 – GEORGE MEDAL**

**45 – ROYAL WEST AFRICAN FRONTIER FORCE: KING'S AFRICAN RIFLES D.C.M.**

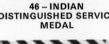

**46 – INDIAN DISTINGUISHED SERVICE MEDAL**

**47 – BURMA GALLANTRY MEDAL**

**48 – DISTINGUISHED SERVICE MEDAL (NAVY)**

**49 – MILITARY MEDAL**

**50 – DISTINGUISHED FLYING MEDAL (CURRENT RIBBON)**

**50A – DISTINGUISHED FLYING MEDAL (FORMER RIBBON)**

**51 – AIR FORCE MEDAL (CURRENT RIBBON)**

**51A – AIR FORCE MEDAL (FORMER RIBBON)**

**QUEEN'S POLICE MEDAL 52 – FOR GALLANTRY**

**QUEEN'S POLICE MEDAL 53 – FOR DISTINGUISHED SERVICE**

**54 – EDWARD MEDAL**

**55 – CONSTABULARY MEDAL (IRELAND)**

**56 – MEDALS FOR SAVING LIFE AT SEA**

**57 – INDIAN POLICE MEDAL FOR MERITORIOUS SERVICE**

**58 – BURMA POLICE MEDAL FOR MERITORIOUS SERVICE**

**COLONIAL POLICE MEDAL**
**59 – FOR GALLANTRY**

**60 – FOR MERITORIOUS SERVICE**

**61 – NAVY GOLD MEDALS**

**62 ARMY GOLD MEDALS AND CROSS**

**63 – SERINGAPATAM 1799**

**64 – NAVAL GENERAL SERVICE (1793–1840)**

**65 – MILITARY GENERAL SERVICE (1793–1814)**

**66 – WATERLOO 1815**

**67 – INDIA MEDAL (1799–1826)**

**68 – CAPTURE OF GHUZNEE 1839**

**69 – JELLALABAD 1842; 1842–43 INDIA MEDALS; KABUL-KANDAHAR STAR 1880**

**70 – CHINA 1842**

**71 – SUTLEJ CAMPAIGN (SIKH WAR) 1845–46**

**72 – NEW ZEALAND 1845–66**

**73 – PUNJAB 1848–49**

**74 – SOUTH AFRICA 1834–35; 1846–47; 1850–53; 1877–79**

**75 – INDIA GENERAL SERVICE 1854–95**

**76 – CRIMEA 1854–56**

**77 – BALTIC 1854–55**

**78 – INDIAN MUTINY 1857–58**

**79 – CHINA 1857–60 (FIRST RIBBON DESIGN)**

**79A – CHINA 1857–60 (RIBBON FINALLY ADOPTED)**

**80 – CANADA GENERAL SERVICE 1866–70**

**81 – ABYSSINIA 1867–68**

**82 – ASHANTEE 1873–74; E. & W. AFRICA 1887–1900**

**83 – AFGHANISTAN 1878–80**

**84 – CAPE OF GOOD HOPE 1880–97**

**85 – EGYPT 1882–89**

**86 – N.W. CANADA 1885**

**87 – MATABELELAND 1893, RHODESIA 1896, MASHONALAND 1897**

**88 – ASHANTI STAR 1896**

**89 – INDIA GENERAL SERVICE 1895**

**90 – CENTRAL AFRICA 1891–98**

**91 – SUDAN 1896–97**

**92 – EAST AND CENTRAL AFRICA 1897–99**

**93 – ROYAL NIGER COMPANY 1886–97**

**94 – BRITISH NORTH BORNEO 1897–98 AND 1915–16**

**95 – BRITISH NORTH BORNEO TAMBUNAN MEDAL 1899–1900**

**96 – QUEEN VICTORIA'S SOUTH AFRICA MEDAL 1899–1902**

**97 – KING EDWARD'S SOUTH AFRICA MEDAL 1901–02**

**98 – KIMBERLEY STAR 1900**

**99 – CAPE COPPER COMPANY MEDAL 1902**

**100 – CHINA 1900**

**101 – ASHANTI 1901**

**102 – TRANSPORT MEDAL**

**103 – AFRICA GENERAL SERVICE 1902**

**104 – ZULU RISING NATAL 1906**

**105 – TIBET 1903–04**

**106 – INDIA GENERAL SERVICE 1908**

**107 – NAVAL GENERAL SERVICE 1915**

**108 – 1914 STAR WITH BAR**

**109 – PROPOSED GALLIPOLI STAR**

**110 – BRITISH WAR MEDAL 1914–20**

**111 – MERCANTILE MARINE MEDAL 1914–18**

**112 – VICTORY MEDAL**

**113 – GENERAL SERVICE MEDAL (ARMY AND R.A.F.)**

**114 – TERRITORIAL FORCE WAR MEDAL 1914–19**

**115 – INDIA GENERAL SERVICE 1936**

**116 – 1939–45 STAR**

**117 – ATLANTIC STAR**

**118 – AIR CREW EUROPE STAR**

**119 – AFRICA STAR**

**120 – PACIFIC STAR**

**121 – BURMA STAR**

**122 – ITALY STAR**

**123 – FRANCE AND GERMANY STAR**

**124 – DEFENCE MEDAL**

**125 – WAR MEDAL 1939–45**

**126 – KOREA 1950**

**127 – UNITED NATIONS MEDAL, KOREA**

**128 – INDIA SERVICE MEDAL 1939–45**

## Canada

**129 – CANADA MEDAL**

**130 – VOLUNTEER SERVICE MEDAL**

**131 – CANADIAN FORCES DECORATION**

**132 – ROYAL CANADIAN MOUNTED POLICE LONG SERVICE AND GOOD CONDUCT MEDAL**

## Australia

**133 – SERVICE MEDAL 1939–45**

## New Zealand

**134 – TERRITORIAL SERVICE MEDAL (OBSOLETE)**

**135 – WAR SERVICE MEDAL 1939–45**

## Southern Rhodesia

**136 – SERVICE MEDAL**

## Union of South Africa

**137 – BOER WAR MEDAL 1899–1902**

**138 – BOER WAR DECORATION FOR DISTINGUISHED SERVICE**

**139 – BOER WAR WOUND RIBBON**

**140 – AFRICA SERVICE MEDAL**

**141 – MEDAL FOR WAR SERVICE**

17

**142 – POLAR MEDALS**

**143 – EMPRESS OF INDIA 1877**

**144 – QUEEN VICTORIA'S JUBILEE & DIAMOND JUBILEE 1887 & 1897**

**145 – QUEEN VICTORIA'S JUBILEE & DIAMOND JUBILEE CIVIL RIBBON**

**146 – POLICE MEDAL: JUBILEE & DIAMOND JUBILEE 1887 & 1897**

**147 – KING EDWARD VII's CORONATION 1902**

**148 – KING EDWARD VII's CORONATION CIVIL RIBBON**

**149 – KING EDWARD VII's CORONATION —POLICE**

**150 – DELHI DURBAR 1903**

**151 – KING EDWARD VII's VISIT TO IRELAND 1903**

**152 – KING GEORGE V's CORONATION 1911 AND DELHI DURBAR**

**153 – KING GEORGE V's CORONATION—POLICE**

**154 – KING'S VISIT TO IRELAND 1911: COMMEMORATION MEDAL**

**155 – TITLE BADGE, INDIA: 1st CLASS**

**156 – TITLE BADGE, INDIA: 2nd CLASS**

**157 – TITLE BADGE, INDIA: 3rd CLASS**

**158 – KING GEORGE V's SILVER JUBILEE 1935**

**159 – KING GEORGE VI's CORONATION 1937**

**160 – QUEEN ELIZABETH II CORONATION MEDAL**

**161 QUEEN VICTORIA FAITHFUL SERVICE MEDAL**

**162 – KING GEORGE V LONG AND FAITHFUL SERVICE MEDAL**

**163 – LONG SERVICE AND GOOD CONDUCT (ARMY)**

**164 – LONG SERVICE AND GOOD CONDUCT, PERMANENT OVERSEAS FORCES (OBSOLETE)**

**165 – ROYAL WEST AFRICAN FRONTIER FORCE & KING'S AFRICAN RIFLES LONG SERVICE AND GOOD CONDUCT**

**166 – LONG SERVICE AND GOOD CONDUCT (NAVY)**

**167 – LONG SERVICE AND GOOD CONDUCT (ROYAL FLEET RESERVE)**

**168 – MERITORIOUS SERVICE MEDAL**

**169 – MERITORIOUS SERVICE MEDAL (R.A.F.)**

**170 – LONG SERVICE AND GOOD CONDUCT (R.A.F.)**

**171 – POLICE LONG SERVICE AND GOOD CONDUCT**

**172 – AFRICAN POLICE MERITORIOUS SERVICE (OBSOLETE)**

**173 – COLONIAL POLICE LONG SERVICE**

**174 – COLONIAL FIRE BRIGADE LONG SERVICE**

**175 – VOLUNTEER OFFICERS' DECORATION; VOLUNTEER LONG SERVICE ETC.**

**176 – NAVAL GOOD SHOOTING MEDAL**

**177 – MILITIA LONG SERVICE**

**178 – IMPERIAL YEOMANRY LONG SERVICE**

**179 – TERRITORIAL AND EFFICIENCY DECORATIONS**

**180 – EFFICIENCY MEDAL**

**181 – H.A.C. SPECIAL RIBBON FOR T.D. AND EFFICIENCY MEDAL**

**182 – SPECIAL RESERVE LONG SERVICE AND GOOD CONDUCT**

**183 – R.N.R. DECORATION**

**184 – R.N.V.R. DECORATION**

**185 – R.N.R. LONG SERVICE AND GOOD CONDUCT**

**186 – R.N.V.R. LONG SERVICE AND GOOD CONDUCT**

**187 – AIR EFFICIENCY AWARD**

**188 – THE QUEEN'S MEDAL FOR CHAMPION SHOTS**

**189 – CADET FORCES' MEDAL**

**190 – COAST LIFE SAVING CORPS LONG SERVICE MEDAL**

**191 – SPECIAL CONSTABULARY MEDAL**

**192 – ROYAL OBSERVER CORPS MEDAL**

**193 – UNION OF SOUTH AFRICA COMMEMORATION MEDAL**

**194 – ST. JOHN OF JERUSALEM SERVICE MEDAL**

**195 – MEDAL FOR SOUTH AFRICA 1899–1902**

**196 – BADGE OF ORDER OF LEAGUE OF MERCY**

**197 – VOLUNTARY MEDICAL SERVICE MEDAL**

**198 – ALLIED SUBJECTS' MEDAL 1914–18**

**199 – KING'S MEDAL FOR COURAGE IN THE CAUSE OF FREEDOM**

**200 – KING'S MEDAL FOR SERVICE IN THE CAUSE OF FREEDOM**

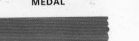

**201 – ROYAL NATIONAL LIFEBOAT INSTITUTION MEDAL**

**202 – STANHOPE GOLD MEDAL**

**ROYAL HUMANE SOCIETY**

**203 – SILVER MEDAL**

**204 – BRONZE MEDAL**

**205 – MEDALS OF THE SOCIETY FOR PROTECTION OF LIFE FROM FIRE**

**206 – LLOYD'S MEDAL FOR SAVING LIFE AT SEA**

**207 – LLOYD'S MEDAL FOR MERITORIOUS SERVICES AND FOR SERVICES TO LLOYD'S**

**208 – LLOYD'S WAR MEDAL FOR BRAVERY AT SEA**

**209 – L.C.C. MEDAL FOR BRAVERY**

**210 – L.C.C. MEDAL FOR ZEAL AND FIDELITY**

**211 – LONDON SALVAGE CORPS: LONG SERVICE MEDAL**

**212 – HONG KONG PLAGUE MEDAL 1894**

**213 – SHANGHAI MUNICIPALITY MEDAL FOR 1937**

**214 – SHANGHAI VOLUNTEER CORPS: LONG SERVICE MEDAL**

**215 – CONSPICUOUS GALLANTRY DECORATION**

**BRITISH FIRE SERVICES ASSOCIATION**

**216 – MERITORIOUS SERVICE DECORATION**

**217 – LONG AND EFFICIENT SERVICE MEDAL**

**218 – FOREIGN HONORARY MEMBERS' DECORATION**

**219 – SYRIA 1840**

**220 – TURKISH MEDAL FOR CRIMEA**

**221 – SARDINIAN MEDAL FOR VALOUR**

**222 – MEDAL FOR CHITRAL. MAHARAJAH OF JUMMOO AND KASHMIR 1895**

**223 – KHEDIVE'S BRONZE STAR 1882–91**

**224 – KHEDIVE'S SUDAN MEDAL 1896–1905**

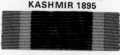

**225 – KHEDIVE'S SUDAN MEDAL 1910–21**

## *Sudan*

**SUDAN DEFENCE FORCE**

**226 – MEDAL FOR GALLANTRY**

**227 – MEDAL FOR MERITORIOUS SERVICE**

## *India*

**228 – INDEPENDENCE MEDAL**

**229 – POLICE INDEPENDENCE MEDAL**

## *Pakistan*

**230 – PAKISTAN INDEPENDENCE MEDAL 1948**

**231 – GENERAL SERVICE MEDAL**

## *Ceylon*

**232 – POLICE MEDAL FOR GALLANTRY**

**233 – POLICE MEDAL FOR MERITORIOUS SERVICE**

## Burma

**234 – AUNG SAN THURIYA**

**235 – THIHA THURA TAZEIT**

**236 – THURA TAZEIT**

**237 – AUNG SAN TAZEIT**

**238 – THIHA BALA TAZEIT**

**239 – CLASS I**

**SIT HMU HTAN GAUNG TAZEIT 240 – CLASS II**

**241 – CLASS III**

**242 – A YE DAW BON TAZEIT**

**243 – LUT LAT YE SI YONE HMU TAZEIT**

**244 – LUT MYAUK YE TAZEIT**

**245 – LUT LAT YE TAZEIT**

**246 – NAINGNGANDAW SIT HMU HTAN TAZEIT**

## Union of South Africa

**247 – CASTLE OF GOOD HOPE DECORATION**

**248 – VAN RIEBEECK DECORATION**

**249 – VAN RIEBEECK MEDAL**

**250 – CROSS OF HONOUR**

**251 – LOUW WEPENER DECORATION**

**252 – STAR OF SOUTH AFRICA**

**253 – JOHN CHARD DECORATION AND MEDAL**

**254 – SOUTHERN CROSS MEDAL**

**255 – UNION MEDAL**

**256 – POLICE GOOD SERVICE MEDAL**

# Ribbons and Medals

## Botswana

**257 – THE ORDER OF HONOUR**

**258 – THE GALLANTRY CROSS**

**259 – CONSPICUOUS SERVICE MEDAL**

**260 – MERITORIOUS SERVICE MEDAL**

**261 – POLICE LONG SERVICE AND GOOD CONDUCT MEDAL**

**262 – PRISON SERVICES LONG SERVICE AND GOOD CONDUCT MEDAL**

## Brunei

**263 – LONG SERVICE MEDAL**

## Ghana

**264 – REPUBLIC COMMEMORATIVE MEDAL**

**265 – LONG SERVICE AND EFFICIENCY MEDAL**

## Guyana

**266 – INDEPENDENCE COMMEMORATIVE MEDAL**

## Kenya

**267 – ORDER OF THE BURNING SPEAR**

**268 – THE HARAMBEE MEDAL**

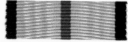

**269 – CAMPAIGN MEDAL**

## Malawi

**270 – ORDER OF THE LION**

## Nigeria

**ORDER OF THE NIGER**

**271 – COMMANDER'S BADGE**

**272 – OFFICER'S MEDAL**

**273 – MEMBER'S MEDAL**

## Sierra Leone

**274 – INDEPENDENCE MEDAL**

10ᴺ

22

## Uganda

**275 – DISTINGUISHED SERVICE ORDER**

**276 – ARMY LONG SERVICE AND GOOD CONDUCT MEDAL**

**277 – POLICE JUBILEE MEDAL**

**278 – POLICE MEDAL FOR GALLANTRY**

**279 – CONSPICUOUS GALLANTRY MEDAL (PRISON SERVICES)**

**280 – SPECIAL CONSTABULARY SERVICE MEDAL**

**281 – PRISON SERVICES LONG SERVICE AND GOOD CONDUCT MEDAL**

## United States of America

**282 – MEDAL OF HONOR**

**283 – DISTINGUISHED SERVICE CROSS (ARMY)**

**284 – BREVET MEDAL MARINE CORPS**

**285 – NAVY CROSS**

**286 – DISTINGUISHED SERVICE MEDAL (ARMY)**

**287 – DISTINGUISHED SERVICE MEDAL (NAVY)**

**288 – SILVER STAR**

**289 – LEGION OF MERIT**

**290 – DISTINGUISHED FLYING CROSS**

**291 – SOLDIER'S MEDAL**

**292 – NAVY AND MARINE CORPS MEDAL**

**293 – BRONZE STAR**

**294 – COMMENDATION (NAVY)**

**295 – COMMENDATION (ARMY)**

**296 – AIR MEDAL**

**297 – THE PURPLE HEART**

**298 – MEDAL FOR MERIT**

**299 – LIFE SAVING MEDAL (ORIGINAL RIBBON) – GOLD**

**300 – LIFE SAVING MEDAL (ORIGINAL RIBBON) – SILVER**

301 – LIFE SAVING MEDAL (PRESENT RIBBON) – GOLD

302 – LIFE SAVING MEDAL (PRESENT RIBBON) – SILVER

303 – GOOD CONDUCT (ARMY)

304 – GOOD CONDUCT (NAVY)

305 – GOOD CONDUCT (MARINE CORPS)

306 – GOOD CONDUCT (COAST GUARD)

307 – NAVAL RESERVE

308 – MARINE CORPS RESERVE

309 – CIVIL WAR 1861–65

310 – INDIAN WARS 1865–91

311 – BATTLE OF MANILA BAY 1898

312 – WEST INDIES NAVAL CAMPAIGN 1898

313 – SPANISH CAMPAIGN 1898

314 – PHILIPPINE CAMPAIGN 1899–1906

315 – CHINA 1900

316 – SPANISH WAR SERVICE

317 – PHILIPPINE CONGRESSIONAL MEDAL 1899–1913

318 – CUBAN OCCUPATION 1898–1902

319 – PORTO RICAN OCCUPATION 1898

320 – CUBAN PACIFICATION 1906–09

321 – NICARAGUA 1912

322 – MEXICAN SERVICE 1911–17

323 – MEXICAN BORDER SERVICE 1916–17

324 – HAITI, 1915, 1919–20

325 – SANTO DOMINGO 1916

326 – NICARAGUA 1926–33

327 – NC-4 MEDAL 1919

328 – BYRD ANTARCTIC EXPEDITION 1928–30

329 – SECOND BYRD ANTARCTIC EXPEDITION 1933–35

330 – ANTARCTIC EXPEDITION 1939–41

331 – YANGTSE SERVICE, 1926–27, 1930–32

332 – CHINA SERVICE 1937–39

**333 – NAVY MEDAL
(EXPEDITIONARY)**

**334 – MARINE CORPS
MEDAL (EXPEDITIONARY)**

**335 – ARMY OF OCCUPATION,
GERMANY 1918–1923
(FINAL RIBBON)**

**335A – ARMY OF OCCUPATION,
GERMANY 1918–1923
(PROVISIONAL RIBBON)**

**336 – AMERICAN
TYPHUS COMMISSION**

**337 – WOMEN'S ARMY
SERVICE CORPS MEDAL**

**338 – AMERICAN DEFENSE
SERVICE 1939–41**

**339 – EUROPEAN-AFRICAN-
MIDDLE EASTERN CAMPAIGN
1941–45**

**340 – ASIATIC-PACIFIC
CAMPAIGN 1941–45**

**341 – AMERICAN
CAMPAIGN 1941–45**

**342 – SECOND WORLD WAR
VICTORY MEDAL**

**343 – ARMY OF
OCCUPATION**

**344 – MEDAL FOR
HUMANE ACTION:
BERLIN AIR LIFT 1948–49**

**345 – KOREA 1950–53**

**346 – ARMED FORCES
RESERVE**

**347 – DISTINGUISHED
UNIT (ARMY)**

**348 – NAVY
(UNIT COMMENDATION)**

**349 – MERCHANT MARINE
COMBAT BAR**

**350 – MERCHANT MARINE
ATLANTIC WAR ZONE**

**351 – MERCHANT MARINE
PACIFIC WAR ZONE**

**352 – MERCHANT MARINE
MEDITERRANEAN AND
MIDDLE EAST WAR ZONE**

*Abu Dhabi*

**353 – UNION DEFENCE
FORCE LOYAL SERVICE
MEDAL**

**354 – GOOD SERVICE
MEDAL**

# Belgium

**355 – ORDER OF LEOPOLD**

**356 – ORDER OF THE CROWN**

**357 – ORDER OF THE CROWN**
(Gold and Silver Palms, and
Medals in gold, silver and
bronze)

**358 – ORDER OF LEOPOLD I**

**359 – ORDER OF THE
AFRICAN STAR**

**360 – ROYAL ORDER OF
THE LION**

**361 – MILITARY CROSS**

**362 – MILITARY DECORATION
(FOR DISTINGUISHED
SERVICE)**

**363 – MILITARY DECORATION
(FOR LONG SERVICE)**

**364 – CROIX DE GUERRE
1914–18**

**365 – MEDAL
''DE LA REINE ELIZABETH''
1916**

**366 – POLITICAL PRISONERS
1914–18**

**367 – CROSS FOR THOSE
DEPORTED 1914–18**

**368 – CROIX DE GUERRE
1941**

**369 – CROIX DES EVADES
1940–44**

**370 – CROSS FOR
POLITICAL PRISONERS
1940–45**

**371 – RESISTANCE MEDAL
1940–45**

**372 – MEDAL FOR
VOLUNTEERS 1940–45**

**373 – COMMEMORATION
MEDAL 1940–45**

**374 – PRISONERS OF WAR
1940–45**

**375 – MARITIME MEDAL
1940–45**

**376 – CIVIC DECORATION
1940–45**

**377 – MEDAILLE DE
REFRACTAIRE**

**378 – MEDAL FOR CIVIL
RESISTANCE**

**379 – MEDAILLE DE LA
RECONNAISSANCE BELGE**

**380 – ABYSSINIA 1941**

**381 – AFRICA 1940–45**

**382 – COLONIAL WAR
1940–45**

**383 – KOREA 1950**

## Brazil

384 – ORDER OF
MILITARY MERIT

385 – ORDER OF
NAVAL MERIT

## Czechoslovakia

386 – ORDER OF THE
WHITE LION

387 – REVOLUTIONARY
CROSS 1918

388 – WAR CROSS 1918

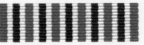
389 – WAR CROSS 1939

390 – MEDAL FOR VALOUR

391 – MILITARY
MEDAL OF MERIT

392 – ORDER OF THE
CZECHOSLOVAK REPUBLIC

## Denmark

393 – ORDER OF
DANNEBROG

394 – SLESVIG
MEDAL, 1920,
AND MEDAL OF
LIBERTY, 1946

395 – MEDAL FOR
PARTICIPATION IN
WAR OF 1940–45

396 – ROYAL MEDAL
OF RECOMPENSE

## Egypt

397 – ORDER OF
MOHAMMED ALÍ

398 – ORDER OF THE NILE

399 – ORDER OF ISMAIL

400 – MILITARY STAR
OF FOUAD I

401 – ORDER OF
AGRICULTURE

402 – ORDER FOR PUBLIC
INSTRUCTION

403 – ORDER FOR
INDUSTRY AND COMMERCE

404 – PALESTINE MEDAL

405 – MEDAL OF
MOHAMMED ALÍ

406 – LIBERATION STAR,
1952

## Ireland (Eire)

**407 – 1916 MEDAL**

**408 – GENERAL SERVICE MEDAL 1916–21**

**409 – GOLD MEDAL FOR VALOUR**

**410 – BRONZE MEDAL FOR VALOUR**

**411 – SCOTT MEDAL FOR VALOUR**

**412 – EMERGENCY SERVICE MEDAL 1939–46 (ARMED FORCES)**

**413 – (EMERGENCY SERVICE MEDAL 1939–46 (EMERGENCY SERVICES)**

**414 – MERCHANT SERVICE MEDAL 1939–46**

**415 – SERVICE MEDAL (10 YEARS)**

**416 – SERVICE MEDAL (15 YEARS)**

**417 – IRISH RED CROSS MEDAL**

## France

**418 – LEGION OF HONOUR**

**419 – MÉDAILLE MILITAIRE**

**420 – CROIX DE GUERRE 1914–18 AND ST. HELENA MEDAL**

**421 – CROIX DE GUERRE 1939–45**

**422 – CROIX DE GUERRE DES THÉATRES D'OPÉRATIONS EXTÉRIEURS**

**423 – MEDAL FOR ITALY, 1859**

**424 – TONKIN 1883–93 AND CHINA 1900–01**

**425 – MADAGASCAR 1885, 1894–95**

**426 – DAHOMEY 1892**

**427 – COLONIAL MEDAL**

**428 – MOROCCO MEDAL 1909**

**429 – MEDAL FOR FRANCO-PRUSSIAN WAR, 1870–71**

**430 – SPECIAL RIBBON FOR WOUNDED**

**431 – MÉDAILLE DE LA RECONNAISSANCE FRANÇAISE**

**432 – MÉDAILLE COMMÉMORATIVE DE LA GRANDE GUERRE 1914–18**

**433 – MEDAL FOR VICTIMS OF THE INVASION**

**434 – MEDAL OF THE ORIENT**

**435 – MEDAL OF THE DARDANELLES**

**436 – MEDAL FOR ESCAPED PRISONERS**

**437 – MEDAL FOR VOLUNTEERS FOR COMBATANT SERVICE**

**438 – COMBATANTS' CROSS**

**439 – VOLUNTARY MILITARY SERVICE MEDAL (1st & 2nd CLASS)**

**439A – VOLUNTARY MILITARY SERVICE MEDAL (3rd CLASS)**

**440 – ORDRE DE LA LIBÉRATION**

**441 – MÉDAILLE DE LA RÉSISTANCE FRANÇAISE**

**442 – COMMEMORATIVE MEDAL OF THE SECOND WORLD WAR**

**443 – MEDAL FOR THOSE DEPORTED DURING THE RESISTANCE 1939–45**

**444 – MEDAL FOR THOSE INTERNED DURING THE RESISTANCE 1939–45**

**445 – MEDAL FOR KOREA, 1952**

**446 – MÉDAILLE COMMÉMORATIVE DE RHÉNANIE**

**447 – MÉDAILLE DE HAUTE SILESIE**

**448 – MÉRITE MARITIME**

**449 – PALMES UNIVERSITAIRES**

**450 – MÉRITE NATIONALE**

**451 – ORDRE DU MÉRITE AGRICOLE**

**452 – ORDRE DU MÉRITE SOCIAL**

**453 – MEDALS FOR SAVING LIFE, ETC.**

**454 – MUNICIPAL AND RURAL POLICE LONG SERVICE MEDAL**

**455 – MÉDAILLE D'HONNEUR DES SAPEURS POMPIERS**

**456 – ORDER FOR PUBLIC HEALTH**

**457 – ORDER FOR PHYSICAL EDUCATION (1st & 2nd CLASS)**

**457A – ORDER FOR PHYSICAL EDUCATION (3rd CLASS)**

**458 – TUNISIAN ORDER OF NICHAN-IFTIKHAR**

**459 – MOROCCAN ORDER OF OUISSAM ALAOUITE**

**ORDRE DU MÉRITE SYRIEN**

**LEBANON – MÉDAILLE COMMÉMORATIVE**

**AWARDS OF THE VICHY GOVERNMENT 1940–44**

**460 – CROIX DE GUERRE**

**461 – CROIX DES COMBATTANTS**

## Germany

**462 – POUR LE MÉRITE**

**463 – IRON CROSS (1813), 1870–71, 1914–18**

**464 – IRON CROSS (1939)**

**465 – CROSS OF HONOUR 1914–18**

**466 – ORDER OF MERIT OF THE GERMAN EAGLE**

**467 – SERVICE MEDAL**

**468 – WAR MERIT CROSS 1939–45**

**469 – MEDAL OF THE WAR MERIT CROSS**

**470 – SUDETENLAND MEDAL 1938**

**471 – RUSSIAN CAMPAIGN 1941–42**

**472 – WEST WALL MEDAL**

**473 – MEDAL FOR THE RETURN OF MEMEL**

**474 – VOLUNTEERS FROM EASTERN COUNTRIES**

**475 – DECORATION FOR NATIONAL WELFARE**

**476 – ORDER OF MERIT, FEDERAL GERMAN REPUBLIC 1951**

## Greece

**477 – ORDER OF THE REDEEMER**

**478 – ROYAL ORDER OF GEORGE I**

**479 – ROYAL ORDER OF THE PHOENIX**

**480 – ROYAL FAMILY ORDER: ORDER OF ST. GEORGE AND ST. CONSTANTINE (MEN)**

**481 – ROYAL FAMILY ORDER: ORDER OF ST. OLGA AND ST. SOPHIA (LADIES)**

**482 – ORDER OF WELFARE (Sash)**

**483 – WAR CROSS 1914–18**

**484 – MEDAL OF MILITARY MERIT**

**485 – CROSS OF VALOUR**

**486 – WAR CROSS 1940–45**

**487 – NAVY CROSS**

**488 – MERCHANT NAVY CROSS**

**DISTINGUISHED FLYING CROSS**

**489 – ORIGINAL RIBBON**     **490 – CURRENT RIBBON**

**491 – AIR FORCE CROSS**

**492 – MEDAL FOR WAR WITH TURKEY 1912**

## Hashemite Kingdom of Jordan

**493 – ORDER OF AN NAHADA**

**494 – ORDER OF ISTIQLAL**

**495 – ORDER OF KAWKAB**

**496 – LONG SERVICE MEDAL**

**497 – MAAN MEDAL (HEDJAZ) 1918**

**498 – CAMPAIGN IN IRAQ AND SYRIA 1942**

**499 – WAR OF 1939–45**

**500 – PALESTINE WAR SERVICE 1947**

**501 – NATIONAL GUARD MEDAL**

## Iraq

**502 – ORDER OF FEISAL I**

**ORDER OF AL RAFIDHAIN**

**503 – MILITARY**

**504 – CIVIL**

**505 – KING FEISAL WAR MEDAL**

**506 – MEDAL FOR BRAVERY**

## Israel

**507 – FREEDOM STAR**

## Italy

**508 – ORDER OF ST. MAURICE AND ST. LAZARUS**

**509 – MILITARY ORDER OF SAVOY**

**510 – ORDER OF THE CROWN OF ITALY**

**511 – ORDER OF MERIT OF THE ITALIAN REPUBLIC**

**512 – MEDAL FOR MILITARY VALOUR**

**513 – MEDAL FOR MARITIME VALOUR**

**514 – MEDAL FOR AERONAUTICAL VALOUR**

**515 – WAR CROSS**

**516 – UNITED ITALY 1848–70**

**517 – CAMPAIGN OF 1859**

**518 – ITALIAN INDEPENDENCE 1848–70; WAR OF 1915–18**

**519 – AFRICA CAMPAIGNS 1891–96**

**520 – CHINA 1900–01**

**521 – MESSINA EARTHQUAKE 1908**

**522 – MESSINA EARTHQUAKE 1908, MEDAL OF MERIT**

**523 – LIBYA 1911**

**524 – VOLUNTEERS, WAR OF 1915–18**

**525 – ETHIOPIAN CAMPAIGN 1935**

**526 – VOLUNTEERS ETHIOPIAN CAMPAIGN 1935**

**527 – SPANISH CIVIL WAR 1936**

**528 – SPANISH CIVIL WAR 1936**

**529 – VOLUNTEERS, SPANISH CIVIL WAR**

**530 – ALBANIA 1939**

**531 – CAMPAIGN AGAINST FRANCE 1940**

**532 – GREECE 1940**

**533 – AXIS MEDAL 1941**

**534 – DALMATIA 1941**

**535 – OCCUPATION OF GREECE 1941**

**536 – AFRICA CAMPAIGN 1940–43**

**537 – WAR MEDAL 1940–43**

**538 – LONG SERVICE MEDAL (ARMY)**

**539 – LONG SERVICE MEDAL (NAVY)**

**540 – THE MARCH ON ROME 1922 (FASCIST)**

**FASCIST MEDALS**

**541**

**542**

## *Japan*

543 – ORDER OF THE RISING SUN 544 – ORDER OF THE SACRED TREASURE 545 – ORDER OF THE GOLDEN KITE 546 – RUSSO-JAPANESE WAR 1904–05

547 – WAR WITH GERMANY 1914–18 548 – MANCHURIA 1931, 1934 549 – CHINA "INCIDENT" 1937

## *Luxembourg*

550 – ORDER OF THE OAK CROWN 551 – CROIX DE GUERRE 552 – MILITARY MEDAL

## *Montenegro*

553 – ORDER OF DANILO 554 – MEDALS FOR BRAVERY

## *Muscat and Oman*

555 – THE OMAN GALLANTRY MEDAL 556 – THE OMAN MEDAL FOR BRAVERY 557 – THE OMAN ACCESSION MEDAL 558 – THE OMAN GENERAL SERVICE MEDAL

559 – THE OMAN CAMPAIGN MEDAL

33

## Netherlands

**560 – MILITAIRE WILLEMSORDE**

**561 – LIFE SAVING MEDAL**

**562 – NEDERLANDSCHE LEEUW**

**563 – ORDE VAN ORANJE NASSAU**

**564 – BRONZEN LEEUW**

**565 – BRONZEN KRUIS**

**566 – KRUIS VOOR VERDIENSTE**

**567 – VLIEGERKRUIS**

**568 – 'EXPEDITION CROSS'**

**569 – WAR COMMEMORATION CROSS 1940–45**

**570 – OFFICERS' LONG SERVICE CROSS**

**571 – KRUIS VOOR RECHT EN VRIJHEID (KOREA 1951)**

**572 – PRINCESS JULIANA WEDDING 1937**

**573 – QUEEN JULIANA CORONATION 1948**

**574 – AIR RAID PRECAUTIONS SERVICE 1940–45**

## Norway

**575 – ROYAL ORDER OF ST. OLAF**

**576 – WAR CROSS**

**577 – WAR MEDAL**

**578 – FREEDOM CROSS**

**579 – KING HAAKON VII 70th ANNIVERSARY MEDAL**

**580 – MEDAL FOR HEROIC DEEDS**

## Philippine Republic

**581 – LEGION OF HONOUR**

**582 – PHILIPPINE DEFENCE MEDAL**

**583 – PHILIPPINE LIBERATION MEDAL**

**584 – PHILIPPINE INDEPENDENCE RIBBON**

## Poland

**585 – ORDER OF THE WHITE EAGLE**

**586 – ORDER OF MILITARY VIRTUE (VIRTUTI MILITARI)**

**587 – ORDER OF POLONIA RESTITUTA**

**588 – INDEPENDENCE CROSS AND MEDAL 1919**

**589 – CROSS OF VALOUR 1920**

**590 – CROSS OF VALOUR 1939**

**591 – CROSS OF MERIT**

**592 – MEDAL FOR WAR OF 1918–21**

**593 – MONTE CASSINO 1944**

**594 – NAVAL ACTIVE SERVICE MEDAL**

**595 – ARMY ACTIVE SERVICE MEDAL**

**596 – AIR FORCE ACTIVE SERVICE MEDAL**

**597 – WARSAW MEDAL 1939–45**

**598 – ODER, NEISSE AND BALTIC MEDAL 1945**

**599 – PARTISAN'S CROSS**

## Portugal

**600 – MILITARY ORDER OF ST. BENEDICT OF AVIZ**

**601 – ORDER OF ST. JAMES OF THE SWORD**

**602 – MILITARY ORDER OF CHRIST**

**603 – MILITARY ORDER OF THE TOWER AND SWORD**

## Russia (Pre-1917)

**604 – ORDER OF ST. ANNE**

**605 – ORDER OF ST. STANISLAS**

**606 – ORDER OF ST. GEORGE**

**607 – ORDER OF ST. VLADIMIR**

**608 – PERSIAN WAR 1826–28**

## Serbia

**609 – ORDER OF THE WHITE EAGLE**

**610 – ORDER OF ST. SAVA**

**611 – STAR OF KARAGEORGE**

**612 – ALL ORDERS AND MEDALS FOR SERVICES DURING WAR OF 1914–18**

## Spain

613 – ORDER OF
THE GOLDEN FLEECE

614 – ORDER OF CHARLES III

615 – ORDER OF
ST. FERDINAND

616 – ORDER OF
ST. HERMENGILDE

617 – ORDER OF ISABELLA
THE CATHOLIC

618 – ORDER OF
MILITARY MERIT

619 – ORDER OF
NAVAL MERIT

620 – ORDER OF
MARIA-LOUISA

## Sweden

621 – ORDER OF
THE SWORD

622 – CROWN PRINCE
GUSTAV'S SILVER
WEDDING 1906

623 – MEDAL FOR
BRAVERY IN WAR

624 – MEDALS FOR
BRAVERY AT SEA,
LAUDABLE ACTIONS, ETC.

## Turkey

625 – ORDER OF THE
MEDJIDIE

626 – ORDER OF THE
OSMANIEH

627 – ORDER OF CHEFAKAT

628 – STAR FOR
GALLIPOLI 1915

## U.S.S.R.

629 – ORDER OF VICTORY

630 – ORDER OF
LENIN

631 – ORDER OF
THE RED
BANNER

632 – ORDER OF
SUVOROV
(1st CLASS)

633 – ORDER OF
KUTUZOV
(1st CLASS)

634 – ORDER OF
ALEXANDER
NEVSKY

635 – ORDER OF
GLORY

636 – ORDER OF
THE PATRIOTIC
WAR

637 – ORDER OF
THE RED STAR

638 – INSIGNIA OF
HONOUR

639 – DEFENCE OF
STALINGRAD

640 – DEFENCE OF
THE CAUCASUS

641 – CAPTURE
OF BERLIN

642 – LIBERATION
OF WARSAW

643 – VALIANT
LABOUR IN
THE GREAT
PATRIOTIC
WAR 1941–45

# Introduction

There is generally a certain amount of mystification attached to the strips of coloured ribbon worn in uniform by the officers and men of Her Majesty's fighting forces and the police. People associate the pieces of coloured silk with Orders, Decorations and Medals, but comparatively few can distinguish them by a mere glance at the ribbons.

Most have their distinctive colourings, and though it is true that many decorations may be won in times of peace, a tolerably complete summary of a man's fighting career may often be obtained by noting the coloured strips on his coat or tunic.

It is laid down that British subjects shall wear the ribbons of their Orders, Decorations and Medals in a certain sequence on their left breasts, the position of priority being in the centre of the chest. Medals awarded by Societies for saving life, if authorized to be worn, are carried on the right breast.

The sequence is as follows:

1. The Victoria Cross.
2. The George Cross.
3. British Orders.
4. British Medals.
5. Foreign Orders in order of date of award.
6. Foreign Decorations in order of date of award.
7. Foreign Medals in order of date of award.

## ORDERS

The British Orders take precedence as shown in the official list of the Central Chancery of the Orders of Knighthood, printed after this Introduction. Here it is sufficient to state that the ribbons of the Orders of the Garter, the Thistle and St. Patrick are not worn in undress uniform, whereas the ribbons of all other Orders, including those of the Orders of Merit and of the Companions of Honour, are so worn.

Unlike many foreign Orders, which have rosettes or other embellishments on the undress ribbons, to indicate their grade, there is nothing to show the class of a British Order when the ribbon is worn alone.

For the order in which the badges of Orders, their miniatures, and the ribbons when they alone are worn in undress, should be displayed, see Note at the top of page **41**.

## DECORATIONS

Generally speaking, anything which is not an Order or a Medal is usually held to be a 'Decoration.' The Victoria Cross and George Cross are in a class by themselves; but the Distinguished Service Cross, Military Cross, Distinguished Flying Cross, Air Force Cross, Royal Red Cross, Order of British India, Kaisar-i-Hind Medal, the Order of St. John of Jerusalem, with the Volunteer and Territorial Officers' Decorations, and the Royal Naval Reserve and R.N. Volunteer Reserve Officers' Decorations are cases in point.

## MEDALS

Medals fall naturally into four distinct groups:

1. Medals for gallantry in action, or for saving life in peace.
2. Medals for war service.
3. Commemoration Medals.
4. Medals for long service and good conduct.

Among the medals for gallantry in action are the Distinguished Conduct Medal and Military Medal for the Army, and their counterparts, the Conspicuous Gallantry Medal and Distinguished Service Medal for the Navy, and the Conspicuous Gallantry and Distinguished Flying Medals for the Royal Air Force. These, all given for war service, are worn immediately before war medals. The Albert Medals, George Medal, the Medal for Saving Life at Sea, the Edward Medal, the Queen's Police Medal, the

Queen's Fire Service Medal, Air Force Medal and the British Empire Medal, among others, are also worn before war medals.

It is to be noted that the Edward Medal, and the Queen's Police Medal and the Queen's Fire Service Medal, for Gallantry, are now only awarded posthumously, their place for living persons having been taken by the George Cross, George Medal, or British Empire Medal.

Immediately after war medals come the Polar medals awarded for Arctic and Antarctic exploration; then the various official Commemoration medals; and, finally, the various decorations and medals awarded for long and meritorious service; or long service and good conduct.

Medals for war service were not issued generally to all the officers and men engaged until well into the nineteenth century, the only exception in Great Britain being the medal for the Battle of Dunbar, 1650, which was awarded by the vote of the House of Commons to all officers and men of the Parliamentary forces who had been present at the battle. In India a medal for the storming and capture of Seringapatam in 1799 was distributed to officers and men, European and native, who had taken part. Details will be found later.

Throughout the Peninsular War (1808–14) medals were only conferred upon senior officers, and it was not until 1848, by which time many of the veterans had died natural deaths, that the Military General Service Medal, with bars for campaigns or engagements in various parts of the world, was issued to the surviving junior officers and men. It seems strange to think that participants in battles like Maida, 4 July 1806, or Albuera, 10 May 1811, went unrewarded for forty-two and thirty-seven years respectively.

The only exception to this was the Battle of Waterloo, 1815, for a medal was issued in 1816 to all officers and men who had taken part in it.

The Navy suffered in much the same way, though, for Lord Howe's victory over the French off Ushant, on 1 June 1794 – 'the Glorious First of June' – the admirals and captains engaged were rewarded with gold medals, a custom which obtained in all subsequent naval actions except Copenhagen. The junior officers and men received no such distinction till 1848, when the Naval General Service Medal, with, among many others, a bar for 'June 1st, 1794,' was issued.

After the Battle of the Nile – 1 August 1798 – Lord Nelson's Prize Agent, a Mr. Davison, issued a medal at his own expense to every officer and man engaged. It was given in gold to admirals and captains, in silver to lieutenants and warrant officers, in bronze-gilt to petty officers, and in bronze to the seamen and marines. The medals were bestowed privately, but were worn and highly prized by their recipients, while the gift cost the donor the best part of £2,000.

For the Battle of Trafalgar, too, a Mr. Boulton of Birmingham requested and received the necessary permission to strike and present a medal to every British officer and man engaged on 21 October 1805. It was given in gold to admirals, in silver to captains and lieutenants and in pewter to junior officers and men. Mr. Davison also gave a special Trafalgar Medal in pewter to the officers and ship's company of Lord Nelson's flagship H.M.S. *Victory*.

According to modern ideas it is surprising to think that it was left for private individuals to reward officers and men who had taken a gallant part in such great and far-reaching victories as the Battles of the Nile and Trafalgar, but no official medal with bars for these battles was issued until 1848, just fifty and forty-three years after they had been fought!

It was in the forties of the last century that it became customary to grant a medal to all officers and men who had taken part in a campaign. At first the rather awkward expedient was adopted of inscribing the name of each important battle on the medal itself, and, as a case in point, we may mention the Candahar, Ghuznee and Cabul Medals of 1842, all given for the same war in Afghanistan. They were worded on the reverse, or back, 'CANDAHAR 1842,' 'GHUZNEE. CABUL 1842,' 'CANDAHAR. GHUZNEE. CABUL. 1842' or 'CABUL 1842,' and, as a consequence, a casual inspection of a recipient's medal, worn obverse to the front, would not reveal whether, for instance, he was the possessor of the Cabul Medal, or the one for Candahar, Ghuznee and Cabul, to earn which he must have seen far more fighting. The system, therefore, was far from satisfactory.

### CLASPS OR BARS

The medals for the Sutlej campaign, 1845–6, all bore the name of a battle on the reverse, and an officer or man who fought in any one engagement received the appropriate medal. For each subsequent battle he received a bar, a silver bar-shaped attachment worn on the ribbon, and inscribed with the name of the engagement.

For the Punjab campaign, 1848–9, however, the medal without a bar was given to all men who served in the Punjab province, i.e. those who were within the sphere of operations, between certain dates. Those who had taken part in the three principal battles, 'Chilianwala,' 'Mooltan' and 'Goojerat,' received, in addition to the medal, bars so worded. In some more modern medals the bars bore dates to cover the periods during which the recipients were on active service, instead of the names of battles or places. See the South African Medal for 1877–9.

Dated bars, 'South Africa 1901,' and 'South Africa 1902,' were issued with Queen Victoria's and King Edward's medals for that campaign to those who qualified for them, while others inscribed 'Natal,' 'Cape Colony,' 'Orange Free State' or 'Transvaal,' were given with the Queen's medal to those officers and men who had served in the territories named within certain dates, but who had not received a bar for a specific engagement fought in that territory. The bars mentioned, therefore, could be earned without actual fighting.

What are known as 'General Service Medals' were first instituted to obviate the multiplication of medals. In other words, the same medal was given for all small wars or expeditions in a certain country or continent, while bars attached to the ribbon denoted the particular service for which the medal was awarded. When we come to count the number of different medals issued for wars in India between about 1839 and 1854 it will be seen that some such expedient was very necessary. Good examples of General Service Medals are the 'India Medal 1854,' the award of which, with twenty-three different bars, continued up till 1895; the East and West Africa Medal, 1887–1900; the Africa General Service Medal of 1902; the Naval General Service Medals of 1848 and 1915; the India General Service Medals of 1908 and 1936; and the General Service Medal of 1918 confined to the Army and the Royal Air Force.

## CAMPAIGN STARS

The award of stars for particular expeditions or operations started in 1843, with the grant of a special star for the Gwalior Campaign. Other examples are the Kabul to Kandahar Star of 1880; the Khedive's Bronze Star for the Egyptian Campaigns of the 1880's; the Ashanti Star, 1896; the 1914 and 1914–15 Stars of the First World War; and the 1939–45, Atlantic, Air Crew Europe, Africa, Pacific, Burma, Italy, and France and Germany Stars awarded for service in the Second World War. No doubt these campaign stars, similar in appearance but with different inscriptions and ribbons, the latter designed by King George VI, were instituted to show at a glance where their recipients had served, and also to obviate the expensive and laborious process of striking and issuing a large number of engagement bars to be worn on the war medal. Details of certain distinctive bars and emblems awarded with the eight campaign stars for the Second World War are to be found in the text.

## UNOFFICIAL AWARDS

Unofficial medals for life-saving, awarded by the Royal Humane Society and the Royal National Lifeboat Institution, with the Life Saving Medal of the Order of St. John of Jerusalem, are allowed to be worn on the right breast in uniform by officers and men of the Royal Navy, Army and Royal Air Force. Otherwise, no unofficial medal may be so worn unless *official* permission has been granted for a gallantry or life-saving medal to be worn *on all occasions*. Not more than one unofficial medal may be worn for any one act of bravery, and not more than two for one act of bravery if an official British or foreign medal has been awarded for the same deed.

There are numerous other unofficial decorations and medals awarded by Societies, Institutions, Corporations, and Local Authorities, for gallantry or long service, which are not officially recognized. Among others these include such awards as those of the Corporation of Lloyd's, the London County Council, the British Fire Services Association, and the Royal Society for the Prevention of Cruelty to Animals.

As the Sovereign is the Fount of Honour, and because a full range of State awards is available for the recognition of gallantry in the shape of the George Cross, the George Medal, the British Empire Medal, and the Queen's Commendation, to name them in descending order, no unofficial awards other than those already named can correctly be worn at Court or in the Queen's uniform, though, as already said, permission may be given in exceptional circumstances for a gallantry or life-saving medal to be worn on all occasions.

The same does not apply to long service or good conduct medals awarded by Local Authorities. A Police Long Service and Good Conduct Medal was instituted by Royal Warrant in June 1951. It applied to full-time serving members of all ranks in the Metropolitan Police; the City of London Police; in Police Forces maintained by local Police authorities in England, Wales and Scotland; in the Royal Ulster Constabulary; in the Police Forces of the Isle of Man and the Channel Islands; in the Constabulary of Government Departments and the British Transport Commission; in the Dock Police Forces of the United Kingdom; and in the Constabulary maintained by the Ulster Transport Authority.

The twelfth paragraph of the Royal Warrant instituting the Police Long Service Medal runs – 'It shall be a condition of the award of the Medal in any Police Force or Constabulary that the grant of the Imperial Service Medal or any unofficial or local long service or good conduct medals for wear in such Force shall be discontinued, and that any unofficial or long service medals, if already granted, shall not be worn by a recipient of our Police Long Service and Good Conduct Medal.'

The Police and members of Fire Brigades are both on the same footing for all the official awards for gallantry or distinguished service, and there has recently been authorised a Long Service and Good Conduct Medal for firemen.

### MINIATURE MEDALS, RIBBONS, ETC.

Miniature medals, small reproductions provided by the wearers themselves, are allowed to be worn by officers in uniform evening dress, and, on special occasions, in plain clothes evening dress. It is not known when the use of these miniatures was authorized by regulation, though photographs of officers taken soon after the Crimean War show them being worn. The earliest miniature medals of all, however, date from about 1817, when officers who had received the Waterloo Medal had small replicas made for their wives to wear.

The custom of wearing ribbons alone in undress seems to have become usual during the late fifties.

There is a widespread belief that medals won by fathers may be worn by sons; but there is nothing to support such an idea. It is true, of course, that medals of deceased officers and men, including the Victoria Cross, are given to their nearest relatives, but this does not imply that they are to be worn.

It is a punishable offence for soldiers and sailors on the active list to sell or otherwise dispose of their medals and decorations, but men who lose them accidentally are usually allowed to purchase duplicates.

British subjects are not allowed to accept and wear foreign Orders and medals without first obtaining Her Majesty's sanction, but no permission is necessary to accept a foreign medal if such medal is not to be worn. Permission to accept and wear foreign decorations is only granted, as a rule, in cases where they have been earned during war or for saving life.

In various books and official documents on the subject the engagement bars worn on the ribbons of medals are variously referred to as 'bars' or 'clasps.' Throughout this small volume the term 'bar' is used to describe the inscribed bar worn on the ribbon; and 'clasp' the means by which the medal is suspended from its ribbon.

I have also used the term 'ribbon' to denote the silk ribbon from which an Order or medal is suspended, and 'riband' to describe the ribbon-like device which may be incorporated in the actual badge of an Order.

The 'obverse' of a medal, too, is the front, or side, generally bearing the Sovereign's head, worn uppermost; and the 'reverse,' the back.

## ORDER OF WEARING

THE FOLLOWING LIST SHOWS THE ORDER IN WHICH ORDERS, DECORATIONS AND MEDALS SHOULD BE WORN. IT IN NO WAY AFFECTS THE PRECEDENCE CONFERRED BY THE STATUTES OF CERTAIN ORDERS UPON THE MEMBERS THEREOF.

VICTORIA CROSS.
GEORGE CROSS.
BRITISH ORDERS OF KNIGHTHOOD, ETC.
  [1] Order of the Garter.
  [1] Order of the Thistle.
  [1] Order of St. Patrick.
  Order of the Bath.
  [2] Order of Merit (immediately after Knights Grand Cross of the Order of the Bath).
  Order of the Star of India.
  Order of St. Michael and St. George.
  Order of the Indian Empire.
  [3] Order of the Crown of India.

Royal Victorian Order (Classes I, II and III).
Order of the British Empire (Classes I, II and III).
  [2] Order of the Companions of Honour (immediately after Knights and Dames Grand Cross of the Order of the British Empire).
Distinguished Service Order.
Royal Victorian Order (Class IV).
Order of the British Empire (Class IV).
Imperial Service Order.
Royal Victorian Order (Class V).
Order of the British Empire (Class V).

NOTE. The Order of Wearing shown above applies to those Orders of similar grades. When the miniature or ribbon of a higher grade of a junior Order is worn with that of a lower grade of a senior Order, the higher grade miniature or ribbon should come first, e.g. the miniature or ribbon of a K.C.I.E. will come before a C.B., and a G.C.M.G. before a K.C.B. Not more than four Stars of Orders and not more than three neck Badges may be worn at any time in Full Dress Uniform. The ribbons of Orders, when the ribbon alone is worn, will be of the width of the ribbons of the Membership of the Order. If there is no Membership Class the ribbon will be of the width of the ribbon of the Companionship of the Order.

BARONET'S BADGE. (The Badge is worn suspended round the neck by the riband in the same manner as the neck badge of an Order and takes precedence immediately after the Badge of the Order of Merit. It is not worn in miniature and the riband is not worn with undress uniform.)

KNIGHTS BACHELOR'S BADGE. (The Badge is worn after the Star of a Knight Commander of the Order of the British Empire. It is not worn in miniature and is not worn with undress uniform.)

[5] INDIAN ORDER OF MERIT (Military).
DECORATIONS.
  Royal Red Cross (Class I).
  Distinguished Service Cross.
  Military Cross.
  Distinguished Flying Cross.
  Air Force Cross.
  Royal Red Cross (Class II).
  Order of British India.
  Kaisar-i-Hind Medal.
  Order of St. John.

MEDALS FOR GALLANTRY AND DISTINGUISHED CONDUCT
  Union of South Africa Queen's Medal for Bravery, in Gold.
  Distinguished Conduct Medal.
  Conspicuous Gallantry Medal.
  George Medal.
  Queen's Police Medal, for Gallantry.
  Queen's Fire Service Medal for Gallantry.
  Edward Medal.
  Royal West African Frontier Force Distinguished Conduct Medal.
  King's African Rifles Distinguished Conduct Medal.
  Indian Distinguished Service Medal.
  Union of South Africa Queen's Medal for Bravery, in Silver.
  Distinguished Service Medal.
  Military Medal.
  Distinguished Flying Medal.
  Air Force Medal.
  Constabulary Medal (Ireland)
  [4] Medal for Saving Life at Sea.

[5]Indian Order of Merit (Civil).
Indian Police Medal for Gallantry.
Ceylon Police Medal for Gallantry.
Colonial Police Medal for Gallantry.
[6]British Empire Medal.
Canada Medal.
Queen's Police Medal, for Distinguished Service.
Queen's Fire Service Medal, for Distinguished Service.
Queen's Medal for Chiefs.

WAR MEDALS (in order of date of campaign for which awarded).
POLAR MEDALS (in order of date).
ROYAL VICTORIAN MEDAL (Gold, Silver and Bronze).
IMPERIAL SERVICE MEDAL.
POLICE MEDALS FOR VALUABLE SERVICES.
Indian Police Medal for Meritorious Service.
Ceylon Police Medal for Merit.
Colonial Police Medal for Meritorious Service.

BADGE OF HONOUR.
JUBILEE, CORONATION AND DURBAR MEDALS.
Queen Victoria's Jubilee Medal, 1887 (Gold, Silver and Bronze).
Queen Victoria's Police Jubilee Medal, 1887.
Queen Victoria's Jubilee Medal, 1897 (Gold, Silver and Bronze).
Queen Victoria's Police Jubilee Medal, 1897.
Queen Victoria's Commemoration Medal, 1900 (Ireland).
King Edward VII's Coronation Medal, 1902.
King Edward VII's Police Coronation Medal, 1902.
King Edward VII's Durbar Medal, 1903 (Gold, Silver and Bronze).
King Edward VII's Police Medal, 1903 (Scotland).
King's Visit Commemoration Medal, 1903 (Ireland).
King George V's Coronation Medal, 1911.
King George V's Police Coronation Medal, 1911.
King's Visit Police Commemoration Medal, 1911 (Ireland).
King George V's Durbar Medal, 1911 (Gold,[7] Silver and Bronze).
King George V's Silver Jubilee Medal, 1935.
King George VI's Coronation Medal, 1937.
Queen Elizabeth II Coronation Medal, 1953.

King George V's Long and Faithful Service Medal.
King George VI's Long and Faithful Service Medal.
Queen Elizabeth II Long and Faithful Service Medal.

EFFICIENCY AND LONG SERVICE DECORATIONS AND MEDALS.
Long Service and Good Conduct Medal.
Naval Long Service and Good Conduct Medal.
Medal for Meritorious Service.
Indian Long Service and Good Conduct Medal (for Europeans of Indian Army).
Indian Meritorious Service Medal (for Europeans of Indian Army).
Royal Marine Meritorious Service Medal.
Royal Air Force Meritorious Service Medal.
Royal Air Force Long Service and Good Conduct Medal.
Indian Long Service and Good Conduct Medal (for Indian Army).
Royal West African Frontier Force Long Service and Good Conduct Medal.
King's African Rifles Long Service and Good Conduct Medal.
Indian Meritorious Service Medal (for Indian Army).
Police Long Service and Good Conduct Medal.
Fire Brigade Long Service and Good Conduct Medal.
African Police Medal for Meritorious Service.
Royal Canadian Mounted Police Long Service Medal.
Ceylon Police Long Service Medal.
Ceylon Fire Services Long Service Medal.
Colonial Police Long Service Medal.
Colonial Fire Brigades Long Service Medal.
Colonial Prison Service Medal.
Army Emergency Reserve Decoration.
Volunteer Officers' Decoration.
Volunteer Long Service Medal.
Volunteer Officers' Decoration (for India and the Colonies)
Volunteer Long Service Medal (for India and the Colonies).
Colonial Auxiliary Forces Officers' Decoration.
Colonial Auxiliary Forces Long Service Medal.
Medal for Good Shooting (Naval).
Militia Long Service Medal.
Imperial Yeomanry Long Service Medal.

Territorial Decoration.
Efficiency Decoration.
Territorial Efficiency Medal.
Efficiency Medal.
Special Reserve Long Service and Good Conduct Medal.
Decoration for Officers of the Royal Naval Reserve.
Decoration for Officers of the Royal Naval Volunteer Reserve.
Royal Naval Reserve Long Service and Good Conduct Medal.
Royal Naval Volunteer Reserve Long Service and Good Conduct Medal.
Royal Naval Auxiliary Sick Berth Reserve Long Service and Good Conduct Medal.
Royal Fleet Reserve Long Service and Good Conduct Medal.
Royal Naval Wireless Auxiliary Reserve Long Service and Good Conduct Medal.
Air Efficiency Award.
Queen's Medal (for Champion Shots in the Military Forces).

Queen's Medal for Champion Shots of the Air Forces.
Cadet Forces Medal.
[8] Coast Life Saving Corps Long Service Medal.
Special Constabulary Long Service Medal.
Canadian Forces Decoration.
Royal Observer Corps Medal.
Civil Defence Medal.
Union of South Africa Commemoration Medal.
Indian Independence Medal.
Pakistan Medal.
Ceylon Armed Services Inauguration Medal.
Service Medal of the Order of St. John.
Badge of the Order of the League of Mercy.
Voluntary Medical Service Medal.
Women's Voluntary Service Medal.
South African Medal for War Services.
Colonial Special Constabulary Medal.
[9] FOREIGN ORDERS (in order of date of award).
[9] FOREIGN DECORATIONS (in order of date of award).
[9] FOREIGN MEDALS (in order of date of award).

**1**   These Orders are not worn in miniature and the ribbons of the Orders are not worn with undress uniform.
**2**   These Orders are not worn in miniature, but are worn round the neck on all occasions except with service dress and certain Orders of undress uniform.
**3**   This Order is not worn in miniature.
**4**   The official medal awarded previously on the recommendation of the Board of Trade, Minister of Shipping or Minister of War Transport and now on the recommendation of the Minister of Transport.
**5**   The Indian Order of Merit (Military and Civil) is distinct from the Order of Merit instituted in 1902.
**6**   Formerly the medal of the Order of the British Empire for Meritorious Service; also includes the medal of the Order awarded before 29 December 1922.
**7**   King George V's Durbar Medal, 1911, in gold, could be worn in the United Kingdom only by those who received it as Ruling Chiefs in India.
**8**   The official medal for service with a Rocket Life-Saving Apparatus Company or Brigade, awarded previously on the recommendation of the Board of Trade, the Minister of Shipping or Minister of War Transport, and now on the recommendation of the Minister of Transport.
**9**   These awards may be worn only when the Queen's permission has been given.

Campaign stars and medals awarded for service during the First World War, 1914–19, should be worn in the following order: 1914 Star, 1914–15 Star, British War Medal, Mercantile Marine War Medal, Victory Medal, Territorial Force War Medal, India General Service Medal (1908) for operations in Afghanistan (1919). Campaign stars and medals awarded for service in the Second World War, 1939–45, should be worn in the following order: 1939–45 Star, Atlantic Star, Air Crew Europe Star, Africa Star, Pacific Star, Burma Star, Italy Star, France and Germany Star, Defence Medal, Volunteer Service Medal of Canada, War Medal 1939–45, Africa Service Medal of the Union of South Africa, India Service Medal, New Zealand War Service Medal, Southern Rhodesia Service Medal, Australia Service Medal. A Pakistan General Service Medal was instituted by King George VI in 1951.

The order of wearing of the Africa General Service Medal (1902), India General Service Medal (1908), Naval General Service Medal (1915), General Service Medal (Army and Royal Air Force) (1918), and India General Service Medal (1936) varies, and depends upon the dates of participation in the relevant campaigns.

## NOTE ON MENTIONS IN DESPATCHES AND KING'S, OR QUEEN'S, COMMENDATIONS

### MENTION IN DESPATCHES, 1914–19

The Emblem of bronze oak leaves, denoting a Mention in Despatches during the First World War, 1914–19, is worn on the ribbon of the Victory Medal. The award of this Emblem ceased as from 10 August 1920.

### MENTION IN DESPATCHES, 1920–39

The single bronze oak leaf Emblem, if granted for service in operations between the two World Wars, is worn on the ribbon of the appropriate General Service Medal. If a General Service Medal has not been granted, the Emblem is worn directly on the coat, after any medal ribbons.*

### MENTION IN DESPATCHES, 1939–45

The single bronze oak leaf Emblem signifying in the armed Forces and the Merchant Navy, either a Mention in Despatches, a King's Commendation for brave conduct, or a King's Commendation for valuable service in the air, if granted for service in the Second World War, 1939–45, is worn on the ribbon of the War Medal, 1939–45. If the War Medal has not been granted, the Emblem is worn directly on the coat, after any medal ribbons.*

### MENTION IN DESPATCHES, 1945, AND SUBSEQUENTLY

The single bronze oak leaf Emblem, if granted for service in operations after the cessation of hostilities in the Second World War, is worn on the ribbon of the appropriate General Service Medal. If a General Service Medal has not been granted, the Emblem is worn directly on the coat after any medal ribbons.*

The single bronze oak leaf Emblem is also used in the Forces to denote a King's or Queen's Commendation for brave conduct or a King's or Queen's Commendation for valuable service in the air granted since the cessation of hostilities in the Second World War.

### KING'S OR QUEEN'S COMMENDATION FOR BRAVE CONDUCT, 1939–45, AND SUBSEQUENTLY

The Emblem of silver laurel leaves granted to civilians, other than those in the Merchant Navy, to denote a King's Commendation for brave conduct during the Second World War, 1939–1945, is worn on the ribbon of the Defence Medal. When the Defence Medal has not been granted or the award is for services subsequent to the war, the Emblem is worn directly on the coat, after any medal ribbons.*

### KING'S OR QUEEN'S COMMENDATION FOR VALUABLE SERVICE IN THE AIR, 1939–1945, AND SUBSEQUENTLY

The oval silver Badge, granted to denote a civil King's or Queen's Commendation for valuable service in the air, is worn on the coat immediately below any Medals or Medal ribbons,* or in civil air line uniform, on the panel of the left breast pocket.

* If there are no medal ribbons, the emblem is worn in the position in which a single ribbon would be worn.

*(Compiled from a list printed in the Supplement to the London Gazette, 27 July 1951.)*

# RIBBONS AND MEDALS

## *British Orders and Decorations*

### 1-2 - THE VICTORIA CROSS

The Victoria Cross, the most highly coveted decoration which it is possible for any sailor, soldier or airman, officer or man, to obtain, was instituted by Queen Victoria in 1856 at, it is said, the suggestion of the Prince Consort. The decoration consists of a bronze cross pattée, 38 mm. across with raised edges. On the obverse, in the centre, is a lion gardant standing upon the Royal Crown, while below the crown are the words, 'FOR VALOUR,' on a semi-circular scroll. The reverse has raised edges like the obverse, and the date of the act for which the decoration is bestowed is engraved in a circle in the centre. The Cross is suspended by means of a plain link from a V, which is part of the clasp, ornamented with laurel leaves, through which the ribbon passes, and on the back of this clasp is engraved the name, rank and ship or regiment of the recipient. The Cross was traditionally and for many years manufactured from the bronze of guns captured in the Crimea, but this supply was exhausted in March 1942. The ribbon, 38 mm. wide; originally blue for the Navy, and crimson for the Army. The latter colour, really a sort of claret, was adopted during the First World War for the Navy, Army and Royal Air Force.

The V.C. was established during the Crimean War for rewarding individual officers and men of the Navy and Army who performed some signal act of valour or devotion to their country in the presence of the enemy. Bars could be awarded for subsequent gallant acts. For recipients below the rank of commissioned officer the Cross was accompanied by a pension of £10 a year with an extra £5 for each bar. From 1898 the pension might be increased to £50 in cases where recipients were in reduced circumstances. In July 1959, the Prime Minister announced that a tax-free annuity of £100 was authorized for all the 220 holders of the V.C., both officers and other ranks, for whom the British Government was responsible. Anyone who has received the V.C., but who is afterwards convicted of treason, cowardice, felony or of any other infamous crime, may have his name erased from the list of recipients. There have been eight such forfeitures since the decoration was instituted, the last in 1908. This number included one midshipman who had won the V.C. in the Crimea.

**1-2 - THE VICTORIA CROSS**

45

In 1857 the European officers and men in the East India Company's Service were declared eligible for the decoration; while in 1858 it was ordained that cases of great bravery performed *not* in the presence of the enemy were admissible. The only cases on record, however, where the V.C. was granted in the latter circumstances were in 1867, when it was bestowed on Private Timothy O'Hea, of the 1st Battalion of the Rifle Brigade, for his courageous behaviour in helping to extinguish a fire in an ammunition railway car during the Fenian Raid in Canada, 1866, and upon a surgeon and four privates of the 24th Regiment of Foot for bravery in saving the lives of companions in a storm at sea in the Andaman Islands in May 1867. In 1858 the award of the Cross was extended to civilians who had distinguished themselves during the Indian Mutiny, and was so granted in four cases, while in 1867 the officers and men of the Colonial Forces were also declared to be eligible. In 1881 the qualification for the decoration was again defined to be 'conspicuous bravery or devotion to the country in the presence of the enemy,' while officers and men of the auxiliary and reserve forces, Navy and Army, and Chaplains, were also declared eligible.

The first distribution of the Victoria Cross was made on 26 June 1856, when Queen Victoria personally decorated sixty-one recipients. Fourteen of these belonged to the Royal Navy, and forty-seven to the Army.

In 1902 King Edward issued an order to the effect that Victoria Crosses earned by soldiers and sailors who had been killed should be delivered to the relatives. Before this date, when officers or men had been recommended for the V.C., but had died before its bestowal, the recipients' names appeared in the official *Gazette*, but the decoration was never actually conferred. The order was made retrospective, so that surviving relatives of men who had won the Cross as far back as in the Crimean War, or the Indian Mutiny, but had died whilst performing their gallant deeds, received the coverted token. During the First and Second World Wars various Victoria Crosses were given posthumously.

In 1912 King George V extended the award to native officers and men of the Indian Army, who up to that time had only been eligible for the Indian Order of Merit for gallant deeds in action. Officers and men of the Merchant Navy serving under Naval, Military or Air Force authority, or who in the course of their duty may become subject to enemy action, are eligible for the award of the Cross, as are women of the three fighting Services, matrons, nursing sisters, nurses and staff nurses, together with members of nursing or other services pertaining to hospitals and nursing, and civilians of either sex serving regularly or temporarily under the orders, direction or supervision of the Navy, Army or Air Force. No woman has so far received the V.C.

If any unit is engaged in an action of outstanding gallantry (for instance, the blocking of Zeebrugge on 23 April 1918) recipients for the V.C. may be chosen by ballot from among the whole number engaged. If less than 100 persons are present, one officer may be chosen by the officers; one warrant officer, petty officer or N.C.O.

by the warrant officers, petty officers or N.C.O.s; and one seaman, marine, soldier or airman by them. With any number between 100 and 200 present the number of seamen, soldiers, etc., selected shall be two. If the number present is more than 200, the case is specially considered by the Admiralty, War Office or Air Ministry. In all cases the ballot is secret.

The Victoria Cross takes precedence of all other Orders and medals. Only 1,343 Crosses (of which 290 were posthumous) and three bars have been awarded from the date of institution in 1856 until the present time. Captain A. Martin Leake, awarded the V.C. in 1902 during the South African War, received a bar for gallantry in France between 20 October and 8 November 1914. Captain N. G. Chevasse, awarded the Cross for bravery at Guillemont, France on August 9, 1916, earned a bar for services at Wieltje, Belgium, between 31 July and 2 August 1917. Second Lieutenant C. H. Upham, of the New Zealand Military Forces, who earned the Cross for bravery in Crete between 22 and 30 May 1941, was awarded a bar for gallantry in the Western Desert on 14 July 1942.

Recipients of the Victoria Cross, when the ribbon alone is worn in undress uniform, bear a miniature replica of the decoration, in bronze, on the ribbon. An additional replica is worn if a bar is subsequently awarded.

Three cases have occurred of the V.C. being bestowed upon father and son. Lieutenant (afterwards Field-Marshal) Earl Roberts, of the Bengal Artillery, was awarded the decoration in 1858 for gallantry during the Indian Mutiny. His son, Lieutenant the Hon. F. H. S. Roberts, of the King's Royal Rifle Corps, won the Cross in the South African War, at the battle of Colenso, Natal, on 15 December 1899.

Captain W. N. Congreve, of the Rifle Brigade, was awarded the V.C. for gallantry in the South African War on 15 December 1899, and his son, Brevet Major W. la T. Congreve, also of the Rifle Brigade, received the decoration for bravery in France between 6 and 20 July 1916.

Major C. J. S. Gough, of the 5th Bengal European Cavalry, was granted the Cross for bravery during the Indian Mutiny on four occasions between August 1857 and February 1858. His son, Captain and Brevet Major J. E. Gough, of the Rifle Brigade, received the coveted decoration for gallantry in Somaliland on 22 April 1903.

There are four cases of the Victoria Cross being bestowed upon brothers – Major C. J. S. Gough, already mentioned, and his brother, Lieutenant H. H. Gough, 1st Bengal European Light Cavalry, for gallantry in November 1857 and February 1858 during the Indian Mutiny.

Major R. W. Sartorius, 6th Bengal Cavalry, Ashanti 1874 and his brother, Captain E. H. Sartorius, 59th Foot, Afghanistan 1874.

2nd Lieut. A. B. Turner, Berkshire Regt., France 1915 and his brother, Major V. B. Turner, Rifle Brigade, Western Desert 1942.

Lieutenant (temporary Lieut-Colonel) R. B. Bradford, of the Durham Light Infantry, earned his V.C. for bravery at Eaucourt l'Abbaye, France, on 1 October 1916, and his brother, Lieutenant-Commander G. N. Bradford, R.N., of H.M.S. *Iris*, for gallantry at the blocking expedition on Zeebrugge, on 23 April 1918.

As various enquiries have been received on the subject, the list which follows shows the number of Crosses awarded over certain periods:

| Service | 1856–1914 | 1914–18 | 1920–38 | 1939–45 | Post-1945 |
|---|---|---|---|---|---|
| Royal Navy<br>Royal Marines<br>R.N.R., R.N.V.R.<br>R.N.A.S. | } 44 | 35 +<br>16 P. | — | 15 +<br>8 P. | — |
| Army | 373 +<br>10 P. | 291* +<br>124* P. | 1 P. | 28 +<br>33 P. | 2 +<br>2 P. |
| R.F.C. and R.A.F. | — | 7 +<br>2 P. | — | 11 +<br>11 P. | — |
| Australia | 5 | 49 +<br>14 P. | — | 11 +<br>8 P. | — |
| Canada | 4 | 40 +<br>22 P. | — | 8 +<br>5 P. | — |
| New Zealand | 2 | 7 +<br>3 P. | — | 7* +<br>2 P. | — |
| Newfoundland | — | 1 | — | — | — |
| South Africa | 19 +<br>2 P. | 4 | — | 2 +<br>1 P. | — |
| Fiji | — | — | — | 1 P. | — |
| King's African Rifles | — | — | — | 1 P. | — |
| Indian Army | 57 +<br>2 P. | 12 +<br>6 P. | 1 +<br>3 P. | 17 +<br>13 P. | — |
| Civilians | 4 | — | — | — | — |
| TOTALS | 508 +<br>14 P. | 446 +<br>187 P. | 1 +<br>4 P. | 99 +<br>83 P. | 2 +<br>2 P. |
| | 522 | 633 | 5 | 182 | 4 |

\* Includes one bar.            1,343 Crosses
P. Indicates a posthumous award.          3 Bars

GRAND TOTAL 1,346

to which should be added the award made to the American Unknown Warrior.

## 3 - THE GEORGE CROSS

The original warrant of 24 September 1940, instituting the George Cross, was cancelled by a new warrant of 8 May 1941, printed in the *London Gazette* of 24 June 1941. It was then laid down that the decoration should consist of a plain silver cross with a circular medallion in the centre bearing a representation of St. George and the Dragon surrounded by the words 'FOR GALLANTRY.' In the angle of each limb of the cross is the Royal cypher 'GVI.' The reverse is plain and bears the name of the recipient and date of award. The Cross hangs by a ring from a silver bar adorned with laurel leaves, and the ribbon, officially described as 'dark blue,' is 38 mm. wide. When awarded to women, the Cross is worn on the left shoulder from a ribbon of the same width and colour and tied in a bow. When the ribbon alone is worn in undress uniform, a silver replica of the Cross is worn in the centre of it. Recipients are entitled to the use of the letters G.C. after their names, while bars may be awarded for further acts of heroism. For each bar awarded a silver replica of the Cross, in addition to that already worn, shall be added to the ribbon when it is worn alone.

The George Cross, which may be awarded posthumously, is awarded 'only for acts of the grestest heroism or of the most conspicuous courage in circumstances of extreme danger.' It superseded the Medal of the Order of the British Empire for Gallantry, and any recipient of that medal was required to return it to the Central Chancery of the Orders of Knighthood and to receive the George Cross instead.

The Cross is intended primarily for civilians throughout the Commonwealth – men and women – and award to members of the Fighting Services is confined to actions for which purely military honours are not normally granted. The George Cross was conferred upon the Island of Malta in recognition of the gallantry of its inhabitants during the war of 1939–45.

Up to the end of 1972 138 awards of the George Cross had been made (excluding that made to Malta), of which four were to women. No bar has yet been awarded.

3 - THE GEORGE CROSS

## BRITISH ORDERS

What may be called the 'full dress insignia' of the highest classes of the various British Orders of Knighthood, i.e. Collars, Mantles, Hoods, Surcoats, Hats, etc., are only worn on special occasions, or when commanded by the Sovereign.

In full dress uniform on ordinary occasions Knights of the Garter, Thistle and St. Patrick; Knights Grand Cross of the Bath, St. Michael and St. George and the Royal Victorian Order; or Knights Grand Commanders of the Star of India and the Indian Empire, wear the stars of their respective Orders on the left breast, and the badge on one hip from a broad sash passing over the opposite shoulder.

Knights of the Garter and Thistle wear their ribbons over the left shoulder, with the badge on the right hip; Knights of St. Patrick and Knights Grand Cross or Grand Commanders of other Orders *vice versa.*

The Collar and Ribbon of an Order are never worn together.

In undress uniform, when ribbons alone are being worn, members of the superior grades of Orders wear the ribbons of Companions, for instance, in undress a G.C.S.I. would wear the 38-mm. ribbon of a C.S.I. sewn on his coat.

The ribbons of the Garter, Thistle and St. Patrick are not worn in undress uniform. Those illustrated in the coloured plates, Numbers 4, 5 and 6, are the ribbons worn by the Prelates of these three Orders, and have been inserted to show the colours.

## 4 - THE MOST NOBLE ORDER OF THE GARTER

This Order, established by King Edward III, in 1348, is the premier Order of Great Britain, and is one of the most ancient in Europe. It comprises the Sovereign and twenty-six Knights only. Extra Knights may be admitted by special statute.

The insignia of the Order comprises:

*A Garter* of dark blue velvet and gold, bearing the motto 'HONI SOIT QUI MAL Y PENSE' in golden letters. It is worn by H.M. the Queen on the left arm above the elbow, and by Knights on the left leg below the knee.

*A Mantle* of blue velvet lined with taffeta, with the star of the Order embroidered on the left breast.

*A Hood* of crimson velvet.

*A Surcoat* of crimson velvet, lined with white taffeta.

*A Hat* of black velvet, lined with white taffeta, and fastened thereto by a band of diamonds, a plume of white ostrich and black heron's feathers.

*A Collar* of gold, composed of alternate buckled garters, each encircling a red enamelled rose, and lovers' knots in gold, though sometimes described as enamelled white.

*The George,* an enamelled figure of St. George fighting the dragon, suspended from the Collar.

*The Lesser George, or Badge,* similar to 'the George,' but encircled by an oval garter bearing the motto, and worn on the right hip from a broad, dark blue ribbon passing over the left shoulder.

**4 - THE MOST NOBLE ORDER OF THE GARTER**
*(Star and Badge)*
*Shown approximately half full size*

*The Star*, a silver, eight-pointed star, bearing in its centre the red cross of St. George on a white ground, surrounded by the garter and motto, and worn on the left breast.

The Garter, Mantle, Hood, Surcoat, Hat, Collar and George are only worn on special occasions, or when commanded by the Sovereign. In ordinary full dress a Knight of the Garter wears the Lesser George and Star only. The ribbon of the Order is not worn in undress uniform. At death the insignia of the Order are returned by the Knight's nearest male relative. The Star of the Order of the Garter is used as a regimental badge by the Coldstream Guards.

## 5 - THE MOST ANCIENT AND MOST NOBLE ORDER OF THE THISTLE

This Order, supposed to have been created in A.D. 787 was revived in 1687 by King James II, and was re-established by Queen Anne, 31 December 1703. It now consists of the Sovereign and sixteen Knights.

The insignia of the Order comprises:

*A Star*, consisting of a silver star in the shape of a St. Andrew's Cross, with other rays issuing between the points of the cross and, in the centre, on a gold background, a thistle enamelled in proper colours surrounded by a green circle bearing the motto, 'NEMO ME IMPUNE LACESSIT' in gold letters, worn on the left breast.

*A Collar* of gold of alternate thistles and sprigs of rue enamelled in proper colours.

*A Mantle* of green velvet bound with taffeta, and tied with cords and tassels of green and gold, and having on its left side a figure of St. Andrew bearing his Cross, surrounded by a circlet of gold bearing the motto of the Order.

*The Badge or Jewel*, a golden image of St. Andrew in green gown and purple surcoat, bearing before him the Cross, enamelled white, the whole surrounded by rays of gold. This is worn pendent from the collar, or on the right hip from a dark green ribbon passing over the left shoulder.

In ordinary full dress the Star, Badge and ribbon alone are worn, the Collar and Mantle being used on special occasions, or when ordered by the Sovereign. The ribbon of the Order is not worn in undress uniform. At death, the insignia of the Order are returned. Among other regiments, the Scots Guards, Royal Scots, Royal Scots Fusiliers and Black Watch, incorporate portions of the insignia of the Order of the Thistle on their colours, badges or appointments.

## 6 - THE MOST ILLUSTRIOUS ORDER OF ST. PATRICK

This Order was instituted by King George III in 1783, and at first consisted of the Sovereign, the Lord-Lieutenant of Ireland and twenty-two Knights; also certain Extra and Honorary Knights.

The insignia of the Order comprises:

*A Star;* a silver, eight-pointed star, having in its centre, on a white field, the Cross of St. Patrick in red enamel charged with a green

**5 - THE MOST ANCIENT AND MOST NOBLE ORDER OF THE THISTLE**
*(Star and Badge)*
*Shown approximately half full size*

51

trefoil, bearing a crown on each leaf, surrounded by a sky-blue enamel circle inscribed with the motto, 'QUIS SEPARABIT,' and the date 'MDCCLXXXIII.'

*A Mantle* of sky-blue satin made in Ireland, lined with white silk, and on the right shoulder a hood of the same. The mantle is fastened by a silk cord of blue and gold, and it has the star of the Order embroidered on the left side.

*The Collar*, of gold, composed of five roses and six harps alternately, each tied together with a knot of gold. The roses are enamelled alternately, white leaves within red, and red within white. In the centre of the Collar is a golden harp surmounted by an Imperial Crown, and from this hangs *the Badge*, similar to the central device of the star, but oval in shape, and surrounded by a wreath of trefoil.

In ordinary full dress the Star and Badge alone are worn, the latter being suspended on the left hip from a sky-blue ribbon, 100 mm. wide, passing over the right shoulder. At death the insignia of the Order are returned by the Knight's nearest male relative. The ribbon of the Order is not worn in undress uniform. The Star of the Order of St. Patrick is worn as a regimental badge by the Irish Guards.

6 - **THE MOST ILLUSTRIOUS ORDER OF ST. PATRICK**
(*Star and Badge*)
(*Shown approximately half full size*)

## 7 - THE ROYAL ORDER OF VICTORIA AND ALBERT

This Order was founded by Queen Victoria in 1862, and comprised the Sovereign and forty-five ladies. It is divided into four classes, the first and second of which are comprised entirely of Royal personages, foreign as well as British. The third class is composed of titled ladies, or 'Honourables.' The badges of the *First* and *Second Classes* consist of an onyx cameo with the busts of Queen Victoria and the Prince Consort, surmounted by an Imperial Crown. They are both set in diamonds, the *Second Class* badge being somewhat smaller. The badge of the *Third Class* is set in pearls, while that of the *Fourth Class* is in the form of a monogram, 'V. & A' set with pearls and surmounted by an Imperial Crown. The ribbon from which the badges are suspended is worn on the left shoulder in the form of a bow, and is white moiré, 38 mm. wide.

## 8 - THE IMPERIAL ORDER OF THE CROWN OF INDIA

This Order was instituted on 1 January 1878, and consisted of the Sovereign, and of such of the Princesses of His Majesty's Royal and Imperial House, the wives or other female relatives of Indian Princes, and other Indian ladies, and of the wives or other female relatives of any of the persons who had held or were holding the offices of Viceroy and Governor-General of India, Governors of Madras or Bombay, or of Principal Secretary of State for India, as the Sovereign might think fit to appoint. The badge consists of the Royal and Imperial monogram in diamonds, turquoises and pearls. It is surrounded by an oval border of pearls and surmounted by a jewelled Imperial Crown. It is worn on the left shoulder hung from a bow of light blue ribbon, edged white.

## THE ROYAL FAMILY ORDERS

(Worn only by the Queen or by the female relatives of the Sovereign.)

King George IV (1820–30) established a Royal Family Order, one such decoration being worn by the King's sister, Charlotte Augusta Matilda, Princess Royal, who married in 1797 Frederick Charles William, King of Wurtemburg. It consisted of a miniature of the King, heavily bordered with diamonds and surmounted by a Crown, also embellished in diamonds. That worn by the King's niece, Augusta Caroline Elizabeth Mary Sophia Louisa, daughter of the King's brother, first Duke of Cambridge, who married H.R.H. Frederick William, Grand Duke of Mecklenburg-Strelitz, had the same miniature with a single border of large diamonds and surmounted by a Crown, also in diamonds. Both these decorations were suspended by diamond loops from a ribbon of sky blue moiré 50 mm. wide, tied in a bow and worn on the left shoulder.

Queen Victoria wore the Royal Order of Victoria and Albert, *First Class*, established in 1862, with the cameo cut with the Prince Consort's head in front.

The Royal Family Order of King Edward VII also consisted of a miniature of the King heavily bordered in diamonds with the diamond Crown above, and was worn from a ribbon, 38 mm. wide, of dark blue bordered by narrow stripes of yellow and broader stripes of crimson with narrow black edges.

A similar Order was established by King George V, and had the King's miniature surrounded by a single border of large diamonds and surmounted by a Crown in diamonds. The ribbon, tied in a bow, was 50 mm. wide and of light blue moiré of a paler shade than that used by King George IV.

The Royal Family Order of King George VI, of similar design to that just described, with the King's miniature, was worn from a bow of pink moiré 50 mm. wide.

## FAMILY ORDER OF QUEEN ELIZABETH II

The Family Order of Queen Elizabeth II, conferred by Her Majesty only upon ladies of the Royal Family, is similar in general design to that of King George VI. It consists of an oval miniature of the Queen, painted on ivory, framed in silver set with diamonds, surmounted by a gold crown of the new reign with red-enamelled cushion. The Order hangs from a bow of very pale yellow silk moiré ribbon 50 mm. wide.

## 9 - THE MOST HONOURABLE ORDER OF THE BATH

The Order of the Bath was founded in 1399, and revived by King George I in 1725. Like the Orders of the Garter, the Thistle and St. Patrick, it originally had one class only, that of Knight, or K.B. Popularly known as the 'Red Riband' it was awarded to senior officers for services in action, and the insignia consisted of a crimson sash worn over the right shoulder with a badge and star similar to that of the present Civil G.C.B. The gold and enamel military badges were not instituted until 1815, when, after the Battle of Waterloo, the Order was extended to three classes for the purpose

*(Shown full size)*

*Star of Military G.C.B.*                    *Star of Military K.C.B.*

*The Military Badge*

# 9 -
# THE MOST HONOURABLE
# ORDER OF THE BATH

*The Civil Badge*

## 9 - THE MOST HONOURABLE ORDER OF THE BATH
(*Shown full size*)

*The Badge of Military K.C.B.*

*The Badge of Military G.C.B.*

of rewarding more junior officers for services in action, and to obviate the issue of the gold medals awarded to senior officers during the Peninsular War. It was later laid down that the C.B. could only be conferred upon officers of or above the rank of Commander in the Navy, or Major in the Army, who had been mentioned in despatches for services in war, and that they might subsequently be advanced to the higher grades of the Order. At the present time all officers of the three Services awarded the C.B. are appointed to the military division.

The civil branch of the Order was established in 1847.

There are three classes in each division, viz. *Knight Grand Cross* (G.C.B.); *Knight Commander* (K.C.B.); and *Companion* (C.B.).

The insignia are as follows:

*The Collar* of gold, composed of nine crowns and eight devices, each consisting of a rose, a thistle and a shamrock issuing from a sceptre all enamelled in their proper colours. The crowns and devices are linked together with gold, white-enamelled knots. From the Collar hangs:

*The Badge. The Military Badge* is a gold Maltese cross of **eight**

55

points, enamelled white, each point tipped with a small gold ball, and in each angle between the arms of the cross a gold lion. In the centre of the cross is a device consisting of the rose, thistle and shamrock issuing from a sceptre, and three Imperial Crowns. This device is surrounded by a red enamel circle, on which is the motto 'Tria Juncta in Uno,' in gold letters. The circle is again surrounded by two branches of laurel, enamelled green, and below is a blue enamel scroll with the words 'Ich Dien' in gold.

*The Civil Badge* is of gold filigree work, and is oval. It consists of a bandlet bearing the motto, and in the centre is the usual device of the rose, thistle and shamrock issuing from a sceptre, and the three crowns.

*A Knight Grand Cross* (G.C.B.) wears the Collar on special occasions only. On ordinary full dress occasions he wears the badge (military or civil, as the case may be) on the left hip, suspended from a broad crimson ribbon passing over the right shoulder.

He wears, in addition, a star on the left breast.

*Star of Military G.C.B.* A gold Maltese cross of the same pattern as the military badge, mounted on a silver flaming star.

*Star of Civil G.C.B.* A silver, eight-pointed star, with a central device of three crowns upon a silver ground, encircled by the motto on a red enamel ribbon.

*A Knight Commander* (K.C.B.) wears a smaller sized badge (military or civil, as the case may be) suspended round the neck from a crimson ribbon, and, in addition, a star on the left breast.

*Star of Military K.C.B.* – A star with the gold Maltese cross omitted, and in the shape of a silver cross pattée.

*Star of Civil K.C.B.* – Similar to that of a Military K.C.B., but without a laurel wreath.

*A Companion of the Order* (C.B.) wears a smaller sized badge (military or civil, as the case may be) suspended round the neck from a crimson ribbon.

In undress uniform a G.C.B. or a K.C.B. wears the ribbon of a C.B.

## 10 - ORDER OF MERIT

This Order was instituted in 1902, and is awarded very rarely to officers of the fighting services and to civilians for very distinguished and conspicuous services either in peace or in war. The badge consists of a gold cross, pattée convexed, enamelled red, edged blue, with, in the centre of the obverse, the words 'For merit' on a blue ground. In the centre of the reverse is the Royal cypher. The cross is surmounted by a Tudor crown, and is worn round the neck from a ribbon, half blue, half crimson, 50 mm. in width. Naval or military recipients of the Order have two silver crossed swords between the arms of the cross in their badge, but in the case of civilian recipients the swords are omitted. Those who have recevied the Order of Merit have the right to use the letters 'O.M.' after their names. The badge is not worn in miniature, but the ribbon is now authorized to be worn on the coat in undress uniform.

**10 - ORDER OF MERIT**

## 11 - THE MOST EXALTED ORDER OF THE STAR OF INDIA

This Order was instituted·by Queen Victoria in 1861, and the dignity of Knight Grand Commander (G.C.S.I.) could be conferred upon Princes or Chiefs of India, or upon British subjects, for important and loyal services rendered to the Indian Empire. The *Second* and *Third Classes* of the Order (K.C.S.I. and C.S.I.) were bestowed for similar services of not less than thirty years' duration. The Order at first consisted of the Sovereign; a Grand Master (the Viceroy of India); 36 Knights Grand Commanders (18 British and 18 Indian); 85 Knights Commander (K.C.S.I.); and 170 Companions (C.S.I.). The badge is an onyx cameo bearing the effigy of Queen Victoria, set in a gold, ornamental oval containing the motto of the Order – 'HEAVEN'S LIGHT OUR GUIDE' – in diamonds, on a pale blue ground, surmounted by a star in chased silver.

The *insignia* of a *G.C.S.I.* consists of a gold collar, formed of lotus flowers, palm branches and united red and white roses, from which the badge is suspended; a star, consisting of golden rays issuing from a centre, having thereon a diamond star resting upon a circular ribbon of light blue enamel, bearing the motto in diamonds and a mantle of light blue satin with a representation of the star on the left side, and tied with a white silk cord with blue and silver tassels. The collar and mantle, however, are only worn on special occasions, and in ordinary full dress uniform a G.C.S.I. wears the star on the left breast, and the badge on the left hip from a broad light blue, white edged ribbon or sash passing over the right shoulder.

A *K.C.S.I.* wears the badge round his neck from a ribbon 50 mm. wide, and a star – similar to that of a G.C.S.I., but in silver – on the left breast.

A *C.S.I.* wears the badge suspended round the neck from a ribbon 38 mm. wide.

In undress uniform G.C.S.I.s and K.C.S.I.s wear the ribbons of a C.S.I.

## 12 - THE MOST DISTINGUISHED ORDER OF ST. MICHAEL AND ST. GEORGE

This Order was founded in 1818 by King George III, and is usually conferred upon British subjects as a reward for services abroad or in the British Commonwealth. The Order is divided into three classes: Knights Grand Cross (G.C.M.G.); Knights Commander (K.C.M.G.); and Companions (C.M.G.). The insignia are as follows:

*The collar* of gold, formed alternately of lions of England, of Maltese crosses in white enamel, and of the cyphers S.M. and S.G., with, in the centre, two winged lions, each holding a book and seven arrows.

*The badge* is a gold seven-pointed star with V.-shaped extremities, enamelled white and edged gold, surmounted by the Imperial Crown. In the centre, on one side is a representation in enamel of St. Michael encountering Satan and on the other, St. George on horseback fighting the dragon. This device is surrounded by a

*Badge or Jewel*

*Star*

**11 - THE MOST EXALTED ORDER OF THE STAR OF INDIA**
*Shown approximately half full size*

## 12 - THE MOST DISTINGUISHED ORDER OF ST. MICHAEL AND ST. GEORGE
*(Shown full size)*

*Star of Knights Grand Cross*

*The ba*

circle of blue enamel, bearing the motto, 'AUSPICIUM MELIORIS ÆVI,' in gold.

*The mantle* is of Saxon blue, lined with scarlet silk, tied with cords of blue and sarlet silk and gold, and having on the left side the star of the Order.

*The chapeau*, or hat, is of blue satin, lined with scarlet, and surmounted by black and white ostrich feathers.

*Knights Grand Cross* (G.C.M.G.) wear the collar, mantle and chapeau on special occasions, or when commanded by the Sovereign; but in ordinary full dress wear the badge on the left hip from a broad ribbon, Saxon blue, with a central scarlet stripe, passing over the right shoulder, and a star on the left breast. This is a silver star of seven rays, with a gold ray between each, and over all the Cross of St. George in red enamel. In the centre is a representation of St. Michael encountering Satan within a blue-

58

circular riband bearing the motto, 'AUSPICIUM MELIORIS ÆVI.'

*Knights Commanders* wear the badge suspended round the neck from a narrower ribbon of the same colours, and, on the left breast, a silver eight-pointed star charged with the red St. George's Cross, and with the same central device as the G.C.M.G. Star.

*Companions* wear the badge suspended round the neck from a ribbon 38 mm. wide. In undress uniform Knights Grand Cross and Knights Commanders wear the ribbon of Companions of the Order.

### 13 - THE ROYAL GUELPHIC ORDER (now obsolete)

This Hanoverian Order was founded by H.R.H. the Prince Regent, afterwards George IV of Great Britain, in 1815, and was not conferred after the death of William IV in 1837. It was more British than Hanoverian, and the last British Grand Cross was the Duke of Cambridge.

The cross or badge was of gold, with a lion between each division. In the centre, on a ground of red enamel, was the white horse of Hanover, surrounded by a circle of light blue enamel with the motto, in gold letters, 'NEC ASPERA TERRENT.' Surrounding the circle was a laurel wreath. On the reverse was the monogram G.R. in gold letters on a red ground, surmounted by the British Crown and surrounded by a gold circle with the date of the institution, 'MDCCCXV.'

The cross was surmounted by the Hanoverian Crown, and below it were two crossed swords.

The star was of silver with eight points, the centre being similar to the centre of the badge, but with two crossed swords between the divisions of the star, in gold, on the silver radiations. The ribbon was of light blue watered silk.

The Civil Order was of the same design as the Military with the exception of the crossed swords which were omitted on the star and badge, while an oak wreath was substituted for the laurel.

There were three classes of the Order in both the Military and Civil divisions – *Knight Grand Cross*, with sash and star; *Knight Commander*, with neck badge and star; and *Knight*, with the badge on the breast. Gold and silver medals were attached to the Order. They had on the obverse the bust of the Prince Regent, and on the reverse the inscription 'VERDIENST UMS VATERLAND,' the whole surrounded by a laurel wreath.

During the twenty-two years of its existence the Royal Guelphic Order was frequently awarded to officers of the British Navy and Army.

**13 - THE ROYAL GUELPHIC
ORDER**
(*Star and Badge*)
*Shown approximately half full size*

### 14 - THE MOST EMINENT ORDER OF THE INDIAN EMPIRE

This Order was instituted by Queen Victoria in 1878 in three classes: Knights Grand Commander (G.C.I.E.); Knights Commander (K.C.I.E.); and Companions (C.I.E.). The insignia of the Order are:

*The collar* of gold, of elephants, lotus flowers, peacocks in their pride, Indian roses and in the centre the Imperial Crown, the whole linked together with chains.

*The badge*, consisting of a gold, five-petalled rose, enamelled crimson and with a green barb between each petal. In the centre an effigy of Queen Victoria on a gold ground, surrounded by a purple ribbon, edged and lettered gold, formerly bearing the legend 'VICTORIA IMPERATRIX,' now reading 'IMPERATRICIS AUSPICIIS'.

*The mantle* of imperial purple (really dark blue) satin, lined with white silk and fastened with a white silk cord with gold tassels, and having on the left side a representation of the Star of the Order.

*Knights Grand Commanders* wear the mantle, and the badge, suspended from the collar, on special occasions, or when ordered by the Sovereign. On ordinary full dress occasions they wear the badge on the left hip, suspended from a broad ribbon of imperial purple, passing over the right shoulder, and, on the left breast, a star. This star is composed of fine rays of silver, having a smaller ray of gold between each, the whole alternately plain and scaled. In the centre, within a purple circle bearing the motto and surmounted by the Imperial Crown in gold, is the effigy of H.M. Queen Victoria on a gold ground.

*Knights Commanders* wear a smaller sized badge, suspended round the neck from a purple ribbon 50 mm. in width, and on the left breast a star similar to that of Knights Grand Commanders, but with the rays fashioned entirely in silver.

*Companions* wear a still smaller sized badge round the neck from a purple ribbon 38 mm. in width. In undress uniform Knights Grand Commanders and Knights Commanders wear the ribbons of Companions.

The Order of the Indian Empire, as its name implies, was only awarded for services in India.

**14 - THE MOST EMINENT ORDER OF THE INDIAN EMPIRE**
*The badge*

## THE ROYAL VICTORIAN CHAIN

Established by King Edward VII in 1902, though sometimes considered as the highest grade of the Royal Victorian Order, mentioned below, has no real connection with it. It is conferred as a special mark of the Sovereign's favour, and then only very rarely, upon Royalty, or other especially distinguished personages, foreign as well as British. The chain consists of three Tudor roses, two thistles, two shamrocks and two lotus flowers, all in gold, connected by a slender double trace of gold chain. At the bottom of the front loop is a centrepiece consisting of the Sovereign's cypher in enamel surrounded by a wreath and surmounted by a crown. From this centrepiece hangs a replica of the badge of a Knight Grand Cross of the Royal Victorian Order.

## 15 - THE ROYAL VICTORIAN ORDER

This Order was established by Queen Victoria in April 1896. There is no limit to the number of members, and the Order, which is conferred for extraordinary, important or personal services to the

*Star of
K.C.V.O.
(Shown full size)*

**15 - THE ROYAL VICTORIAN
ORDER**
*Shown approximately half full size*

Sovereign or to the Royal Family, can be bestowed upon foreigners as well as upon British subjects. Ladies were made eligible for the Order in 1936. The insignia consists of:

*A mantle*, of dark blue silk, edged with red satin, lined with white silk, and fastened by a cordon of dark blue silk and gold.

*A collar*, of gold, composed of octagonal pieces and oblong perforated and ornamental frames alternately linked together with gold. The pieces are edged and ornamented with gold, and each contains upon a blue-enamelled ground a gold rose jewelled with a carbuncle. The frames are gold, and each contains a portion of the inscription 'VICTORIA BRITT. DEF. FID. IND. IMP.,' in letters of white enamel. In the centre of the collar within a perforated and ornamental frame of gold is an octagonal piece enamelled blue, edged with red, and charged with a white saltire, thereon being a gold medallion of Queen Victoria's effigy from which hangs the badge.

*The badge*, a white-enamelled Maltese cross of eight points, in the centre of which is an oval of crimson enamel with the cypher 'V.R.I.' in gold letters. Encircling this is a blue enamel riband with the name 'VICTORIA' in gold letters, and above this is the Imperial Crown enamelled in proper colours.

The Order has five classes:

*Knights Grand Cross* and *Dames Grand Cross* (*G.C.V.O.*) the Knights wearing the badge on the left hip from a broad ribbon worn over the right shoulder, and, on the left breast, a silver chipped star of eight points, with the white-enamelled badge in the centre. Dames Grand Cross wear a somewhat narrower ribbon over the right shoulder with the badge, and a star similar to that of Knights.

*Knights Commanders* and *Dames Commanders* (*K.C.V.O.* and *D.C.V.O.*) the former wearing the badge suspended round the neck, and, on the left breast, a silver chipped star in the shape shown. Dames Commanders wear the same star, with the badge on the left shoulder from a ribbon tied in a bow.

*Commanders* (*C.V.O.*) (men), wear the same badge round the neck, and ladies on the left shoulder.

*Members of the Fourth Class* (*M.V.O.*) (men), wear a smaller badge on the left breast in line with other decorations and medals, and ladies on the left shoulder from the ribbon tied in a bow.

*Members of the Fifth Class* (*M.V.O.*) (men and ladies), wear the same except that the badge is of frosted silver instead of white enamel.

All the badges of the Royal Victorian Order are numbered on the reverse.

## THE ROYAL VICTORIAN MEDAL

This medal, in silver-gilt, silver or bronze, may be awarded to those below the rank of officers who perform personal services to the Sovereign or to members of the Royal Family. It bears on the obverse the effigy of the reigning Sovereign, with the usual legend, and on the reverse the Royal cypher upon an ornamental shield within a wreath of laurel. The medal is worn by women on the left shoulder from a bow of the ribbon. Any person in possession of the bronze medal to whom a silver medal is awarded, can wear both, and the silver-gilt medal in addition if such be conferred upon him. Clasps may be awarded for further services to each class of medal, while the medals may be worn in addition to the insignia of the Order if the latter is subsequently conferred. When awarded to foreigners, the medal has a 3 mm. white stripe down the centre of the blue.

## 16, 17, 18, 19 - THE MOST EXCELLENT ORDER OF THE BRITISH EMPIRE

The Most Excellent Order of the British Empire was founded by King George V in June 1917 for services to the Empire at home, in India and in the Dominions and Colonies, other than those rendered by the Navy and Army. It could be conferred upon officers of the fighting services for services of a non-combatant character. The Order ranks in precedence to the Royal Victorian Order, and can be conferred upon ladies as well as upon men. In December 1918 His Majesty created a Military Division of the Order to date from its creation. The following classes of persons were declared eligible for the Military Division: all commissioned, warrant and subordinate officers subject to the Naval Discipline Act, or employed under the orders of the Admiralty, and all commissioned and warrant officers recommended by any Commander-in-Chief in the field or elsewhere, or by the G.O.C., Independent Force, R.A.F., or employed under the War Office or Air Ministry, or under the Administrative Headquarters of Dominion or Oversea Forces, or employed under the Ministry of Munitions or the Ministry of

(*Obverse*)

**ROYAL VICTORIAN MEDAL**
(*Reverse*)

*The former Star*

*The badge*

## THE MOST EXCELLENT ORDER OF THE BRITISH EMPIRE

National Service on work which, but for the creation of these departments, would have been performed by the War Office. Also all members of the Naval, Army, Dominion or Overseas Nursing Services, the Women's Royal Naval Service, Queen Mary's Army Auxiliary Corps, or the Women's Royal Air Force, and such commandants of the Women's Legion or similar organizations as are under contract with, or employed by, the Admiralty, War Office or Air Ministry. Persons who, between June 1917 and December 1918, had been appointed to the Order, and by subsequent regulations were qualified for the Military Division, could be transferred to the same on the recommendation of the First Lord of the Admiralty, the Secretary of State for War or the Secretary of State for the Royal Air Force, as the case may be.

## THE MOST EXCELLENT ORDER OF
## THE BRITISH EMPIRE

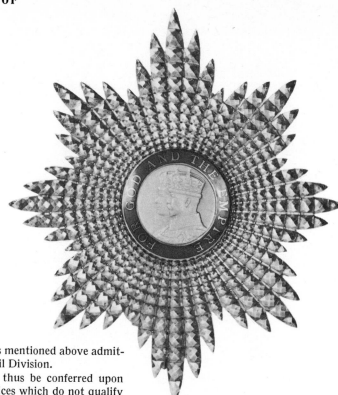

All persons employed otherwise than as mentioned above admitted to the Order are appointed to the Civil Division.

The Order – Military Division – can thus be conferred upon members of the fighting services for services which do not qualify them for some other Order or decoration awarded for services in the field or before the enemy, though during the Second World War the Order was not infrequently conferred for service in action.

*Star of G.B.E.*

The insignia for both the Military and Civil Divisions are identical. The ribbon was originally purple, a narrow scarlet stripe down the centre being added in the case of the Military Division when it was instituted in December 1918. In 1936 the ribbon was altered to rose-pink edged with pearl-grey for the Civil Division, a central narrow stripe of pearl-grey being added for the ribbon of the Military Division.

*The collar* is of silver-gilt, with medallions of the Royal Arms and of the Royal and Imperial cypher of King George V alternately linked together with cables. In the centre is the Imperial Crown between two sea lions. The collar for Dames Grand Cross is somewhat narrower than that for Knights Grand Cross.

*The mantle* is of rose-pink satin lined with pearl-grey silk, tied by a cord of pearl-grey silk, with two rose-pink and silver tassels attached. On the left side of the mantle is a representation of the star of the *First Class* of the Order.

*The badge* is a cross patonce. As worn by members of the first three classes it is of silver-gilt, with the arms enamelled pearl-grey.

In the centre, within a circle enamelled crimson, are the conjoint busts of King George V and Queen Mary facing left. The circle contains the motto of the Order – 'FOR GOD AND THE EMPIRE.' The badge for the *Fourth Class* (O.B.E.) is similar, but is rather smaller in size and is in silver-gilt without enamel. That of the *Fifth Class* (M.B.E.) is executed in silver.

*The stars* worn by members of the *First* and *Second Classes* are shown in the illustrations. The central device is the same as that for the badge. (Until 1935 the central device had a representation of Britannia within the circle bearing the motto.) The five classes are as follows, the members of which have the right of using the appropriate letters after their names:

MEN

1. Knights Grand Cross (G.B.E.)
2. Knights Commanders (K.B.E.)
3. Commanders (C.B.E.)
4. Officers (O.B.E.)
5. Members (M.B.E.)

LADIES

1. Dames Grand Cross (G.B.E.)
2. Dames Commanders (D.B.E.)
3. Commanders (C.B.E.)
4. Officers (O.B.E.)
5. Members (M.B.E.)

The ladies of the *First* and *Second Classes* have the right to use the title 'Dame' before their Christian names. Thus: 'Dame Mary Jones, G.B.E.'

G.B.E.s (Ladies) have precedence before wives of G.C.B.s; D.B.E.s, before wives of K.C.B.s; C.B.E.s, before the wives of C.B.s; O.B.E.s, before wives of M.V.O. (*Fourth Class*); and M.B.E.s before wives of M.V.O. (*Fifth Class*).

*Star of K.B.E.*

**THE MOST EXCELLENT ORDER OF
THE BRITISH EMPIRE**

The insignia are worn as follows:

*G.B.E.* (*Men*) – Star on the left breast, and the badge on the left hip from the ribbon, 95 mm. wide, passing over the right shoulder.

*G.B.E.* (*Ladies*) – Star on the left side, not higher than 15 cm. above the waist. The broad ribbon, 57 mm. wide, over the right shoulder with the badge resting just below the waist.

*K.B.E.* (*Men*) – Star on the left breast, and the badge suspended round the neck from a ribbon 44 mm. wide.

*D.B.E.* (*Ladies*) – A bow of the ribbon, 44 mm. wide, with badge attached on the left side, the star being affixed below the badge on the same side.

*C.B.E.* (*Men*) – The ribbon with the badge attached round the neck as for K.B.E.

*C.B.E.* (*Ladies*) – The bow with the badge attached on the left side as for D.B.E.

*O.B.E.* (*Men*) – The smaller, silver-gilt badge on the left breast with other orders, decorations and medals from a ribbon 38 mm. wide.

*O.B.E.* (*Ladies*) – The same badge on the left side from the ribbon tied in a bow.

*M.B.E.* (*Men*) – The silver badge worn as by O.B.E. (Men).

*M.B.E.* (*Ladies*) – The silver badge as worn by O.B.E. (Ladies).

## BRITISH EMPIRE MEDAL

A silver medal of the Order, bearing on one side a representation of Britannia within the circle and motto, and on the other the Royal cypher, and suspended by a ring, was instituted in 1917. It had a Military as well as a Civil Division from 1918 onwards, with the difference only in the ribbon. In 1922 the award of this medal was discontinued, and two other medals were issued in its place:

(*a*) *The Medal of the Order of the British Empire for Gallantry* (E.G.M.), and

(*b*) *The Medal of the Order of the British Empire for Meritorious Service.*

Each of these had a Military and a Civil Division, the difference in each case being confined to the ribbon, which was the same as for the Military and Civil Divisions of the Order. The width of the medal ribbon was 32 mm., that of the Order being 38 mm.

The Empire Medal for Gallantry was abolished on the institution of the George Cross in September 1940, while in a supplement to the *London Gazette* of 22 April 1941, it was laid down that a recipient of the Empire Gallantry Medal living on 24 September 1940 should return it to the Central Chancery of the Orders of Knighthood and become instead a holder of the George Cross. A similar change was made in relation to any posthumous grant of the E.G.M. made subsequent to the outbreak of war on 3 September 1939. The same gazette laid down the rules for the British Empire Medal when it was ordained that the Military or Civil Medal was for award to persons who rendered meritorious service warranting such mark of Royal appreciation who were not already members of any of the five classes of the Order of the British Empire, and were not eligible

(*Obverse*)

**BRITISH EMPIRE MEDAL**
(*Original Medal*)            (*Reverse*)

for appointment thereto. If the holder of the medal were subsequently appointed a member of the Order, he, or she, could wear
both the medal and the insignia of the Order.

The medal is silver. The obverse has a representation of Britannia
with the motto of the Order, and in the exergue the words 'FOR
MERITORIOUS SERVICE.' The reverse has the Royal and Imperial
cypher of the Sovereign and the words 'INSTITUTED BY KING
GEORGE.' It is suspended from a clasp ornamented with oak leaves,
the ribbons of the Military and Civil Medals being the same as for
the Order, but 32 mm. wide instead of 38 mm. When the medal is
worn by a woman it may be worn on the left shoulder with the
ribbon tied in a bow. Recipients use the letters B.E.M. after their
names. Bars may be awarded for further acts and a silver rose,
one for each bar, carried on the ribbon when it is worn alone.

To clarify the situation regarding the appointments, promotions
and awards for gallantry, the relevant announcement in the *London
Gazette* of January 1958 is quoted in full: 'Appointments to, or
promotions in, the Order of the British Empire and awards of the
British Empire Medal, granted after 14 January 1958, for gallantry,
are so described, and a silver oak-leaf emblem is worn on the ribbon.
When the ribbon only is worn the emblem is worn in miniature.
Classification of an award as made for gallantry has no effect on
seniority or precedence in the various classes of the Order. A person
appointed to the Order after 14 January 1958, for gallantry, and
subsequently promoted in the Order, retains and wears the emblem
whether promoted for gallantry or otherwise. A holder of the British
Empire Medal, for gallantry, granted since 14 January 1958, if
subsequently appointed to the Order, continues to wear the emblem
on the ribbon of the Medal and wears the emblem also on the ribbon
of the Order only if appointed to the Order for gallantry.'

The emblem consists of two silver oakleaves crossed, and can be
awarded either with the Military or Civil Division of the Order and
Medal, for gallantry.

*(Obverse)*

**BRITISH EMPIRE MEDAL**
*(Reverse)*

## 20 - ORDER OF THE COMPANIONS OF HONOUR

This Order was instituted in June 1917 at the same time as the Order
of the British Empire. It carries no title or precedence and consists
of the Sovereign and one class of members. Not more than fifty
persons, men or women who have rendered conspicuous service of
national importance, are to be admitted. The Order ranks immediately after the *First Class* of the Order of the British Empire.
Members of the Order will 'upon all great and solemn occasions'
wear an oval-shaped badge consisting of a gold medallion with an
oak tree, hanging from one branch being a shield of the Royal Arms,
and on the right a knight armed and in armour, mounted on a horse.
The badge has a blue border with the motto 'IN ACTION FAITHFUL
AND IN HONOUR CLEAR' in gold letters, and is surmounted by the
Imperial Crown. The ribbon is 38 mm. wide and is carmine in
colour with borders of gold thread. By men the badge is worn suspended round the neck, and by women from a bow of the ribbon
on the left shoulder. Companions of Honour use the letters C.H.
after their names.

*Issue of King George VI (Obverse)*    *Issue of King George VI (Reverse)*

## 21 - DISTINGUISHED SERVICE ORDER

This Order was established in 1886 for rewarding individual instances of meritorious or distinguished service in war. Statutes amended in 1902, 1903, 1916, 1918 and 1931. No person is eligible for this distinction who does not actually hold at the time of his nomination a commission in the Royal Navy, the Army, the Royal Marines, the Royal Air Force, or a commission in one of the departments of the above entitling him to honorary or relative Naval, Military or Air Force rank, though since September 1942 the D.S.O. may be conferred upon officers of the Merchant Navy who perform gallant or meritorious acts before the enemy while serving in close contact with the Royal Navy. No person shall be eligible for the award whose services have not been marked by the special mention of his name in despatches for 'distinguished services under fire, or under conditions equivalent to service in actual combat with the enemy.' Foreign officers who have been associated with British forces are eligible for honorary membership. Any recipient of the Order who subsequently performs an approved act of gallantry which, if he had not received the Order, would have entitled him to it, shall be awarded a bar to be attached to the ribbon, and for every additional such act, a further bar. The D.S.O. ranks immediately after the Order of the Companions of Honour, and Companions of the D.S.O. take precedence after Commanders of the British Empire (C.B.E.). The badge consists of a gold cross, enamelled white, edged gold, having on one side thereof in the centre, within a wreath of laurel enamelled green, the Imperial Crown in gold, and on the reverse, within a similar wreath, and upon a similar ground, the Royal cypher. It hangs from its ribbon by a gold clasp ornamented with laurel, while another similar clasp is worn at the top of the ribbon. The number of members of the Order is unlimited. Companions of the D.S.O. who have been awarded bars wear on

*Issue of King George V (and bar) (Obverse)*

*Issue of King George V (Reverse)*

the ribbon, when it alone is worn in undress uniform, a small silver rose; one or more according to the number of bars awarded. Any person admitted to membership of the Order who shall be convicted of treason, cowardice, felony or any infamous crime, or if he be accused of any such offence, and does not after a reasonable time surrender himself to be tried for the same, shall have his name erased from the register of members.

## 22 - IMPERIAL SERVICE ORDER
## IMPERIAL SERVICE MEDAL

This Order and Medal were instituted by King Edward in August 1902 as a means of rewarding meritorious services on the part of members of the administrative or clerical branches of the Civil Service throughout the British Empire. The number of Companions is limited, and at least twenty-five years' meritorious service is the usual qualification for companionship, twenty years for Europeans in India, or sixteen years in unhealthy places abroad. The Order can, however, be bestowed upon those who have performed, 'eminently meritorious service' irrespective of any qualifying period.

There is only one class of the Order, and companionship does not carry the honour of Knighthood. Companions use the letters I.S.O. after their names. The badge consists of a circular plaque of gold having in its centre the Royal cypher, and round its circumference the words 'FOR FAITHFUL SERVICE,' both in dark blue lettering. The badge for men is surrounded by a seven-pointed star of silver, surmounted by a crown; that for women has a silver laurel wreath in place of the star. Members of the Civil Service who are not eligible for the I.S.O. may be granted the 'Imperial Service Medal' under the same conditions as the Order. The Medal was originally the same as the badge of the Order, except that the centre plaque was silver with the star or laurel wreath in bronze. It was later issued in silver, and circular in shape, with the Sovereign's head on the obverse, and the legend 'FOR FAITHFUL SERVICE' on the reverse. The name of the recipient is engraved on the edge. Both Order and Medal have rings for suspension, and are worn by men on the left breast in the ordinary way, and by women on the left shoulder from the ribbon tied in a bow.

## 23 - BARONET'S BADGE

In 1629 King Charles I instituted a badge for baronets of Scotland, who were authorized to wear and carry round their necks 'an orange tawny ribbon whereon shall be pendent an escutcheon argent, a saltire azure with an Imperial Crown above the escutcheon, and enclosed with the motto in an oval band,' the motto being 'FAX MENTIS HONESTAE GLORIA.' After the Union of 1707, Baronets of Scotland properly charged their arms with the badge of Ulster, the red hand, being created Baronets of the United Kingdom. No Baronets of Scotland have been created since 1707, or of Ireland since 1801. Later Baronets are of Great Britain, or of the United Kingdom.

A Baronet's badge, worn round the neck from an orange ribbon 44 mm. wide with narrow edges of blue, was created in 1929. The ribbon is not worn in undress uniform. The badge consists of a shield of the arms of Ulster, i.e. on a silver field a left-hand gules (or red), surmounted by an Imperial Crown in its proper colours, the whole enclosed by an oval border embossed with gilt scroll work having a design of shamrocks, and of roses and thistles combined, for those Baronets who were created Baronets of England, Ireland and Great Britain respectively, and for all other Baronets other than those of Scotland a design of roses, thistles and shamrock combined.

## KNIGHTS BACHELOR'S BADGE

This is a badge worn on the left side of the coat or on the garment like the star of an Order. It is about 76 mm. long and 50 mm. wide, and consists of an oval medallion of vermilion, enclosed by a scroll, bearing a cross-hilted sword, belted and sheathed, pommel up-wards, between two spurs, rowels upwards, the whole set about with the sword-belt, all gilt.

## BRITISH DECORATIONS

### 24 - THE ROYAL RED CROSS

This decoration was instituted by Queen Victoria on 27 April 1883, and is the first example of a British Military Order solely for ladies. It may be conferred upon members of the Nursing Services, with-out restriction as to rank, or upon other persons engaged in nursing duties, whether British or foreign, who may be recommended for special devotion and competency in their nursing duties with the Army in the field, or in Naval and Military Hospitals and Hospital Ships, as well as upon any ladies, British or foreign, who may be recommended as having voluntarily undertaken the duties of estab-lishing, conducting or assisting in hospitals for sick or wounded personnel of the fighting services or as having performed valuable services with the Red Cross or kindred societies at home or abroad, or as having otherwise rendered eminent services in a similar connection.

Recipients of the *First Class* are designated 'Members' and are entitled to use the letters R.R.C. after their names. Those awarded the *Second Class* are 'Associates,' and use the letters A.R.R.C. It is further ordained that if any recipient shall by her conduct become unworthy of it, her name may be erased from the register.

The badge of the *First Class* is a gold cross pattée (38 mm. wide), enamelled red, edged gold, having on the arms the words 'FAITH, HOPE, CHARITY,' and the date of institution, '1883.' In the centre, in relief, was originally a symbolic female effigy. This has since been replaced by the head of the reigning Sovereign. The reverse has the Royal Crown and cypher. The badge of the *Second Class* is in silver, with the Sovereign's head in the centre and the inner portion of the arms enamelled red. The reverse has the Royal Crown and cypher in the centre, and the same wording and date on the four arms as

**THE ROYAL RED CROSS**

those which appear on the obverse of the *First Class*.

The cross of either class hangs from a ring, and may be worn on the left shoulder from a bow of the ribbon, or with other decorations and medals.

Members of the *First Class* who render further services of a similar nature may be awarded a bar to be attached to the decoration.

## 25 - THE DISTINGUISHED SERVICE CROSS
### (Late Conspicuous Service Cross)

The Conspicuous Service Cross was instituted by King Edward in 1901 as a means of 'recognizing meritorious or distinguished services before the enemy,' performed by warrant officers, acting warrant officers, or by subordinate officers of His Majesty's Fleet. No person could be nominated unless his name had been mentioned in despatches, while the award of the decoration carried with it the right to use the letters C.S.C. In October 1914 the name of this decoration was altered to the 'Distinguished Service Cross,' and its award was extended to all Naval and Marine officers below the relative rank of Lieutenant-Commander, 'for meritorious or distinguished services which may not be sufficient to warrant the appointment of such officers to the Distinguished Service Order.' The letters after a recipient's name, too, were altered to D.S.C. while the proviso that a recipient must have been mentioned in despatches still held good. In the *London Gazette* of 22 December 1939 it was announced that the King had been pleased to approve that Commanders and Lieutenant-Commanders of the Royal Navy and officers of equivalent rank should also be eligible for the award of the Distinguished Service Cross. The decoration itself, which is suspended from its ribbon by a ring, is a plain silver cross pattée convexed with the reverse side plain. On the obverse it bears the cypher of the reigning Sovereign surmounted by the Crown. Bars are awarded for further services, as is the case with the D.S.O., and the same regulations are in force as to the wearing of the silver rose on the ribbon in undress uniform. Only eight 'Conspicuous Service Crosses' were awarded from the date of its institution in 1901 until the opening of the First World War, when it was renamed the 'Distinguished' Service Cross.

The D.S.C. is the only purely Naval decoration, as opposed to medals, and as such was awarded to the town of Dunkirk for the gallant behaviour of its inhabitants during the First World War. Officers of the Royal Air Force serving with the Fleet Air Arm are eligible for the D.S.C., as are officers of the Women's Royal Naval Service for gallantry and distinguished conduct on shore during enemy action. Officers of the Merchant Navy were awarded the D.S.C. during the First World War for gallant services in action, and an Order in Council of 19 May 1931 legalized its grant to the Merchant Navy. The Conspicuous Gallantry and Distinguished Service Medals described later, are available in similar circumstances to men of the Merchant Navy.

*Issue of King George V (and bar)*
*(Obverse)*

*Issue of Queen Elizabeth II*
**25 - THE DISTINGUISHED SERVICE CROSS**

*Issue of King George V I (early type) and bar*

*Issue of King George V*

## 26 - MILITARY CROSS

This decoration was instituted on 31 December 1914. It is an Army decoration, and no person is eligible to receive it unless he is a captain, a commissioned officer of a lower grade, or a warrant officer in the Army, Indian Army or Colonial Forces. The cross can be awarded to officers and warrant officers of the R.A.F. for gallant service on the ground as opposed to flying. The decoration consists of an ornamental silver cross, on each arm of which is an Imperial Crown. In the centre is the Royal cypher and the cross hangs by its top arm from the plain silver clasp through which the ribbon passes. The Military Cross is worn after British Orders and before war medals, but does not carry with it any individual precedence. Recipients are entitled to use letters M.C. after their names. Bars are also awarded for further services as with D.S.O., and the same regulations are in force as to the wearing of the silver rose on the ribbon in undress uniform. The original warrant of December 1914 provided for the award of the M.C. 'in recognition of distinguished and meritorious services in time of war.' An amending warrant, of 5 February 1931, laid it down that it should be awarded to officers not above the substantive rank of major 'for gallant and distinguished services in action.'

## 27 - DISTINGUISHED FLYING CROSS

Established in June 1918 for award to officers and warrant officers of the Air Forces recommended for 'an act or acts of valour, courage, or devotion to duty performed whilst flying in active operations against the enemy.' It is silver and consists of 'a cross flory terminated in the horizontal and base bars with bombs, the upper bar terminating with a rose, surmounted by another cross composed of aeroplane propellers charged in the centre with a roundel within a wreath of laurels a rose winged ensigned by an Imperial Crown thereon the letters R.A.F. On the reverse the Royal cypher above the date 1918.' It hangs from the clasp and ribbon by two sprigs of laurel.' Ribbon, 32 mm. wide, in colour, violet and white in alternate diagonal stripes 3 mm. in width, running at an angle of 45 degrees, from left to right. The stripes were originally horizontal (Ribbon 27a). The letters D.F.C. are used after a recipient's name, and bars may be awarded for further acts with a silver rose on the ribbon in undress uniform.

**27 - DISTINGUISHED FLYING CROSS**          **28 - AIR FORCE CROSS**
   (*and bar*)

## 28 - AIR FORCE CROSS

This decoration is granted to officers and warrant officers of the Air Force for 'an act or acts of valour, courage or devotion to duty whilst flying, though not in active operations against the enemy, and may also be granted to individuals not belonging to the Air Force (whether Naval, Military or Civil) who render distinguished service to aviation in actual flying.' It is silver, and consists of a thunderbolt in the form of a cross, the arms conjoined by the wings, base bar terminating with a bomb, surmounted by another cross composed of aeroplane propellers, the four ends enscribed with the Royal cypher. In the centre a roundel, thereon a representation of Hermes mounted on a hawk bestowing a wreath. On the reverse the Royal cypher above the date 1918. The whole ensigned by a Crown. It hangs from the clasp and ribbon by two sprigs of laurel. The letters A.F.C. are used after a recipient's name, and the usual bars may be awarded for further acts. The ribbon has diagonal stripes of crimson and white. The stripes were originally horizontal (Ribbon 28a).

In February 1970 the Air Force Cross was awarded to a naval officer for the first time.

*First Class*

## 29 - ORDER OF BRITISH INDIA

This Order was originally created in 1837 for native officers of the Indian Army for long and faithful service. The conditions of award were amended in September 1939, and appointments to the *Second Class* were made by the Viceroy from those on the active list of the Armed Forces in India, including Frontier Guards, Military Police and Indian States' Forces. Appointments to the *First Class* were made only from members of the *Second Class*. The badge of the *First Class* consists of a gold star of the design shown in the illustration with, in the centre, on a ground of light blue enamel, the words 'ORDER OF BRITISH INDIA' encircling a lion and surrounded by a laurel wreath in gold. The *Second Class* badge is slightly smaller, with the light blue enamel in the centre replaced by dark blue. Both badges are worn round the neck from a ribbon of dark red. When the ribbons alone are worn on the breast, that of the *First Class* has two thin vertical lines of light blue in the centre, and that of the *Second Class* one thin vertical line of light blue. Recipients of both classes use the letters O.B.I. after their names; those of the *First Class* using the title of 'Sardar Bahadur,' and those of the *Second Class* – 'Bahadur.' It was originally intended that the colour of the ribbon should be sky blue, but this was altered in 1838 to crimson, because, owing to the habit of all classes of natives of oiling their hair, the light ribbon would soon have been soiled.

*Second Class*

**29 - ORDER OF BRITISH INDIA**

## 30, 31 - INDIAN ORDER OF MERIT

This Order was instituted in 1837 for rewarding conspicuous acts of individual gallantry in battle on the part of officers, N.C.O.s and soldiers of the Indian Army. It is quite distinct from the British Order of Merit established in 1902. There were originally three classes; but the highest was abolished in 1912 on the extension of the award of the Victoria Cross to Indian officers, N.C.O.s and men of the Indian Army. The conditions of award were further modified in September 1939. There was a Civil Division of one class only awarded to persons of Indian origin for acts of conspicuous personal bravery in aid of public authority or the safety of others. The civil badge consists of a silver eight-pointed star with a circular ground of dark blue enamel in the centre, surrounded by a laurel wreath in gold. On the enamel centre is the Royal cypher and Crown encircled by the words 'FOR BRAVERY' all in gold. The badge is worn on the left breast from a ribbon of dark red with blue edges.

The Military Division had two classes, bestowed upon Indian officers, warrant officers, N.C.O.s and men of the Armed Forces for acts of conspicuous gallantry in connection with their duties. Appointments to the *First Class* were made only from members of the *Second Class*, for any similar act performed by them. The badge consists of a silver eight-pointed star, 38 mm. in diameter, of the design shown in the illustration. The centre is of dark blue enamel with the crossed swords surrounded by the words 'REWARD OF GALLANTRY' and a laurel wreath outside. In the *First Class* the swords, inscription and laurel wreath are worked in gold. In the *Second Class* the badge is all silver. Recipients of both the Civil and Military Divisions use the letters I.O.M. after their names. The military badges are worn on the left breast from a dark blue ribbon with red edges.

**30, 31 – INDIAN
ORDER OF MERIT**

## 32 - THE KAISAR-I-HIND MEDAL

This medal was instituted in May 1900, and might be given to any person, irrespective of race, occupation, position or sex, who had distinguished himself, or herself, by important or useful service in the advancement of the public interest in India. There were three classes, gold, silver and bronze, and bars might be awarded for further services. The decoration consists of an oval badge. The obverse bears the Imperial cypher in the centre, and the reverse the words 'KAISAR-I-HIND, FOR PUBLIC SERVICE IN INDIA.' The medal, when awarded to ladies, is worn attached to the left shoulder by a bow of the ribbon, and when given to men is suspended from the left breast in the usual manner.

## 33 - THE ORDER OF BURMA (now obsolete)

This Order was established by King George VI for award to Governor's commissioned officers of the Burma Army, the Burma Frontier Force and the Burma Military Police, for long, faithful and honourable service. Appointments were made by the Governor of Burma within a fixed establishment of twenty-eight, sixteen for the Burma Army and twelve for the Burma Frontier Force and Military Police, vacancies being filled once annually as they occurred. Recipients may use the letters O.B. after their names. The Order had one class only and the award carried with it an allowance of one rupee a day for life unless forfeited for misconduct. The badge is worn round the neck from a ribbon of green, 38 mm.

**32 - THE KAISAR-I-HIND
MEDAL**

wide, edged with light blue a 6 mm. wide. The badge, 38 mm. in diameter, is composed of rays of gold issuing from a gold medallion charged with a peacock in his pride azure, within a circle of azure inscribed with the words 'ORDER OF BURMA,' also in gold; the whole ensigned with the Imperial Crown proper.

## ST. JOHN OF JERUSALEM

### 34, 34a - THE GRAND PRIORY IN THE BRITISH REALM OF THE MOST VENERABLE ORDER OF THE HOSPITAL OF ST. JOHN OF JERUSALEM

It is impossible in the space at our disposal to give a full and complete account of the work carried on under the auspices of the Grand Priory in the British Realm of the Order of the Hospital of St. John of Jerusalem. It is principally concerned with hospital and ambulance work. The St. John Ambulance Association provides for: (1) The dissemination of instruction in 'first aid,' home nursing, and hygiene. (2) The deposit in convenient places of stretchers, splints, bandages, etc. (3) The development of ambulance corps for the transport of sick and wounded. The Order itself is of very ancient origin, dating from the eleventh century. It has branches in nearly all European countries, and was incorporated in England by Queen Victoria under Royal Charter, 14 May 1888. The Order was granted the title of 'Venerable' in 1926, at which time it was reorganized into five classes like certain other Orders. Both men and women are eligible for membership, and the badge consists of a true Maltese cross, embellished alternately in each of its principal angles with a lion and a unicorn. We are principally concerned with the various decorations of the Order which may be worn in public by its members. Her Majesty the Queen is the *Sovereign Head*

*Star of Bailiffs and Dames Grand Cross*

*Badge for all grades except Serving Brother and Sister.*

**THE MOST VENERABLE ORDER OF THE HOSPITAL OF ST. JOHN OF JERUSALEM**

and Patron of the Order. Next in authority is the *Grand Prior*. Apart from the mantle of black velvet worn on special occasions, the *Grand Prior* wears the badge or cross, in white enamel, set in and embellished with gold, and surmounted by an Imperial Crown, round the neck from a black-watered silk ribbon.

*Bailiffs Grand Cross* and *Dames Grand Cross* wear the badge suspended from a black ribbon over the right shoulder, and on the breast a star which is a replica of the badge set in gold without embellishment, that is the cross without the lions and unicorns between the limbs. The sash ribbon for Bailiffs is 102 mm. wide, and that for Dames 57 mm.

*Knights and Dames of Justice.* Knights wear the badge round the neck from a ribbon 50 mm. wide, and on the breast the plain eight-pointed star set in silver-gilt without embellishment. Dames wear the badge on the breast from a bow of the ribbon, 32 mm. wide, and below it the same star as the Knights.

*Knights and Dames of Grace.* The badges are worn in the same manner as Knights and Dames of Justice; but they are set in and embellished in silver. Their stars are also in silver, and have in silver the lions and unicorns in the four principal angles.

N.B. – The Order of St. John of Jerusalem is essentially aristocratic, and at one time members had to have sixteen quarterings of nobility on their coats of arms. The term 'Knights of Justice,' originally meant Knights who were noble by birth, while 'Knights of Grace' were those of non-noble birth admitted to the Order for their attainments.

*Commanders* (Brothers) wear the badge embellished in silver round the neck, and Commanders (Sisters) a slightly smaller badge worn from a bow of the ribbon in the left breast.

*Officers* of both sexes wear the badge on the left breast, ladies from a bow.

*Serving Brothers and Serving Sisters* wear a circular badge on the left breast. It consists of the cross of the Order in white enamel and silver on a black-enamelled background set in a silver rim, with a silver link at the top for suspension.

The ribbons for *Commanders, Officers* and *Serving Brothers and Sisters* are 38 mm. wide for men, and 32 mm. for ladies.

For all grades of the Order, when the ribbon only is worn, a small Maltese Cross in silver is carried on the ribbon in order that it may be distinguished against a dark background.

*Associates.* Persons not eligible to be made members of the Order by reason of not being British subjects or being non-Christians, may be attached to the Order as associates if they have rendered conspicuous service to the Order, or if their attachment would be to the benefit of the Order, or to the benefit of its work *pro utilitate hominum.* They may be attached to any grade, though their initial attachment is usually in the grade of Serving Brother or Serving Sister. They wear the badges of their respective grades from a ribbon of black watered silk with a central white stripe one-twelfth of its breadth.

*Donats* are selected from persons who, from an appreciation of

*Badge of Serving Brother and Sister (Note. The Badge is incorrectly mounted on the suspender: the right hand limb of the Cross should be at the bottom.)*

the works of the Order, have contributed to its funds. They are not enrolled either as members or associates of the Order. The badges are given in gold, silver or bronze, and are the same as the badge of the Order with the upper arm of the cross replaced by an ornamental piece of metal for suspension. The ribbon, with its central white stripe, is the same as that for associates.

## 35 - ST. JOHN OF JERUSALEM LIFE-SAVING MEDAL

This medal, in gold, silver and bronze, was originally instituted in 1874, and is awarded by the Order for gallantry in saving life on land. It is circular in shape, and bears on the obverse the cross of the Order surrounded by the legend, 'FOR SERVICE IN THE CAUSE OF HUMANITY.' The reverse has a sprig of the plant known as St. John's Wort, with which is entwined a scroll bearing the words, 'JERUSALEM, ENGLAND,' the whole surrounded by the words, 'AWARDED BY THE GRAND PRIORY IN THE BRITISH REALM OF THE ORDER OF THE HOSPITAL OF ST. JOHN OF JERUSALEM.' The medal hangs from its ribbon by means of a ring; is worn on the right breast from a ribbon 38 mm. wide, formerly black, but now with a 25 mm. black centre, with 1 mm. white and 2 mm. scarlet stripes at each edge, and is only awarded to those who, by a conspicuous act of gallantry, have endangered their own lives. Since the institution of the medal, 11 gold, 145 silver and 326 bronze medals have been awarded, also 329 Certificates of Honour. This medal should not be confused with the Service Medal of the Order of St. John, worn from a black ribbon with two white stripes, and dealt with later.

# British Medals for Gallantry and Distinguished Conduct

## 36, 37, 38, 39 - THE ALBERT MEDALS

Albert Medal in Gold for Gallantry in saving life at sea.
Albert Medal for Gallantry in saving life at sea.
Albert Medal in Gold for Gallantry in saving life on land.
Albert Medal for Gallantry in saving life on land.

These decorations, said to have been designed by Prince Albert, were originally established by Queen Victoria in 1866 for distinguishing the 'many heroic acts performed by mariners and others who endanger their own lives in saving, or endeavouring to save, the lives of others from shipwrecks and other perils of the sea'; while in 1877 they were extended to cover 'the many heroic acts performed on land by those who endanger their lives in saving or endeavouring to save the lives of others from accidents in mines, or railways, and at fires, or other peril within Her Dominions, other than perils of the sea.' The decorations were known as the 'Albert Medal of the First Class,' and the 'Albert Medal of the Second Class,' inscribed 'FOR GALLANTRY IN SAVING LIFE AT SEA,' and similar decorations inscribed 'FOR GALLANTRY IN SAVING LIFE ON LAND.'

In 1905 the rules of award were amended, and it was ordained that the grant of decorations of the *First Class* should be 'confined to cases of extreme or heroic daring,' and those of the *Second Class* should be given 'in cases which, though falling within the cases contemplated by this warrant, are not sufficiently distinguished to deserve the Albert Medal of the *First Class*.' In August 1917 the designations of the Albert Medals of the *First* and *Second Class* were altered, respectively, to 'The Albert Medal in Gold,' and 'The Albert Medal.' The Albert Medal in Gold for Gallantry in saving life at sea consists of an oval gold badge, enamelled in dark blue, with a monogram in the centre composed of the letters 'V' and 'A' in gold, interlaced with an anchor in gold. The badge is encircled by a bronze garter, inscribed in raised gold letters, 'FOR GALLANTRY IN SAVING LIFE AT SEA,' and is surmounted by a representation in bronze of the crown of H.R.H. the late Prince Consort. At the top of the crown there is a ring through which the ribbon passes. The Albert Medal for Gallantry in saving life at sea is worked entirely in bronze, instead of in gold and bronze. The two varieties of the Albert Medal for saving life on land follow the same design, except that the anchor is omitted and the background is enamelled crimson. In 1904 the *Second Class* ribbons were increased in width from 16 mm. to 35 mm. Any subsequent act of gallantry which is considered worthy of recognition by the award of the Albert Medal may be recorded by a bar. It is ordained, further, that any recipient of the Albert Medal who may be guilty of any crime or disgraceful conduct shall have his name erased from the register of recipients, and shall be required to return the decoration. Every person on receiving the medal, moreover, is required to enter into an engagement to return it if his name is so erased. His Majesty King George V approved recipients of the Albert Medals using the letters A.M. after their names.

In 1971 the award of the Albert Medal was discontinued, its place being almost exclusively taken by the award of the George Cross. Previous holders of the Albert Medal were asked to return their insignia in exchange for the George Cross. It had been considered by many that acts for which the Albert Medal had been awarded were not adequately recognised in the relatively low position of the Medal in the order of wearing, a situation wholly redeemed by substitution of the Cross. Furthermore, former holders of the Albert Medal are now entitled to receive the £100 annual bounty applicable to holders of the George Cross.

## 40 - UNION OF SOUTH AFRICA QUEEN'S MEDALS FOR BRAVERY

This medal, sometimes known as the 'Woltemade Medal,' was instituted by the Union Government in 1939 to be awarded for individual acts of bravery in civilian life. The obverse bears the crowned head of King George VI with the usual legend in Latin.

The reverse depicts one of the most notable instances of spontaneous courage in South African history – the rescue on horseback by Wolraad Woltemade of drowning men from the Dutch East India Company's ship, *Jonge Thomas*, which ran ashore in Table Bay on 17 June 1773. Seven times the horse and rider made the dangerous journey between the ship and the shore, saving fourteen lives. At the eighth attempt both perished in the heavy surf. For acts of supreme personal bravery the medal may be issued in gold, otherwise in silver. Both are suspended by a ring from a ribbon of dark blue with narrow edges of orange.

## 41 - DISTINGUISHED CONDUCT MEDAL

A medal for 'meritorious service' was instituted in 1845. It was awarded on the recommendation of the Commander-in-Chief only to sergeants, while serving or after discharge, with or without a pension. The 'D.C.M.', as it is usually called, for N.C.O.s and men, was sanctioned in 1854 to replace the old 'Meritorious Service Medal' for gallantry in action. It is suspended from its ribbon by an ornamental scroll clasp, and bears on one side the effigy of the reigning Sovereign, and on the other the embossed words 'FOR DISTINGUISHED CONDUCT IN THE FIELD.' The date of the action for which the medal is given sometimes engraved upon it, while bars bearing the dates of any subsequent gallant actions may be awarded. Non-commissioned officers and men who have been given this medal either receive a gratuity of £20 on discharge, or an increase of pension of 6*d.* a day. Bars are also awarded for further services, and the usual regulations are in force as to the wearing of the silver rose on the ribbon in undress uniform. Recipients use the letters D.C.M. after their names. In January 1943, airmen of non-commissioned rank became eligible for this medal for distinguished conduct in action on the ground. It is a superior award to the Military Medal.

*(Obverse)*

## 42 - CONSPICUOUS GALLANTRY MEDAL

(Royal Navy)

This medal, which, before 1943, was awarded only to petty officers and men of the Royal Navy, and non-commissioned officers and men of the Royal Marines who might at any time distinguish themselves by acts of conspicuous gallantry in action with the enemy, is now available to men of the Merchant Navy. It is the Naval counterpart of the Army medal for Distinguished Conduct in the Field. It was originally sanctioned for the Crimean War only, but was reinstituted in 1874, and is now available for any war. The medal is of silver, and has on one side the effigy of the reigning Sovereign with the usual legend, and on the other, in raised letters, the words 'FOR CONSPICUOUS GALLANTRY,' with a crown above, and the whole design encircled by laurel branches. Medals awarded before 1874 had an ornamental scroll clasp for suspension, but those issued since this date have a plain clasp. Petty officers of the Navy and sergeants of the Royal Marines may be awarded an annuity not exceeding £20 with this medal, while men of junior grades may be awarded a gratuity of £20 on discharge from the

*(Reverse)*

**41 - DISTINGUISHED CONDUCT MEDAL**

service, or on promotion to a commission. Bars are also awarded for further services, and the usual regulations are in force as to the wearing of the silver rose on the ribbon in undress uniform. Recipients use the letters C.G.M. after their names. Women of the W.R.N.S. are eligible for the award of the C.G.M. for gallantry on shore during enemy action.

Ten C.G.M.'s were awarded in 1855. Since its reinstitution in 1874 no more than 233 medals and one bar have been granted.

The ribbon, originally blue, white, blue in equal stripes, exactly similar to that of the D.S.C., was altered in 1921 to the ribbon of the old Naval General Service Medal, 1793–1840.

## 43 - CONSPICUOUS GALLANTRY MEDAL
(Royal Air Force)

Airmen of non-commissioned rank, glider pilots, observers and other Army personnel are eligible for the award of the Conspicuous Gallantry Medal for gallantry in air operations against the enemy. The medal is of the same design as the Naval C.G.M., but has a ribbon of light blue with dark blue edges. The award is superior to the Distinguished Flying Medal, described later.

Since its institution early in 1943 a total of 104 C.G.M.'s (Flying) have been awarded, including one to a member of the Royal Australian Air Force in Korea during 1968.

## 44 - THE GEORGE MEDAL

This medal is awarded in similar circumstances to the Cross, where the services are not so outstanding as to merit the award of the latter. Though more freely awarded than the Cross, a very high standard is set for the award of the George Medal. It carries with it the right to the use of letters G.M., and takes precedence immediately after the Conspicuous Gallantry Medal.

42 - CONSPICUOUS GALLANTRY MEDAL (Royal Navy)

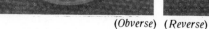
*(Obverse)* *(Reverse)*

**44 - THE GEORGE MEDAL**

The Medal is in silver. Its obverse bears the crowned effigy of His Majesty surrounded by the inscription 'GEORGIUS VI D.G.BR. OMN. REX ET INDIÆ IMP,' and is thus identical with that of services medals in general.

The reverse depicts St. George slaying the Dragon on the coast of England, and was modelled and adapted by Mr. George Kruger Gray, C.B.E., A.R.C.A., F.S.A., after the bookplate designed by Mr. Stephen Gooden, A.R.A., for the Royal Library, Windsor Castle. The design is circumscribed 'THE GEORGE MEDAL.'

### 45 - THE ROYAL WEST AFRICAN FRONTIER FORCE DISTINGUISHED CONDUCT MEDAL

The obverse of this silver medal shows the effigy of the reigning Sovereign, while the reverse bears the inscription 'FOR DISTINGUISHED CONDUCT IN THE FIELD,' encircled by the words 'ROYAL WEST AFRICAN FRONTIER FORCE.'

### THE KING'S AFRICAN RIFLES DISTINGUISHED CONDUCT MEDAL

The ribbon and medal are the same as those mentioned above except for the wording on the reverse, which reads 'KING'S AFRICAN RIFLES.'

### 46 - INDIAN DISTINGUISHED SERVICE MEDAL
(now obsolete)

This medal was instituted in 1907 for rewarding distinguished services in the field of Indian commissioned and non-commissioned officers and men of the Indian Regular forces, the Reserve of the Indian Army, Border Militia and Levies, Military Police and Imperial Service troops employed under the Indian Government. An amendment of 6 July 1917 extended the grant of the medal to Indian non-combatants engaged on field service, and authorized the issue of bars for further distinguished service as in the case of the British D.C.M. The Indian D.S.M. has on one side the effigy of the reigning Sovereign with the usual legend, and on the other a laurel wreath with the words 'FOR DISTINGUISHED SERVICE.'

### 47 - BURMA GALLANTRY MEDAL (now obsolete)

This medal was established by King George VI for award by the Governor of Burma upon Governor's commissioned officers, N.C.O.s and other ranks of the Burma Army; the Burma Frontier Force, Military Police, Royal Naval Volunteer Reserve and Auxiliary Air Force for any act of conspicuous gallantry performed in connection with their duties in peace or in war. The medal is of silver with the King's effigy on the obverse. On the reverse is a laurel wreath with the words 'BURMA' and 'FOR GALLANTRY' in relief. The medal is worn before war medals, and hangs from a green ribbon, 32 mm. wide, with a 6 mm. crimson stripe in the centre. A bar may be awarded for a further act of gallantry, in which case a silver rose is added to the ribbon when it alone is worn in undress uniform.

## 48 - THE DISTINGUISHED SERVICE MEDAL
(Royal Navy)

This medal was established on 14 October 1914, during the First World War. It is designed to be awarded in the numerous cases of courageous service in war by petty officers and men of the Royal Navy, and non-commissioned officers and men of the Royal Marines, and all other persons holding corresponding positions in the naval forces, who 'may at any time show themselves to the fore in action, and set an example of bravery and resource under fire, but without performing acts of such pre-eminent bravery as would render them eligible for the Conspicuous Gallantry Medal.' It can also be awarded for similar services to men of the Merchant Navy, and airmen of non-commissioned rank, glider pilots, observers and other Army personnel are now eligible for the award of the D.S.M., as are also women of the Women's Royal Naval Service for gallantry or distinguished conduct ashore during enemy action. The medal bears on one side the effigy of the Sovereign with the usual legend, and on the reverse the inscription 'FOR DISTINGUISHED SERVICE,' surmounted by a crown, and encircled by a wreath of laurel. It hangs from its ribbon by means of a straight silver clasp. Bars are also awarded for further services, and the usual regulations are in force as to the wearing of the silver rose on the ribbon in undress uniform. Recipients use the letters D.S.M. after their names.

## 49 - THE MILITARY MEDAL

This medal was instituted in March 1916 for award to non-commissioned officers and men of the Army for individual or associated acts of bravery brought to notice by the recommendation of a Commander-in-Chief in the field. The medal, which is silver, bears on the obverse the Royal effigy, and on the reverse the words 'FOR BRAVERY IN THE FIELD,' encircled by a wreath and surmounted by

**48 - THE DISTINGUISHED
SERVICE MEDAL**
(Royal Navy)

**49 - THE MILITARY MEDAL**

the Royal cypher and Crown. By a warrant dated 21 June 1916 women became eligible for award of the Military Medal for devotion to duty under fire. Bars are also awarded for further services, and the usual regulations are in force as to the wearing of the silver rose on the ribbon in undress uniform. Recipients use the letters M.M. after their names. The Military Medal can be awarded to warrant officers, First Class and Second Class, for acts of bravery in the field in the same conditions as are prescribed for other ranks, as well as to personnel of the R.A.F. for gallant service on the ground.

### 50 - DISTINGUISHED FLYING MEDAL
Awarded to non-commissioned officers and men of the Air Forces in the same conditions as is the D.F.C. to officers. It is in silver and oval, with the Sovereign's effigy on the obverse, and on the reverse a representation of Athena Nike seated on an aeroplane, a hawk rising from her right hand above the words 'FOR COURAGE.' The medal is surmounted by a bomb attached to the clasp and ribbon by two wings. The ribbon is 32 mm. wide, with alternate diagonal stripes of violet and white, 1 mm. wide, running at an angle of 45 degrees from left to right. The stripes were originally horizontal (Ribbon No. 50a). The letters D.F.M. are used after a recipient's name, and bars may be awarded for subsequent acts, with the silver rose on the ribbon in undress uniform.

　　　　　　(Obverse)　　(Reverse)　　　　　　　　(Reverse)

*Issue of King George VI*

**50 - DISTINGUISHED FLYING MEDAL**　　　**51 - AIR FORCE MEDAL**

## 51 - AIR FORCE MEDAL

Awarded to N.C.O.s and men of the Air Forces, and to others, in the same conditions as the A.F.C. It is silver and oval, with the same obverse as the D.F.M. The reverse has a representation of Hermes mounted on a hawk bestowing a wreath. The ribbon has alternate diagonal stripes of crimson and white. The stripes were originally horizontal (Ribbon No. 51a). The letters A.F.M. are used after a recipient's name and bars may be awarded for subsequent acts.

Foreign officers and men associated with British, Indian, Dominion or Colonial Forces are eligible for the D.F.C., A.F.C., D.F.M. and A.F.M. in the same conditions as the R.A.F., while the same applies to officers and men of the Fleet Air Arm serving with the R.A.F., and to glider pilots, observers and other Army personnel engaged on flying duties.

## 52 - THE QUEEN'S POLICE MEDAL FOR GALLANTRY

## 53 - THE QUEEN'S POLICE MEDAL FOR DISTINGUISHED SERVICE

A King's Police Medal was established in 1909 for award to officers of Police or Fire Brigades throughout His Majesty's Dominions for conspicuous gallantry; distinguished administrative or organizing work; special or valuable services in various different capacities; and prolonged service when distinguished by very exceptional ability and merit. The medal, in silver, has the Sovereign's effigy and usual legend on the obverse, and on the reverse the design shown in the illustration, a watchman leaning on a sword and holding a shield inscribed 'To GUARD MY PEOPLE' with a fortified city in the background. The ribbon is dark blue with white edges and a white stripe in the centre. (No. 53.)

The original warrant was amended in 1916, 1930, 1933 and twice in 1936. British subjects and others serving in recognized Police Forces or Fire Brigades in colonies, protectorates and mandated territories became eligible, as did those in any Dominion whose Government so desired.

Since 1933 there have been two distinct medals—'*For Gallantry*' and '*For Distinguished Service.*' The first has the words 'FOR GALLANTRY' in the exergue, or space at the foot of the figure, while a thin red line was added in each white stripe of the ribbon. (No. 52.) The old ribbon was retained on the medal for Distinguished Service, which has the words 'FOR DISTINGUISHED POLICE SERVICE' round the figure of the watchman on the reverse.

Both these awards take precedence before war medals.

The medal became known as the 'King's Police and Fire Service Medal' during the war of 1939–45, and became 'The Queen's Police Medal' in May, 1954, when a separate medal was instituted for the Fire Services, described next.

The Queen's Police Medal, *for Gallantry*, is now only awarded posthumously. Gallantry on the part of the Police, in common with other citizens, is now recognized by the award, in descending order according to the degree of gallantry, of the George Cross, George Medal, the British Empire Medal, or the Queen's Commendation for brave conduct.

## THE QUEEN'S FIRE SERVICE MEDAL FOR GALLANTRY
## THE QUEEN'S FIRE SERVICE MEDAL FOR DISTINGUISHED SERVICE

Established in 1954. Circular medals in silver with the Sovereign's effigy on the obverse, and on the reverse the same designs and wording as the Police Medals but with the word 'FIRE' substituted for 'POLICE' on the D.S.M. It is laid down that the medal shall be awarded only to those 'who have either performed acts of exceptional courage and skill at the cost of their lives, or exhibited conspicuous devotion to duty' as members of a recognized fire brigade in the United Kingdom, the Colonies, etc., as for the Queen's Police Medal.

The ribbon is scarlet with narrow yellow edges and a narrow yellow stripe in the centre. When awarded for acts of exceptional courage, each yellow stripe of the ribbon has a thin dark blue line down the middle. Like the Police medal *'for Gallantry'* the equivalent Fire Servide medal is only awarded posthumously.

## 54 - EDWARD MEDAL

This medal was established in 1907 for distinguishing heroic acts performed by miners and quarrymen who endanger their own lives in saving, or endeavouring to save, the lives of others from perils in mines or quarries within the King's Dominions. In 1909 the award was extended to British subjects who, in the course of industrial employment, endangered their own lives in saving, or endeavouring to save, the lives of others from perils incurred in connection with such industrial employment.

The medals are of silver and bronze, and were originally known as the Edward Medals of the *First* and *Second Class*. In August 1917, however, their designations were altered respectively to 'The Edward Medal in Silver,' and 'The Edward Medal.' The obverses of both bear the Royal effigy. The design on the reverse of the miners' and quarrymen's medal, designed by Mr. Reynolds Stephens, shows a miner rescuing a stricken comrade and bears the words 'FOR COURAGE.' The reverse of the industrial medal shows a classical female figure holding a wreath, with the words 'FOR COURAGE,' and a suggestion of a manufacturing town in the background.

The cost of these medals is not provided from Imperial funds, but from the income of a capital sum subscribed by a few gentlemen of position interested in the subject. Whenever possible the medals are presented by the Sovereign in person. Bars could be granted for subsequent acts of gallantry, two such bars having been awarded, both to Silver Medals and both for actions in mines. Recipients were entitled to use the letters E.M. after their names.

The Edward Medals, among the rarest of British awards, are now granted only posthumously. As awards for living recipients their

places have now been taken by the George Cross and the George
Medal.

## QUEEN'S MEDAL FOR CHIEFS

This medal was instituted in 1920 as The King's Medal for Chiefs.
It was an oval badge with the crowned head of the sovereign on the
obverse, and on the reverse the name of the territory with a design
symbolic of the territory. It was awarded in silver-gilt (first class)
and silver (second class) and was worn round the neck from a silver
chain. The Queen's Medal, in silver-gilt or silver, is circular, and is
worn from a yellow ribbon with two white central stripes for the
silver-gilt medal, and a yellow ribbon with a single white central
stripe for the silver. As it may be appropriate for some persons
to wear the medal on the left breast together with other medals,
it is the intention that where it may be more suitable, a smaller
breast medal should be awarded rather than one worn round the
neck. It is worn before war medals.

## 55 - CONSTABULARY MEDAL - IRELAND

(now obsolete)
In the centre of the obverse is the Irish Harp surmounted by a crown,
the lower half of the harp being surrounded by a wreath of shamrock
and laurel. Above the crown the words 'REWARD OF MERIT,' and
below the wreath the words 'IRISH CONSTABULARY.' The reverse
bears the name of the recipient, surrounded by a wreath of shamrock
and laurel.

## 56 - MEDALS FOR SAVING LIFE AT SEA

The obverse of these medals bears the head of the Sovereign, with
the legend 'AWARDED BY THE MINISTRY OF TRANSPORT FOR

**SEA GALLANTRY MEDAL**

(*Large Medal*)          (*Obverse*)          (*Reverse*)

**MEDAL FOR GALLANTRY IN SAVING LIFE AT SEA**

87

GALLANTRY IN SAVING LIFE,' and the Royal cypher. The reverse shows the figure of a man holding on to a spar in the sea, and signalling to a lifeboat in the distance; a man supporting a rescued seaman, and a woman and child seated on a rock. The medals, awarded in gold, silver or bronze according to circumstances, are worn before war medals on the left breast, and are suspended from their ribbons by means of ornamental scroll clasps. They are given not only for individual gallantry in saving life, but also for collective cases of heroism, as, for instance, to members of a boat's crew. The Ministry of Transport's authority to confer such medals is derived not from Royal Warrant, but from the Merchant Shipping Acts of 1854 and 1894. They are the only medals now current issued under the authority of Parliament. Holders are entitled to use the letters S.G.M. (Sea Gallantry Medal) after their names. Awards of the gold medal are extremely rare, while a very high standard of gallantry is also required for the bestowal of the silver and bronze specimens.

## 56 - GOLD AND SILVER MEDALS 'FOR FOREIGN SERVICES'

These medals are issued by the Ministry of Transport through the Foreign Office, to foreigners only. The medals are four in number, each having on the obverse the head of the reigning Sovereign with the usual titular legend. The reverse bears the words 'PRESENTED BY (in the case of No. 3, 'FROM') THE BRITISH GOVERN-MENT,' within a wreath of oak leaves surmounted by a crown, with legend as follows: (1) For Saving the Life of a British Subject. (2) For Saving the Lives of British Subjects. (3) For Gallantry and Humanity. (4) For Assisting a British Vessel in Distress. The medals are given in gold to officers and in silver to men. They are small, approximately 32 mm. in diameter, and were originally suspended from plain crimson ribbons, since altered to ribbons precisely similar to that of the Ministry of Transport for Saving Life at Sea.

## INDIAN POLICE MEDAL FOR GALLANTRY
(now obsolete)

This medal was in bronze. On the obverse is the effigy of the King Emperor crowned, and facing left. The reverse shows a wreath of laurel surmounted by a small Imperial Crown. Across the wreath is a band inscribed 'FOR DISTINGUISHED CONDUCT.' Above this band is the word 'INDIAN,' and below the word 'POLICE.' (See pages 182-3 Police Medal, India.)

## 57 - INDIAN POLICE MEDAL FOR MERITORIOUS SERVICE
## BURMA POLICE MEDAL FOR GALLANTRY
## 58 - BURMA POLICE MEDAL FOR MERITORIOUS SERVICE
## 59 - COLONIAL POLICE MEDAL FOR GALLANTRY
## 60 - COLONIAL POLICE MEDAL

This medal was established in 1938 for award in the Colonies to all members of the Police Forces and properly organized Fire Brigades for (1) conspicuous gallantry, or (2) valuable services characterized by resource and devotion to duty, including long service marked by exceptional ability, merit and exemplary conduct. Bars may be awarded for further acts, with the usual silver rose on the ribbon when it alone is worn. The ribbon of the gallantry medal has narrow red stripes down the green edges.

# *British War Medals*

### 61 - NAVY GOLD MEDALS (1794–1815)

The Naval Gold Medals were instituted on the occasion of Lord Howe's victory over the French Fleet on 'the glorious first of June' 1794, and their award continued until 1815.

The large medal, conferred only upon admirals, was circular and 50 mm. across. On the obverse was part of an antique galley, on the prow of which was the winged figure of Victory placing a wreath on the head of Britannia, who stands on the galley with her right foot on a helmet, and holding a spear in her left hand. Behind her is the Union shield. The reverse was engraved with the name of the recipient and the event for which the medal was conferred within a wreath of oak and laurel. The medal was suspended by a plain gold ring and was worn round the neck from a ribbon, 44 mm. wide, of white with blue borders.

The smaller medal, 32 mm. in diameter, awarded to captains, has the same obverse, while the reverse is the same as for the large medal with the wreath omitted. It is mounted from a plain gold ring and bar from the same ribbon as for the admirals, and has a gold buckle on the ribbon. It was ordered to be worn from a button-hole on the left breast.

On the return of the British fleet to Spithead after the battle of 1 June 1794, King George III went on board the *Queen Charlotte* and presented Lord Howe with a diamond-hilted sword as a mark of His Majesty's approbation. He also gave gold chains, to which medals were afterwards to be attached, to Lord Howe and five of his subordinate flag officers. The medals awarded to the admirals and to the fourteen captains honourably mentioned in Lord Howe's despatch were not distributed until November 1796.

Similar medals were later awarded for various fleet actions, including the battles of Cape St. Vincent, 1797; Camperdown, 1797; the Nile, 1798; and Trafalgar, 1805, as well as for a number of outstanding single ship actions, up till 1815. In all, 22 large and 117 small gold medals were granted.

Nelson set an extremely high value on medals, and there was much heart-burning on the part of himself and his officers when the Government refused to sanction the medal for the battle of Copenhagen in 1801 because it might offend the Danes.

It must be emphasized that these gold medals were only awarded to admirals and captains, though on two occasions to lieutenants who had succeeded to the command of a ship after the captain had been killed in action. They were not given to other officers or men. Large or small, they could be earned on each and every separate occasion, so it was possible for one officer to wear as many as three.

Their award ceased after the expansion of the Order of Bath into three classes in 1815.

As mentioned in the Introduction, medals were privately struck and presented for the battle of the Nile by Mr. Davison, Nelson's Prize Agent, and for the battle of Trafalgar, by Mr. Boulton. Though they may occasionally have been worn in uniform, their use was never officially sanctioned.

## 62 - ARMY GOLD MEDALS AND CROSS (1806-14)

The grant of a gold medal for the battle of Maida, in Calabria, Italy, where the French were defeated with heavy loss by a small British force under Major-General Sir John Stuart, was doubtless suggested by the award of the Naval gold medals already described. It was given to the thirteen senior officers engaged, and is a gold medal, 38 mm. in diameter, bearing the laureated head of George III on the obverse with the legend 'GEORGIUS TERTIUS REX.' On the reverse is the figure of Britannia casting a spear with her right hand, and on her left arm the Union shield. Above is the flying figure of Victory holding out a wreath. In front of Britannia is the lettering 'MAIDA. JUL. IV. MDCCCVI,' and behind her the triquetra, or trinacria (the three legs joined as in the arms of the Isle of Man), the symbol of the island of Sicily. Below the figure of Britannia are crossed spears. The medal hangs from a gold bar from a ribbon of crimson with narrow blue borders, and was worn on the left breast from a button of the coat.

In 1810 the principle was adopted of giving gold medals of uniform design, differing only in the name of the action on the reverse, to commemorate the battles of Roleia and Vimiera, the cavalry operations at Sahagun and Benevente, and the battles of Corunna and Talavera, in Spain in 1808 and 1809. There were two medals, a large one for general officers, and a smaller one for field officers; also for those who had succeeded to the command of a battalion in consequence of the death or removal of the original commander; for officers commanding artillery and engineers; adjutant and quartermaster-generals; and the military secretaries.

The large medal, 54 mm. in diameter, has on the obverse the figure of Britannia seated on a globe and wearing a helmet. Her right hand is extended and holds a laurel wreath, and in her left hand is a palm branch. Beside her appears the head of the British lion, while her left hand rests on an oval shield charged with the crosses of the Union. The reverse has the name of the engagement for which the medal was granted within a wreath of laurel. The large medal, for general officers exclusively, is hung from a ring and was worn round the neck by a crimson ribbon with blue edges, 44 mm. wide.

The small medal, 35 mm. in diameter, is of exactly the same

**62 - ARMY GOLD MEDAL**
*(Large Medal)*     *(Shown full size*

design and hangs from a bar with a gold buckle half-way up the ribbon. It was ordered to be worn from the buttonhole.

Medals, large and small, were subsequently given for the capture of Martinique and Guadaloupe, in the West Indies, 1809–10; Busaco, Barrosa, Fuentes d'Onor, and Albuera, in Spain, 1810–11; Java, 1811; Ciudad Rodrigo, Badajoz and Salamanca, in Spain, 1812; Fort Detroit, America, 1812; Vittoria, the Pyrenees and San Sebastian, 1813; Chateauguay, America, 1813; Nivelle, 1813; Chrystler's Farm, America, 1813; Nive, 1813; Orthes and Toulouse, 1814.

*Bar* 'GUADALOUPE'

In 1813 it was ordered that only one medal should be worn by each officer. For the second and third events in which he participated and for which a medal was authorized, a gold bar, of massive gold, 50 mm. long and 16 mm. wide, with a laureated border and bearing the name of the battle in raised capital letters, was mounted on the ribbon.

Upon a claim to a fourth mark of distinction being admitted, a gold cross was awarded in place of the medal and bars, with the names of the four engagements on the arms of the cross. Bars for further victories were authorized to be worn on the ribbon of the cross.

THE GOLD CROSS is of Maltese shape, 38 mm. square, having in the centre in high relief a British lion statant. In each limb is inscribed the name of a battle, and the cross is edged by laurel leaves with a double raised border. It is attached to the top swivel by a highly ornamental ring.

Of the large and small medals 469 were awarded without bars, 143 with one bar, and 72 with two bars. Sixty-one gold crosses without bars were distributed, 46 with one bar, 18 with two bars, 17 with three, 8 with four, 7 with five, 3 with six, 2 with seven. The cross which belonged to the Duke of Wellington alone had nine bars, which, with the four names inscribed on the arms of the cross, represented thirteen engagements.

The bars awarded with these Army gold medals and crosses established a precedent for the issue of engagement bars with future campaign medals, while the crimson ribbon with blue edges, which came to be known as 'the military ribbon,' was later used for the Waterloo Medal, and for the Army General Service Medal of 1793–1814, authorized in 1848, and is now perpetuated in the ribbon of the Distinguished Service Order instituted in 1886.

### 63 - SERINGAPATAM MEDAL 1799

Medals for service in India had been awarded to individuals by the East India Company as early as 1668; but the first occasion of the general distribution of a medal by the Indian Government was in 1784, on the return home of a detachment of the Bengal Army from active service in the West of India. The next occasion was in the following year, on the return of another detachment of the same army from service in the Carnatic. Further awards followed – for the Mysore War of 1791–2; the expedition to Ceylon in 1795–6; the Mysore campaign, including the capture of Seringapatam, in

### 62 - ARMY GOLD CROSS
'VITTORIA,' 'PYRENEES,' 'NIVE,' 'ORTHES'
*Bars:* 'PYRENEES,' 'NIVELLE'

1799; the expedition to Egypt in 1801; the capture of the French islands of Rodriguez, Bourbon and Mauritius in 1809–10; the capture of Java, 1811; the Nepaul campaign of 1814–16; and the Burmese War of 1824–5. Before the Battle of Waterloo in 1815, therefore, the general grant of medals was a well-established practice under the government of the Honourable East India Company.

All of these earlier medals, with the exception of that for the capture of Seringapatam, were given to *native troops only.*

The Seringapatam medal, ordered by the Directors of the East India Company in 1801, was presented to all the officers and men, British and native, engaged under Lieutenant-General George Harris at the capture of Seringapatam on 4 May 1799. The medals were struck in England; but for some reason which is not apparent were not sent to India for distribution until 1809. They were presented in gold for generals and other senior officers; silver-gilt for field officers and the general staff; silver for captains and subalterns; bronze for native commissioned and European non-commissioned officers; and pure tin for the privates.

**63 - SERINGAPATAM MEDAL**

The Royal sanction for wearing this medal, in respect of the Company's officers, was given in 1815. There does not seem to have been any similar official sanction for the British Army until 1851.

The medal has, on the reverse, a representation of the storming of the breach at Seringapatam, with the meridian sun denoting the time of assault. At the foot, in Persian characters, the inscription – 'The Fort of Seringapatam, the gift of God, the 4th May, 1799.' The obverse has the British lion subduing the tiger, the emblem of Tippoo Sultan's government, and on a banner the Union badge with the Arabic inscription 'The Lion of God is the Conqueror.' Below is the date, 'IV. May. MDCCXCIX.'

The medal was worn by general officers round the neck, and by others on the left breast. Some were worn with the crimson, blue-edged ribbon like that of the Army gold medals and crosses already described, others from a ribbon of pale orange moiré, the shading of which was intended to represent the stripes in the fur of a tiger, Tippoo Sultan's favourite emblem.

## 64 - NAVAL GENERAL SERVICE MEDAL (1793–1840)

One side of this medal, authorized in 1847, bears the diademed head of Queen Victoria, the usual legend and the date, '1848.' The other side shows a figure of Britannia seated on a sea-horse, with a trident in her right hand and a laurel branch in the left. The artist was Mr. W. Wyon, R.A. There is a plain silver clasp for suspension. Engagement bars for no less than 230 different engagements, actions and cutting-out expeditions were authorized. These either bear the name of an action, the name of a vessel capturing or defeating an enemy's ship, or the words 'BOAT SERVICE' with the date. It is impossible to mention all the bars here, but among them there are those inscribed '1ST JUNE, 1794,' for Lord Howe's action on the 'GLORIOUS FIRST OF JUNE,' 1794; 'CAMPERDOWN,' for the battle of 11 October 1797; 'NILE,' for Lord Nelson's battle in Aboukir Bay,

**64 - NAVAL GENERAL SERVICE MEDAL (1793–1840)** *(Obverse)*

1 August 1798; 'COPENHAGEN,' 2 April 1801; 'TRAFALGAR,' 21 October 1805; 'SHANNON WITH CHESAPEAKE,' 1 June 1813; 'NAVARINO,' 20 October 1827. The last bar issued was that inscribed 'SYRIA,' for the operations of November 1840. This medal was not issued until 1848. Included in the list of recipients of the medal with the bar for '1ST JUNE, 1794,' was Daniel Tremendous McKenzie, of H.M.S. *Tremendous.* He was officially styled as 'Baby.' At that time a certain proportion of the seamen were allowed to take their wives to sea with them, and 'Tremendous McKenzie' was born at sea shortly before the action. A woman, Jane Townshend, of H.M.S. *Defiance* at Trafalgar, claimed the medal and bar for the battle of Trafalgar, as the Gazette directed that all who were present in this action should have a medal, 'without any restrictions as to sex.' However, as noted in handwriting on the Admiralty Medal Rolls, 'upon further consideration this cannot be allowed.' If the grant had been approved for Jane Townshend, numbers of other women who had been on board ships during any Naval action between 1793 and 1840 might also have claimed the award. Various Army officers and soldiers received the Naval medal and bars, for during the wars for which it was issued troops were not infrequently embarked on board men-of-war instead of Royal Marines. Naval General Service Medals, with amongst others, bars of the following actions were issued to certain officers and men of the Army who were serving on board His Majesty's ships: '1ST JUNE, 1794'; 'ST. VINCENT,' 14 September 1797; 'COPENHAGEN,' 2 April 1801; 'ST. SEBASTIAN,' August–September 1813; 'ALGIERS,' 27 August 1815; 'NAVARINO,' 20 October 1827; 'SYRIA,' November 1840.

A full list of bars to the Naval General Service Medal (1793–1840) is given in Appendix 1.

**64 - NAVAL GENERAL SERVICE MEDAL**
(1793–1840)     (*Reverse*)

## 65 - MILITARY GENERAL SERVICE MEDAL
(1793–1814)

The obverse of this medal is the same as that of the Naval General Service Medal just described. Upon the reverse appears an upright figure of Queen Victoria standing on a dais. She is crowning the kneeling figure of the Duke of Wellington with a wreath of laurel. By the side of the dais is the British lion couchant. Round the top circumference are the words 'TO THE BRITISH ARMY'; '1793–1814' at the bottom. Mr. W. Wyon, R.A., was the artist. The ribbon for suspension passes through a plain clasp at the top of the medal. Twenty-nine different engagement bars were issued, and though the medal was to be bestowed for services from 1793 till 1814, it will be noticed that no bars were awarded for services before 1801, or between 1801 and 1806. The following is a list of the bars awarded: 'EGYPT.' This bar, for the campaign of 1801, was granted in 1850, to those soldiers who had taken part in the operations and 'were still alive.' 'MAIDA,' for the battle in Calabria of 4 July 1806. 'ROLEIA,' for the engagement of 17 August 1808, Peninsular War. 'VIMIERA,' for the battle of 21 August 1808, Peninsular War. 'SAHAGUN,' 21 December 1808, Peninsular War. 'BENEVENTE,'

**65 - MILITARY GENERAL SERVICE MEDAL**
(1793–1814)     (*Obverse*)
'CHATEAUGUAY '

29 December 1808, Peninsular War. (A single bar inscribed 'SAHAGUN & BENEVENTE' was given to those men who had fought in both engagements.) 'CORUNNA,' 16 January 1809, Peninsular War. 'MARTINIQUE,' 24 February 1809, West Indies. 'TALAVERA,' 27–28 July 1809, Peninsular War. 'GUADALOUPE,' January–February 1810, West Indies. 'BUSACO,' 27 September 1810, Peninsular War. 'BARROSA,' 5 March 1811, Peninsular War. 'FUENTES D'ONOR,' 5 May 1811, Peninsular War. 'ALBUERA,' 16 May 1811, Peninsular War. 'JAVA,' August–September 1811. 'CIUDAD RODRIGO,' 19 January 1812, Peninsular War. 'BADAJOZ,' 17 March–6 April 1812, Peninsular War. 'SALAMANCA,' 22 July 1812, Peninsular War. 'FORT DETROIT,' 16 August 1812, North America. 'CHATEAUGUAY,' 26 October 1812, North America. 'CHRYSTLER'S FARM,' 11 November 1813, North America. 'VITTORIA,' 21 June 1813, Peninsular War. 'PYRENEES,' 28 July–2 August 1813, Peninsular War. 'ST. SEBASTIAN,' August–September 1813, Peninsular War. 'NIVELLE,' 16 November 1913, Peninsular War. 'NIVE,' 9–13 December 1813, Peninsular War. 'ORTHES,' 17 February 1814, Peninsular War; and 'TOULOUSE,' 10 April 1814, Peninsular War. As already mentioned, senior officers of the Army had previously been granted gold medals and bars for all the engagements and battles mentioned above, but no medal had been bestowed upon the junior officers or the rank and file. There was considerable feeling in the matter, and no little discussion in the Houses of Parliament, and to rectify the omission the Army General Service Medal was eventually sanctioned by Queen Victoria in 1847, and was issued the following year to all surviving officers and men who had been in any of the battles mentioned. The Duke of Richmond was almost entirely responsible for the award, and the officers interested in the grant presented him with a piece of plate to the value of 1,500 guineas. One Naval officer, Lieutenant Carroll, received the Army medal and bar for 'MAIDA,' while a few other officers of the Royal Navy and Royal Marines were awarded it with the 'GUADALOUPE' and 'JAVA' bars.

'BADAJOZ,' 'SALAMANCA,' 'VITTORIA,' 'ST. SEBASTIAN'

65 - MILITARY GENERAL SERVICE MEDAL (1793–1814) (*Reverse*) 'EGYPT.' 'MARTINIQUE,' 'GUADALOUPE'

#### 66 - WATERLOO MEDAL (1815)
The ribbon is 38 mm. wide. This medal bears on the obverse the effigy of H.R.H. the Prince Regent, with the words 'GEORGE P. REGENT.' On the reverse is a winged figure of Victory seated on a plinth, the base of which bears the word 'WATERLOO.' Round the top circumference is the name 'WELLINGTON,' and at the bottom the date 'JUNE 18TH, 1815.' The artist was Mr. Thomas Wyon. When issued the medal was suspended by means of a large steel ring through which the ribbon passed, but many officers and men had the ring removed and an ornamental silver bar substituted. No engagement bars were issued, as the medal bears the name of the battle. The medal was issued in 1816–17, at the suggestion of the Duke of Wellington, and besides being bestowed upon all officers and men who had been at Waterloo, was given to those who had fought at the battle of Ligny on 16 June, and at Quatre Bras on 16 June.

66 - WATERLOO MEDAL (1815) (*Obverse*)

**66 - WATERLOO MEDAL** (1815)
(*Reverse*)

**66 - FIRST BURMAH MEDAL**
(1824–26)       (*Reverse*)

**66 - FIRST BURMAH MEDAL** (1824–26)
One side of this medal shows the white elephant of Ava kneeling before a victorious lion. In the background is a Union Jack and palm trees. Below is a Persian inscription reading, 'The elephant of Ava submitting to the British lion. 1826.' On the obverse is shown an attacking party advancing towards a pagoda. In the foreground is the dismounted figure of Sir A. Campbell directing the operations from beneath a palm tree. A steamer is in the left background. Below, in Persian, is the inscription, 'The Standard of the Victorious Army of England in Ava.' The ribbon, which was 38 mm. wide, passed through a steel ring like that of the Waterloo Medal. This medal was issued by the East India Company in 1826, to the Madras and Bengal native troops.

It was given in gold to officers, and in silver to others, and no engagement bars were issued. Naval officers and men who had served in the Irrawaddy flotilla during the campaign subsequently received the 'India Medal, 1799–1826,' with a bar for 'AVA.'

'KIRKEE AND POONA:'

**67 - FIRST INDIA MEDAL** (1799–1826)
On the obverse of this medal is the head of Queen Victoria with the legend 'VICTORIA REGINA.' The reverse has a seated winged figure of Victory in the foreground. She holds a laurel wreath in one hand and a wreath in the other. Above appears the inscription 'TO THE ARMY OF INDIA,' and below the dates '1799–1826.' The artist was Mr. W. Wyon, R.A. The ribbon passes through an ornamental scroll clasp at the top of the medal. This medal was the counterpart for the troops in India of the Army General Service Medal. It was issued in 1851 at the request and expense of the Hon. East India Company. Bars for the following battles were issued: 'ALLIGHUR:' storming of Allighur, 4 September 1803. 'BATTLE OF DELHI,' 11

**67 - FIRST INDIA MEDAL**
(1799–1826) 'NEPAUL:' (*Obverse*)

September 1803, Mahrattas defeated by British. 'ASSAYE:' 23 September 1803, Mahrattas defeated by Wellesley. 'ASSEERGHUR:' siege of Asseerghur, 21 October 1803. 'LASWARREE,' 1 November 1803. 'ARGAUM:' battle of Argaum, 26 November 1803. 'GAWIL-GHUR:' siege and storming of Gawilghur, 15 December 1803. 'DEFENCE OF DELHI:' 7–16 October 1804, besieging force of Mahrattas defeated by British. 'BATTLE OF DEIG,' 13 November 1804. 'CAPTURE OF DEIG,' 23 December 1804. 'NEPAUL:' war in Nepaul, 1814–16. 'KIRKEE,' November 1817. 'POONA:' battle and capture of Poona, November 1817. 'KIRKEE AND POONA:' battles of Kirkee and Poona, November 1817. 'SEETABULDEE:' battle of Seetabuldee, 26–7 November 1817. 'NAGPORE:' battle and capture of Nagpore, November and December 1817. 'SEETABULDEE AND NAGPORE.' 'MAHEIDPOOR:' battle of Maheidpoor, 21 December 1817. 'CORYGAUM:' defence of Corygaum, 1 January 1818. 'AVA:' war in Ava, 1824–6. 'BHURTPOOR:' siege and storming of Bhurtpoor, January 1826. Bars for this medal, contrary to usual practice, are worn in reverse order, reading from top down.

**67 - FIRST INDIA MEDAL**
(1799–1826)                    'AVA.'

## 68 - MEDAL FOR THE CAPTURE OF GHUZNEE
(July 1839)

This medal has on one side a representation of the gateway of the fortress of Ghuznee, with the word 'GHUZNEE' in a scroll below. On the other side are two branches of laurel with, inside them, a mural crown. Above, '23RD JULY,' below, '1839.' The ribbon passes through a plain clasp at the top of the medal. No engagement bars were issued. This medal was originally to have been conferred by the Shah Shoojah-ool-Moolk on the troops engaged in the capture of Ghuznee. The Shah Shoojah died, however, before the medal was issued, and it was subsequently bestowed in 1842 in the name of the Indian Government. The ribbon was originally intended to be half green and half yellow, instead of crmison and green. How the change came to be made is not known.

**68 - MEDAL FOR THE
CAPTURE OF GHUZNEE**

## 69 - JELLALABAD MEDAL (1842)

On one side of this medal is the head of Queen Victoria with the legend 'VICTORIA VINDEX.' On the other side is a winged figure of Victory flying over the fortress of Jellalabad. She carries a Union Jack in one hand and laurel wreath in the other. Above is 'JELLALABAD. VII APRIL,' and below, the year 'MDCCCXLII.' The artist was Mr. W. Wyon, R.A. The medal was hung from its ribbon by means of a plain german-silver clasp, and no engagement bars were issued. A Jellalabad medal was first issued in December 1842 to the European and native troops who defended the fortress. It did not bear the effigy of Queen Victoria, and was of a very rough design, and the medal described above was intended to supersede it. The men, however, preferred the original medal first issued, and comparatively few of the later ones were applied for in exchange. This ribbon is supposed to represent an Eastern sky at sunrise: pink merging into yellow, and yellow into blue. Its colouring is most striking, and the ribbon was revived in narrower form for the 'Kabul to Kandahar Bronze Star' of 1880.

**69 - FIRST JELLALABAD
MEDAL (1842)**

(*Obverse*)

**69 - CANDAHAR, GHUZNEE
AND CABUL MEDAL**
(1842)       (*Reverse*)

## 69 - CANDAHAR, GHUZNEE AND CABUL MEDALS
(1842)

The obverse of these medals bears the diademed head of Queen Victoria with the wording 'Victoria Vindex.' There are four different reverses: (1) A crown, the word 'Candahar,' and the date, '1842,' inside a wreath of laurel. (2) A crown, the words 'Ghuznee' and 'Cabul,' each in a laurel wreath, with '1842' below. (3) The same as No. 1, but with the names 'Candahar,' 'Ghuznee' and 'Cabul.' (4) The same as No. 1, but with the name 'Cabul' only. The medals are suspended from their ribbons by means of plain steel clasps, and were designed by Mr. W. Wyon, R.A. They were given for the operations in Afghanistan in 1842, and were issued by the Indian Government.

## 69 - MEDAL FOR THE DEFENCE OF KELAT-I-GHILZIE (1842)

This medal was specially struck for the heroic defence of the fort of Kelat-i-Ghilzie, May 1842. The garrison consisted of 950 men, and of these one irregular regiment of Shah Shoojah's force, in recognition of its gallant conduct during the siege, was specially brought to the strength of the Bengal Army under the name of the 'Regiment of Kelat-i-Ghilzie.' Its regimental colours were composed of the three colours of the military medal ribbon of India, red, yellow and blue. The Kelat-i-Ghilzie Medal has on one side a shield bearing the word 'Kelat-i-Ghilzie,' surmounted by a mural crown and encircled by branches of laurel. On the reverse appears a trophy of arms and below it a tablet with the word 'Invicta' and the date 'MDCCCXLII.' The medal has a steel clasp for suspension.

## 69 - SINDE MEDAL (1843)

This medal was awarded for Sir Charles Napier's conquest of Sinde. It bears on one side the head of Queen Victoria, with the legend

**69 - SINDE MEDAL (1843)**

'VICTORIA REGINA.' There are three different reverses: (1) A laurel wreath surrounding a crown, the word 'MEEANEE,' and the date, '1843.' (2) The same, but with the word 'HYDERABAD' instead of 'MEEANEE.' (3) The same, but with 'HYDERABAD' in addition to 'MEEANEE.' The artist was Mr. W. Wyon, R.A., and the medal is provided with a plain steel clasp for suspension. The action at Meeanee was fought on 17 February 1843, and that at Hyderabad on 24 March the same year. The appropriate medals were awarded to the officers and men who had been in one or both of the battles. The officers and crew of the Hon. East India Company's vessels, *Comet, Planet, Meteor* and *Satellite,* also received it, as these four ships formed the flotilla which took part in the campaign. The cost of these medals was borne by the Home Government, this being the only case on record where medals for Indian Service were not paid for by the Indian Government.

**69 - SINDE MEDAL** (1843)
(*Reverse*)

### 69 - STARS FOR GWALIOR CAMPAIGN (1843)

Stars made of bronze from guns captured at the battles of Maharajpoor and Punniar during the Gawlior campaign of 1843, were presented by the Government of India to all officers and men present at those engagements. They consist of six-pointed bronze stars, 50 mm. in diameter, with small silver stars in the centre. Round the centre of the silver stars are the names and year, 'MAHARAJPOOR. 1843,' or 'PUNNIAR. 1843,' as the case may be, and in the centre, the date, 'DEC. 29TH.' The back of the stars are quite plain except for name of recipient and regiment. When first issued these decorations were fitted with hooks and were intended to be worn on the breast of the coat like the stars of Orders of Knighthood. The recipients later fitted suspension clasps or rings, according to their individual fancies, and wore them as medals with the then usual Indian ribbon.

**69 - STARS FOR GWALIOR CAMPAIGN** (1843)

'PUNNIAR. 1843'

'MAHARAJPOOR. 1843'

## 70 - CHINA MEDAL (1842)

This medal was granted to the men of the Navy and Army who had taken part in the following operations in China: in the Canton River, 1841; at Chusan in 1841 and 1842; at Amoy, Ningpo, Chinpae, Tsekee Chapoo; in the Yang-tse-kiang; in the Woosung River; and in the assult upon Ching-Kiang-Foo. No engagement bars were issued. The medal bears on one side the effigy of Queen Victoria with the usual legend, and on the other a palm tree, an oval shield with the Royal Arms, and a trophy of weapons. Round the top circumference is the inscription, 'ARMIS EXPOSCERE PACEM,' and at the bottom the word 'CHINA,' and the date '1842.' A plain german-silver clasp was provided for suspension. The artist was Mr. W. Wyon, R.A. The crimson in this ribbon is said to represent the heraldic colour of Great Britain and the yellow the imperial colour of China.

**70 - CHINA MEDAL** (1842)
*(Reverse)*

## 71 - MEDAL FOR SUTLEJ CAMPAIGN (SIKH WAR) (1845–46)

The obverse of this medal has the effigy of Queen Victoria and the usual wording. Upon the reverse appears a figure of Victory holding out a laurel wreath in her right hand. In her left is a palm branch, and at her feet a pile of captured weapons. The words 'ARMY OF THE SUTLEJ' round the top circumference, and at the bottom the name and date of the battle for which the medal was struck. The medal was provided with an ornamental scroll clasp for suspension from its ribbon. The artist was Mr. W. Wyon, R.A. Medals with the following battles inscribed on the reverse were issued. 'MOODKEE 1845,' 'FEROZESHUHUR 1845,' 'ALIWAL 1846,' 'SOBRAON 1846.' For his first engagement a soldier received the medal with the corresponding inscription, and if he subsequently took part in another he was given an engagement bar bearing the name of the second. Similarly with second and third bars for his third and fourth engagements. This was the first instance of bars being granted with any Indian medal, the first Indian medal, 1799–1826, with bars for battles previous to 1845, not being authorized until 1851.

*(Obverse)*

**71 - MEDAL FOR SUTLEJ CAMPAIGN (SIKH WAR)**

'MOODKEE 1845,' 'FEROZESHUHUR
'SOBRAON          (*Reverse*)

## 72 - NEW ZEALAND MEDAL (1845–66)

The obverse and reverse of this medal are shown in the illustration. The new Zealand Medal was not authorized until 1869, and was then issued to the officers and men of the Navy and Army for services against the Maoris between 1845 and 1847, and again for the operations carried out from 1860 to 1866. The medal hangs from its ribbon by an embossed silver clasp. No engagement bars were given, but the medal bears on the reverse the dates between which the recipients served, or a single date or no date.

## NEW ZEALAND CROSS

This cross was instituted by the New Zealand Government in 1869 for award to members of the Militia, Volunteers and Armed Constabulary who had particularly distinguished themselves by bravery in action, or devotion to duty while on service during the war against the Maoris. In communicating the order establishing the cross to the Secretary of State for the Colonies in London, the Governor of New Zealand observed he was aware that the Queen was the fount of honour and could alone institute orders of distinction. The New Zealand Government did not pretend to any powers of this kind; but the proposed distinction was simply a local honour and the Governor's responsible advisers had urged there should be no delay in its award, particularly as the defence of the country had fallen upon the local forces. In his reply the Secretary of State observed that the Governor had overstepped the limits of his authority, and that it was necessary to point this out so that no precedent might be established for the institution of similar awards in New Zealand or any other Colony. In the very exceptional circumstances, however, the Queen had been pleased to sanction the institution of the decoration and the rules governing its award. The decoration consists of a silver Maltese cross with a gold star on each limb. In the centre, in a circle within a wreath of laurel in gold, are the words, 'NEW ZEALAND.' The cross is surmounted by a crown in gold which is attached by a ring and a V to silver bar

**NEW ZEALAND CROSS**
*(Obverse)*

ornamented with gold laurel leaves, through which the ribbon passes. The ribbon, 38 mm. wide, is crimson. As the New Zealand Cross was awarded to no more than twenty-three officers and men of the New Zealand Forces, and has not been used since 1869, it is probably one of the rarest decorations in the world.

NOTE – Other medals awarded in New Zealand are described later in this book.

## 73 - PUNJAB MEDAL (1848–49)

The obverse of this medal has the effigy of Queen Victoria with the usual wording. On the reverse is a party of Sikhs laying down their arms to General Sir Walter Raleigh Gilbert, who appears on horse-back. To the right is a file of British troops with colours flying, and in the background a hill surmounted by palm trees. 'TO THE ARMY OF THE PUNJAB' round the top; 'MDCCCXLIX' at the bottom. The medal hangs from an ornamental scroll clasp. This decoration was given to the officers and men of the Navy and Army for the war which ended in the annexation of the Punjab. Three engagement bars were issued, inscribed respectively 'MOOLTAN,' 'CHILIANWALA,' and 'GOOJERAT.' The first was awarded for the operations before Mooltan, 27 December 1848 to 21 January 1849; the second, for the battle of Chilianwala, 13 January 1849; and the third, for the battle of Goojerat, 21 February 1849. The bars were awarded according to whether the recipient had been in one, or more battles, but a large number of medals were given without them.

## 74 - INDIA GENERAL SERVICE MEDAL (1854)

This medal has on the obverse the usual head of Queen Victoria with the customary legend. The reverse shows a winged figure of Victory crowning a seated warrior with a wreath of laurel. Below a lotus flower and leaves, emblematic of the East. An ornamental scroll clasp is provided for suspension. This medal was first issued in 1854, to 'commemorate the services rendered against the Burmese in 1852–3.' It was used subsequently, however, for many campaigns and expeditions against the native tribes, and was not finally dis-continued until 1895. It was Lord Dalhousie, the Governor-General of India, who, in 1852, first suggested that a general service medal for India should be adopted, and that the medal, with appropriate bars, should be given for all succeeding campaigns in India. Medals had recently become very numerous, and the idea was to limit their number. The medal was issued for a large number of small wars and expeditions, with the following bars: 'PEGU,' 'PERSIA,' 'NORTH-WEST FRONTIER,' 'UMBEYLA,' 'BHOOTAN,' 'LOOSHAI,' 'PERAK,' 'JOWAKI 1877–8,' 'NAGA 1879–80,' 'BURMA 1885–7,' 'SIKKIM 1888,' 'HAZARA 1888,' 'BURMA 1887–89,' 'CHIN-LUSHAI 1889–90,' 'SAMANA 1891,' 'HAZARA 1891,' 'N.E. FRONTIER 1891,' 'HUNZA 1891,' 'BURMA 1889–92,' 'LUSHAI 1889–92,' 'CHIN HILLS 1892–3,' 'KACHIN HILLS 1892–3,' 'WAZIRISTAN 1894–5.'

## 75 - MEDALS FOR SOUTH AFRICA
(1834–35, 1846–47, 1850–53, 1877–79)

A medal for the campaigns against the Kaffirs of 1834–5, 1846–7

**NEW ZEALAND CROSS**
(*Reverse*)

**73 - PUNJAB MEDAL**
(1848–49) (*Obverse*)
'CHILIANWALA,' 'GOOJERAT.'

**74 - INDIA GENERAL
SERVICE MEDAL** (1854)
(*Obverse*) 'JOWAKI 1877–8'

and 1850–3, was issued in 1854. They all bore the date '1853.'
The same medal, with bars inscribed '1877,' '1877–8,' '1878,'
'1878–9,' '1879,' and '1877–8–9,' was again given for the campaigns
of 1877–9 against the Galeka, Gaika, Zulu and other Kaffir tribes,
the principle being that the date or dates on the bar covered all the
operations in which the recipients were engaged. The medal without bars was also given to the troops employed in Natal during the
Zulu War. The obverse of all the medals is the same, and bears the
diademed head of Queen Victoria with the customary inscription.
The reverse shows a British lion crouching behind a bush with the
words 'SOUTH AFRICA' above. The medal issued in 1854 has the
date '1853' below the lion, but in the '1877–9' specimen the date
is replaced by a Zulu shield, and assegais. They both have an ornamental scroll clasp for suspension.

**74 - INDIA GENERAL
SERVICE MEDAL** (1854)
'HAZARA 1888,'
'HAZARA 1891' (*Reverse*)

**75 - MEDALS FOR SOUTH AFRICA** (1834–53)

**75 - MEDAL
FOR SOUTH AFRICA** (1877–79)
(*Reverse*)     '1877–8–9'

**76 - CRIMEA MEDAL** (1854–56)
*(Reverse)*

### 76 - CRIMEA MEDAL (1854–56)

The obverse of this medal bears the head of Queen Victoria, the usual wording, and the date '1854.' The reverse shows a flying figure of Victory crowning with a laurel wreath a Roman warrior armed with a shield and sword. The word 'CRIMEA' is inscribed vertically on the left. The medal is hung from its ribbon by an ornamental foliated clasp, and its issue, with bars inscribed, 'INKERMANN' and 'ALMA' for those two battles, was authorized in December 1854, while the Crimean War was yet in progress. Subsequent orders, however, authorized additional bars being granted for 'BALAKLAVA' and 'SEBASTOPOL,' while another, 'AZOFF,' was awarded to the Navy for the operations in the Sea of Azoff. Medals with the 'BALAKLAVA' bar awarded to the 17th Lancers, 13th Light Dragoons, 11th Hussars, 4th Light Dragoons and the 8th Hussars, are most highly prized by collectors on account of the historic charge of the Light Brigade. The bars for the Crimean Medal are in the form of oak leaves, with the name of the engagement in raised letters. They are most unusual and artistic. The British medal was given to a limited number of French soldiers who fought as our Allies during the campaign.

**76 - CRIMEA MEDAL** (1854–56)
*(Obverse)* 'ALMA' 'BALAKLAVA'
'INKERMANN' 'SEBASTOPOL'

### 77 - BALTIC MEDAL (1854–55)

The Baltic Medal bears the usual head of Queen Victoria and legend. On the reverse is a seated figure of Britannia holding a trident, with a representation of the fortress of Bomarsund and Fort Sveaborg in the background. The word 'BALTIC' appears at the top, and at the bottom the dates '1854–1855.' The medal hangs from an ornamental scroll clasp, and no engagement bars were issued. It was issued to the officers and men serving on board H.M. ships which were in the Baltic in the years 1854 and 1855, and was also given to two officers and ninety men of the Sappers and Miners who served on board the flagship.

**77 - BALTIC MEDAL** (1854–55)
*(Reverse)*

**78 - INDIAN MUTINY MEDAL**
(1857–58)

'DEFENCE OF LUCKNOW'

**78 - INDIAN MUTINY MEDAL** (1857–58)
This medal has the usual Queen's head and legend on the obverse. On the reverse is a standing figure of Britannia with a shield. Her right hand is outstretched with a wreath of laurel. The British lion appears in the background. The word 'INDIA' appears round the top circumference, and below the dates '1857–1858.' The artist responsible for the reverse is Mr. Leonard Wyon. The medal is suspended from its ribbon by an ornamental clasp. The decoration was awarded to the British troops employed in the Indian Mutiny, and, amongst others, was given to the officers and men of H.M.S. *Pearl* and *Shannon*, and to the crews of the Hon. East India Company's vessels *Calcutta* and *Sans Pareil*. It was the last medal given by the Hon. East India Company in the name of the British Government. The following bars were issued: 'DELHI.' Granted to those employed in the operations against, and at the assault of Delhi, 30 May–14 September 1857. 'DEFENCE OF LUCKNOW.' Granted to all those who formed part of the original garrison under Major-General Sir John Inglis; and to those who succoured them, and continued the defence under Major-Generals Havelock and Outram, until relieved by Lord Clyde, 29 June–17 November 1857. 'RELIEF OF LUCKNOW.' Granted to the troops engaged in the operations against Lucknow, under the immediate command of Lord Clyde, November 1857. 'LUCKNOW.' Granted to those engaged in the operations against Lucknow, under the immediate command of Lord Clyde, November 1857 and March 1858. 'CENTRAL INDIA.' Granted to the troops employed in the operations against Jhansi, Calpee and Gwalior, and to those employed in Central India, January–June 1858.

**79, 79a - CHINA MEDAL** (1857–60)
This medal is of exactly the same design as that given for China 1842, except that the date '1842' on the reverse is omitted. It is suspended from its ribbon by an ornamental clasp. It was authorized

(*Reverse*) 'LUCKNOW.'
'RELIEF OF LUCKNOW'

**79, 79a - CHINA MEDAL** (1857–60)

'CANTON, 1857,'
'FATSHAN, 1857'

(*Reverse*) 'TAKU FORTS, 1860,'
'PEKIN, 1860'

**80 - CANADA GENERAL
SERVICE MEDAL**
(1866–70)       *(Obverse)*

'RED RIVER, 1870.'

*(Reverse)* 'FENIAN RAID, 1866'

in 1861, and was first issued with a ribbon of five equal stripes: blue, yellow, red, white and green, eventually to be replaced by the crimson ribbon with yellow edges. The medal was given to officers and men of both the Navy and Army, and the following bars were issued: 'CHINA, 1842,' to those entitled to the new medal who were already in possession of the one for 1842. 'CANTON, 1857,' to those who were employed in the operations against that city. 'TAKU FORTS, 1858,' to those present at the capture, 23 May 1858. 'TAKU FORTS, 1860,' to those employed in the capture of the forts, 21 August 1860. 'PEKIN, 1860,' to those employed in the operations resulting in the capture of Pekin, October 1860. 'FATSHAN, 1857,' to those Naval officers and men present at the battle. The first proof of this medal, which was not issued as it was thought that it might give offence to the Chinese, showed on the reverse the British lion trampling upon the Chinese dragon.

**80 - CANADA GENERAL SERVICE MEDAL** (1866–70)
The issue of this medal, which was presented by the Canadian Government, was not authorized until January 1899. It was given to soldiers of the British Army, and to those of the Canadian Militia, who were employed on active service during the Fenian Raids of 1866 and 1870, and the Red River expedition of 1870. Three bars were issued, inscribed respectively: 'FENIAN RAID, 1866,' 'FENIAN RAID, 1870' and 'RED RIVER, 1870.' The medal bears on one side the effigy of Queen Victoria, crowned and veiled, with the legend 'VICTORIA REGINA ET IMPERATRIX,' and on the other, the Canadian flag surrounded by a wreath of maple. The word 'CANADA' appears at the top, and the medal hangs from a straight clasp. The same ribbon is used for the 'Canada Medal' established in 1943.

**81 - ABYSSINIAN MEDAL** (1867–68)
The obverse of this medal has a small bust of Queen Victoria

**81 - ABYSSINIAN MEDAL**
(1867–68)     *(Obverse)*

within a beaded circle. The circle forms the centre of a nine-pointed star, the points of which reach to the circumference of the medal. The triangular spaces between the points of the star contain the nine letters of the word 'ABYSSINIA.' On the obverse there is a laurel wreath, inside of which are the name, rank and ship or regiment of the recipient in raised letters. The medal is surmounted by an Imperial Crown, and a large silver ring through which the ribbon passes. It was awarded to the soldiers and sailors who took part in the Abyssinian operations of 1867–8, which resulted in the capture of Magdala. It is the only medal on which the name of the recipient is embossed on the reverse, the usual custom being for the name, rank, etc., of the recipient to be engraved or stamped upon the rim.

### 82 - ASHANTEE MEDAL (1873–74)

This medal was given to all the men of Her Majesty's Forces who were employed on the Gold Coast during the operations against the King of Ashantee, 1873–4. The obverse bears the head of Queen Victoria with the usual wording, and the reverse a scene in high relief, representing a fight in the bush between British soldiers and a party of natives. The design, which is considered by experts to be one of the finest seen on British medals, was executed by Sir Edwin Poynter, R.A. A plain silver clasp is provided for suspension from the ribbon. An engagement bar, inscribed 'COOMASSIE,' was awarded to all those who were present at the battle of Amoaful, and the actions between that place and Coomassie, including the capture of the latter. Also to those who, during the five days of those battles, were engaged north of the Prah in maintaining and protecting the lines of communication of the main army.

**82 - ASHANTEE MEDAL**
(1873–74) (*Obverse*)
'COOMASSIE'

### 82 - EAST AND WEST AFRICA MEDAL (1887–1900)

The Ashantee Medal, 1873–4, was again used for many expeditions in East and West Africa between 1887 and 1900. It is impossible here to mention all these small campaigns, but the medal with the following bars was issued to the officers and men of the Navy and Army: '*1887–8*,' for operations against the Yonnie tribe, November 1887–January 1888. – '*Witu 1890*,' for Witu expedition of 1890, carried out by men from His Majesty's ships with marines. – '*1891–2*,' expedition up the Gambia. – '*1892*' expeditions against Tambi, March–April; against Toniataba, March–April, and against the Jebus, May. – '*Witu, August 1893*,' for the Pumwani and Iongeni expeditions, carried out by 236 officers and men of H.M.S. *Blanche, Sparrow* and *Swallow*. – '*Juba River 1893*,' for the expedition of August 1893, carried out by one officer and forty men of H.M.S. *Blanche*. – '*Liwondi 1893*,' February–March 1893, three officers and thirty-four men of H.M.S. *Herald* and *Mosquito*. – '*Lake Nyassa 1893*,' November 1893, H.M.S. *Adventurer* and *Pioneer*. – '*1893–4*,' fifty men of West India Regiment who took part in Gambia expedition, 1894. – '*Gambia 1894*,' February–March, men of H.M.S. *Alecto, Magpie, Raleigh, Satellite* and *Widgeon*. – '*Benin River 1894*,' August–September 1894, H.M.S. *Alecto, Philomel, Phoebe* and

**82 - ASHANTEE MEDAL**
(1873–74)          (*Reverse*)

*Widgeon.* – '*Brass River 1895*,' February 1895, H.M.S. *Barossa, St. George, Thrush* and *Widgeon.* – '*1896–7*,' '*1896–8*,' operations in the Gold Coast, Lagos, Borgu and in various other operations between 1896 and 1898; recipient received a bar according to the date of the operations in which he had taken part. – '*1896–9*,' to all officers and men on military duty in the northern territory of the Gold Coast, or in the Hinterland of Lagos, November 1896–May 1899. – '*Niger 1897*,' Egbon, Bida and Ilorin expeditions, January–February 1897. – '*Benin 1897*,' Benin expedition, officers and men of H.M.S. *Forte, Philomel, St. George, Barrosa, Phoebe, Theseus, Widgeon, Magpie* and *Alecto.* – '*Dawkita 1897*,' to the men of the Gold Coast Constabulary engaged in the Defence of Dawkita. – '*1897–8*,' same as '*1896–8*.' – '*1898*,' same as '*1869–98*.' – '*Sierra Leone 1898–9*,' military operations in Sierra Leone; February, 1898–March 1899. – '*1899*,' for Bula and other expeditions of 1899. – '*1900*,' Munshi and Kaduna expeditions, January–May 1900. Men already in possession of the medal received the bar only on taking part in a subsequent expedition. For one expedition, that against M'wele in 1895–6, the medal was issued with no bar, but with the word 'M'WELE' and the date impressed on the claw. The possession of the medal usually means that the wearer has seen a good deal of hard bush fighting, for, as a rule, the decoration was not issued to those who had not served ashore, and had not been in action. As many as five bars are sometimes seen attached to the ribbon, while two, three and four are by no means rare.

### 83 - MEDAL FOR AFGHANISTAN (1878–80)

The obverse of this medal has the head of Queen Victoria with the legend 'VICTORIA REGINA ET IMPERATRIX.' On the reverse a column of British troops are shown on the march. They are accompanied by native cavalry, and an officer rides in the foreground. In the centre is an elephant carrying a mountain-gun on its back. A mountain with a castle on its summit is in the background. The word 'AFGHANISTAN' appears round the top circumference, and below the dates '1878–79–80.' The medal hangs from its ribbon by a plain silver clasp. The following engagement bars were issued: 'ALI MUSJID.' For the capture of Ali Musjid, 21 November 1878. 'PEIWAR KOTAL.' For the forcing of the Peiwar Kotal of 2 December 1878. 'CHARASIA.' For the action of 6 October 1879. 'AHMED KHEL.' For the battle of 19 April 1880. 'KABUL.' For the operations at and around Kabul, 10–23 December 1879. 'KANDAHAR.' To the troops under Sir Frederick Roberts's command who fought in the action against Sirdar Mahomed Ayub Khan on 1 September 1880. It was first proposed to issue the 'India Medal, 1854,' with bars for 'Afghanistan,' 'Ali Musjid' and 'Peiwar Kotal,' for this campaign, but Queen Victoria subsequently decided to give a separate medal. The crimson in the ribbon is said to represent the heraldic colour of Great Britain, and the green the sacred colour of the Prophet.

**83 - MEDAL FOR AFGHANISTAN** (1878–80) (*Obverse*) 'PEIWAR KOTAL.' 'CHARASIA.' 'KABUL.'

**83 -** (*Reverse*)

**69 - KABUL TO KANDAHAR STAR** (1880)

**84 - CAPE OF GOOD HOPE GENERAL SERVICE MEDAL** (*Obverse*)
'TRANSKEI' 'BASUTOLAND'

## 69 - KABUL TO KANDAHAR STAR (1880)

This decoration consists of a bronze, five-pointed star with radiations. In the inner angles of the points are small balls. In the centre of the star is the Imperial cypher 'V.R.I.' encircled by the words 'KABUL TO KANDAHAR.' The back of the star is plain bronze with a hollow centre, and is generally inscribed with the name, rank and regiment of the recipient. The star is surmounted by a crown and a ring, and the ribbon for suspension passes through the latter. No bars were issued. The decoration was given to all the troops who took part in Lord Roberts's celebrated march from Kabul to Kandahar, 3–31 August 1880, and the bronze of which it is made came from guns taken from Ayub Khan at the battle of Kandahar, 1 September 1880. The ribbon is 38 mm. wide.

## 84 - CAPE OF GOOD HOPE GENERAL SERVICE MEDAL

On the obverse is the head of Queen Victoria with the legend 'VICTORIA REGINA ET IMPERATRIX.' On the reverse are the arms of Cape Colony, with the words 'CAPE OF GOOD HOPE' round the top circumference. The medal hangs from its ribbon by means of a straight clasp, and was issued by the Cape of Good Hope Government in 1900, with the approval of the home Government. It was awarded to the Colonial troops and to a small number of British officers and men who took part in the Basutoland and Transkei operations of 1880–1, and in Bechuanaland in 1896–7. Three bars were awarded: 'BASUTOLAND,' 'TRANSKEI' and 'BECHUANALAND.'

**84 - CAPE OF GOOD HOPE GENERAL SERVICE MEDAL** (*Reverse*)

## 85 - EGYPTIAN MEDAL (1882–89)

The obverse of this medal bears the head of Queen Victoria with the usual legend 'VICTORIA REGINA ET IMPERATRIX,' and the reverse a representation of the Sphinx on a pedestal, with the word 'EGYPT' above it. The medal, issued in 1882, bears the date on the reverse, but in subsequent issues the date was omitted. It hangs from its ribbon by a straight clasp. The medal was awarded to all soldiers and sailors who took part in the operations in Egypt and the Sudan, 1882–9, and the blue and white stripes in the ribbon are sometimes said to typify the Blue and White Niles. The following bars were issued: 'ALEXANDRIA, 11TH JULY.' To those present at the bombardment of Alexandria. 'TEL-EL-KEBIR.' For the engagement of 13 September 1882. 'SUAKIN, 1884.' To those who were landed at Suakin or Trinkitat between 19 February and 26 March 1884, and had already received the 1882 medal. Those who had not been awarded the 1882 medal received a medal with no bar. 'EL-TAB.' To those present at the battle on 29 February 1884. 'TAMAAI.' To those present at the battle of 13 March 1884. 'EL-TEB. TAMAAI.' To those present at both the above battles. 'THE NILE. 1884–85.' To those officers and men who served south of Assouan on or before 7 March 1885. 'ABU KLEA.' To those who fought in the battle on 17 January 1885. 'KIRBEKAN.' For the battle of 10 February 1885. 'SUAKIN, 1885.' To those who were engaged in the operations at Suakin between 1 March and 14 May 1885. 'TOFREK.' For the action of 22 March 1885. 'GEMAIZAH, 1888.' To those who were landed at Suakin before the battle of Gemaizah on 20 December 1888, and were present at the engagement. 'TOSKI, 1889.' For the battle of Toski, 3 August 1889. Many medals without bars were issued to the soldiers serving in Egypt, and to the sailors who served on board ships in Egyptian waters.

## 86 - NORTH-WEST CANADA MEDAL (1885)

The obverse of this medal bears the head of Queen Victoria with the words 'VICTORIA REGINA ET IMPERATRIX.' The reverse has the words 'NORTH-WEST CANADA, 1885,' surrounded by a wreath of maple. The medal hangs from its ribbon by a plain silver clasp. The medal was given by the home Government to the Canadian troops who were engaged in suppressing Riel's rebellion in North-West Canada in 1885. It was also awarded to members of the N.W. Mounted Police. No British troops took part in the expedition. One bar, 'SASKATCHEWAN,' was awarded to those men who were present at the operations in the vicinity of the Saskatchewan Rivers.

## 87 - MEDALS AWARDED BY CHARTERED COMPANY OF SOUTH AFRICA FOR SERVICE IN MATABELELAND (1893); RHODESIA (1896); and MASHONALAND (1897)

The obverse of these medals bears the head of Queen Victoria with the usual legend, and the reverse shows the British lion charging and trampling upon native weapons. The lion is wounded in front by an

**85 - EGYPTIAN MEDAL**
(1882–89) *(Reverse)*
'THE NILE. 1884–85 ' 'ABU KLEA.'

**86 - NORTH-WEST
CANADA MEDAL** (1885)
*(Reverse)* 'SASKATCHEWAN '

**MATABELELAND** (1893)
(*Reverse*)

**RHODESIA** (1896)
(*Reverse*)

assegai. In the background is a bush. Above are the words 'MATA-
BELELAND, 1893,' 'RHODESIA, 1896,' or 'MASHONALAND, 1897,' as
the case may be. Below 'BRITISH SOUTH AFRICA COMPANY.' The
medal hangs from an ornamental floreated clasp. The Matabeleland
Medal was given to those Imperial and Colonial troops who were
engaged with the Matabele under King Lobengula between October
and December 1893. That for Rhodesia was awarded to those who
served in the operations in that place between March and December
1896, and that for Mashonaland to those who took part in the
expeditions and operations of 1897. Men who were already in
possession of the medal received bars inscribed, 'RHODESIA, 1896,'
or 'MASHONALAND, 1897,' for the subsequent operations. The medal
with bar for 'MASHONALAND, 1890' was issued in 1926. The cost of
the medal was defrayed by the Chartered Company of South
Africa, but its issue was sanctioned by Queen Victoria.

87 - (*Obverse*)
'MASHONALAND, 1897.'

**88 - ASHANTI STAR** (1896)
This decoration was awarded to the officers and men who took part
in the expedition of 1895–6 to suppress slavery and human sacrifices,
and to punish King Prempeh for his refusal to carry out his part of
the treaty of 1874. The force had a very difficult march through
swamps and dense forests, but the King was compelled to render
public submission to the Governor, and, with his principal chiefs,
was made a prisoner and deported. The bad climate occasioned
many deaths, and Prince Henry of Battenberg was one of the
victims. It is understood that Princess Henry designed the bronze
star which was awarded by the Queen for the expedition. It consists of a four-pointed star with a St. Andrew's cross between the
arms. In the centre of the obverse is a crown encircled by a band,

**88 - ASHANTI STAR** (1896)

on which are the word 'Ashanti' and the date '1896.' The reverse is plain, but bears the words 'FROM THE QUEEN.' The star is surmounted by a ring through which the ribbon passes, and no engagement bars were issued.

## 89 - INDIA MEDAL (1895)

The obverse of this medal bears the effigy of Queen Victoria with the legend 'VICTORIA REGINA ET IMPERATRIX.' The reverse shows a British and an Indian soldier each supporting the British standard. At the sides the word 'INDIA' and the date '1895.' An ornamental scroll clasp is provided for suspension. This medal – sanctioned in 1896 – owed its origin to the Chitral Expedition of 1895. The India General Service Medal of 1854 had been issued with no fewer than twenty-three different bars between the date of its institution and 1895, and as many officers and men were in possession of it with as many as five or ten of its different bars, it had lost, in their eyes, a considerable amount of its value as a record of their campaigns. It was considered, therefore, that the time had come to start a new one. For the Chitral campaign, accordingly, the new medal was issued with bars for 'DEFENCE OF CHITRAL 1895' and 'RELIEF OF CHITRAL 1895.' In 1898 it was again given with bars 'PUNJAB FRONTIER 1897–98,' 'MALAKAND 1897,' 'SAMANA 1897,' and 'TIRAH 1897–98,' to the officers and men who had taken part in the different expeditions. Again, in March 1903, with King Edward's effigy on the obverse, the date, 1895, on the reverse deleted, and a bar inscribed 'WAZIRISTAN 1901–2,' it was awarded for the operations carried out between November 1901 and the following February. Those officers and men who had already received Queen Victoria's medal were awarded the bar only.

**89 - INDIA MEDAL** (1895)
'PUNJAB FRONTIER 1897–98 '

**89 - INDIA MEDAL** (1895)
(*Reverse*)      'PUNJAB
FRONTIER 1897–98,' 'TIRAH 1897–98 '

(*Obverse*)      'WAZIRISTAN 1901–2

*Issue of King Edward VII*

'RELIEF OF CHITRAL 1895.'

(*Reverse*)

### 90 - CENTRAL AFRICA MEDAL (1891–98)

The obverse and reverse of this medal are exactly the same as those of the Ashantee Medal, 1874, but as the ribbon is different it is a separate decoration. The first medal, sanctioned in 1895, was awarded for various expeditions in Eastern and Central Africa between 1891 and 1894. No bars were given, and there was a ring in the top of the medal through which the ribbon passed. The greater number of recipients were members of native regiments and their British officers, so the medal is rather rare. In 1899 the same medal was again issued for operations in British Central Africa between 1894 and 1898. This time, however, it was fitted with a plain silver clasp for suspension, while a bar inscribed 'CENTRAL AFRICA 1894–98' was added. Those officers and men who had already received the 1891–4 medal received the bar only, and had the rings of their medals removed and the plain silver clasp for suspension substituted. The black in this ribbon is said to allude to the Zanzibar troops employed in the expeditions; the terra-cotta to the Sikhs; and the white to the Europeans.

### 91 - SUDAN MEDAL (1896–97)

This medal has a half-length figure of Queen Victoria on the obverse with the words 'VICTORIA REGINA ET IMPERATRIX.' On the reverse appears a seated figure of Victory and a trophy of draped flags. The figure holds in her right hand a palm leaf, and in her left a wreath of olive. Below is the word 'SUDAN.' The medal hangs from a plain clasp, and no engagement bars were awarded. The black in this ribbon is said to represent the dervish enemy; the yellow, the desert; and the scarlet stripe, the 'thin red line' of British troops. The medal was given in 1899 and was bestowed on all those who had taken part in the operations for the reconquest of the Sudan.

### 92 - EAST AND CENTRAL AFRICA MEDAL (1897–99)

The obverse of this medal is exactly the same as that of the Sudan Medal for 1896–7 just described. The reverse has a standing figure of Britannia with a trident in her right hand and a palm branch and scroll in her left. The left arm is extended towards the sun which is just rising over the horizon. The British lion stands beside the figure of Britannia, and the words 'EAST AND CENTRAL AFRICA' appear below. The medal hangs from a straight clasp. It was given to the soldiers employed in the military operations in Uganda in 1897–8; to those who took part in the expedition against the Ogaden Somalis, April–August 1898; and to those troops employed in the operations against Kabarega in Uganda between March and May 1899. The following bars were issued: 'LUBWA'S.' For those who took part in the expedition against the Sudanese mutineers, September 1897 to February 1898. 'UGANDA 1897–98.' To those who took part in military operations in Uganda between July 1897 and March 1898. '1898.' For the expedition against the Ogaden Somalis, April–August 1898. 'UGANDA 1899.' To those employed in the expeditions against Kabarega. This medal superseded the Central Africa Medal, 1891–8.

90 - CENTRAL AFRICA
MEDAL (1891–98)
'CENTRAL AFRICA 1894–98'

91 - SUDAN MEDAL (1896–97)

**92 - EAST AND CENTRAL AFRICA MEDAL** (1897–99) 'Lubwa's.' 'Uganda 1897–98.'

**93 - ROYAL NIGER COMPANY'S MEDAL** (1886–97) 'Nigeria 1886–1897'

**94 - BRITISH NORTH BORNEO COMPANY'S MEDAL** (*Reverse*) *Punitive Expedition Medal* (1897–8)

## 93 - ROYAL NIGER COMPANY'S MEDAL (1886–97)

Following the example of the British South Africa Company, the Royal Niger Company, in 1899, decided, with Government approval, to issue a medal to those troops and constabulary who had taken part in expeditions in their territory between 1886 and 1897. The medal was only given to men who had been in expeditions in which casualities had occurred, and was awarded in silver to Europeans, and in bronze to natives. For the silver medal, one bar, inscribed 'Nigeria 1886–1897' was issued. The medal itself bears on its obverse the head of Queen Victoria wearing a wreath of laurel, with the words 'Victoria Regina et Imperatrix.' On the reverse is a shield inscribed with the words 'Pax,' 'Jus' and 'Ars,' the three words forming the letter Y. Behind the shield is a trophy of swords, guns and flags, and the whole design is surrounded by a wreath of laurel. This medal was very rare indeed in the British Army. The bar issued for the bronze medal bears the word 'Nigeria' only.

## 94–95 - BRITISH NORTH BORNEO COMPANY'S MEDALS (1897–1916)

Medals were issued by the British North Borneo Company to all those who took part in expeditions in their territory between 1897 and 1916.

(*a*) *Punitive Expedition Medal* (1897–8). Ribbon No. **94**. Awarded to all those present at any of the following actions: 'Inanam,' July 1897; 'Ranau,' August 1897, December 1897 and January 1898;

**95 - BRITISH NORTH BORNEO COMPANY'S MEDAL** (*Obverse*) *Tambunan Medal* (1899–1900)

'AMBONG,' during 1897; and 'LABUK' and 'SUGUT' during 1897 and 1898.

Presented to officers in silver (twelve issued), and to N.C.O.s and men in bronze (seventy-four issued). The rank and file were natives, Indians or Dyaks, and their bronze medals were exchanged for silver ones in 1906.

The medal bears on the obverse the arms of the Company, a Jacobean shield bearing, azure, a six-oared galley sailing on the sea, argent. On a chief, or, a lion passant guardant, argent. Supported on either side of the shield by a wild man of Borneo; above, the crest of two arms (one nude and the other clothed), issuing from wreath and supporting the Company's flag; below shield the motto of the Company, 'PERGO ET PERAGO' ('I advance and accomplish'). The reverse has the British lion standing in front of the flag of the Colony, a large bush in the background; in the exergue, a wreath between 'SPINK & SON' and 'LONDON.' Round the top circumference, 'BRITISH NORTH BORNEO.' A bar inscribed 'PUNITIVE EXPEDITION' was issued with each medal. War Office sanction was granted for the medal to be worn in uniform, but it is extremely rare. The ribbon was formerly watered orange, but was altered in 1917 to the one shown.

(b) *Punitive Expeditions Medal* (1897–8). Ribbon No. **94**. Awarded to officers in silver (five issued), and to men in bronze (forty-seven issued). Bronze medals exchanged for silver ones in 1906. Granted to those who took part in two or more of the actions mentioned above, and worn in addition to (a). It is also of the same pattern, and is worn from the same ribbon as (a), but has a bar 'PUNITIVE EXPEDITIONS.'

(c) *Tambunan Medal* (1899–1900). Ribbon No. **95**. Presented to officers in silver (eight issued), and to men in bronze (106 issued). Bronze medals exchanged for silver, 1906. Awarded with bar to all who took part in the Tambunan expedition, and the taking of Mat Saleh's fort in 1899–1900. The medal bears on the obverse the arms of the Company and the date, 1900, while the reverse shows two arms (one nude and the other clothed) supporting the Company's flag, within a laurel wreath with legend around, 'PERGO ET PERAGO.'

(d) *Rundum Medal* (1915–16). Presented in silver to all those who took part in the Rundum Expeditions of 1915–16 (113 issued). Issued with bar inscribed 'RUNDUM,' and those already in possession of any of the previous medals received the bar only. The medal is of similar pattern to those mentioned above but the ribbon, formerly of watered orange, is now the same as No. 94.

## 96 - SOUTH AFRICAN MEDAL (1899–1902)

This medal bears on one side the head of Queen Victoria with the customary legend. On the reverse there is a figure of Britannia with a flag in her left hand, and extending her right hand with a laurel wreath towards an advancing party of soldiers. In the background is the sea with men-of-war upon it; above are the words 'SOUTH AFRICA.' The medal hangs from a plain silver clasp. It was granted to all officers and men of the Navy and Army, and to all hospital

**95 - BRITISH NORTH BORNEO COMPANY'S MEDAL**    *Rundum Medal*

**96 - SOUTH AFRICAN MEDAL** (1899–1902) (*Obverse*) 'CAPE COLONY,' 'ORANGE FREE STATE,' 'JOHANNESBURG,' 'DIAMOND HILL,' 'BELFAST'

nurses, who actually served in South Africa between 11 October 1899 and 31 May 1902; also to troops in Cape Colony and Natal at the outbreak of hostilities, and to the soldiers guarding Boer prisoners at St. Helena between 14 April 1900 and 31 May 1902. A similar medal with the same ribbon, but with the word 'MEDITERRANEAN' on the reverse, was given to the officers and men of the Militia battalions who served in the Mediterranean garrisons during the war. It is impossible to give full details of all the different actions for which bars were awarded, but the following were issued: 'CAPE COLONY,' 'NATAL,' 'RHODESIA,' 'RELIEF OF MAFEKING,' 'DEFENCE OF KIMBERLEY,' 'TALANA,' 'ELANDSLAAGTE,' 'DEFENCE OF LADYSMITH,' 'BELMONT,' 'MODDER RIVER,' 'TUGELA HEIGHTS,' 'RELIEF OF KIMBERLEY,' 'PAARDEBERG,' 'ORANGE FREE STATE,' 'RELIEF OF LADYSMITH,' 'DRIEFONTEIN,' 'WEPENER,' 'DEFENCE OF MAFEKING,' 'TRANSVAAL,' 'JOHANNESBURG,' 'LAING'S NEK,' 'DIAMOND HILL,' 'WITTEBERGEN,' 'BELFAST,' 'SOUTH AFRICA 1901,' 'SOUTH AFRICA 1902.' The bars of 'SOUTH AFRICA 1901' and 'SOUTH AFRICA 1902' were awarded to those officers and men who had served in South Africa during those years, but who were not eligible for the medal subsequently given by King Edward (see the next medal described). The 'CAPE COLONY,' 'NATAL,' 'ORANGE FREE STATE,' and 'TRANSVAAL' bars were given to troops who were employed in the territories named between certain dates who did not receive any other bar for an engagement in Cape Colony, Natal, the Orange Free State or the Transvaal. Nobody, however, could be awarded both the 'NATAL' and 'CAPE COLONY' bars. Officers and men in the ships on the Cape of Good Hope station received the medal, but those who did not land on duty received it without bars.

### 97 - KING EDWARD'S SOUTH AFRICAN MEDAL (1901–02)

The obverse of this medal has the head of King Edward VII with the legend 'EDWARDUS VII REX. IMPERATOR.' The reverse and mounting are the same as Queen Victoria's medal for the same campaign. It was given to all officers and men, doctors and nursing sisters who were actually serving in South Africa on or after 1 January 1902, provided they had completed eighteen months' war service on that date, or afterwards completed it before 1 June 1902. Bars inscribed 'SOUTH AFRICA 1901' and 'SOUTH AFRICA 1902' were given with it, and those who did not qualify for the King's medal were eligible to receive them with their Queen's medals. The green, white and orange ribbon of King Edward's South African medal is never seen except in conjunction with the red, blue and orange ribbon of the Queen's, for if a man was awarded the former, he must also have been eligible for the latter. Very few King's medals were awarded to the Royal Navy, for by the middle of 1901 most of the naval brigades had returned to their ships, and men who were not ashore on war service did not receive them.

**96 - SOUTH AFRICAN MEDAL** (1899–1902) (*Reverse*) 'CAPE COLONY,' 'WEPENER,' 'TRANSVAAL,' 'WITTEBERGEN '

**96 - SOUTH AFRICAN MEDAL** (1899–1902) (*Reverse*) 'MEDITERRANEAN'

## 98 - KIMBERLEY STAR

This star was presented in 1900 by the Mayor of Kimberley to the defenders of the town who served during the three months' siege, ending on 15 February 1900. The star, shown in the illustration, has a plain reverse with the inscription 'MAYOR'S SIEGE MEDAL, 1900.' The ribbon, about 25 mm. wide, is of black and yellow, divided by a band of red, white and blue. The decoration was allowed to be accepted by officers and men, though it or its ribbon are not allowed to be worn in uniform.

## 99 - THE CAPE COPPER COMPANY MEDAL (1902)

A bronze medal, awarded to the Cape Copper Company, to those who defended the O'Okiep Mine, in South-West Africa during the South African War. The medal has a scroll suspender, and on the obverse, a miner and shovel, with his left hand on a truck on rails running into the adit of the mine, against a background of the setting sun, the whole encirled by the legend 'THE CAPE COPPER COMPANY LIMITED, 1888.' On the reverse, in relief, in ten lines, is the inscription 'Presented to the officers, non-commissioned officers and men of the garrison of O'Okiep in recognition of their gallant defence of the town under Lt.-Col. Shelton, D.S.O., against a greatly superior force of Boers, April 4th to May 4th, 1902.'

This medal is not officially recognized, and was not allowed to be worn; but is, nevertheless, a rarity. The ribbon is dark copper colour, watered, with a green stripe down the centre.

NOTE – For medals authorized by the Government of the Union of South Africa for award to officers and men of the forces of the Boer Republic who served against the British in the war of 1899–1902, see under 'South Africa.'

## 100 - CHINA MEDAL (1900)

This medal was sanctioned in 1902 for the men of the Navy and Army who had been employed in North China during the so-called 'Boxer Rebellion' of 1900. It was given to all officers and men who were employed in North China and in the valley of the Yang-tse-Kiang between 11 June and 31 December 1900, and also to those Indian troops who served in China under the orders of General Sir A. Gaselee. The medal bears on the obverse the head of Queen Victoria with the usual legend, while the reverse is the same as for the China Medal of 1842, with the date altered to '1900.' It is suspended from its ribbon by means of a plain silver clasp. The following bars were issued: 'TAKU FORTS,' to those engaged in the capture of the forts at the mouth of the Peiho, 17 June 1900. 'DEFENCE OF LEGATIONS,' to those who defended the Pekin Legations between 10 June and 14 August 1900. 'RELIEF OF PEKIN,' to those employed ashore in the operations between 10 June and 14 August 1900, which culminated in the relief of Pekin.

Admiral of the Fleet Sir Edward Seymour, the Naval Commander-in-Chief on the China Station, who led an unsuccessful allied expedition for the relief of the Pekin Legations in June 1900, received this medal and bar for 'Relief of Pekin.' As a young

**98 - KIMBERLEY STAR**

**100 - CHINA MEDAL** (1900)
(*Obverse*)

**100 - CHINA MEDAL** (1900)
(*Reverse*) 'RELIEF OF PEKIN'

officer he had also earned the medal and bars for the China War of 1857–60.

As a matter of interest, H.M.S. *Terrible* (Captain Percy Scott), whose men and guns had been landed in South Africa in 1899 and early 1900, sailed for China in April of the latter year. She again landed men and guns in North China in June, and was the only vessel in the Navy whose ship's company as a whole earned both the South African and China Medals with the appropriate bars.

### 101 - ASHANTI MEDAL (1901)

This medal was sanctioned in October 1901, and granted to the men of the Ashanti field force who were employed in quelling the rebellion of the native tribes between 31 March and 25 December 1900. During this time, also, the capital, Kumassi, was besieged by the rebels. The medal has on its obverse the bust of King Edward with the usual wording, and on the reverse a representation of the British lion looking to the left towards a rising sun. A native shield and two spears lie at the feet of the lion, and below, in an oblong, is the word 'ASHANTI.' A plain silver clasp is provided for suspension from the ribbon. A bar, inscribed 'KUMASSI,' was given to those who took part in the defence and relief of that place.

**102 - TRANSPORT MEDAL**
(*Obverse*) 'S. AFRICA 1899–1902'

### 102 - TRANSPORT MEDAL

This medal was instituted by King Edward in 1903, and was first awarded to certain officers of the specially chartered transports who had been employed in carrying troops during the South African War, 1899–1902, and during the China campaign of 1900. It was officially stated that it would be granted 'in future wars to the officers of the Mercantile Marine serving in the transports' whenever a medal was issued to the troops taking part in the campaign. The medal bears on the obverse the bust of King Edward in Naval uniform with the usual legend. The reverse shows a map of the Southern Hemisphere with a liner steaming through the ocean. Below is the inscription, 'OB PATRIAM MILITIBUS PER MARE TRANSVECTIS ADJUTAM.' The medal hangs from its ribbon by a straight silver clasp, and bars inscribed, 'CHINA 1900,' or 'S. AFRICA 1899–1902,' were issued. No bars have been issued since, and in the First World War the medal was more or less superseded by the Mercantile Marine War Medal, awarded to all officers and men of the Merchant Navy. In the Second World War officers and men of the Merchant Navy received the same awards as the Royal Navy.

**102 - TRANSPORT MEDAL**
(*Reverse*)

### 103 - AFRICA GENERAL SERVICE MEDAL (1902)

The obverse of this medal is the same as that of the Ashanti Medal just described, while the reverse is identical with that of the East and Central Africa Medal of 1899, but with the word 'AFRICA.' It is suspended from its ribbon by means of a plain silver clasp. The medal, as its name implies, was awarded for all the expeditions and small wars in Africa carried out by the Navy and Army between 1901 and the time of King Edward's death. It is impossible to give the details of all these different expeditions, but the following bars

**103 - AFRICA GENERAL SERVICE MEDAL (1902)**

were awarded: 'N. NIGERIA,' for operations of 1900–1; 'N. NIGERIA 1902'; 'N. NIGERIA 1903'; 'N. NIGERIA 1903–4'; 'N. NIGERIA 1904'; 'N. NIGERIA 1906'; 'S. NIGERIA,' for operations of 1901; 'S. NIGERIA 1902'; 'S. NIGERIA 1902–3'; 'S. NIGERIA 1903'; 'S. NIGERIA 1903–4'; 'S. NIGERIA 1904'; 'S. NIGERIA 1904–5'; 'S. NIGERIA 1905'; 'S. NIGERIA 1905–6'; 'EAST AFRICA 1902'; 'EAST AFRICA 1904'; 'EAST AFRICA 1905'; 'EAST AFRICA 1906'; 'WEST AFRICA 1906'; 'WEST AFRICA 1908'; 'WEST AFRICA 1909–10'; 'SOMALILAND 1901'; 'SOMALILAND 1902–4'; 'SOMALILAND 1908–10'; 'JUBALAND'; 'UGANDA 1900'; 'B.C.A. 1899–1900'; 'GAMBIA'; 'ARO 1901–2'; 'LANGO 1901'; 'JIDBALLI'; 'KISSI 1905'; 'NANDI 1905–6.'

Another issue of the Africa General Service Medal with the effigy and titular legend of King George V on the obverse was sanctioned in 1916. The medal is not issued without bars, and the following bars were authorized: 'SHIMBER BERRIS 1914–15,' to all officers and men who took part in the operations against the dervishes at Shimber Berris, Somaliland, 19–25 November 1914, and 2–9 February 1915. 'NYASALAND 1915,' to the forces engaged in the operations against the rebels in the Shire Highlands of Nyasaland between 24 January and 17 February 1915. Recipients already in possession of King Edward's Medal received the new bars only. A new bar, 'EAST AFRICA 1913—14,' was sanctioned in 1916. In December 1917 the same medal with further bars, 'EAST AFRICA 1913,' and 'EAST AFRICA 1914,' were authorized respectively for those who took part in the operations against the Dodinga tribe, June–August 1913, and for those who took part in the operations against the Turkania tribe, April–July 1914. Officers and others already in possession of King Edward's or King George's General Africa Medals received the bars only. Bars subsequently issued were 'EAST AFRICA 1915,' 'JUBALAND 1917–18,' 'NIGERIA 1918,' 'EAST AFRICA 1918,' 'SOMALILAND 1920.'

It was announced in February, 1955, that the Africa General Service Medal, with the effigy of the Queen on the obverse and the bar 'KENYA' would be awarded to the troops and others who had taken part in operations against the Mau Mau in the Colony of Kenya.

N.B. – The Africa General Service Medal is never seen without a bar.

**103 - AFRICA GENERAL SERVICE MEDAL** (1902) 'NYASALAND 1915 '

**104 - MEDAL FOR ZULU RISING IN NATAL** (1906)

## 104 - MEDAL FOR ZULU RISING IN NATAL (1906)

A silver medal was granted by the Natal Government in 1908 to all those who had taken part in suppressing the native revolt of 1906. It hangs from a straight clasp, and has on the obverse the head of King Edward with the usual wording, and on the reverse an erect female figure representing Natal with the sword of justice in her right hand and a palm branch in the left. She treads upon a heap of native weapons, and is supported by Britannia, who holds the Orb of Empire in her left hand. In the background there is a group of natives, while the sun is bursting forth from behind receding storm clouds. One bar, inscribed '1906' was issued with the medal.

**104 -** (*Reverse*)

## 105 - TIBET MEDAL (1903–04)

This medal was awarded to all members of the Tibet Mission and the accompanying troops who served at, or beyond, Siliguri, between 13 December 1903 and 23 September 1904. The medal bears on the obverse the head of King Edward VII, with the usual inscription, and on the reverse a representation of the hill city of Lhasa with 'TIBET 1903–4' below. A silver scroll clasp is provided for suspension. A bar inscribed 'GYANTSE' was given with the medal to all those who were present at the operations near Gyantse between 3 May and 6 July 1904. Comparatively few British troops received the award.

105 - TIBET MEDAL (1903–04)

## 106 - INDIA GENERAL SERVICE MEDAL (1908)

In December 1908 a new Indian General Service Medal was issued for the North-West Frontier campaign of that year. It bears the bust of King Edward, in military uniform, with the legend 'EDWARDUS VII. KAISAR-I-HIND.' The reverse shows a fort on a hilltop with mountains in the background, and below the word 'INDIA' inside branches of oak and laurel. The medal hangs from an ornamental scroll clasp, and one bar, 'NORTH WEST FRONTIER 1908' was granted. It was the last medal issued during the reign of King Edward. After the Abor Expedition of 1911–12, the same medal, but with King George's effigy on the obverse, was issued to the troops who had taken part. A bar inscribed 'ABOR 1911–12' was awarded with it, and those men who already possessed King Edward's medal received the bar only. Bars issued later were: 'AFGHANISTAN N.W.F. 1919'; 'WAZIRISTAN 1919–21'; 'MAHSUD 1919–20'; 'MALABAR 1921–22'; 'WAZIRISTAN 1921–24'; 'WAZIRISTAN 1925' (Royal Air Force only); 'NORTH WEST FRONTIER 1930–31'; 'BURMA 1930–32'; 'MOHMAND 1933'; 'NORTH WEST FRONTIER 1935.' A new India General Service Medal, with the effigy of King George VI was issued in 1936, and is described later.

## 107 - NAVAL GENERAL SERVICE MEDAL (1915)

Instituted by King George V in 1915 'for service in minor operations, whether in the nature of belligerency or police, which may be considered of sufficient importance to justify the award of a medal in cases where no other medal would be awarded.' It was first issued with a bar or clasp 'PERSIAN GULF, 1909–1914' to officers and men of H.M. ships employed in the suppression of the arms traffic in the Arabian Sea or Persian Gulf between 19 October 1909 and 1 August 1914. The same award was later extended to fourteen British officers of the Indian Army who had taken part in the suppression of the arms traffic.

The medal with clasps 'IRAQ, 1919–20' and 'NORTH WEST PERSIA 1920' were later issued to Naval personnel.

The obverse bore the head of King George V in Naval uniform with the usual legend, and the reverse a striking representation of Britannia and two sea-horses travelling through the sea.

In May 1940 with the effigy of King George VI and the clasp 'PALESTINE,' the medal was authorized for officers and men of the

106 - INDIA GENERAL SERVICE MEDAL (1908)

Royal Navy or Royal Marines present in Palestine, or serving in ships at Haifa, or on duty ashore, also to personnel of the Hospital Ship *Maine* and of Royal Fleet Auxiliaries, between the dates 19 April 1936 and 3 September 1939. Officers and men of H.M.S. *Weston* were also eligible for their services in the Gulf of Akaba and adjacent waters from the end of September to mid-November 1938.

The next issue, in 1947, with clasp 'S.E. ASIA 1945–46' was authorized for Naval personnel on operational duty in Java and Sumatra from 3 September 1945 to 30 November 1946, or in French Indo-China from the same starting date to 28 January 1946.

With clasp 'MINESWEEPING 1945–51,' the medal was granted to Naval personnel engaged in six months' post-war minesweeping service in the following areas up to the terminal date mentioned— East Indies, S.W. Pacific and China coast, 30 December 1946: N.W. Europe and British Isles, including the North Sea but excluding Thames Estuary, 30 October 1947: Thames Estuary, 21 October 1948: Mediterranean, except Greek waters, and approaches to Gibraltar, 15 August 1947: Greek waters, 30 September 1951: Red Sea, 15 April 1948.

The medal, with clasp 'BOMB-MINE CLEARANCE, 1945–1953,' was authorized for Naval personnel actively engaged for an aggregate of not less than twenty-six working weeks on the actual excavation down to, removal of, or final disposal of unexploded bombs; on the clearance of live minefields inside the perimeter fencing; the disarming of live mines; acting as water-jet operator; or service with the Mediterranean Fleet Clearance Diving Team. The areas and terminal dates finally laid down were as follows: *Pacific—* Hong Kong Island, Kowloon, and small islands adjoining, 16 December 1946; Singapore and Malayan area, 31 December 1949; New Guinea, 31 October 1946; Solomon Islands, 28 April 1953; Queensland coast of Australia, 31 May 1950. *East Indies—* Ceylon, Andaman and Nicobar Islands, and Cocos Islands, 30 June 1948. *Mediterranean—* Palestine, 30 June 1948; Malta, and the N. Africa coast (except Marsamxett, Marsaxlokk, Tobruk and Tripoli Harbours), 31 March 1950; Marsamxett, Marsaxlokk, Tobruk and Tripoli, 30 September 1951.

Though here mentioned out of its chronological order, the medal with clasp 'BOMB-MINE CLEARANCE 1955–?,' and the Queen's Head on the obverse, was authorized by an Admiralty Fleet Order, 1943, of 27 July 1956, for bomb and mine clearance by the Mediterranean Fleet Clearance Diving Team since 1 January 1955. The clasp was not to be manufactured until the operations abated and the terminal date was known. Qualifications are the same as for the Bomb-Mine Clearance clasp 1945–53, and qualifying service of less than six months on or before 30 September 1951, by those who had *not* been granted the medal for minesweeping and bomb or mine clearance could be aggregated towards eligibility for the new award. The new clasp, if earned by anyone in possession of the medal and clasp MINESWEEPING 1945–51, or BOMB-MINE-CLEARANCE 1945–53, or both, will be worn in addition.

Other awards of the medal since 1945, bearing the effigy of King

**107 – NAVAL GENERAL SERVICE MEDAL** (1915)
'PERSIAN GULF, 1909–1914'
*Issue of King George V*

'MINESWEEPING 1945–51'
*Issue of King George VI*

George VI, are as follows:

With the clasp 'PALESTINE 1945–1948,' to Naval or Royal Fleet Auxiliary personnel for 28 days' service afloat in Palestinian waters between 27 September 1945 and 30 June 1948; for service in ships acting in close support of the Army or those on the Palestine Patrol against illegal immigration by sea; as Naval armed guards in merchant ships carrying illegal immigrants from Haifa to Cyprus. Officers and men of the Royal Navy, Royal Marines and the Royal Fleet Auxiliaries landeu for duty ashore became eligible for the medal and clasp under the Army rules, e.g. by entry, as did Naval aircrew based ashore, and, under certain conditions, civilian members of various Admiralty Departments employed ashore in uniform.

With clasp 'YANGTSE 1949,' the medal was granted to officers and men of the following ships for service on the dates or within the periods mentioned: H.M.S. *Consort*, 20 April 1949; H.M.S. *London*, 21 April 1949; H.M.S. *Black Swan*, 21 April 1949; H.M.S. *Amethyst*, 20 April to 31 July 1949, both dates inclusive. Officers and Army personnel carried to the *Amethyst* on 21 or 22 April in a Sunderland aircraft of the R.A.F., with the crew of the Sunderland and a medical officer of the R.A.F. transferred to the *Amethyst* were eligible for the Naval medal and clasp.

With the clasp 'MALAYA' the Naval General Service Medal, with the effigy of King George VI, was authorized for 28 days' service afloat subsequent to 16 June 1948 in ships or craft patrolling off the Malayan coast in support of operations against bandits, or one journey up a creek or river in close support of the same. For service ashore the qualifying period was one day or more on duty in the Federation of Malaya employed as an integral part of the Security Forces, i.e. 3 Commando Brigade Royal Marines, 848 Naval Air Squadron, Royal Marine detachments employed in their infantry rôle. The qualifying period for Naval personnel attached to the Security Forces for training or jungle warfare familiarization was 28 days, while members of the Royal Naval Police, Singapore, the Malaya Naval Force and Malaya R.N.V.R. qualified in the same conditions as the Royal Navy. Awards of the medal since 1953, bearing the effigy of H.M. Queen Elizabeth II, have been authorized as follows:

With the clasp 'CYPRUS,' to naval personnel employed in or off Cyprus during the emergency following after 1 April 1955. The normal qualification period was four months, 120 days. This award was announced in a White Paper, Cmnd. 190, of June 1957.

With the clasp 'NEAR EAST,' to naval personnel engaged during the period 31 October to 22 December 1956, in the 'Suez Incident,' either ashore in Egypt or in ships operating off the Egyptian coast in the Mediterranean or Red Sea. Authority for this award was also contained in the above White Paper.

Naval personnel who already held the Naval General Service Medal (1915) for service before the war of 1939–45 and later qualified for another clasp, continued to wear the ribbon before those of the campaign stars, etc., 1939–45. A rose emblem was not added to the

'NEAR EAST,' 'CYPRUS '
(*Reverse*)

ribbon. Those who qualified for the medal for the first time after the end of the Second World War wear the ribbon immediately after that of the War Medal, 1939–45, if awarded, or after the Korea or United Nations' Service Medal is these have been previously earned.

The single oak leaf emblem is worn on the ribbon of the Naval General Service Medal to denote the award of a Mention in Despatches or the King's or Queen's Commendation.

# Campaign Stars 1914~15

### 108 - 1914 STAR

In 1917 the grant of the 1914 Star, sometimes, though erroneously, known as the 'Mons Star,' was approved for award to all those officers and men of the British and Indian Expeditionary Forces, including civilian medical practitioners, nursing sisters, nurses and others employed with military hospitals, who actually served in France or Belgium on the establishment of a unit between 5 August 1914 and midnight on 22–23 November 1914. Officers and men of the Royal Navy, Royal Marines, Royal Naval Reserve and Royal Naval Volunteer Reserve who served on the establishment of a unit landed for shore service in France or Belgium between the same dates were also eligible, but not those who served afloat.

On 19 October 1919 it was announced that the King had approved the issue of a bar to those already awarded the 1914 Star 'who actually served under the fire of the enemy in France or Belgium' between the dates mentioned above.

The decoration is a four-pointed star in bright bronze. The reverse is plain, and is stamped with the name and unit of the recipient. The bar is of the same metal as the star, and is of simple design with the inscription '5th AUG.–22nd Nov. 1914' on a frosted ground. It is not fitted to slide over the ribbon in the customary manner, but has four small holes pierced at the corners for sewing to the ribbon, a somewhat clumsy expedient which might result in accidental loss.

The ribbon is red, white and blue, shaded and watered, and is worn with the red nearest the centre of the breast. In undress uniform recipients of the bar wear a small silver rose on the ribbon.

There are thus two varieties of the 1914 Star, with and without the bar. Except for the slight difference in the decoration itself, there is therefore nothing to differentiate between an officer or man who received the 1914 Star without bar, or the subsequently authorized 1914–15 Star.

**108 - 1914 STAR**
'5th AUG.–22nd Nov. 1914'

### 108a - 1914-15 STAR

This star, sanctioned in 1918, is similar in shape and design to that just described. The only difference is that the date '1914–15' appears on the centre scroll, while the smaller scrolls bearing the words 'AUG.' and 'NOV.' are omitted. The ribbon is identical with that of the 1914 Star.

So far as the Royal Navy was concerned, it was issued to: All officers and men of the R.N., R.M., R.N.A.S., R.N.R., R.N.V.R., R.I.M. and Dominion Naval forces, who were mobilized and served at sea, or on shore within the theatres of military operations; to officers and men of the R.N.A.S. employed flying from Naval air stations on overseas patrols; to personnel of the Mercantile Marine serving under special Naval engagements; to canteen staffs who had served in a ship of war at sea.

In the Army, the star was awarded to all officers, warrant officers, N.C.O.s and men of the British, Dominion, Colonial and Indian Forces, including civilian medical practitioners, nursing sisters, nurses and others employed with military hospitals, who actually served on the establishment of a unit in a theatre of war. Individuals in possession of the '1914 Star' were not eligible for the award of the '1914–15 Star.'

### 109 - THE GALLIPOLI STAR

As a result of representations made on behalf of the Governments of Australia and New Zealand it was originally intended to issue a special star and ribbon to members of the 1914 contingents of the Australian Imperial Force and the New Zealand Expeditionary Force who had fought in Gallipoli and had embarked in Australia or New Zealand on or before 31 December 1914. The award was never issued as it was felt to be somewhat unfair to British, Indian and other troops who had fought in Gallipoli or in other theatres of war. The eventual result was the issue of the 1914–15 Star to all those of the British, Dominion, Colonial and Indian Forces, including the Naval Forces, who had served in any theatre of war up till 31 December 1915, and had not already been awarded the 1914 Star. The Gallipoli Star was to have been a bronze eight-pointed star with a circular centre inscribed 'GALLIPOLI 1914–15' with a crown above. The yellow in this striking ribbon represented the wattle of Australia; the grey, the fern leaf of New Zealand; the red, the Army; and the blue, the Navy.

108a - 1914-15 STAR

# *War Medals 1914~70*

### 110 - BRITISH WAR MEDALS (1914–20)

This medal was approved by King George V in 1919 to record the bringing of the war to a successful conclusion, and the arduous services rendered by His Majesty's Forces. The award was later extended to 1919–20 to cover the post-war mine clearance at sea, as well as service in North and South Russia, the Eastern Baltic, Siberia, Black Sea and Caspian. The medal, which hangs from its ribbon by a straight clasp, without swivel, bears on the obverse the effigy of His Majesty with the legend 'GEORGIVS V: BRITT: OMN: REX ET IND: IMP:' The reverse represents St. George on horseback trampling underfoot the eagle shield of the Central Powers and a skull and cross-bones, the emblems of death. Above is the risen sun of victory. The male figure, rather than a symbolical female one, was chosen because man had borne the brunt of the fighting. The figure was mounted on horseback as symbolic of man's mind controlling a force (represented by the horse) of greater strength than his own. The design was thus also symbolic of the mechanical and scientific appliances which helped so largely to win the war. The ribbon has an orange watered centre with stripes of white and black at each side and borders of royal blue. It is stated that the colours have no particular significance.

As regards the Royal Navy, the medal was granted to those of the undermentioned classes who performed twenty-eight days' mobilized service, or lost their lives in active operations before completing that period, between 5 August 1914 and 11 November 1918, both dates inclusive.

(a) Officers, warrant officers, petty officers, non-commissioned officers and men of the Royal Navy, Royal Marines, Royal Naval Air Service, Royal Indian Marine, Royal Naval Reserve (including Trawler and Fishery Sections), Royal Naval Volunteer Reserve and Dominion and Colonial Naval Forces.

(b) Mercantile Marine officers and men serving in His Majesty's commissioned ships and auxiliaries on Special Naval Engagements.

(c) Officers and enrolled members of the Women's Royal Naval Service who proceeded and served overseas.

(d) Members of Queen Alexandra's Royal Naval Nursing Service and Royal Naval Nursing Service Reserve, and recognized official nursing organizations, who served in a hospital ship at sea or proceeded overseas and served in a Naval hospital abroad.

(e) Canteen staffs who served in a ship of war at sea.

(f) Non-nursing members of medical units, e.g. dispensers, storekeepers, clerks, wardmaids, etc., who served in a hospital ship at sea or proceeded overseas and served in a Naval hospital abroad.

In the Army, the medal was issued to the following classes who either entered a theatre of war on duty, or who left places of residence and rendered approved service overseas, other than the waters dividing the different parts of the United Kingdom, between 5 August 1914 and 11 November 1918, both dates inclusive:

(a) Officers, warrant officers, attested non-commissioned officers and men of British, Dominion, Colonial and Indian military forces.

(b) Members of women's formations who had been enrolled under a direct contract of service for service with His Majesty's Imperial forces.

(c) All who served on staffs of military hospitals and all members of recognized organizations who actually handled sick and wounded.

(d) Members of duly recognized or authorized organizations.

(e) Enrolled and attested followers on the establishment of units of the Indian Army.

As regards the Royal Air Force the medal was granted to the

**110 - BRITISH WAR MEDAL**
(1914–20)          (*Obverse*)

undermentioned classes who either entered a theatre of war on duty, or who left their places of residence and rendered approved service overseas, other than the waters dividing the different parts of the United Kingdom, between 5 August 1914 and 11 November 1918, both dates inclusive:

(a) Officers, warrant officers, attested and enrolled non-commissioned officers and men of the Royal Naval Air Service, Royal Flying Corps or Royal Air Force.

(b) Members of women's formations employed under a direct contract of service with the Royal Air Force Medical Service.

(c) Members of duly recognized or authorized organizations.

The medal was also granted to all officers, warrant officers, attested and enrolled non-commissioned officers and men of the Royal Naval Air Service, Royal Flying Corps and Royal Air Force who –

(i) Had been actively engaged in the air against the enemy whilst borne on the strength of an operational unit in Great Britain.

(ii) Had been employed in flying new aircraft to France.

(iii) Had formed part of the complement of an aircraft-carrying ship.

It will be noted that officers and members of the Women's Air Force were not specifically referred to above. There might, however, be many who are qualified for the medal by reason of services with other women's formations prior to their having joined the W.R.A.F.

No members of the W.R.A.F. served overseas as such.

### THE MERCANTILE MARINE MEDALS FOR FIRST WORLD WAR

In July 1919 it was announced that the British War Medal which had been granted to His Majesty's Forces, would be granted also to the British, Dominion, Colonial and Indian Mercantile Marine.

In the United Kingdom the medal was given to those who had served at sea for not less than six months between the 4 August 1914 and 11 November 1918. Licensed pilots, fishermen and crews of pilotage and lighthouse authorities' vessels, and of post office cable ships were included.

In other parts of the Empire the qualifying service was the same, but all details were determined by the several Governments.

It was also announced that a Mercantile Marine War Medal be granted to the persons mentioned above who were qualified for the British War Medal, and who, in adddition, could supply evidence of having served at sea on at least one voyage through a danger zone.

Officers, men and women who, whilst serving at sea were captured by the enemy or lost their lives through enemy action or were precluded by disablement through enemy action from further service at sea, before being able to complete their qualifying service for one or both of the medals, were deemed to have qualified.

The medals earned by deceased officers, men and women, were issued to their legatees or next of kin.

**111 - MERCANTILE MARINE WAR MEDAL**   *(Obverse)*

Officers, men and women, who had served during part of the war in the Royal Navy, R.N.R., or under special Naval engagements, in the Army, or in the Royal Air Force, had in many cases performed service during some other part of the war which would entitle them to the Mercantile Marine War Medal. Such officers, men and women were awarded the Mercantile Marine War Medal if their claims were approved, apart from any further medal which might be awarded under the regulations of the Admiralty, War Office or Air Ministry.

Qualifying service in all cases was service at sea, and not service in harbours, rivers or other inland waters.

### 111 - MERCANTILE MARINE WAR MEDAL
The obverse of this medal, which is of bronze, bears His Majesty's effigy, as on the British War Medal, with the usual legend. The design of the reverse shows a merchant steamer ploughing through an angry sea, with a sinking submarine and sailing vessel in the background. The ribbon, red and green with a white central stripe, is typical of the port, starboard and steaming lights of a steamer. It is worn with the green farthest from the left shoulder.

### 112 - VICTORY MEDAL
This medal, of bronze, bears on the obverse a winged figure of Victory. On the reverse is an inscription, 'THE GREAT WAR FOR CIVILIZATION.' The rim is plain, and the medal hangs from a ring. The ribbon is red in the centre, with green and violet on either side shaded to form the colours of two rainbows. It was approved that any officer or man who had been 'mentioned in despatches' should wear a small bronze oak leaf on the ribbon of this medal. Only one oak leaf is so worn, no matter how many 'mentions' the wearer may have received. The oak leaf was issued in two sizes. The larger, worn with the medal, was affixed to the centre of the ribbon at an angle of sixty degrees from the inside edge of the ribbon, stem to the right. The smaller was worn, when the wearer was in service dress, transversely across the ribbon.

The medal was designed to obviate the exchange of Allied commemorative war medals, and was awarded as follows:

To the personnel of the Royal Navy of the undermentioned classes who were mobilized and rendered approved service either (i) at sea between midnight, 4–5 August 1914, and midnight, 11–12 November 1918; or (ii) on the establishment of a unit *within a theatre of military operations* –

(*a*) All officers and men of the R.N., R.M., R.N.A.S., R.I.M., R.N.R., R.N.V.R., R.N.A.S.B.R., and Dominion and Colonial Naval Forces. Trained pilots and observers and men of the R.N.A.S. employed in actual flying from Naval Air Stations at home on oversea patrols will be eligible.

(*b*) Mercantile Marine officers and men serving under special Naval engagements in H.M. Ships of War and Commissioned Fleet Auxiliaries.

**112 - VICTORY MEDAL**
(*Reverse*)

(c) Members of Queen Alexandra's Royal Naval Nursing Service, and Royal Naval Nursing Service Reserves.

(d) Officers and enrolled members of the W.R.N.S.

(e) Canteen staffs who served in a ship of war at sea.

The following services were not approved as qualifying:

(a) Service in depot ships, except those which go to sea; boom defence vessels, examination vessels and other craft employed on harbour service.

(b) Service at shore bases and depots, except those within theatres of active military operations.

(c) Services of a temporary and special nature at sea, or in theatres of military operations, e.g. casual inspections and inquiries, purchase of materials, trials, passage, etc.

(d) Service at sea, subsequent to midnight, 11–12 November 1918, except in certain specified cases, with regard to which a further announcement would be made.

For the Army the Victory Medal was granted to all officers, warrant officers, non-commissioned officers and men of the British Dominion, Colonial and Indian Forces, members of women formations who had been enrolled under a direct contract of service for service with His Majesty's Imperial forces, civil medical practitioners, nursing sisters, nurses and others employed with military hospitals, who actually served on the establishment of a unit in a theatre of war and within certain specified periods.

In the Royal Air Force the medal was granted to all officers and airmen who had either:

(a) Been posted and served with a unit in any theatre of war outside the British Islands, within certain periods.

(b) Served with an operational unit in the British Islands or overseas and have been actively engaged in the air against the enemy. This included service in airships, aeroplanes, seaplanes, kite balloons employed on fleet or coastal reconnaissance, convoy or antisubmarine work, or to protect the British Isles against air-raids.

(c) Been employed on flying new aircraft to France.

(d) Served as part of the complement of aircraft-carrying ships.

The claims of officers, airmen and women who became eligible on account of services rendered with the Royal Navy or Army, excluding the R.N.A.S. and R.F.C., prior to transfer to the R.A.F., were dealt with under the regulations of the Royal Navy or Army respectively.

## 113 - GENERAL SERVICE MEDAL (ARMY AND ROYAL AIR FORCE)

This medal was instituted in 1918, for award with distinctive bars, like the India and Naval General Service Medals, for minor campaigns which do not warrant the issue of a separate medal. The medal hangs from an ornamental suspender, and has on the obverse the effigy of the Sovereign with the usual legend, and on the reverse a winged figure of Victory with a trident in one hand and a wreath in the other.

The following bars have been issued up to date:

**113 - GENERAL SERVICE MEDAL**     *(Obverse)*
'KURDISTAN'
*Issue of King George V*

'PALESTINE 1945–48'     *(Obverse)*
*Issue of King George VI*

*(Obverse)*     *(Reverse)*

**113 - GENERAL SERVICE MEDAL**
*Issue of Queen Elizabeth II*

'IRAQ,' 'KURDISTAN,' 'N.W. PERSIA,' 'S. PERSIA,' 'NORTHERN KURDISTAN,' 'SOUTHERN DESERT: IRAQ,' for service in these countries at various dates from 1918 onwards; 'PALESTINE,' for services within the geographical limits of Palestine and/or Trans-Jordan between 19 April 1936 and 3 September 1939; 'S.E. ASIA. 1945-6,' in similar conditions to those for which the Naval General Service Medal with this bar was awarded to the Navy; 'BOMB & MINE CLEARANCE 1945-49,' as for the Navy; 'PALESTINE 1945-48,' as for the Navy; 'MALAYA,' for service of one day or more on duty on shore in the Federation of Malaya in operations against bandits since 16 June 1948, or, in the case of the Royal Air Force, for one operational sortie against bandits.

It is of interest to note that fourteen British officers of the Indian Army were awarded the *Naval* General Service Medal with bar, 'PERSIAN GULF. 1909-1914,' for their services in connection with the suppression of the arms traffic, while a few personnel of the Army and Royal Air Force were awarded this same medal with bar, 'YANGTSE 1949,' for their services in connection with H.M.S. *Amethyst* on 21 or 22 April 1949. (See under Naval General Service Medal.)

**114 - TERRITORIAL FORCE WAR MEDAL**
This medal was established in April 1920 for award to members of the Territorial Force and Territorial Force Nursing Service who volunteered for service overseas on or before 30 September 1914, and who rendered such service during the First World War.

**114 - TERRITORIAL FORCE WAR MEDAL** *(Obverse)*

The medal was granted to members of the forces mentioned who:

(*a*) Were serving with the Territorial Force on 4 August 1914; or

(*b*) had completed a period of not less than four years' service with the Territorial Force before 4 August 1914, and rejoined that Force on or before 30 September 1914.

Provided that they:

(i) Undertook either verbally or by written agreement, on or before 30 September 1914 to serve outside the United Kingdom, such agreement being operative after 4 August 1914; and

(ii) served outside the United Kingdom between 5 August 1914 and 11 November 1918, both dates inclusive; and

(iii) did not qualify for the award of the '1914 Star' or the '1914–15 Star.'

The medal is in bronze, with a straight bar suspender, and the effigy of King George V with the usual legend on the obverse. On the reverse is the inscription 'TERRITORIAL WAR MEDAL, VOLUNTARY SERVICE OVERSEAS 1914–1919.'

**114 - TERRITORIAL FORCE WAR MEDAL** (*Reverse*)

### 115 - INDIA GENERAL SERVICE MEDAL (1936)

On the obverse of this medal is a crowned effigy of the King; on the reverse a tiger to the left with the word 'INDIA' above and a view of the North-West Frontier below. Bars issued were 'NORTH-WEST FRONTIER, 1936–37,' 'NORTH-WEST FRONTIER, 1937–39.'

(*Obverse*)　　　　　　　　　(*Reverse*)

**115 - INDIA GENERAL SERVICE MEDAL** (1936)

'NORTH-WEST FRONTIER, 1936 -37 '

# *Campaign Stars, 1939~45*

The eight campaign stars awarded for service in the Second World War were all of similar design and were made of a yellow copper zinc alloy in the form of a six-pointed star measuring 44 mm. between opposite points. The Royal and Imperial cypher is in the centre, surmounted by a crown. The cypher is surrounded by a circlet bearing the name of the particular star.

Abbreviated conditions of award are set forth below.

### 116 - 1939–45 STAR

Granted for service in operations from 3 September 1939 to 15 August 1945, the date on which active operations against Japan ceased in the Pacific.

For the Royal Navy, the qualification was six months' service afloat in areas of active operations, and for the Army six months in an operational command, which did not include the United Kingdom. In the Royal Air Force the star was awarded to all air crews who had taken part in active operations against the enemy subject to the completion of two months in an operational unit, while non-crew personnel had to serve for six months in operational areas. In the Merchant Navy the same conditions applied as for the Royal Navy except that six months' service at sea qualified provided that at least one voyage had been made through an area of active operations. Lifeboatmen of the Royal National Lifeboat Institution qualified if they were out on service twenty-five times or more during the war, while women of the W.R.N.S., the A.T.S. and W.A.A.F. qualified on exactly the same basis as sailors, soldiers or airmen.

**116 - 1939–45 STAR**

Time spent as a prisoner of war was allowed to count, while those who had taken part in certain specified operations who had won an honour, decoration or mention in despatches; had died on service; or were evacuated as the result of wounds or sickness incurred on service, were eligible for the 1939–45 Star irrespective of the six months' qualification period. The same applied to personnel evacuated from Norway, Dunkirk, Greece, Crete, etc. Others eligible for the star were those enrolled in the maritime Royal Artillery, or serving with the A.A. defence of merchant shipping, provided they had completed six months' sea-going duty in certain specified 'dangerous waters.'

Special grants of the star were made to those responsible for operational decisions, such as chiefs of staff, commanders-in-chief, and commanders.

A bar to the 1939–45 Star was authorized for the air crews of fighter aircraft engaged in the Battle of Britain between 10 July and 31 October 1940, this award being uniquely denoted by a gilt rose emblem on the ribbon when it alone is worn.

The ribbon, 32 mm. wide, is unwatered and of three equal stripes

**117 - ATLANTIC STAR**

of dark blue, red, and light blue, representing the Royal and Merchant Navies, the Army, and the Royal Air Forces.

## 117 - ATLANTIC STAR

The ribbon, 32 mm. wide, in blue, white and sea green, worn with the blue farthest from the left shoulder, was designed as a symbol of service in the Atlantic. The star commemorates the Battle of the Atlantic and was designed primarily for those serving in convoys, escorts and anti-submarine forces, and for fast merchant ships sailing unescorted.

It was awarded in the Royal Navy for six months' service afloat between 3 September 1939 and 8 May 1945, in the Atlantic or Home Waters, and to personnel employed with the convoys to North Russia and in the South Atlantic west of longitude twenty degrees east, provided that the 1939–45 Star had first been earned for six months' service in an operational area. Those of the Merchant Navy qualified in much the same conditions as the Royal Navy.

118 - AIR CREW EUROPE STAR

Air crews qualified for the award if they had taken part in operations against the enemy in the areas specified within the dates mentioned; but subject to two months' service in an operational unit, and the prior award of the 1939–45 Star.

Notwithstanding the above, anyone who served for twelve months in operational areas any six months of which were in the Atlantic or, in the case of air crew, four months' operational service, any two months of which were in the area qualifying for the Atlantic Star was awarded both the Atlantic and 1939–45 Stars.

Those qualifying for the Atlantic Star, the France and Germany Star and the Air Crew Europe Star, or two of these, were awarded only the star first earned and a bar, or clasp, with it to denote that service qualifying for the second star had been rendered. A silver rose emblem is worn on the ribbon to denote the award of the France and Germany, the Atlantic or Air Crew Europe bar.

## 118 - AIR CREW EUROPE STAR

The ribbon, 32 mm. wide, is pale blue with black edges and a narrow yellow stripe on either side, symbolic of the continuous day and night service of the Air Forces. The star was awarded for operational flying from United Kingdom bases over Europe and including the United Kingdom, for a period of two months from the outbreak of war on 3 September 1939 to 4 June 1944. Service by air crews in operations at sea was not a qualification. Those qualifying for the Air Crew Europe, Atlantic and France and Germany Stars, or two of these, were awarded only the first star earned with a bar, or clasp, denoting service which would have qualified for the second star. A silver rose emblem worn on the ribbon denotes the award of the Atlantic, France and Germany, or Air Crew Europe bar as the case may be.

## 119 - AFRICA STAR

This star was awarded to the Armed Forces and Merchant Navy, and to women of the A.T.S., W.R.N.S., and W.A.A.F., for entry

119 - AFRICA STAR

into an operational area in North Africa between 10 June 1940 (the date of Italy's entry into the war) and 12 May 1943 (the end of operations in North Africa); also for service in Abyssinia, Somaliland, Eritrea, and Malta. The ribbon, 32 mm. wide and unwatered, is pale buff, a symbol of the sand of the desert. It has a wide red stripe in the centre, a dark blue stripe on the left and a light blue stripe on the right, both narrower than the centre stripe; the dark blue representing the Naval Forces and Merchant Navy, the red, the Armies, and the light blue, the Air Forces. A silver, Arabic '8' or 'I' worn on the ribbon indicates service with the Eighth Army between 23 October 1942 and 12 May 1943, or the First Army between 8 November 1942 and 12 May 1943. Naval and Merchant Navy service anywhere at sea in the Mediterranean between the dates 10 June 1940 and 12 May 1943 qualified. A silver rose emblem is worn on the ribbon by personnel of the Royal Navy Inshore Squadrons and Merchant Navy vessels which worked inshore between the dates 23 October 1942 and 12 May 1943, and by personnel of the R.A.F. serving between the same dates. The Eighteenth Army Group H.Q. also wear this emblem for service between 15 February 1943 and 12 May 1943.

120 - PACIFIC STAR

## 120 - PACIFIC STAR

The ribbon is dark green with red edges, a central yellow stripe and stripes of dark blue and light blue. The green and yellow represents the forests and beaches of the Pacific, the red the Armies, the dark blue the Naval Forces and Merchant Navies, and the light blue the Air Forces. The ribbon is worn with the dark blue stripe farthest from the left shoulder. It was awarded for operational service in the Pacific theatre of war from 8 December 1941. Service with the Royal Navy and Merchant Navy in the Pacific Ocean, the Indian Ocean, and the South China Sea and service on land qualified. The defined limits for the Indian Ocean are east of a line running due south from Singapore round the south-east coast of Sumatra through Christmas Island and southward along the meridian 110 degrees east. For land service eligibility was restricted to operational service between specified dates in territories invaded by Allied or enemy forces. These territories included:

Hong Kong, Malaya, Nauru, Ocean Island, Gilbert and Ellice Islands, Borneo and Sarawak, Celebes, Bismarck Archipelago, Molucca Islands, Solomon Islands (British Solomon Islands and Australian Mandated Territory), Sumatra, Timor, Java, New Guinea.

The award was made to air crews for service in operations against the enemy, and to Naval shore personnel and R.A.F. ground personnel for entry into the area of land operations.

Personnel qualifying for both the Pacific and Burma Stars received only the first star earned with a clasp, or bar, on the ribbon of the other, in which event a silver rose emblem is worn on the ribbon of the first star when it is worn alone.

121 - BURMA STAR

## 121 - BURMA STAR

The ribbon is dark blue with a wide central stripe of red flanked on either side by stripes of orange in the centre of the blue. The red stripe represents the British Commonwealth Forces, the blue the Royal and Merchant Navies, and the orange the sun.

Qualifying service in the Burma campaign counted as from 11 December 1941. For land operations the award was made for service in Burma, and for service on land in Bengal or Assam from 1 May 1942 to 31 December 1943, and from 1 January 1944 onwards, in those parts of Bengal or Assam east of the Brahmaputra. For the Royal and Merchant Navies awards were confined to service in the Bay of Bengal enclosed by lines running from a point 300 miles off the southernmost point of Ceylon, thence to a point 300 miles from the southernmost point of Sumatra and continuing to the western side of the Sunda Straight. The Malacca Strait was included. Air crew service in operations against the enemy qualified as did entry into the prescribed areas of land operations by Naval personnel and non air crew personnel of the R.A.F.

Persons qualifying for both the Burma and the Pacific Stars were awarded the first star earned with a clasp or bar on the ribbon to denote that qualifying service for the second star had been rendered. The possession of a bar is indicated by a silver rose emblem on the ribbon when it is worn alone.

122 - ITALY STAR

## 122 - ITALY STAR

The ribbon is of five equal stripes of red, white, green, white, and red representing the Italian colours. The star was awarded for operational service on land in Italy or Sicily, Greece and Yugoslavia, the Aegean and the Dodecanese, Corsica, Sardinia and Elba. It was granted to those on service at any time during the campaign from the capture of Pantellaria on 11 June 1943, until V.E. Day, 8 May 1945. Service in Sicily after 17 August 1943, in Sardinia after 19 September 1943, and Corsica after 4 October 1943, did not qualify. Service with the Royal Navy or Merchant Navy in operations, and air crew service in operations against the enemy in the Mediterranean, including sorties, both qualified, as did Naval personnel ashore and Air Force ground forces entering the prescribed areas.

The Italy Star was awarded in addition to any other star or stars granted.

## 123 - FRANCE AND GERMANY STAR

The ribbon is in five equal stripes of blue, white, red, white and blue, the colours of the Union flag and also of the flags of France and the Netherlands. The star was awarded for entry into operational service in France, Belgium, Holland, or Germany from 6 June 1944 to 8 May 1945. In the Royal and Merchant Navies service afloat in the North Sea south of a line from the Firth of Forth to Kristiansand (south), in the English Channel, in the Bay of Biscay east of longitude 6° west, was a qualification if service was in support of land operations. Air crews were eligible for service against the

123 - FRANCE AND GERMANY STAR

enemy over Europe from 6 June 1944 to 8 May 1945, as were Naval personnel on shore and ground members of the Royal Air Force who took part in land operations within the prescribed areas.

Service afloat in the Mediterranean in support of operations off the south of France was not a qualification in the case of the Royal and Merchant Navies, as such service qualified for the Italy Star.

The France and Germany Star was not awarded in addition to the Atlantic or Air Crew Europe Star, while sorties from the Mediterranean area over Europe did not qualify, as those taking part were awarded the Italy Star.

In the event of a person qualifying for both the Atlantic and Air Crew Europe Star, only the first one earned was awarded. If he later qualified for the France and Germany Star, he was granted a bar worn with the Atlantic or Air Crew Europe Star. This bar is indicated by a silver rose emblem when the ribbon alone is worn.

# *War Medals, 1939~45*

### 124 - DEFENCE MEDAL

The ribbon is flame coloured with green edges with a narrow black stripe in each green edge. The colours symbolize the enemy attacks upon our green and pleasant land, and the black the black-out all over the country.

The medal is in cupro-nickel with a straight bar suspender, and has on the obverse the uncrowned effigy of King George VI with the usual legend.

Service to qualify for the award counted from 3 September 1939 to 8 May 1945 in Great Britain; and to forces overseas until the end of active hostilities in the Pacific, 15 August 1945. Civil Defence Services in military operational areas subjected to enemy air attack were included, as were Civil Defence Services in areas in the British Commonwealth or the Colonial Empire subjected to air attack or closely threatened. Service in Civil Defence Services in West Africa or the West Indies did not qualify.

In general terms the Defence Medal was granted for three years' service at home, or six months' overseas in territories subjected to air attacks or closely threatened. In the case of mine and bomb disposal units of the Forces the time qualification was three months. The medal could be awarded in addition to the campaign stars already mentioned.

The following categories were eligible:

Members of the Forces who had served in the United Kingdom.

Personnel of Anti-Aircraft Command.

R.A.F. personnel other than operational air crews.

**124 - DEFENCE MEDAL**

Dominion Forces serving in the United Kingdom.

The Home Guard.

United Kingdom Forces serving in West Africa, Palestine, and India.

Dominion Forces in non-operational areas outside their own countries.

Malta Home Guard – part-time service.

Wardens Service including Shelter Wardens.

Rescue Service (including former First-Aid Party Service).

Decontamination Service.

Report and Control Service.

Messenger Service.

Ambulance Service.

First-Aid Service, including First-Aid Posts and Points, Public Cleansing Centres, Mobile Cleansing Units, and the Nursing Service for public air-raid shelters.

Rest Centre Service.

Emergency Food Service (including Queen's Messenger Convoy Service).

Canteen Service.

Emergency Information Service.

Mortuary Service.

National Fire Service (including service in a local authority Fire Brigade or the Auxiliary Fire Service prior to nationalization).

Police, Royal Marine Police Special Reserve, Admiralty Civil Police, War Department Constabulary, Air Ministry Constabulary, Railway and Dock Police.

American Ambulance, Great Britain.

Civil Air Transport and Air Transport Auxiliary.

Civil Defence Reserve, Kent County Civil Defence Mobile Reserve, and West Sussex County Civil Defence Mobile Reserve.

Civil Nursing Reserve.

Civilian Technical Corps.

Coast Guard.

Fire Guards performing duties under the local authorities, or at Government or business premises.

Lighthouse Keepers serving under the three Lighthouse Authorities, and Keepers of Light-Vessels under those Authorities, who do not qualify for the 1939–45 Star.

Nurses in hospitals for which Government Departments or local authorities are responsible, or in the recognized voluntary hospitals.

Port of London Authority River Emergency Service. Clyde River Patrol.

Royal Observer Corps.

Women's Voluntary Services for Civil Defence. Members of the W.V.S. may qualify if (*a*) they are enrolled in an eligible local authority Civil Defence Service; (*b*) they perform duties analogous to those of one of the eligible local authority Civil

Defence Services and the section of the W.V.S. to which they belong is one which functions operationally during or immediately after enemy attacks.

## THE QUEEN'S (OR KING'S) COMMENDATION EMBLEM

This badge, awarded to civilians for brave conduct, consists of an emblem of silver laurel leaves worn on the ribbon of the Defence Medal. If that medal has not been granted the emblem is to be worn on the coat after any ribbons that may be worn. A small silver oval badge is authorized for award to civilians granted King's or Queen's Commendations for valuable service in the air. It is worn on the coat immediately below any medal ribbons or, in the case of civil air line uniform, on the panel on the left breast pocket. In the Forces the single bronze oak leaf emblem is used to denote the King's or Queen's Commendation for bravery.

## 125 - WAR MEDAL, 1939–45

This medal was awarded to full-time personnel of the Armed Forces of the British Commonwealth (excluding the Home Guard) wherever they served during the war; the qualification being twenty-eight days' service, operational or non-operational. In the Merchant Navy the twenty-eight days must have been served at sea. The period covered by service is 3 September 1939 to 2 September 1945. The medal was granted in addition to the campaign stars and the Defence Medal. A few categories of civilians, such as war correspondents and civil air transport air crews who had served or flown in operational theatres, received the award.

The medal is of cupro-nickel, except the Canadian issue which is of silver.

The ribbon is red, white and blue. It has a narrow red stripe in the centre with a narrow white stripe on either side, broad red stripes at either edge, with two intervening stripes of blue.

**125 - WAR MEDAL, 1939–45**

## MENTION IN DESPATCHES

A bronze oak leaf emblem signifying a Mention in Despatches is ordered to be worn on the ribbon of the War Medal, 1939–45, with the stalk farthest from the shoulder. Only one emblem is worn no matter how many times the wearer may have been 'mentioned.'

The same emblem, if granted for service in operations after the end of the Second World War, is worn on the ribbon of the appropriate General Service Medal. If a medal has not been granted, the oak leaf emblem is worn directly on the coat after other medal ribbons.

In the Forces the emblem also denotes a King's or Queen's Commendation for brave conduct.

## 126 - KOREA MEDAL

This medal was instituted in July 1951 to recognize the services of British Commonwealth Forces on behalf of the United Nations in repelling aggression in Korea subsequent to 2 July 1950. The medal is of cupro-nickel with the Sovereign's effigy on the obverse, and the ribbon is yellow, blue, yellow, blue, yellow in five equal stripes, the blue being that of the United Nations flag. The medal issued by Canada is in silver and has the word 'CANADA' beneath the Queen's head on the obverse. The qualifying service for the Royal Navy was twenty-eight days' afloat in ships or craft engaged in operations off the Korean coast, or one day or more on duty ashore. For the Army the necessary qualification was one day or more on the posted strength of a unit or a formation in Korea, and for the Air Force one operational sortie over Korea or Korean waters, otherwise as for the Navy and Army. Members of certain civilian categories were also eligible in the same conditions.

Service in Japan, or on the way to Japan from anywhere outside Korea or Korean waters did not qualify.

A single bronze oak leaf emblem is worn on the ribbon by those Mentioned in Despatches.

It was originally announced that the obverse of this medal would bear the crowned effigy of King George VI. As it would be contrary to custom to issue any medal bearing the crowned effigy of Queen Elizabeth II until after Her Majesty's Coronation, Her Majesty approved that her classical effigy should be shown instead. The design on the reverse, approved by the Queen in March 1952, shows Hercules fighting the Hydra, a mythical monster with nine or more heads, which serves as a symbolic representation of the Communist menace.

**126 - KOREA MEDAL**
'CANADA'

## 127 - UNITED NATIONS SERVICE MEDAL

Instituted by the General Assembly of the United Nations on 12 December 1950 – 'in recognition of the valour and sacrifice of the men and women who have served on behalf of the United Nations in repelling the aggression in Korea.' The full title of this medal is the 'United Nations Service Medal, with clasp "Korea," for service in Defence of the Principles of the Charter of the United Nations,' from which it appears that it is intended that it shall be a general service award with separate clasps, or bars, for all campaigns in which the forces of the United Nations may be called upon to take part.

The medal is circular and is made of a bronze alloy. The reverse has the inscription 'FOR SERVICE IN DEFENCE OF THE PRINCIPLES OF THE CHARTER OF THE UNITED NATIONS,' and the obverse the emblem of the United Nations. A bar, constituting part of the suspension from the ribbon, bears the word 'KOREA.' The ribbon is of seventeen alternate stripes of pale blue, described as 'United Nations blue,' and white.

In general, the medal was earned by one day's service under United Nations command in Korea or the adjacent areas, which included Japan and Okinawa.

An aggregate of thirty days, which need not have been consecutive, spent on official visits or inspections to the qualifying area qualified for the medal.

The medal was awarded to members of the land, sea and air forces of *all* nations sent to Korea or adjacent areas for service on behalf of the United Nations.

**127 - UNITED NATIONS
SERVICE MEDAL**

## WAR MEDALS, 1939–45, OF INDIA, CANADA, AUSTRALIA, NEW ZEALAND, THE UNION OF SOUTH AFRICA, AND SOUTHERN RHODESIA

The forces of all the nations of the British Commonwealth mentioned above as well as all Colonial forces, qualified for the Campaign Stars, the Defence Medal and the War Medal, 1939–45 awarded to the strictly British forces, and in the same conditions. In addition, India, Canada, Australia, New Zealand, the Union of South Africa, and Southern Rhodesia, had their own special war medals.

During or since the war the Governments of Canada and the Union of South Africa instituted decorations or medals which are now permanent awards. For convenience in arrangement all of these, with the war medals, and in some cases awards for long service and good conduct, etc., have been grouped together in the following pages. In the descriptions the decorations and medals are not listed in their order of priority or precedence, and the reader is particularly referred to the Index, and to the Order of Precedence printed at the beginning of this book.

DECORATIONS AND MEDALS INSTITUTED IN INDIA, BURMA AND EIRE SINCE THEY ATTAINED INDEPENDENCE ARE DESCRIBED LATER.

### 128 – INDIA SERVICE MEDAL (1939–45)

This medal was awarded for three years' non-operational service with the Indian forces between 3 September 1939 and 2 September 1945. It was not awarded to anyone who qualified for the Defence Medal, but was granted in addition to the War Medal and the Campaign Stars. The ribbon is in the blue colours of the Order of the Star of India and the Order of the Indian Empire.

### 129 – THE CANADA MEDAL

This medal was established in October 1943 with the approval of His Majesty King George VI, on the recommendation of the Canadian Government. It was the first distinctly Canadian decoration intended for the recognition of 'meritorious service above and beyond the faithful performance of duties' by citizens of Canada, whether as civilians or as members of the Armed Forces or the Merchant Navy, or by citizens of other countries whom Canada desired to honour. The medal is silver with the effigy of the Sovereign on the obverse, and on the reverse the arms of Canada with the word 'CANADA' on a scroll beneath, and on each side a spray of maple. The word 'MERIT' in French or English appears on the clasp from which the medal is suspended, the ribbon being the same as that of the Canada General Service Medal of 1866–70, No. 80 in this book. The award confers no individual precedence, but recipients may use the letters 'C.M.' or 'M. du C.' after their names, as English- or French-speaking Canadians. The Canada Medal is officially listed as taking precedence before all war medals.

### 130 – CANADA VOLUNTEER SERVICE MEDAL

This medal was authorized in 1943 for men and women of all ranks

*(Obverse)*

**128 – INDIA SERVICE MEDAL** (1939–45)

*(Reverse)*

in the Canadian Armed Services who volunteered for service during the Second World War. A minimum of eighteen months' service must have been honourably completed, though those honourably discharged or retired after having proceeded outside the territorial limits of Canada received the medal irrespective of any time limit. Recipients who served abroad were entitled to wear a silver maple leaf on a straight bar on the ribbon. The medal could be awarded posthumously to those of any rank in the Naval, Military or Air Forces of Canada who had been killed, or died of wounds sustained in action or on duty. The medal is silver, and has on the obverse seven marching figures representing the Services (men and women and nurses), with the inscription 'CANADA' above and 'VOLUNTARY SERVICE VOLONTAIRE' below, while the reverse bears the Canadian coat-of-arms.

## THE CANADIAN STAR OF COURAGE

### 131 - THE CANADIAN FORCES DECORATION

This decoration was instituted in June 1950 after approval by King George VI, for award to all ranks of both the Regular and Reserve Forces who complete twelve years' service in certain stipulated conditions. The decoration and ribbon are identical whether awarded to the Regular or Reserve Forces.

As from 1 July 1950 personnel other than those serving in the Permanent, Regular or Reserve Armed Forces of Canada on or before 1 September 1939 ceased to be eligible for the Canadian Medal for Long Service and Good Conduct (Military); the Royal Canadian Navy and Royal Canadian Air Force Long Service and Good Conduct Medals; the Canadian Efficiency Decoration and Medal for Long Service and Good Conduct (Military); the Royal Navy (Reserve) Long Service and Good Conduct Medal; and the Air Efficiency Award which were formerly used in common with Britain and the various other nations of the British Commonwealth.

The decoration is in silver-gilt in the form of a decagon, with the head of the Sovereign and usual inscription on the obverse, and on the reverse the design shown in the illustration. Each of the ten sides represents one of the provinces of Canada. The initials 'C.D.' are used to indicate the possession of this decoration.

### 132 - ROYAL CANADIAN MOUNTED POLICE LONG SERVICE AND GOOD CONDUCT MEDAL

This medal is awarded to personnel of the R.C.M.P. who have served with the Force for twenty years and have carried out their duties efficiently. It is circular and in silver, and bears the Sovereign's effigy and legend on the obverse, and on the reverse the crest of the R.C.M.P. encircled by the words 'LONG SERVICE AND GOOD CONDUCT.'

### 133 - AUSTRALIA SERVICE MEDAL (1939–45)

This medal was instituted in November 1949 for award to members of the Australian Armed Forces, the Mercantile Marine and civilian

THE CANADIAN
STAR OF COURAGE

133 - AUSTRALIA SERVICE
MEDAL (1939–45)

personnel serving in operational areas, who took part in the Second World War. Eligibility was not affected by the grant of any other general award for war service – e.g. the Campaign Stars, the Defence Medal or the War Medal, 1939–45 – and in general the qualifying period for the Australia Service Medal was eighteen months in Australia or overseas.

The obverse bears the King's head and the usual legend, and the reverse the Australian coat-of-arms with the words 'THE AUSTRALIA SERVICE MEDAL, 1939–45.' The dark blue of the ribbon represents the Navy; the khaki, the Army; the pale blue, the Air Force; and the red, the Mercantile Marine.

NOTE – In common with those from New Zealand, Canada, South Africa, India and the Colonies, members of the Australian Forces and the Mercantile Marine were entitled to the Campaign Stars; the Defence Medal (under special conditions); and the War Medal, 1939–45, authorized for the British Forces.

*(Obverse)*

## NEW ZEALAND
### NEW ZEALAND LONG AND EFFICIENT SERVICE MEDAL

This medal is now obsolete, but was originally awarded to all members of the New Zealand Military Forces who had served efficiently for sixteen consecutive years, or for a total period of twenty years which did not need necessarily to be consecutive. Active service overseas in the First World War counted double. The medal was in silver, and was worn from a crimson ribbon with two central stripes of white.

### 134 - NEW ZEALAND TERRITORIAL SERVICE MEDAL

This medal is now obsolete, but was originally awarded for twelve years' service in the Territorial Force. Active service overseas in the First World War counted double. It was replaced by the Efficiency Decoration and Efficiency Medal when New Zealand abandoned compulsory military training in 1936. It is a silver medal with the effigy of King George V on the obverse, surrounded by the words 'NEW ZEALAND TERRITORIAL. 12 YEARS SERVICE,' and on the reverse the representation of a kiwi encircled by two sprays of fern tied at the bottom.

**134 - NEW ZEALAND TERRI-TORIAL SERVICE MEDAL**

### 135 - NEW ZEALAND WAR SERVICE MEDAL (1939–45)

A silver medal with the uncrowned effigy of King George VI on the obverse with the usual legend, and on the reverse the inscription 'FOR SERVICE TO NEW ZEALAND. 1939–1945' over the representation of a New Zealand fern leaf. The medal is hung from a black moiré ribbon with white edges by a clasp composed of two fern leaves. It was issued to all officers and men of the Navy, Army, Air Force, the Home Guard and other ancillary services who had completed at least six months' service in New Zealand by the end of the war. New Zealand personnel who served overseas were eligible for the same Campaign Stars and medals as were awarded to the British Forces.

**135 - NEW ZEALAND WAR SERVICE MEDAL** *(Obverse)*

## NEW ZEALAND MEMORIAL CROSS

This cross was instituted by the New Zealand Government in December 1946 for award to the widows and mothers of New Zealand sailors, soldiers, airmen and merchant seamen who were killed or died on active service during the Second World War. The Government had for some time been anxious to ensure that the widows and mothers received some individual token of the one they had lost. 'I trust,' said the Prime Minister, 'that those who receive this Cross will accept it as a very small tribute of gratitude from the Government and people of New Zealand in memory of one who gave his life for his country.' The cross is of dull silver and surmounted by a crown, having at the foot and at the end of either arm a fern leaf, with King George VI's Royal cypher in the centre. A wreath of laurel appears between the arms of the cross. The ribbon is of purple satin, and the cross was issued in a suitable case.

135 - NEW ZEALAND WAR SERVICE MEDAL *(Reverse)*

## SOUTHERN RHODESIA
## 136 - SOUTHERN RHODESIA SERVICE MEDAL

This medal was awarded to members of the Armed Forces of Southern Rhodesia who served in the Second World War in much the same way as the Australia and New Zealand Service Medals.

## THE UNION OF SOUTH AFRICA
## 137 - ANGLO-BOER WAR

This silver medal was instituted by the Government of the Union of South Africa in 1920 for award to officers and men of the Boer Forces who served against the British in the War of 1899–1902. It bears on one side the arms of the Transvaal, and on the other the arms of the Orange Free State.

## 138 - DEKORATIE VOOR TROUWE DIENST
## (DECORATION FOR DISTINGUISHED SERVICE)

This decoration, in the form of a silver medal, was awarded by the Government of the Union of South Africa in 1920 to officers who served with the forces of the Boer Republics during the War of 1899–1902, and rendered distinguished service. The reverse has the arms of the Orange Free State and an inscription. The obverse has the same inscription with the arms of the Transvaal.

NEW ZEALAND
MEMORIAL CROSS

## 139 - ANGLO-BOER WAR - WOUND RIBBON

Simultaneously with the institution of the awards just described a ribbon was prescribed for all officers and men of the burgher forces of the South African Republic and Orange Free State who were wounded during the South African War of 1899–1902. It has no medal. The ribbon is ordered to be worn after that of the Decoration for Distinguished Service.

## 140 - THE AFRICA SERVICE MEDAL

This medal was established in 1943 for award to all members of the Union Defence Forces or other Uniformed Services of the Union who attested for service in Africa before 13 May 1943 the day on which

137 - ANGLO-BOER WAR

Africa was finally cleared of the enemy. Men and women of all ranks were eligible. The medal is silver and bears a map of Africa with the inscription 'AFRICA SERVICE MEDAL,' and on the other side a leaping springbok. The ribbon is orange with the green and gold springbok colours in vertical stripes at the edges.

### 141 - SOUTH AFRICAN MEDAL FOR WAR SERVICES

This medal was awarded to persons who, during the period 6 September 1939 to 15 February 1946, for a minimum aggregate period of two years, one at least of which should have been a continuous period, rendered voluntary and unpaid service in one or more of the organizations, associations, institutions or other approved bodies, e.g. Civilian Protective Services, Civic Guards, Red Cross of South Africa, etc. Persons who served in the Union Defence Forces, or part-time Military Units, did not qualify for this award. The medal is circular and in silver, and inside the circumference of the obverse are the words 'FOR WAR SERVICES SOUTH AFRICA. VIR OORLOG DIENSTE SUID AFRIKA.' The inscription forms a complete circle, inside of which are interleaved protea flowers with the date '1939–1945' in the centre. The other side has the Union coat-of-arms in relief.

### 142 - POLAR MEDALS

The first Arctic Medal, established in 1857, was awarded to all officers and men of a number of ships which had been engaged in Arctic expeditions between 1818 and 1855. The silver medal, which is octagonal, has on the obverse the head of Queen Victoria with the usual legend, and on the reverse a ship in the ice with icebergs right and left and a sledge party in the foreground. Above appear the words 'For Arctic Discoveries,' and below the dates '1818–1855.' Above the medal is a five-pointed star, surmounted by a ring through which passes the white moiré ribbon, 38 mm. wide. The next medal was issued in 1876 to all those who had served in H.M. ships *Alert* and *Discovery* during the Arctic Expedition of 1875–6, and to the officers and crew of the steam yacht *Pandora* during her voyage in the Arctic, June–November 1876. The medal is circular, and has on the obverse the effigy of Queen Victoria with the usual legend and date '1876,' and on the reverse a ship in the ice-pack with clouds overhead. It hangs from a straight silver clasp from a white unwatered ribbon 32 mm. wide.

Another medal, now known as the 'Polar Medal,' was instituted by King Edward VII in 1904 for members of Captain R. F. Scott's 'National Antarctic Expedition' of 1901–4. It is octagonal, and has on the obverse the effigy of the King in naval uniform, with legend, and on the reverse Scott's *Discovery* in winter quarters and a sledging party on skis in the foreground. The ribbon is white, 32 mm. wide, and the medal hangs from a scroll attachment. All those serving in the *Discovery* and with the landing party received the award in silver with a clasp 'ANTARCTIC 1901–1904,' while

**142 - FIRST ARCTIC MEDAL**
*Issue of Queen Victoria* (*Obverse*)

officers and men of the relief ships *Morning* and *Terra Nova* had the medal in bronze with no clasp.

With a clasp 'ANTARCTIC 1907–1909' the medal was again awarded for Sir Ernest Shackleton's 'British Antarctic Expedition 1907,' the members of which received it in silver. Those in the *Nimrod*, which did not winter in the Antarctic had the medal in bronze with no clasp. Any of the *Nimrod* men, however, who had served in the relief ships in Scott's expedition received a bronze clasp with the same wording as the silver one.

With King George V's effigy on the obverse and the clasp 'ANTARCTIC 1910–1913' the medal was next awarded for Captain Scott's last expedition. It was given to all members of the landing party and to the officers and men of the *Terra Nova*, who had made three hazardous voyages to the Antarctic from New Zealand. About sixty silver medals and clasps were given on this occasion. Four men who had made only one summer voyage received the medal in bronze.

The same medal in silver, with clasp 'ANTARCTIC 1912–1914,' and in bronze without clasp, was granted for the Mawson Expedition of those years. For Sir Ernest Shackleton's 'Imperial Trans-Antarctic Expedition' of 1914–16, thirty silver medals with clasp 'ANTARCTIC 1914–16' were given to officers and men of the *Endurance* and *Aurora*; five silver clasps went to those who already possessed the silver medal; eleven bronze medals were awarded to men who did not land. The medal with clasps 'ARCTIC 1930–31'; 'ANTARCTIC 1929–30'; 'ANTARCTIC 1929–31'; 'ANTARCTIC 1930–31'; 'ANTARCTIC 1935–37' was issued for expeditions which took place in those years.

In October 1941 King George VI approved the award of the medal in bronze for service in the Antarctic between 1925 and 1929 in the Royal Research Ships *Discovery II* and *William Scoresby*. One clasp and four medals were awarded posthumously; three officers and men received clasps to the medals already earned; eighty-nine others received the medal for the first time.

In January 1943 the medal in silver, with the effigy of King George VI and clasp 'ARCTIC 1940–42,' was awarded to eight members of the crew of the Royal Canadian Mounted Police schooner *St. Roche* for exploration of the North-West Arctic waters in 1940–42. Three clasps and eight medals in silver were awarded to personnel of the same vessel for exploration in 1944. The clasp is engraved 'ARCTIC 1944.'

The bronze medals are no longer issued, and since July 1953 the medal in silver bearing the effigy of Queen Elizabeth II, with clasps 'ANTARCTIC' or 'ARCTIC' and the appropriate dates, has been awarded. (The dates quoted here are those of the announcements in the *London Gazette*.) 17/vii/53: 54 medals (2 posthumous) and 1 clasp, Falkland Is. Dependencies Survey in Antarctic 1944–50. 30/xi/54: 29 medals (1 posthumous) and 1 clasp, British N. Greenland Expedition 1952–1954. 1/iii/55: 13 medals and 1 clasp, Falkland Is. Dependencies Survey. 2 medals to Australian observers with French Antarctic Expedition to Adelie Land 1951–1952. 24/i/56:

**142 - FIRST ARCTIC MEDAL**
*Issue of Queen Victoria   (Reverse)*

143

5 medals (2 posthumous) and 1 clasp to Commonwealth members of Norwegian-British-Swedish Antarctic Expedition 1949–52. 9 medals (1 to a French observer) and 1 clasp for Australian National Antarctic Research Expedition to Mawson, 1954–55. 30/x/56: 15 medals for ditto 1955–56.

The silver and bronze medals were different decorations and could be worn simultaneously. In the event of a second award of the same sort a man received a silver or bronze clasp only. In 1945 King George VI approved a silver rose emblem being worn on the ribbons of the silver and bronze medals to denote the award of a second clasp. A third clasp is denoted by a second emblem.

Recommendations for the Polar Medal are made by the First Lord of the Admiralty, or the appropriate Minister of State of any oversea country of the British Commonwealth.

(The precise conditions of award are laid down in a Royal Warrant published in the *London Gazette* of 18 May 1954.)

# *Commemoration Medals*

## 143 - EMPRESS OF INDIA MEDAL

A large medal, 58 mm. in diameter, was struck in gold and silver for presentation to high English officials, Indian native princes, and others on the occasion of the proclamation of Queen Victoria as Empress of India, at Delhi, on 1 January 1877. The medals, in silver, were presented to selected noblemen and gentlemen, European and native, and to a selected soldier of each British and native regiment in India.

The medal, intended to be worn round the neck from a straight bar suspender, bore the bust of the Queen on the obverse with the legend 'VICTORIA 1ST JANUARY 1877.' The reverse had an ornamental border, with the inscription 'EMPRESS OF INDIA' in Persian, English and Hindi. The medal was not permitted to be worn by officers or soldiers of the Regular Army or Auxiliary Forces when in uniform.

## BADGE OF HONOUR

Awarded to Chiefs and other non-European dignitaries in Colonies and Protectorates, for loyal and valuable service, though in exceptional circumstances to Europeans also.

There are two types. The first, granted in African territories, is an oval bronze badge, worn round the neck from a bright yellow watered silk ribbon 38 mm. wide. In European dress it may be worn on the breast with other medals in a reduced size from a ribbon 32 mm. in width. The obverse bears the crowned effigy of the Sovereign, and the reverse the name of the territory and a special design, officially described as follows: *Aden*, sailing boat of local rig; *Basutoland, Bechuanaland Protectorate, Swaziland,* cypher of the Sovereign with a crown above; *Gambia, Gold Coast, Sierra Leone,* elephant and palm tree; *Kenya,* lion rampant; *Nigeria,* crown within a design formed of two triangles; *Northern Rhodesia,* eagle holding in its talons a fish; *Nyasaland Protectorate,* leopard and the rising sun; *Somaliland Protectorate,* head of a kudu (a species of antelope); *Tanganyika Territory,* head of a giraffe; *Uganda Protectorate,* golden-crested crane and the sun.

The other type of Badge, granted in non-African territories, is circular, in silver-gilt, and 41 mm. in diameter. It is suspended round the neck from a ribbon of bright yellow watered silk 38 mm. wide when awarded in the *British Solomon Islands, Cyprus, Fiji* and the *Gilbert and Ellice Islands,* or a ribbon of red, white and blue in equal stripes when granted in *Hong-Kong, North Borneo, Sarawak,* or *Singapore.* In European dress the badge may be worn on the breast in a reduced size with other medals from a ribbon 32 mm. wide. The obverse has the crowned effigy of the Sovereign, and the reverse varies; that for the British Solomon Islands, Cyprus, Fiji, the Gilbert and Ellice Islands and Singapore having the name of the territory and its armorial bearings; Hong-Kong having the name with shipping, etc.; and North Borneo and Sarawak, the name with armorial bearings and the inscription 'FOR LOYAL SERVICE.'

The Badge of Honour, which is worn immediately before Jubilee and Coronation medals, must not be confused with the Queen's Medals for Chiefs, described earlier.

## 144, 145 - QUEEN VICTORIA'S JUBILEE AND DIAMOND JUBILEE MEDALS (1887 and 1897)

The former has on one side the bust of Queen Victoria with the legend, 'VICTORIA D.G. REGINA ET IMPERATRIX F.D.,' and on the other, the inscription, 'IN COMMEMORATION OF THE 50TH YEAR OF THE REIGN OF QUEEN VICTORIA, 21 JUNE 1887.' The inscription is surmounted by a crown, and is encircled by a wreath of roses, thistles and shamrock. The medal was struck in gold, silver and bronze. The latter (1897) is the same, but the wording on the reverse has '60TH' instead of '50TH,' and '20 JUNE 1897' instead of the other date. On the occasion of the Queen's Jubilee in 1887, and the Diamond Jubilee in 1897, these medals were bestowed upon members of the Royal Family and the Royal guests; upon members of the Royal household, ladies, gentlemen and servants; upon the officers commanding the various guards of honour along the route of the Royal processions; and officers who commanded ships present at the Naval reviews at Spithead. It was also awarded to certain other officers and officials who took part in any Jubilee ceremonial at which the Queen was present. It was given in bronze to certain of the soldiers and sailors who took part in the processions through London, and who were serving on board the men-of-war when the fleets were reviewed by the Queen. Those who had already received the 1887 decoration were awarded a bar, dated '1897' on the occasion of the Diamond Jubilee. The ribbon passes through a ring in the top of the medal, and is worn by ladies attached to a bow of the ribbon. A similar medal with the colours of the ribbon reversed, No. **145**, was conferred upon civilians who took a prominent part in the various Jubilee ceremonies.

Special medals in gold and silver (fourteen gold and 512 silver) were struck for presentation to Lord Mayors and Lord Provosts, and later to Mayors and Provosts, on the occasion of Her Majesty's Diamond Jubilee in 1897. The medal is diamond shaped, and has on the obverse the crowned and veiled bust of the Queen surrounded by the inscription 'VICTORIA ANNVM REGNI SEXAGESIMVM FELICITER CLAVDIT XX–IVN–MDCCCXCVII,' and on the reverse the earlier bust of the Queen as used on the coinage from 1837 to 1897, with the head set above a spray of laurel and the date '1837.' To the left of the head is the wording 'LONGITUDO DIERVM IN DEXTERA EVIS,' and, on the right, 'ET IN SINISTRA GLORIA.' The medal, which is of unusual design, hangs by a ring from a ribbon of the same colouring as the Jubilee Medal but reversed – i.e. the stripes are dark blue and the ground pale blue.

### 146 - QUEEN VICTORIA'S POLICE MEDALS FOR THE JUBILEE AND DIAMOND JUBILEE OF 1887 AND 1897

These medals, which are suspended by plain clasps, bear on one side the head of Queen Victoria. On the other there is an oak wreath and a crown with, inside, the words, 'JUBILEE OF HER MAJESTY QUEEN VICTORIA,' and outside, 'CITY OF LONDON POLICE,' or 'METROPOLITAN POLICE,' as the case may be. Below is the date '1887,' or '1897,' with a heraldic rose on either side. The medals were given in silver or bronze – according to rank – to all members of the police forces who were on duty in London during the Jubilee processions of 1887 and 1897. A bronze medal, hung from the same ribbon, was awarded to the Dublin Metropolitan Police and men of the Royal Irish Constabulary who were on duty during the Royal visit in 1900. The obverse bears the head of the Queen with the usual legend, and the reverse a figure of Hibernia and a view of Kingstown Harbour, with the date '1900.'

### 147, 148 - KING EDWARD VII'S CORONATION MEDAL (1902)

This medal bears on the obverse the busts of King Edward and Queen Alexandra side by side, crowned and facing to the right. On the other side it has the Royal cypher 'E.R. VII.' with a crown above it, and the date 'JUNE 26TH 1902.' It is oval with a raised ornamental rim, is rather smaller than ordinary war medals, and is surmounted by a crown and a ring through which the ribbon passes. The medal, in silver and bronze, was awarded in much the same way as Queen Victoria's Jubilee medals. Amongst other recipients it was given in bronze to one seaman or marine of 'very good' character on board each of the ships present at the Naval review at Spithead on 16 August 1902. A rather similar medal was bestowed upon provincial mayors and others who took part in the Coronation ceremony. It has a raised rim, with no crown between the ring and

**146 - QUEEN VICTORIA'S POLICE MEDALS FOR THE JUBILEE AND DIAMOND JUBILEE OF 1887 AND 1897** 'METROPOLITAN POLICE' (*Reverse*)

the medal, and is circular, not oval. The ribbon has a narrow white stripe down the centre with a blue stripe on either side, and wide scarlet edges, No. **148**.

### 149 - KING EDWARD'S POLICE CORONATION MEDAL (1902)

This medal has on the obverse the head of King Edward, with the usual wording. On the reverse is the inscription 'CORONATION OF HIS MAJESTY KING EDWARD VII, 1902,' and the words 'METRO-POLITAN POLICE.' Below is a crown with a branch of oak with laurel on either side. It was issued in silver or bronze, according to rank, to all members of the police forces who were on duty during the Coronation procession through London. The same medal, with the words 'CITY OF LONDON POLICE'; 'COUNTY AND BOROUGH POLICE'; 'L.C.C. Metropolitan Fire Brigade' (actual inscription 'L.C.C.M.F.B.'); 'ST. JOHN AMBULANCE BRIGADE' and 'POLICE AMBULANCE SERVICE,' was given to members of these services on duty during the Coronation.

### KING EDWARD'S POLICE MEDAL (1903) (SCOTLAND)

This bronze medal was struck to commemorate the King's visit to Scotland in 1903. The design on the obverse is the same as that of the Police Coronation Medal, 1902, just described. The reverse is also similar except that the inscription round the upper rim reads 'SCOTTISH POLICE,' while in the centre, in three lines, are the words 'FROM HIS MAJESTY KING EDWARD VII,' and below the date '1903.' The ribbon, 32 mm. wide, is plain red: 2,975 medals were issued.

### 150 - KING EDWARD'S DELHI DURBAR MEDAL (1903)

On one side of this medal is the bust of King Edward with the words 'EDWARD VII., DELHI DURBAR, 1903.' On the reverse is a native inscription which reads, 'BY THE FAVOUR OF THE LORD OF DOMI-NION, EDWARD THE SEVENTH, EMPEROR OF INDIA.' This medal was awarded in gold, silver or bronze, according to the rank of the recipient. It was given to officers, civil officials, prominent civilians and to certain of the soldiers and others who took a prominent part in the Durbar. It is suspended by means of a ring.

### 151 - KING EDWARD'S MEDAL (IRELAND) (1903)

This medal bears on one side the bust of the King with the usual wording. On the other appears a figure of Hibernia, with a view of the Royal yacht entering Kingstown Harbour. At the feet of the figure is a harp, rose and shamrock with the date '1903' below. It was given in silver and bronze on the occasion of King Edward's visit to Ireland in 1903. Most of the recipients were members of the police forces.

### 152 - KING GEORGE V'S CORONATION MEDAL (1911)

This medal, which is suspended from its ribbon by means of a ring,

bears on one side the busts of King George and Queen Mary, side
by side, facing left. On the other side appears the Royal cypher,
'G.R.v.' surmounted by an Imperial Crown, with the date '22 JUNE
1911' below. A beaded circle runs round the circumference. The
medal, which was struck in silver only, was awarded during the
Coronation festivities in 1911, in much the same way as Queen
Victoria's Jubilee medals, and that for King Edward's Coronation.
King George's Medal for the Delhi Durbar of 1911 is suspended
from the same ribbon, but is somewhat larger and of a different
design. Both these medals were awarded to ladies, and are worn
by them on the left shoulder, attached to a bow of the ribbon.

### 153 - KING GEORGE V'S POLICE CORONATION MEDAL (1911)

This medal was awarded in silver in much the same way as King
Edward's Police Coronation Medal. There were nine variations
of the inscription on the reverse, viz.: 'CITY OF LONDON POLICE';
'METROPOLITAN POLICE'; 'COUNTY AND BOROUGH POLICE'; 'LON-
DON FIRE BRIGADE'; 'ROYAL PARKS'; 'ST. JOHN AMBULANCE
BRIGADE'; 'ROYAL IRISH CONSTABULARY'; 'SCOTTISH POLICE';
'ST. ANDREW'S AMBULANCE.' It is possible that a tenth inscription,
'POLICE AMBULANCE SERVICE,' may exist.

### 154 - KING'S VISIT COMMEMORATION MEDAL (IRELAND) (1911)

This medal was awarded to prominent officials in Ireland, and to
members of the Irish Police Forces in much the same way as King
Edward's Medal, 1903.

### 155, 156, 157 - TITLE BADGES (INDIA)

What were known as Title Badges were instituted by the King
Emperor, George V, at the Coronation Durbar at Delhi on 12
December 1911. They were awarded, in three classes, to civilians
and Viceroy's commissioned officers of the Indian Army for faithful
service or acts of public welfare, the badges in each case bearing
the name of the title, as follows:

*First Class.*    'Diwan Bahadur,' for Muslims.
                  'Sardar Bahadur,' for Hindus.
*Second Class.*   'Khan Bahadur,' for Muslims.
                  'Rai' or 'Rao Bahadur' for Hindus.
*Third Class.*    'Khan Sahib' for Muslims.
                  'Rai' or 'Rao Sahib' for Hindus.

A man had to be awarded the lowest grade before being advanced
to a senior grade, and if he received two decorations only the senior
title was used. If he eventually became a knight, the title was
dropped. The title carried with the decorations was used before
the name but after any rank held, e.g. Subadar Major 'Khan
Bahadur' Mohammed Khan.

The badges were worn round the neck from ribbons 38 mm.
wide. That for the *First Class*, with a ribbon of pale blue with dark
blue edges, was in silver-gilt; and the *Second Class*, with a ribbon
of red with darker red edges, of silver with the centre medallion in

silver. The *Third Class*, with a ribbon of dark blue with light blue edges, was worked entirely in silver with the circle bearing the title in blue enamel.

The design of the badge was the same for all three classes except for the wording of the title, and the reverse was plain and had the name of the recipient. The ribbons were worn in undress uniform, and miniature badges on the breast with other miniature decorations and medals. The 'Title Badges' took precedence after all British and British Indian Orders and decorations, and before war medals.

## EDWARD, PRINCE OF WALES' INDIA MEDAL
(1921–22)

This medal was conferred upon approximately eighty Indian officers and police, but not to any British officers or officials, in commemoration of the Royal Tour in India, 1921–2, carried out by the Prince of Wales, later King Edward VIII and Duke of Windsor. The medal, intended to be worn round the neck, is of frosted silver, 41 mm. in diameter. The obverse shows the Prince's head facing left, and around the circumference are the words 'EDWARD PRINCE OF WALES, INDIA 1921/22.' The reverse has in the centre the badge of the Heir Apparent surrounded by an oval garter with motto, the whole being surmounted by the Prince's coronet. The ribbon, 57 mm. wide, is very dark red with a 3 mm. dark blue stripe towards each edge.

## 158 - KING GEORGE V'S SILVER JUBILEE MEDAL

Some 84,400 medals were issued over the whole Empire on the occasion of King George V's Silver Jubilee in 1935. The medal, which is of silver, was designed by Sir William Goscombe John, R.A. It is suspended from a ring, and has on the obverse the conjoint busts of their Majesties King George V and Queen Mary, crowned, robed and looking to the left. Inscription round the obverse 'GEORGE V AND QUEEN MARY. MAY VI—MCMXXXV.' The reverse bears the Royal cypher 'G.R.I.' surmounted by the crown, the dates 'MAY 6, 1910' and 'MAY 6, 1935' on either side of the cypher, the whole within an ornamental border. The medal is worn by ladies attached to a bow of the ribbon. The medals, like other Jubilee and Coronation medals, were issued as personal souvenirs to persons selected throughout the Empire. The white in the ribbon was regarded as representing silver.

## 159 - KING GEORGE VI'S CORONATION MEDAL (1937)

Some 95,000 medals were issued as personal souvenirs over the whole Empire to representative persons on the occasion of King George VI's Coronation. The medal was designed by Mr. Percy Metcalfe, and the obverse has the conjoint busts of their Majesties the King and Queen, crowned and robed and looking to the left. The reverse bears the Royal cypher surmounted by the crown, and below the cypher the inscription 'CROWNED 12 MAY, 1937,' the whole surrounded by the inscription 'GEORGE VI. QUEEN ELIZABETH.'

*(Obverse)*

**158 - KING GEORGE V'S SILVER JUBILEE MEDAL**    *(Reverse)*

*(Obverse)*

**159 - KING GEORGE VI'S CORONATION MEDAL**    *(Reverse)*

## 160 - QUEEN ELIZABETH II'S CORONATION MEDAL

This medal, to commemorate the Coronation, was struck in silver at the Royal Mint for issue as a personal souvenir from Her Majesty to selected persons in the Crown Services and others in Britain and in other parts of the Commonwealth and Empire. The medal, designed by Mr. Cecil Thomas, is 32 mm. in diameter and bears on the obverse the effigy of the Queen, crowned and robed and looking to the right. The reverse bears the Royal cypher, 'E II R,' surmounted by the crown, surrounded by the inscription 'QUEEN ELIZABETH II, CROWNED 2ND JUNE, 1953.' The medal hangs from a ring, and the ribbon, 32 mm. wide, is dark red with narrow white stripes at each edge and two narrow stripes of dark blue near the centre.

The Coronation Medal, engraved round the rim with the words 'MOUNT EVEREST EXPEDITION,' was presented by the Queen to all the fourteen members of the expedition at Buckingham Palace on 16 July 1953. The award was Her Majesty's own happy idea to mark the coincidence of the conquest of the mountain with her Coronation. The only other instance where a medal was granted with the name of an expedition engraved on the rim was when the East and West Africa Medal of 1887–1900 was awarded to officers and men of the Naval brigades, to native troops, and to certain consular and civil officers, who were employed in suppressing the Mazrui rebellion in East Africa in 1895-6. The medal carried no bar, but was issued with 'MWELE 1895' or 'MWELE 1895–96' on the rim with the name of the recipient.

*(Re*

*(Obverse)*

160 - QUEEN ELIZABETH II'S CORONATIO MEDAL

# *Long Service Decorations and Medals*

## 161 - QUEEN VICTORIA'S FAITHFUL SERVICE MEDAL

A silver medal, smaller than usual, with the effigy of the Queen and legend on the obverse, and on the reverse the name of the recipient. Attached to the top of the medal is a bar consisting of a rose between two sprays of leaves. Above is the cypher, 'V.R.I.' surmounted by a Tudor crown, the top of which is attached by two links to a bar pin for suspension, ornamented with two sprays of laurel. This medal, awarded for twenty-five years' faithful service to members of the staff of the Royal Household, was not originally intended to have a ribbon. As presented, however, it had a narrow strip of ribbon in the colours of the Royal Stewart tartan behind the crown and cypher between the top and bottom bars. The ribbon was not intended to be worn without the medal. In the coloured illustra-

161 - QUEEN VICTORIA'S FAITHFUL SERVICE MEDAL

tion the horizontal stripes of yellow and white appeared just beneath the brooch pin at the top. Further down, above the bar over the medal, half hidden by the Royal cypher, were three similar horizontal stripes of black, white, black.

### 162 - KING GEORGE V'S LONG AND FAITHFUL SERVICE MEDAL

A silver medal, with the uncrowned head of the King on the obverse with the usual legend, and on the reverse the words 'FOR LONG AND FAITHFUL SERVICE' surrounded by two sprays of laurel tied at the bottom. The medal is surmounted by the Royal cypher and crown, the crown being attached to a straight suspension bar engraved with the dates for which the award was made. It was granted to members of the staff of the Royal Household for twenty-five years' service, and the ribbon, 28 mm. wide, is of crimson with broad royal blue diagonal stripes descending from left to right. Straight bars bearing the words 'THIRTY YEARS,' 'FORTY YEARS,' 'FIFTY YEARS' could be awarded for further periods of service.

### 162 - KING GEORGE VI'S LONG AND FAITHFUL SERVICE MEDAL

This medal is exactly similar to the above, but with the head of King George VI on the obverse, and the diagonal stripes on the ribbon descending from right to left.

### QUEEN ELIZABETH II HOUSEHOLD LONG SERVICE MEDAL

A silver medal awarded in similar conditions to those already described. The obverse has the effigy of Her Majesty, and the reverse 'FOR LONG AND FAITHFUL SERVICE.' It hangs by the Royal cypher, 'E. II R.' from a ribbon of royal blue with three narrow stripes of red; one near each edge and one in the centre.

### KING EDWARD VII'S MEDAL FOR SCIENCE, ART AND MUSIC

This medal was instituted in 1902 and discontinued in 1906. It is not known how many of these medals were awarded. A circular silver medal with the obverse bearing the conjoint heads of King Edward and Queen Alexandra, and the reverse a group of symbolic figures with an inscription and the words 'SCIENCE, ART AND MUSIC' beneath. Except at the bottom, the circumference of the medal on both obverse and reverse is formed of sprays of laurel joined at the top. The medal hangs from a ring, and the ribbon of scarlet moiré has a 9 mm. central stripe of dark blue with white stripes 3 mm. wide 3 mm. in from each edge.

### 163 - LONG SERVICE AND GOOD CONDUCT MEDAL (ARMY)

A medal for long service and good conduct was instituted by King William IV in 1830, to be granted to soldiers of irreproachable

*(Reverse)*          *(Obverse)*

**163 - LONG SERVICE AND GOOD CONDUCT MEDAL (ARMY)** *(Original Medal)*

character who had served twenty-one years in the infantry, or twenty in the cavalry. It was worn from a plain crimson ribbon and bore on the obverse a trophy of arms surrounding the Royal escutcheon, and on the reverse the inscription 'FOR LONG SERVICE AND GOOD CONDUCT.' There have been various alterations since 1830. When King Edward VII came to the throne the design on the obverse was replaced by the effigy of the reigning Sovereign, while during the First World War, because of its similarity to that of the Victoria Cross, the present ribbon – crimson with white edges – was adopted.

This medal is now common to the Regular Army and other Permanent Military Forces throughout the British Commonwealth except in Canada and South Africa; a 'subsidiary title' inscribed on a bar attached to the mount of the ribbon denoting whether service was in the Regular Army or in one of the Permanent Forces. It is awarded to warrant officers, N.C.O.s and men of eighteen years' service whose character and conduct throughout have been irreproachable. A similar medal with the same ribbon and the 'subsidiary title' 'Bechuanaland' is awarded in the same conditions to members of the BECHUANALAND PROTECTORATE POLICE. Service under the age of eighteen can be reckoned as qualifying service, while service in West Africa and certain parts of the Sudan counted as double. Officers commissioned after 3 September 1939 with a minimum of twelve years' service in the ranks on a Regular Army engagement may qualify on completion of eighteen years' Service.

Dominion and Colonial Long Service and Good Conduct Medals used formerly to be issued with distinctive ribbons. The ribbon was crimson, with a narrow central stripe of colour – dark green for the Commonwealth of Australia; light blue for New South Wales and Queensland; pink for Tasmania; orange for the Cape of Good Hope and Natal; white for Canada; green for New Zealand. Victoria used a crimson ribbon with a broad white central stripe, and New Guinea scarlet with a light blue stripe. These ribbons were rendered obsolete by the general issue of the 'Permanent Overseas Forces L.S. and G.C. Medal' with its crimson ribbon and central narrow stripe of blue flanked by two narrow stripes of white, which has now been replaced by the medal just described.

In Canada the Long Service and Good Conduct Medal was superseded by the Canadian Forces Decoration, No. 131, in 1950, and in South Africa by the John Chard Medal No. 253 and the Union Medal No. 255.

## 163 - INDIAN LONG SERVICE AND GOOD CONDUCT MEDAL (for Europeans of the Indian Army)

This medal is similar to the above, but is now obsolete.

## 163 - INDIAN LONG SERVICE AND GOOD CONDUCT MEDAL (for Indian Army)

Awarded in much the same conditions as that just described. The reverse had a wreath of lotus leaves and flowers encircling one of

*(Obverse)*

**163 - INDIAN LONG SERVICE AND GOOD CONDUCT MEDAL** *(Reverse)*

palm leaves with the inscription 'FOR LONG SERVICE AND GOOD CONDUCT' and the word 'INDIA.' The medal is now obsolete.

## 164 - LONG SERVICE AND GOOD CONDUCT MEDAL, PERMANENT OVERSEAS FORCES (now obsolete)

## 165 - ROYAL WEST AFRICAN FRONTIER FORCE LONG SERVICE AND GOOD CONDUCT MEDAL
This medal is the same as for the British Army, but with the words 'WEST AFRICAN FRONTIER FORCE' added to the inscription on the reverse. The ribbon is crimson with a central green stripe.

## 165 - KING'S AFRICAN RIFLES LONG SERVICE AND GOOD CONDUCT MEDAL
The ribbon and medal are the same as No. 165 above, but with 'KING'S AFRICAN RIFLES' on the reverse.

## 166 - LONG SERVICE AND GOOD CONDUCT MEDAL (NAVY)
A medal for good conduct was first established by King William IV, in 1831, and was worn with a ribbon of dark blue. In 1848 a medal of a different type was introduced and is now granted to petty officers and men of the Royal Navy, and to non-commissioned officers and men of the Royal Marines, who have served for fifteen years with very good characters. Gratuities, varying with the rank of the recipients, may also be granted. The medal, which hangs from a straight clasp, bears on its obverse the head of the Sovereign, and on the reverse the design shown in the illustration.

Recipients are entitled to a clasp on completion of a further fifteen years' service in the conditions governing the original award. Possessors of the clasp wear the rosette on the ribbon when it is worn alone.

Women of the W.R.N.S. are eligible for the award in the same conditions as men.

## 167 - ROYAL FLEET RESERVE LONG SERVICE AND GOOD CONDUCT MEDAL
Men of the Royal Fleet Reserve who are not in possession of the R.N. Long Service and Good Conduct Medal are eligible for the award of the Royal Fleet Reserve Long Service and Good Conduct Medal provided that they have completed at least fifteen years' service in the Fleet and Royal Fleet Reserve combined; have satisfactorily carried out the prescribed training; and have been of good character during the fifteen years preceding the award.

Men in possession of the Royal Fleet Reserve Long Service and Good Conduct Medal who subsequently re-enter the Royal Navy or Royal Marines or any of the Dominion Navies and qualify for the award of the Active Service Long Service and Good Conduct Medal, will be required to surrender the Reserve Medal on being awarded the Active Service Medal.

The medal is suspended by a ring. The obverse bears the bust of

*(Obverse)*

**166 - LONG SERVICE AND GOOD CONDUCT MEDAL (NAVY)**                    *(Reverse)*

the Sovereign, the reverse a battleship with the legend 'DIUTURNE FIDELIS,' and exactly the same as the R.N.R. L.S. and G.C. Medal. As in the case of the Naval Long Service and Good Conduct Medal, recipients of the R.F.R. Medal are entitled to a clasp for a further fifteen years' qualifying service.

## 168 - MEDAL FOR MERITORIOUS SERVICE

This medal was instituted on 19 December 1845 for the Army and four years later for the Royal Marines, its award in these cases being accompanied by an annuity not exceeding twenty pounds a year. The ribbon was crimson for the Army and dark blue for the Royal Marines.

*Army.* Previous to the First World War the medal was awarded to specially selected warrant officers and sergeants of long and meritorious service, and then very rarely. It was also awarded for gallantry. It was worn from the same ribbon as the Long Service and Good Conduct Medal, but instead of it, and bore the Sovereign's head in military uniform on the obverse, and on the reverse a wreath with a crown at the apex encircling the inscription 'FOR MERITORIOUS SERVICE.' In October 1916 the grant was extended to sergeants, and other N.C.O.s and men, irrespective of length of service, 'for valuable and meritorious services.' In January 1917 the conditions were changed to cover 'warrant officers, N.C.O.s and men who are duly recommended for the grant in respect of gallant conduct in the performance of military duty otherwise than in action with the enemy, or in saving or attempting to save the life of an officer or soldiers, or for devotion to duty in a theatre of war.' It was also laid down that it could be worn in addition to the Long Service and Good Conduct Medal, and the ribbon was altered to crimson with narrow white edges and a central stripe of white. Bars could be awarded for further acts and recipients were entitled to an annuity of ten pounds. The use of the medal for these latter purposes ceased in 1917 and 1922, when its place was taken by the British Empire Medal.

The medal is still awarded to specially selected warrant officers and sergeants for long and meritorious service, with gratuities to those chosen when gratuities become vacant.

*Royal Marines.* Instituted in 1849. A similar medal, but with the blue ribbon, was originally granted to warrant officers and N.C.O.s of the Royal Marines, with gratuities when they became vacant, as rewards for distinguished or meritorious service. It is no longer awarded.

*Royal Navy and Royal Marines.* In 1919 King George V approved the adoption by the Royal Navy of the Army Meritorious Service Medal and ribbon. Its grant was limited to chief petty officers, petty officers, men and boys of the Royal Navy, warrant officers, N.C.O.s and men of the Royal Marines, and others holding corresponding positions in the Naval service who might be considered deserving of award (1) for arduous and specially meritorious service either afloat or ashore not in action with the enemy; (2) for a specific act of gallantry in the performance of his duty when not in the

*(Obverse)*

**168 - MEDAL FOR MERITORIOUS SERVICE**
*(Reverse)*

presence of the enemy. The holder of a Meritorious Service Medal might receive a bar to the medal in question for either (*a*) a second act of gallantry, or (*b*) for such an act performed by a petty officer or man who had already obtained the medal for long and meritorious service.

Awarded in these conditions the Meritorious Service Medal did not carry any annuity or additional pension. When granted to men of the Royal Navy it bore the King's head on the obverse in Naval uniform, otherwise it was exactly the same as that awarded to the Army, with the same ribbon. It was discontinued in 1928, and its place taken by the British Empire Medal.

Naval and Royal Marine recipients of the M.S.M. were allowed by custom to use the letters M.S.M. after their names.

## INDIAN MERITORIOUS SERVICE MEDAL
(for Europeans of Indian Army). This medal is now obsolete.

## 168 - INDIAN MERITORIOUS SERVICE MEDAL
(for Indian Army)
This medal had the same ribbon as that already described, and was of the same pattern as the Indian Long Service and Good Conduct Medal with the inscription 'FOR MERITORIOUS SERVICE' on the reverse. It is now obsolete.

**168 - INDIAN MERITORIOUS SERVICE MEDAL**   (*Reverse*)

## NEW ZEALAND MERITORIOUS SERVICE MEDAL

## 169 - ROYAL AIR FORCE MERITORIOUS SERVICE MEDAL
The Meritorious Service Medal was also granted to warrant officers, N.C.O.s and men of the Royal Air Force 'for the recognition of valuable services rendered in the field as distinct from actual flying services.' The reverse of this medal was exactly the same as that for the Army and Navy, but the obverse bore His Majesty's effigy, without uniform, as used upon coins, with the usual legend. The R.A.F. M.S.M. with its distinctive ribbon, was abolished in 1928, and its place taken by the British Empire Medal.

## 170 - ROYAL AIR FORCE LONG SERVICE AND GOOD CONDUCT MEDAL
The medal is of silver, circular, and bears on the obverse His Majesty's effigy with the usual legend, and on the reverse the words 'FOR LONG SERVICE AND GOOD CONDUCT,' surrounding an eagle surmounted by the crown. The ribbon is worn with the blue to the right, i.e, farthest from the left shoulder.

## MERITORIOUS SERVICE MEDAL (SOUTH AFRICAN PERMANENT FORCES) (now obsolete)
This medal was established on 18 January 1929 on the recommendation of the officer commanding the Union Defence Force for

(*Obverse*)

**NEW ZEALAND MERITORIOUS SERVICE MEDAL**

award on discharge to warrant and non-commissioned officers of the South African Permanent Force above the rank of corporal for long, valuable and meritorious service of not less than twenty-one years; for valuable services in the execution of duty either in peace or in war; or some outstanding meritorious service above that usually rendered, such as by personal example and energy assisting in the successful carrying out of a military operation, or by consistent devotion to duty in peacetime, thereby rendering special assistance to a superior officer. This award became obsolete in December 1939 on the extension of the Efficiency Decoration, the Efficiency Medal, and the Long Service and Good Conduct Medal to the Military Forces of the Union. The medal was of silver with the effigy of the Sovereign on the obverse, and on the reverse the words 'FOR MERITORIOUS SERVICE' encircled by a wreath and surmounted by a crown. The ribbon was crimson with blue edges, and in the centre a blue stripe flanked by narrower stripes of white.

This same medal, in similar conditions, was formerly available for all the permanent military forces of the Commonwealth.

*(Obverse)*

## 171 - POLICE LONG SERVICE AND GOOD CONDUCT MEDAL

This medal was established in June 1951 for twenty-two years' pensionable or approved police service with very good character and conduct to – 'full-time serving members of all ranks in the Metropolitan Police Force, in the City of London Police Force, in Police Forces maintained by local police authorities in England, Wales and Scotland, in the Royal Ulster Constabulary, in the Police Forces of the Isle of Man and the Channel Islands, in the Constabulary of Government Departments and the British Transport Commission, in the Dock Police Forces of the United Kingdom, and in Constabulary maintained by the Ulster Transport Authority.'

The Royal Warrant also laid down that it should – 'be a condition of the award of the Medal in any Police Force or Constabulary that the grant of the Imperial Service Medal or any unofficial or local long service or good conduct medals for wear in such Force shall be discontinued, and that any unofficial or local long service medals, if already granted, shall not be worn by a recipient of Our Police Long Service and Good Conduct Medal.'

The medal is in cupro-nickel and circular, and bears on the obverse the crowned effigy of the Sovereign, and on the reverse the inscription 'FOR EXEMPLARY POLICE SERVICE,' with 'a design showing the figure of Justice holding with outstretched hand an emblem of laurel, thus honouring the forces of law and order.'

**MALTA POLICE LONG SERVICE AND GOOD CONDUCT MEDAL** *(Reverse)*

## 172 - AFRICAN POLICE MEDAL FOR MERITORIOUS SERVICE (now obsolete)

This medal, instituted in 1915 for award to non-European members of the Police Forces of East and West Africa, has now been superseded by the Colonial Police Medal. It bore the King's effigy on the obverse, and on the reverse a crown surmounted by a lion and surrounded by a laurel wreath and appropriate inscription.

**173 - COLONIAL POLICE LONG SERVICE MEDAL** *(Reverse)*

**MALTA POLICE LONG SERVICE AND GOOD CONDUCT MEDAL**

**173 - COLONIAL POLICE LONG SERVICE MEDAL**

**174 - COLONIAL FIRE BRIGADES LONG SERVICE MEDAL**

These medals are awarded for eighteen years' long service and good conduct. The ribbons for Police and Fire Brigades differ as shown. The obverse of both medals has the Sovereign's effigy. The reverse of that for the Police shows a truncheon through a wreath around the words 'COLONIAL POLICE: FOR LONG SERVICE AND GOOD CONDUCT'; and that for Fire Brigades a helmet and hatchet and 'COLONIAL FIRE BRIGADE: FOR LONG SERVICE AND GOOD CONDUCT.'

**COLONIAL SPECIAL CONSTABULARY MEDAL**

Instituted in 1958, and granted in recognition of nine years' unpaid service or fifteen years' paid service. A clasp is given for each further ten years.

**FIRE BRIGADE LONG SERVICE AND GOOD CONDUCT MEDAL**

In a Royal Warrant of 1 June 1954 it was announced that the Queen had approved the award of an official medal for long service and good conduct to full-time and part-time members of all ranks of Local Authority Fire Brigades, other than members of the Auxiliary Fire Service; as well as to full-time and certain part-time members of Fire Brigades and services maintained by certain Government Departments. The qualifying period is twenty years' whole or part-time service in one brigade or service, or the same in one or more brigades or services. Service in Local Authority Brigades no longer in existence; in the Auxiliary Fire Service between 3 September 1939 and 18 August 1941 (or in Northern Ireland, 1 April 1942); and service in the National Fire Service are also treated as qualifying service. A certificate of good character and conduct is necessary.

The medal is in cupro-nickel and circular, and has on the obverse the crowned effigy of the Sovereign, and on the reverse the inscription 'FOR EXEMPLARY FIRE SERVICE,' with a design showing two firemen handling a hose. The name of the recipient is engraved or stamped on the rim. The ribbon is red with, on each side, a yellow stripe divided by a narrow stripe of red.

**175 - VOLUNTEER OFFICERS' DECORATION** (1892) (now obsolete)

This decoration was instituted in July 1892 for the purpose of rewarding 'efficient and capable' officers of the Volunteer Force who had served for twenty years. Two years later a similar distinction was introduced for officers of Volunteer Forces in India and the Colonies, but in the case of India the qualifying service was reduced to eighteen years. The badge consists of an oval oak wreath in silver,

**174 - COLONIAL FIRE BRIGADES LONG SERVICE MEDAL**      (*Reverse*)

(*Obverse*)

**COLONIAL SPECIAL CONSTABULARY MEDAL**

tied in gold, and having in the centre the Royal cypher surmounted by the Imperial Crown, both in gold. It is suspended from its ribbon by a silver ring, while the ribbon itself is 38 mm. wide, and has a silver bar brooch with oak leaves at the top. In the decoration for British volunteer officers the cypher was 'V.R.' or 'E.R. VII.' according to the reign in which it was issued, while that for Indian and Colonial officers had 'V.R.I.' or 'E.R.I. VII.' The award of the decoration entitled the recipient to use the letters V.D. after his name. The V.D., except for India, became obsolete when the Volunteer Force was disbanded in 1908.

### 175 - VOLUNTEER LONG SERVICE MEDAL (1894)
(now obsolete)

This medal was instituted in 1894 for men of the Volunteer Forces who had completed twenty years' service. In 1896 its issue was extended to the Indian and Colonial Forces, eighteen years' service being the qualification in India. The medal has on the obverse the effigy of the reigning Sovereign, with the usual legend. The reverse has laurel branches and intertwined scrolls bearing the words, 'FOR LONG SERVICE IN THE VOLUNTEER FORCE.' In the Indian and Colonial medals the obverse had 'ET IMPERATRIX' or 'ET IMPERATOR,' added to the legend. This medal became obsolete in Great Britain on the disbandment of the volunteers in 1908, but, with the effigy of the reigning Sovereign on the obverse, the words on the reverse altered to 'FOR LONG SERVICE IN THE COLONIAL AUXILIARY FORCES,' and the laurel branches surmounted by the Imperial Crown, was still issued in the Colonies. The Honourable Artillery Company had a special ribbon for this medal. It was half scarlet, half dark blue with narrow yellow edges, the racing colours of King Edward VII. (See later under Efficiency Decoration and Medal.)

### 175 - COLONIAL OFFICERS' AUXILIARY FORCES DECORATION (now obsolete)

This decoration was established in 1899 for commissioned officers in the Colonial Auxiliary Forces who had served for twenty years, service on the West Coast of Africa counting double. It superseded the V.D. for Colonial officers. The oval badge has in the centre the Imperial cypher 'E.R.I. VII.' or 'G.R.I. V.' as the case may be. The cypher is surrounded by a band bearing the words 'COLONIAL AUXILIARY FORCES,' while the badge is surmounted by an Imperial Crown. It hangs from a green ribbon, 38 mm. wide, by means of a ring.

This decoration has been superseded by the Efficiency Decoration.

### 176 - NAVAL GOOD SHOOTING MEDAL (1903)
(no longer awarded)

This medal, which is suspended by a plain clasp, bears the effigy of the reigning Sovereign in Naval uniform on one side with the usual inscription. On the reverse appears a figure of Neptune turned towards the right. He grasps thunderbolts in each hand,

*(Obverse)*

**175 - VOLUNTEER LONG SERVICE MEDAL**
*(Reverse)*

and the right arm is drawn back in the act of throwing them. In the background is the prow of a Roman trireme drawn by three sea-horses. Above is a trident, with the wording 'AMAT VICTORIA CURAM.' This medal was authorized by King Edward in August 1903, and was given annually to seamen who attained a certain very high percentage of hits with each type of gun during the annual target practice carried out by the Fleet. The medal was first awarded without a bar, but if a man qualified for it again, he received a bar on which appeared the name of his ship, the calibre or denomination of the gun with which he fired, and the year. The Naval Good Shooting Medal is rare, and was most highly prized.

### 177 - MILITIA LONG SERVICE AND GOOD CONDUCT MEDAL (1904–08)
This medal was granted by King Edward VII to all non-commissioned officers and men of good character in the Militia who were serving on, or after, 9 November 1904. Eighteen years' service and at least fifteen annual trainings were required to qualify. It is oval, and has on its obverse the head of King Edward VII with the usual legend, and on the reverse the words 'MILITIA. FOR LONG SERVICE AND GOOD CONDUCT.' It hangs from a light blue ribbon by a ring in the top of the medal.

### 178 - IMPERIAL YEOMANRY LONG SERVICE AND GOOD CONDUCT MEDAL (1904–08)
This medal was formerly given to members of the Imperial Yoemanry after ten years' service with a minimum of ten trainings. It is oval, and bears on one side the head of the reigning Sovereign, and on the other, 'IMPERIAL YEOMANRY. FOR LONG SERVICE AND GOOD CONDUCT.' It hangs by a ring from a yellow ribbon. It is now obsolete, those entitled to it receiving the Efficiency Medal.

### 179 - TERRITORIAL DECORATION (now obsolete)
This decoration, instituted in 1908 to replace the volunteer officers' decoration of 1892, when the Territorial Force was established, is of much the same design as the V.D. It has the cypher 'E.R. VII.' or 'G.R. V.' according to the reign in which it was issued, and hangs from a green ribbon, 38 mm. wide, with a yellow stripe down the centre. Recipients are entitled to use the letters T.D. after their names.

### ARMY EMERGENCY RESERVE DECORATION
This decoration was established during the summer of 1951 for award to officers of the Army Emergency Reserve for twelve years' service, though the qualifying period is ten years if they were commissioned on or after 8 August 1924 or before 15 May 1928, if transferred to the Royal Army Officers Reserve. Active service counts double. Worn after 174, it takes precedence to the Efficiency Decoration; but is of the same design with the crown and Royal cypher 'E. II. R.' surrounded by the oval oak wreath. The ribbon is dark blue, 38 mm. wide, with a 6 mm. central stripe of yellow, and hangs from a top suspender bar bearing the words 'ARMY EMERGENCY RESERVE' in two lines.

**176 - NAVAL GOOD SHOOTING MEDAL**
(*Reverse*)

## 179 - EFFICIENCY DECORATION

This decoration was established in 1930 to replace the Volunteer Officers' Decoration (1892), the Colonial Auxiliary Forces Decoration (1899) and the Territorial Decoration (1908). The conditions of award were amended in 1940, 1946, twice in 1949, 1951 and by a Royal Warrant printed as a Special Army Order, No. 136, of 24 November 1952

The order is too long and complicated to be quoted in detail. In brief, the decoration is conferred for twelve years' continuous efficient commissioned service on the active list in the Territorial Army, the New Zealand Territorial Force, and authorized Volunteer Forces in British colonies and territories under British protection, or in any other part of Her Majesty's Dominions where the Government so desire. For Auxiliary Military Forces of the Commonwealth the qualification is twenty years' commissioned service on the active list which need not necessarily be continuous. Half the time served in the ranks, or as a cadet over the age of seventeen is reckoned as qualifying service, while war service counts double. A clasp or bar is awarded to recipients of the decoration for each six years' additional continuous efficient service.

The decoration consists of an oval oak wreath (39 x 32 mm.) in silver tied with gold, with the Royal cypher and crown, also in gold. There is a bar brooch at the top of the ribbon bearing a subsidiary title showing whether the recipient served in the Territorial Army or one of the other Auxiliary Military Forces of the Commonwealth. The illustration shows this 'subsidiary title,' with two clasps, in gold, each denoting six years' additional service. The decoration confers no individual precedence, but entitled an officer of the Territorial Army to use the letters T.D. after his name, and an officer of one of the Auxiliary Military Forces of the Empire the letters E.D. King Edward VII gave permission to members of the Honourable Artillery Company to wear a special ribbon with the old Volunteer Decoration. Its use is still continued, though the privilege is not automatic. Recipients must fulfil certain qualifications of service in the H.A.C. and be granted permission by the colonel-commandant. Composed of the King's racing colours, the special ribbon is half scarlet, half dark blue, with corded edges of bright yellow.

## 180 - TERRITORIAL EFFICIENCY MEDAL

(1908–21 and 1921–30)
This medal was instituted by King Edward on the establishment of the Territorial Force in 1908–9. It really superseded the old Volunteer Long Service Medal, and was awarded to men of the Territorial Force after twelve years' service, provided they had undergone at least twelve trainings. The medal, which is oval, bears on its obverse the head of the reigning Sovereign with the usual legend. The inscription 'TERRITORIAL FORCE EFFICIENCY MEDAL' appears on the reverse of the earlier medal, but on the later issue the word 'FORCE' is omitted. The ribbon was originally the same as that of the Territorial Decoration, though 32 mm. wide instead of 38, but in 1920 was changed to green with narrow yellow edges. The ribbon

*(Obverse)*

**180 - TERRITORIAL EFFICIENCY MEDAL**
*(Original Medal) (Reverse)*

**180 - EFFICIENCY MEDAL**
'INDIA'    *(Obverse)*
*Issue of King George V*

'MILITIA.'
*(Obverse)*
*Issue of King George VI*

passes through a ring at the top of the medal.
This medal was superseded in 1940 by the Efficiency Medal.

## 180, 181 - EFFICIENCY MEDAL

This medal superseded the old Volunteer Long Service Medal, the Colonial Auxiliary Forces Medal, the Militia and Special Reserve Long Service Medals and the Territorial Efficiency Medal. It is awarded to warrant officers, N.C.O.s and men of the Territorial and Auxiliary Military Forces throughout the Commonwealth, except in Canada and South Africa, who complete twelve years' efficient service. A clasp worn on the ribbon is awarded after a total of eighteen years, with a further clasp for twenty-four years. Service in West Africa and during war is reckoned as double, while cadet service is allowed to count.

**180 - EFFICIENCY MEDAL**
'MALAYA' *and Second Bar*

The medal is now awarded to officers and other ranks of the Territorial Army who were serving on the active list of that force on 2 September 1939, and who have completed twelve years' qualifying service, whether their service has been wholly in the ranks or partly as an emergency commissioned officer. As the Second World War lasted nearly six years and war service counts double, this means that practically everyone in the Territorial Army on 2 September 1939 became eligible for the medal. It is *not* awarded to officers who already possess the Efficiency Decoration; but if a Territorial officer is awarded the medal (twelve years) and the first clasp (eighteen years) he can, after twenty years' total service, be awarded the decoration. Though he cannot wear both, he is not called upon to surrender the medal.

Women are eligible for the medal in the same conditions as men.

The medal, of silver, is oval, and bears on the obverse the Royal effigy, and on the reverse the inscription 'FOR EFFICIENT SERVICE.'

*(Reverse)*

It bears a subsidiary title inscribed on the mount denoting whether it is awarded for service in the Territorial Army or in one of the other Auxiliary Forces of the Commonwealth. For certain units of the Supplementary Reserve, until the Army Emergency Reserve was established in 1950, the mount bore the word 'MILITIA.' Members of the H.A.C. may be permitted to wear the special ribbon described under the Efficiency Decoration, except that it is 32 mm. in width instead of 38 mm.

## ARMY EMERGENCY RESERVE MEDAL

This medal, which follows the same lines as the Efficiency Medal, hangs by two foliated branches from a scroll bar with the words 'ARMY EMERGENCY RESERVE.' The ribbon is dark blue with three narrow central stripes of yellow.

## 182 - SPECIAL RESERVE LONG SERVICE AND GOOD CONDUCT MEDAL (1908)

This medal was formerly awarded to members of the Special Reserve of the Army after fifteen years' service with good character. It was similar to the Territorial Efficiency Medal, but had different wording on the reverse, and hung from a dark blue ribbon with a light clue central stripe.

## 183 - ROYAL NAVAL RESERVE DECORATION (1908)

The Royal Naval Reserve Officers' Decoration may be conferred on officers who have total officers' service in the R.N.R. of at least fifteen years. All officers' time counts except time in the rank of midshipman. Commissioned officers must have completed the voluntary or obligatory training laid down; though officers, other-wise qualified, who have not undergone such training, but who have performed specially good service may, at the discretion of the Admiralty, be granted the decoration.

War service as an officer in any branch of the Naval Forces, or in the Army or Royal Air Force, counts as double time for the award of this decoration. The letters R.D. are inserted in the Navy List against the names of officers upon whom it is conferred.

The decoration consists of an oval medallion in gilt, formed of the Royal cypher surrounded by a loop of cable tied at the bottom and surmounted by a crown. The ribbon was originally dark green. This did not show up on a dark blue uniform, and was the same colour as the ribbon of the R.N.R. Long Service and Good Conduct Medal for men. In October 1941 the ribbon of the R.D. was therefore altered to dark green with white borders.

## 184 - ROYAL NAVAL VOLUNTEER RESERVE DECORATION

This decoration is awarded to officers of the R.N.V.R. for twenty years' service, which need not be continuous. Honorary service is not allowed to count. All officers' service over the age of seventeen in the R.N.V.R. is reckoned towards the twenty years, as is all commissioned service in the R.N.R., the Army Volunteer or

Territorial Force, in a contingent of the Officers' Training Corps, or in qualifying for the Colonial Auxiliary Forces Decoration. In general, half the time served as a rating in the R.N.R. or R.N.V.R. or in the ranks of any of the units mentioned above is allowed to count. War service counts as double time.

The letters V.R.D. are inserted in the Navy List after the names of officers to whom the decoration has been given, while those who have been previously granted the R.N.V.R. Long Service and Good Conduct Medal for twelve years' service may wear both medal and decoration.

The design of the V.R.D. is the same as the R.D. The ribbon used to be plain green, like that of the original R.N.R. decoration. At the general request of the R.N.V.R. for a distinctive ribbon it was altered to its present colouring in about 1919. The ribbon, with that of the R.N.V.R. Long Service and Good Conduct Medal, was designed by the writer. The blue represents the sea; the red the Royal crimson; and the green the old volunteer colour.

Following the merging of the R.N.V.R. and R.N.R. into one Service in 1958, the R.N.V.R. Decoration lapsed in 1966 when the R.N.R. Decoration took its place.

### 185 - ROYAL NAVAL RESERVE LONG SERVICE AND GOOD CONDUCT MEDAL (1908)

This medal may be granted to men of the Royal Naval Reserve who satisfactorily complete fifteen years' service, with the necessary periods of Naval training, provided their characters have never been assessed below 'Very good.' The medal bears on one side the bust of the Sovereign, and on the other a representation of a battleship, with the legend 'DIUTURNE FIDELIS.' It hangs from its ribbon, 32 mm. wide, by means of a straight clasp. War service usually counts double towards the period of qualifying service, while a bar may be awarded for a second period of fifteen years. When the ribbon alone is worn the possession of a bar is denoted by a silver rose. The ribbon, originally plain green, was altered in October 1941.

### 185 - ROYAL NAVAL AUXILIARY SICK BERTH RESERVE LONG SERVICE AND GOOD CONDUCT MEDAL

This medal is awarded by the Chief Commissioner, St. John Ambulance Brigade. It is of the same design as the R.N.R., L.S. and G.C. Medal, and is worn from the same ribbon.

### 186 - ROYAL NAVAL VOLUNTEER RESERVE LONG SERVICE AND GOOD CONDUCT MEDAL

The R.N.V.R. Long Service and Good Conduct Medal is granted to men of the R.N.V.R. after twelve years' qualifying service, war service usually counting double, provided that during such service their character has never been assessed below 'Very good.' Those who serve for a further period which would again qualify them for the award of a medal may be awarded a bar, in which case a silver rose is worn on the ribbon when it is worn alone. The clasp may also

*(Obverse)*

**185 - ROYAL NAVAL RESERVE LONG SERVICE AND GOOD CONDUCT MEDAL**            *(Reverse)*

be granted under the same conditions to officers who have received the medal, provided they are not eligible for the award of the Volunteer Officers' Decoration. The medal or clasp may be granted to men who have quitted the R.N.V.R., if they are qualified.

The medal is similar to that for the R.N.R., but has its own special ribbon.

## 186 - ROYAL NAVAL WIRELESS AUXILIARY RESERVE LONG SERVICE AND GOOD CONDUCT MEDAL

This medal is similar to that for the R.N.V.R. and is worn from the same ribbon. The conditions of award are twelve years' qualifying service in the R.N.V.R. or the Royal Naval Volunteer Reserve or Royal Naval Wireless Auxiliary Reserve. Bars may be awarded for further periods of service, with the usual silver rose on the ribbon when it is worn alone.

## 187 - AIR EFFICIENCY AWARD

This award was established in September 1942 to reward long and meritorious service in the Auxiliary and Volunteer Air Forces of the Commonwealth, though the award is no longer applicable to Canada or South Africa. The medal is oval and of cupro-nickel with the uncrowned effigy of the Sovereign on the obverse, and on the reverse the words 'AIR EFFICIENCY AWARD' in large capital lettering. It hangs from a clasp formed by the outstretched wings of an eagle. The main qualification is ten years' efficient service, and a bar is awarded for a further ten years.

# *Miscellaneous British Awards*

## 188 - THE QUEEN'S MEDAL

(for champion shots in the Military Forces)

A medal for the best shot in the British Army was authorized in 1869. It had on one side the head of Queen Victoria, with the usual inscription, and on the other a figure of Fame standing on a dais. She has a horn in her left hand, and with her right is crowning a kneeling warrior with a wreath of laurel. The warrior is armed with a bow, and holds a shield pierced by three arrows. The medal was instituted in 1869, and was awarded each year, with a gratuity of £20, to the best rifle shot in the British Army. It was issued in bronze until 1872, and then in silver, and was worn on the right breast. It became obsolete in 1883, and as only seventeen of the Victoria Queen's Medal were awarded, specimens are very rare indeed. A somewhat similar medal, with the same ribbon, was at one time presented to the best rifle shot in the Indian Army. The original ribbon had a centre of dark crimson, watered, with black, white and black stripes at each edge.

A King's Medal, for champion shots in the Military Forces, the counterpart of the older medal, was re-instituted in 1923. Now known as the Queen's Medal it is awarded each year to the champion rifle shots in the Regular and the Territorial Armies in Great Britain, as well as in each Dominion. A bar, with the appropriate date, is worn upon the ribbon. The medal, worn on the left breast, has the Royal effigy on the obverse with the usual legend, and on the reverse the same design as that of the older medal of 1869.

### THE QUEEN'S MEDAL
(for champion shots of the Air Forces)

This medal was instituted in August 1953 for the purpose of encouraging skill in small arms shooting in the Air Forces, 'not only on account of the need for the effective defence of airfields in war, but also because such skill has an important bearing on the standard of shooting in the air on which the air defence battle so largely depends.'

The medal, in silver and circular in shape, is worn on the left breast and has on the obverse the crowned effigy of the Queen with the usual legend, and on the reverse the title of the medal round the circumference surrounding a representation of Hermes, throwing a javelin, and mounted on a hawk in flight.

The ribbon is 32 mm. wide and is of dark crimson, with, at each edge, stripes 3 mm. wide of dark blue, light blue, dark blue. It is unfortunate that the colours and arrangement chosen are so similar to those of King George V's Jubilee Medal of 1935.

*(Obverse)*

Each medal granted bears a clasp, or bar, affixed to the ribbon with the date inscribed thereon. Should a recipient of the award again qualify, a clasp only is awarded, in which case he wears a silver rose emblem on the ribbon when it is worn by itself.

One medal only is awarded annually to members of the Air Forces of the United Kingdom and Northern Ireland, and one other to such of the several nations of the Commonwealth as may desire to participate.

### 189 - CADET FORCES MEDAL
A cupro-nickel medal, established in February 1950, bearing the crowned effigy of the Sovereign on the obverse, and on the reverse the inscription 'THE CADET FORCES MEDAL' and the representation of a torch. Those eligible are persons who have been granted commissions in 'Reserve or Auxiliary or Volunteer Forces, and persons given appointments prior to 1st February, 1942, as Officers by the Navy League or the Air League of the British Empire, for service in Units of or with Services Cadets, who have so served . . . on or after 3rd September, 1939, and Chief Petty Officer Instructors and adult Warrant Officers of Services Cadets who were serving as such on or after "the same date in cadet formations raised in Great Britain and Northern Ireland, any British Colony or territory under British protection," or within "Any other part of our Dominions Our Government whereof shall desire to take part in the grant of the award."'

**189 - CADET FORCES
MEDAL**          *(Reverse)*

The qualifying period of service is twelve years subsequent to 3 September 1926, qualifying service during the Second World War between 3 September 1939 and 2 September 1945 counting as double. Service which has been, or may be, reckoned as qualifying for the Efficiency Decoration or Efficiency Medal or its clasps, or any other efficiency or long service award may not be reckoned towards the award of the Cadet Forces Medal. Qualifying service must be continuous, though a special award may be made where service had been terminated by disability of a permanent nature due to qualifying service during the war period mentioned above, provided that the individual had completed service which could be reckoned as eleven years.

A clasp, or bar, may be awarded for each additional twelve years' service, and for each clasp a silver rose is worn on the ribbon when it only is worn. (The details governing the award are to be found in the Royal Warrant, H.M.S.O. Cmd. 7879 February 1950.)

### 190 - COAST LINE SAVING CORPS
### (formerly ROCKET APPARATUS VOLUNTEER)
### LONG SERVICE MEDAL

This silver medal was established in 1911 by the Board of Trade for rewarding long service with the Rocket Life-Saving Apparatus. The control of these companies was transferred to the Ministry of Transport in 1942. The obverse bears the Sovereign's effigy and usual legend with the date of establishment, and the reverse the inscription 'To . . . for LONG SERVICE WITH THE ROCKET LIFE-SAVING APPARATUS.' The medal hangs from its watered azure ribbon with broad scarlet edges by means of a scroll clasp. The regulations for the grant of this medal to an enrolled volunteer lay down: (*a*) He must have served for at least twenty years in a Volunteer L.S.A. Company or Brigade. (*b*) His character must have been uniformly good during his period of service. (*c*) He must have been prompt and regular in rendering service when called out on wreck duty. (*d*) He must have regularly attended the drills during his period of membership. (*e*) He must be recommended by the Inspector of Coastguard under whom he is serving at the date of application.

### 191 - THE SPECIAL CONSTABULARY
### LONG SERVICE MEDAL

This medal was established by King George V in August 1918 'in consideration of the faithful and devoted service' of the Special Constabulary during the First World War, 'and also of providing a means of recognizing continued and efficient service' in the future. The regulations were amended in 1920, 1929, 1930, 1937, 1940 and 1945.

The medal is in bronze with the Sovereign's effigy on the obverse, and on the reverse there is an inscription, 'FOR FAITHFUL SERVICE IN THE SPECIAL CONSTABULARY,' half surrounded from bottom to right by a semi-circular spray of laurel.

To qualify during the two World Wars a special constable must

**191 - THE SPECIAL CONSTABULARY LONG SERVICE MEDAL**
(*Obverse*)

have served without pay for not less than three years, and during that period have performed at least fifty police duties a year, and be recommended by a chief officer of Police as willing and competent to discharge the duties of special constable as required. A bar, 'THE GREAT WAR. 1914–18' was awarded with the medal to those who qualified.

In peace the medal is granted after nine years' service provided the fifty duties a year have been performed, and the candidate is recommended by a chief officer of Police. A bar, worded 'LONG SERVICE,' is awarded for each successive period of ten years, provided the fifty duties a year have been performed. It is to be noted that service in both World Wars counts treble.

**191 - THE SPECIAL CONSTABULARY LONG SERVICE MEDAL**
(*Reverse*)

### 192 - THE ROYAL OBSERVER CORPS MEDAL

This medal was established in January 1950. It is a circular medal in cupro-nickel with the uncrowned effigy of Queen Elizabeth II on the obverse, facing right, surrounded by the inscription 'ELIZABETH II. DEI GRA: BRITT. OMN. REGINA. F:D.' On the reverse a representation of an Elizabethan coast-watcher, holding aloft a torch and standing beside a signal fire, the whole surrounded by the words 'THE ROYAL OBSERVER CORPS MEDAL.' The medal hangs from the ribbon by a suspender consisting of two wings.

In general, the medal may be conferred upon officers and observers of the Royal Observer Corps, male and female, who have completed a total of twelve years' satisfactory service. (The precise details of reckoning service for the award are to be found in the Royal Warrant. H.M.S.O. Cmd. 7878 of January 1950.) A clasp may be awarded on the completion of each additional twelve years' service.

### 193 - UNION OF SOUTH AFRICA COMMEMORATION MEDAL (1910)

This medal was awarded to those who took a prominent part in the ceremonies in connection with the union of the various South African states and provinces by H.R.H. the Duke of Connaught in 1910; also to certain officers of H.M.S. *Balmoral Castle*, which vessel – a Union Castle liner – was specially commissioned as a man-of-war to convey His Royal Highness to the Cape of Good Hope. The obverse bears the effigy of King George V with the usual legend, and the reverse a figure at an anvil welding together the links of a chain, typical of the uniting of the various South African territories into one.

### 194 - ST. JOHN OF JERUSALEM SERVICE MEDAL

This medal, in silver, is awarded for conspicuous services to the Grand Priory in the British Realm of the Venerable Order of St. John of Jerusalem and its departments, and for fifteen years' efficient service in the St. John Ambulance Brigade. It has on the obverse Queen Victoria's effigy surrounded by the usual legend. In the centre of the reverse is a small circle containing the Royal Arms surrounded by the garter and motto. At the top, bottom, right and left of this are four small circles containing an Imperial Crown, the

167

Prince of Wales' feathers and the badges of the Order. Between the circles are sprigs of St. John's Wort. Round the circumference is the inscription, 'MAGNUS PRIORATUS ORDINIS HOSPITALIS SÁNCTI JOHANNIS JERUSALEM IN ANGLIA,' in old English lettering. The medal is worn on the left breast. A bar may be awarded for each successive five years' efficient service, and when the ribbon is worn alone a small silver cross indicates one bar; two silver crosses, two bars; three silver crosses, three bars; a gilt cross, four bars, etc.

## 195 - MEDAL FOR SOUTH AFRICA, 1899–1902, GIVEN TO MEMBERS OF THE ST. JOHN AMBULANCE BRIGADE

This bronze medal bears on one side the bust of King Edward VII, with the usual legend, and on the other the arms of the Order of St. John of Jerusalem, with the words, 'SOUTH AFRICA 1899–1902' above, and the motto, 'PRO FIDE: PRO UTILITATE: HOMINUM' on a scroll below. It was awarded to members of the St. John Ambulance Brigade who served in South Africa during the war; also to those who had to do with the despatch of medical comforts, stores, etc.

## 196 - BADGE OF THE ORDER OF THE LEAGUE OF MERCY

The badge of this Order consists of a red cross surmounted by the badge of the Heir Apparent – a plume of ostrich feathers enfiled by a coronet – and has in the centre a group of figures representing 'Charity.' Appointments to the Order are approved and sanctioned by the Sovereign on the recommendation of the Grand President of the League of Mercy, as a reward for distinguished personal service on behalf of the League in assisting the support of hospitals, or in connection with the relief of suffering, poverty or distress. Ladies or gentlemen who have rendered gratuitously the required services to the League for five years at least, are eligible. Late in 1917, the King instituted a bar to be awarded to those who, for a long period of years, have continued their services to the League after having received the Order of Mercy.

**196 - BADGE OF THE ORDER OF THE LEAGUE OF MERCY**

## 197 - VOLUNTARY MEDICAL SERVICE MEDAL

To qualify for this medal members of the British Red Cross Society and the St. Andrews' Ambulance Association must have rendered fifteen years' active efficient service. A bar bearing the Geneva Cross or the St. Andrew's Cross on a plain background is granted for each five years' additional service. The medal is in silver with a bust symbolic of Florence Nightingale on the obverse, and on the reverse the Geneva and St. Andrew's Crosses with the words 'LONG AND EFFICIENT SERVICE.'

## 198 - ALLIED SUBJECTS MEDAL

This medal was instituted in 1922, in silver and in bronze, with the effigy and legend of King George V on the obverse, for award to Allied personnel, men or women, who, at the risk of their own lives or liberty, assisted British soldiers behind the enemy lines during the First World War.

## 199 - THE KING'S MEDAL FOR COURAGE IN THE CAUSE OF FREEDOM
## 200 - THE KING'S MEDAL FOR SERVICE IN THE CAUSE OF FREEDOM

The institution of these medals was announced in August 1945. They were intended only for Allied or other foreign persons, mainly civilians, for services 'in furtherance of the interests of the British Commonwealth in the Allied cause during the war.' There were no distinctions of status or rank. The Medal for *Courage* was intended for some of those who helped members of the British forces in occupied territories to escape from or to evade the enemy, and for other services to the British Commonwealth entailing risk to life or involving dangerous work in hazardous circumstances. The Medal for *Service* was awarded for civilian services to the Allied cause in a variety of ways, the King having made the first award to Mr. Winthrop Aldrich for his outstanding work as national president of the British War Relief Society in the United States of America. The ribbons of both these medals have a background of white, and are 32 mm. wide. The first has broad red edges and in the centre two narrow stripes of blue divided by a thinner stripe of white. The second has a narrow red stripe in the centre flanked on either side by narrow stripes of blue equidistant between the centre and the edge.

Both medals are in silver with rings for suspension and have the crowned effigy of King George VI and the usual legend on the obverse. The reverse of the Medal for *Courage* has its title surrounded by a circle of chain, and that for *Service* the figure of a knight with a broken lance standing over his helm and being offered sustenance by a lady. The words 'THE KING'S MEDAL' appears below, and 'FOR SERVICE IN THE CAUSE OF FREEDOM' round the upper circumference.

# Medals awarded by British Institutions, Societies, Associations, &c.

## 201 - MEDAL OF THE ROYAL NATIONAL LIFE-BOAT INSTITUTION

Gold, silver and bronze medals are voted by the Committee of Management of the Royal National Life-Boat Institution, founded in 1824, to 'persons whose humane and intrepid exertions in saving life from ship-wreck on our coasts, etc., are deemed sufficiently conspicuous to merit these honourable distinctions. Since its institution the obverse of this medal has borne the effigies of King George IV, Queen Victoria, King Edward VII, and King George V. Since the accession of King George VI it has borne the effigy of Sir William Hillary, Bart., founder of the Institution, as the award is not made by the Sovereign. When the ribbon of the gold medal is worn alone it carries a miniature of the head of the founder. In the case of the silver and bronze medals nothing is worn on the ribbon to show which it is. Bars may be awarded for further acts, in which case a miniature of the head of the founder is added to the ribbon for each bar.

### 202 - STANHOPE GOLD MEDAL

The Stanhope Gold Medal is awarded by the Royal Humane Society for the bravest deed of life-saving of the year, either ashore or afloat. It is not awarded for bravery in saving life in fires, as cases of this kind are dealt with by another Society. The medal bears on the obverse a boy blowing an extinguished torch, in the hope, as expressed by the motto round the top circumference, 'LATEAT SCINTILLULA FORSAN. – 'Peradventure a little spark may yet lie hid.' Under the figure of the boy is the following inscription abbreviated: 'SOCIETAS LONDINI IN RESUSCITATIONEM INTER-MORTUORUM INSTITUTA, MDCCLXXIV. – 'The (Royal Humane) Society, established in London for the recovery of persons in a state of suspended animation, 1774.' The reverse shows a Civic Wreath, which was the Roman reward for saving life, while the inscription round it, 'HOC PRETIUM; CIVE SERVATO TULIT' – 'He has obtained this reward for saving the life of a citizen' – expresses the merit which obtains this honour from the Society. Inside the wreath is the inscription, abbreviated, 'VITAM OB SERVATAM DONO DEDIT SOCIETAS REGIA HUMANA' – 'The Royal Humane Society presented this gift for saving life.' There is another reverse, with the Civic Wreath only, which is used when the medal is presented to persons who have endeavoured to save the lives of others, at the risk of their own, but without success. The inscription reads, 'VITA PERICULO EXPOSITA DONO DEDIT SOCIETAS REGIA HUMANA' – 'The Royal Humane Society presented this to ——, his life having been exposed to danger.' The Stanhope Gold Medal is worn on the right breast, and is suspended from its ribbon by means of a straight gold clasp bearing the words, 'STANHOPE MEDAL.'

### 203 - ROYAL HUMANE SOCIETY'S SILVER MEDAL

### 204 - ROYAL HUMANE SOCIETY'S BRONZE MEDAL

Besides the Stanhope Medal, the Royal Humane Society also awards silver and bronze medals for rescues, or attempted rescues, from drowning, dangerous cliffs, mines where a fall of roof has occurred, or from suffocation by foul gas in mines, etc., provided that such cases are reported to the Society within two months of their occurrence. The Royal Humane Society's Medals are highly prized, and are eagerly sought after, and the silver medal is awarded for a more gallant deed than a bronze one. Bars may be awarded for any subsequent acts of bravery in saving, or attempting to save, life. The medals themselves are similar in design to the Stanhope Medal, already described, and are worn on the right breast, suspended

*(Obverse)*

**201 - MEDAL OF THE ROYAL NATIONAL LIFE-BOAT INSTITUTION**
*(Reverse)*

from their ribbons by means of a scroll clasp. If the Stanhope Medal is subsequently awarded for a deed which has already been recognized by the Society by the bestowal of a silver medal, the former is worn in place of the silver medal, not in addition to it. Awards of the silver medal are about six annually, and of the bronze medal about fifty.

Both medals were originally worn from a plain dark blue ribbon; but the silver medal now has white edges with a yellow stripe down the centre.

### 205 - MEDALS OF THE SOCIETY FOR THE PROTECTION OF LIFE FROM FIRE

Medals, certificates, watches and money awards are granted by the Trustees of the Society to those who display gallantry in saving life at fires. The medals, which are granted comparatively rarely, are given in silver or bronze, according to the merit of the deed, and are worn on the right breast – with other life-saving medals – attached to a scarlet ribbon. One side of the medal bears two branches of oak encircling the inscription: 'DUTY AND HONOR' with, round the circumference, the words 'THE SOCIETY FOR THE PROTECTION OF LIFE FROM FIRE,' and, below, the date, '1843.' On the other side is a group of figures representing a rescue from fire.

### MEDALS OF THE SHIPWRECKED FISHERMEN AND MARINERS ROYAL BENEVOLENT SOCIETY

This Society, established in 1839, besides giving assistance to the shipwrecked, and relief to widows and orphans of seamen and fishermen, grants gold and silver medals, and other honorary and pecuniary rewards for 'heroic and praiseworthy exertions to save life from shipwreck, etc., on the high seas, or coasts of India and the Colonies.' The medals are not, however, awarded so frequently as they used to be, cases of heroism at sea being usually recognized either by the Government, the Ministry of Transport, the Royal Humane Society, or the Royal National Life-Boat Institution. The design of both varieties is the same and is shown in the illustration. The medal is suspended from its navy blue ribbon, 25 mm. wide, by means of a silver clasp surmounted by two dolphins. A buckle is worn two-thirds of the way up the ribbon.

### 206 - LLOYD'S MEDAL FOR SAVING LIFE AT SEA

The medal of the Society is presented by the Corporation of Lloyd's as an honorary acknowledgement to those who have by extraordinary exertions contributed to the saving of life at sea. The subject of the medal is taken from the Odyssey, where Ulysses, after various adventures during his return to his native Ithaca, subsequent to the fall of Troy, is described as being rescued from the perils of a storm by Leucothöe:

> 'A mortal once,
> But now, an azure sister of the main.'

The words addressed by Leucothöe to the shipwrecked hero represent the action on the obverse side:

> 'This heavenly scarf beneath thy bosom bind,
> And live: give all thy terrors to the wind.'

*(Obverse)*

**204 - ROYAL HUMANE SOCIETY'S BRONZE MEDAL**    *(Reverse)*

The obverse also bears round the top circumference the words 'LEUCOTHÖE NAUFRAGO SUCCURRIT,' while in the exergue appears the name of the designer, Allan Wyon.

The reverse is taken from a medal of Augustus; a crown of oak being the reward given by the Romans to him who saved the life of a citizen, and within is inscribed the motto derived from the same authority, 'OB CIVES SERVATOS.' Round the top circumference of the reverse is the embossed wording 'PRESENTED BY LLOYD'S,' while in small letters at the bottom is the name of the designer, 'A. WYON.'

This very handsome medal is issued in silver and in bronze, the medal in both cases being suspended from its ribbon by means of a ring. One example was struck in gold for presentation to Captain E. R. G. R. Evans of H.M.S. *Carlisle* (afterwards Admiral Lord Mountevans) for gallantry at the wreck of the steamer *Hong Moh* in China in 1921.

### 207 - LLOYD'S MEDAL FOR MERITORIOUS SERVICES

In 1893 the Committee of Lloyd's decided to bestow a medal upon ships' officers and others who, by extraordinary exertions, had contributed to the preservation of vessels and cargoes from perils of all kinds. The medal is struck in silver and in bronze, and bears on the obverse, within a border, the shield of the Corporation of Lloyd's. Round the top circumference are the words 'PRESENTED BY LLOYD'S' and, at the bottom, a floral spray of the rose, thistle and shamrock. The reverse bears a wreath of oak leaves, with, in the centre, a scroll on which are engraved the words 'FOR MERITORIOUS SERVICES.' Both the silver and bronze medals are suspended from the ribbon by means of a silver ring, while the official colouring of the ribbon is 'blue and silver.'

MEDAL OF THE SHIPWRECKED FISHERMEN AND MARINERS ROYAL BENEVOLENT SOCIETY

### 207 - LLOYD'S MEDAL FOR SERVICES TO LLOYD'S

In November 1913 the Committee of Lloyd's decided that a medal should be instituted for bestowal in recognition of services to Lloyd's. The obverse of this medal, which is struck in gold, silver and bronze, bears a very spirited representation of Neptune in a chariot drawn through the sea by four prancing horses. The reverse is the same as that of the medal for meritorious services, except that the wording on the scroll is altered to 'FOR SERVICES TO LLOYD'S.' The ribbon is the same as for the meritorious service medal, and the medals are suspended by means of rings.

### 208 - LLOYD'S WAR MEDAL FOR BRAVERY AT SEA

In December 1940 it was announced that the Committee of Lloyd's had decided, with the approval of the Admiralty and the Ministry of Shipping, to strike a new medal to be bestowed on officers and men of the Merchant Navy and fishing fleet in cases of exceptional gallantry at sea in time of war. It was known as 'Lloyd's War Medal for Bravery at Sea.'

206 - LLOYD'S MEDAL FOR SAVING LIFE AT SEA

The designer was Mr. Allan G. Wyon, F.R.B.S. All Lloyd's medals have been designed by the members of the Wyon family, the first ('For Saving Life at Sea') having been instituted in 1836.

The obverse shows a heroic figure symbolizing courage and endurance seated looking out over the sea, on which is seen in the distance a vessel of the mercantile marine. In his right hand the figure holds a wreath. The inscription is 'AWARDED BY LLOYD'S.' On the reverse is a trident, symbolizing sea power, surrounded by an endless wreath of oak leaves and acorns. On a ribbon across the centre is the single word 'BRAVERY.' The ribbon is in blue and silver, similar in design to that of the ribbon for Lloyd's Meritorious Medal, but with the colours reversed.

The first awards of this medal to fifty-four merchant seamen of all grades from thirty-one ships were announced by Lloyd's on 18 March 1941.

This medal or its ribbon may be worn on the right breast by officers and men of the Merchant Navy in uniform; but it is not worn at all by Service personnel as it is not awarded by the Crown. It therefore follows that an officer or rating of the Royal Naval Reserve serving for training in H.M. ships or establishments will not wear the ribbon while in R.N.R. uniform.

### 209 - LONDON COUNTY COUNCIL MEDAL FOR BRAVERY

This medal, in silver, was granted to members of the London Fire Brigade by the L.C.C. for extraordinary bravery at fires. It bears on one side a seated female figure and an inscription in raised lettering 'AWARDED BY THE LONDON COUNTY COUNCIL FOR BRAVERY.' The other side has a representation of the front portion of a fire-engine drawn by two prancing horses, with, in the exergue, the words 'LONDON FIRE BRIGADE.' The name and rank of the recipient appears on the edge of the medal, which hangs from its red and white striped ribbon by means of an ornamental scroll clasp.

As this medal is unofficial, the Sovereign being the Fount of Honour, it is presumed it is now superseded by the George Cross, George Medal, or British Empire Medal as mentioned earlier in this book.

### 210 - LONDON COUNTY COUNCIL MEDAL FOR ZEAL AND FIDELITY

This medal, in bronze, is awarded to every officer, fireman and driver of the London Fire Brigade who serves for fifteen years with zeal and fidelity. The pattern of the medal and clasp is the same as that just described, except that the lettering on the side bearing the figure bears the inscription 'AWARDED BY THE LONDON COUNTY COUNCIL FOR GOOD SERVICE.' The ribbon is orange moiré.

Presumably this award and the one which follows have now been superseded by the Official Fire Brigade L.S. and G.C. Medal authorized in 1954.

**207 - LLOYD'S MEDAL FOR MERITORIOUS SERVICES**

**207 - LLOYD'S MEDAL FOR SERVICES TO LLOYD'S**

## 211 - LONDON SALVAGE CORPS (LONG SERVICE MEDAL)

This medal is awarded to officers and men of the London Salvage Corps who have completed fifteen years' consecutive service without blemish. The obverse shows a kneeling fireman in uniform being crowned by a female figure with a wreath of laurel. A salvage cart, fireman and buildings are in the background. The reverse bears the name of the recipient with the embossed inscription 'FOR LONG AND EFFICIENT SERVICE IN THE LONDON SALVAGE CORPS,' the whole being surmounted by a wreath of laurel. The medal hangs from its ribbon by means of a straight clasp, the ribbon being half maroon, half grey with narrow edges of white.

## LONDON COUNTY COUNCIL (AMBULANCE SERVICE MEDAL)

*(Obverse)*

This medal was established in July 1938 by the London County Council on the recommendation of the then Hospitals and Medical Services Committee, that an award on the lines of those available to the London Fire Brigade should be instituted for 'Any officer or employee in the London Ambulance Service whose conduct in the execution of his duty is considered to be sufficiently meritorious.'

The medal is in silver and hangs from a scroll clasp. The obverse has the words 'LONDON AMBULANCE SERVICE' running round the circumference, and in the centre a design showing a Greek Cross resting on a laurel wreath with the L.C.C. arms in its centre. The reverse is filled with the inscription 'AWARDED BY THE LONDON COUNTY COUNCIL FOR MERITORIOUS SERVICE.' The ribbon is 32 mm. wide in blue and white, with the stripes, reading from edge to edge, as follows: 6 mm. blue, 4 mm. white, 1.5 mm. blue, 1.5 mm. white, 4.5 mm. blue, 1.5 mm. white, 1.5 mm. blue, 4 mm. white, 6 mm. blue. A narrow ornamental clasp is worn at the top of the ribbon. The medal has only once been awarded.

## LIVERPOOL SHIPWRECK AND HUMANE SOCIETY'S MARINE MEDALS

These medals, established in 1839, are awarded by the Society in gold, silver and bronze for gallantry and heroism in saving life at sea. The design of the medal is shown in the illustration. Gold, silver and bronze bars are granted for further acts of gallantry, and sextants, telescopes, binoculars, barometers and testimonials are given in cases where the award of a medal is not suitable. The ribbon is dark blue, and has a buckle at the top.

## LIVERPOOL SHIPWRECK AND HUMANE SOCIETY'S MEDALS FOR SAVING LIFE FROM FIRE

These medals, established in 1882, are awarded by the Society in gold, silver and bronze for gallantry in saving life from fire in much the same way as the Society's marine medals. Bars are given for further acts of heroism, and money awards can also be granted. The obverse of the medal is shown in the illustration, and the reverse is

**LIVERPOOL SHIPWRECK AND HUMANE SOCIETY'S MARINE MEDAL** *(Reverse)*

similar to that of the marine medal. The ribbon is scarlet, similar to that awarded by the Society for the Protection of Life from Fire, and has a buckle at the top.

## LIVERPOOL SHIPWRECK AND HUMANE SOCIETY'S GENERAL MEDALS

These medals, established in 1894, are awarded by the Society for gallantry in saving life on land in much the same way as their marine and fire medals. Bars are given for further acts of gallantry, and money awards can also be granted. The obverse is shown in the illustration, and the reverse is similar to that of the two medals just described. These medals are sometimes given to those who endanger their lives by stopping runaway horses, and for other acts of gallantry which take place on shore. The ribbon is of five equal stripes, red, white, red, white, red and a buckle is worn at the top.

## 212 - PLAGUE MEDAL (HONG-KONG) (1894)

This medal was awarded by the community of Hong-Kong to 300 men of the Shropshire Light Infantry, to several officers and men of the Royal Engineers, to a few men of the Royal Navy, and also to certain nursing sisters and civilians who volunteered their help in combating a serious outbreak of plague in 1894. The design of obverse and reverse are shown in the illustration. The medals issued to the officers (thirteen in number) were struck in gold, and had no ribbons or attachments. Those awarded to the men were in silver, and were suspended from their ribbons by means of a ring. The medals were not allowed to be worn in uniform.

In all 150 gold medals were issued to civilians and officers, and 381 silver medals to other service personnel and civilians.

## 213, 214 - SHANGHAI MUNICIPALITY MEDALS (1937–38)

These medals are in the form of an eight-pointed bronze star. In the centre of the obverse is a circle with the arms and title of the Shanghai Municipal Council, and on the reverse, within a wreath, the words – 'FOR SERVICES RENDERED—AUGUST 12 TO NOVEMBER 12, 1937.' They were awarded to employees of the municipality, and to Police and members of the Shanghai Volunteer Force, for their work during the invasion of China by the Japanese. The ribbon is red, white, red with narrow edges of yellow, all these colours being divided by very narrow stripes of black. Ribbon No. 214 is that of the Volunteer Long Service Medal awarded by the Shanghai Municipality Council.

## BRITISH FIRE SERVICES ASSOCIATION

This Association incorporates the former National Fire Brigades Association and the Professional Fire Brigades Association, whose awards, though *unofficial*, are still sometimes worn in Fire Brigade uniform. The British Fire Services Association has four awards, which are worn on the right breast. It is not known to what extent they have been superseded by the official Fire Brigade Long Service and Good Conduct Medal instituted in 1954.

FOR SAVING LIFE
FROM FIRE

LIVERPOOL SHIPWRECK
AND HUMANE SOCIETY'S
GENERAL MEDAL

212 - PLAGUE
MEDAL (HONG-KONG)

### 215 - CONSPICUOUS GALLANTRY DECORATION

This is an oval wreath in bronze, bound at top and bottom, in the centre of which is a circular garter bearing the word 'GALLANTRY' surrounding the Union flag within a wreath, the badge of the B.F.S.A. The decoration hangs from two foliated branches in low V-shape bearing a scroll with the letters 'B.F.S.A.' The ribbon is that of the old National Fire Brigades Association's gallantry medal, crimson shading from each side to white in the centre. Plain bronze bars, with 'B.F.S A ' in an oblong in the centre, are available for further awards.

### 216 - MERITORIOUS SERVICE DECORATION

This decoration is of the same design as that first described, but in silver with the words 'FOR MERITORIOUS SERVICE' on the garter. Bars are available for further awards.

### 217 - LONG AND EFFICIENT SERVICE MEDALS

These medals, in silver and bronze, are awarded for twenty and ten years' service respectively. The obverses show a female figure standing before a portico and holding in her right hand a wreath over the uncovered head of a kneeling fireman, his helmet under his arm. In the rear is a manual fire-engine. The reverses show the Union flag within a wreath, surrounded by a garter bearing the words 'FOR LONG SERVICE AND EFFICIENCY.' Outside the garter project axes and ladders, bound by a circular rope with a helmet at the top, with the words 'BRITISH FIRE SERVICES ASSOCIATION' around all.

The medals are suspended from bars with 'B.F.S.A.—TWENTY YEARS,' or 'B.F.S.A.' in the case of the bronze medal.

Small silver rosettes are worn on the undress ribbon to indicate the addition of bars to the silver medal for further periods of five years, and to indicate the holding of the silver medal itself. Thus the silver medal with two bars will have three rosettes on the undress ribbon. There is also a bronze bar for fifteen years' service, though no addition is made to the undress ribbon.

### 218 - FOREIGN HONORARY MEMBERS DECORATION

This is a silver eight-pointed star resting on a wreath, with a large circular centre with a blue-enamelled garter with the words 'BRITISH FIRE SERVICES ASSOCIATION' surrounding a green wreath and the Union flag in proper colours. The reverse has the name of the recipient. The decoration hangs from a fish-tailed bar with the words 'FOREIGN HONORARY MEMBER.'

# *Foreign Medals for War Services awarded to British Personnel*

## 219 - SYRIA (1840)

In 1832 the city of Acre, in Palestine, then in the hands of the Turks, was captured and wrecked by Ibrahim Pasha of Egypt. On 4 November 1840 it was recaptured for the Turks after a three hours' bombardment by a combined British, Austrian and Turkish fleet under Sir Charles Napier. A medal, usually known as the 'St. Jean d'Acre Medal' was issued by the Sultan of Turkey in commemoration of this event. It was issued in gold to captains of the Navy and field officers of the Army; in silver to other officers; in bronze to seamen and marines. A few artillery and engineer officers who accompanied the expedition also received it.

The obverse shows a fortress with the Turkish flag flying and six stars above. Below is the inscription in Turkish 'The People of Syria: and the Citadel of Acre, A.H. 1258.' The reverse has the Sultan's cypher surrounded by branches of laurel.

## 220 - TURKISH MEDAL FOR THE CRIMEAN WAR (1854–55)

After the Crimean War, the Turkish Government presented a silver medal to certain of the soldiers and sailors of the Allied Forces – British, French and Sardinians – who had taken part in the campaign. The medal bears on the obverse a field gun, upon which is spread a map of the Crimea. In the background are the British, French, Sardinian and Turkish flags, and below is the inscription, 'CRIMEA 1855' in English, French or Italian. The reverse has the Sultan's cypher within a laurel wreath, with the word 'Crimea' in Turkish, and the date in Arabic. Permission to wear the medals was granted to the British recipients, and they were generally fitted with a ring for suspension, or else with silver clasp attachments. The medals intended for the British had the British and Turkish flags to the fore on the obverse, with the inscription in English; those for the French troops the French and Turkish flags to the front, with the wording in French; and those for the Sardinians the Sardinian and Turkish flags to the fore, and the inscription in Italian. Owing, however, to the ship bringing home the British medals being wrecked, many British soldiers and sailors received French or Sardinian medals instead of the ones originally intended for them. The original ribbon was only 16 mm. wide.

## 221 - SARDINIAN MEDAL FOR VALOR

After the Crimean War the King of Sardinia also awarded a silver medal to 450 specially selected officers and men of the Navy and Army. The obverse has the arms of Savoy, surmounted by the

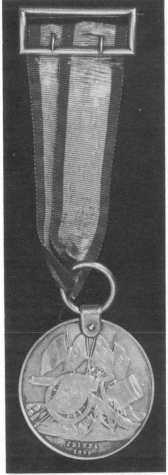

**220 - TURKISH MEDAL FOR THE CRIMEAN WAR** (*Obverse*)

177

crown of Sardinia, within two branches of palm and olive. Round the circumference is the legend 'AL VALORE MILITARE.' On the reverse is the name, and regiment or ship, of the recipient, within a laurel wreath, and outside the wreath are the words, 'SPEDIZIONE D'ORIENTE. 1855–56.' The blue watered ribbon, which passes through a broad loop at the top of the medal, is identical with the present Italian medal 'Al Valore Militare.'

## 222 - MEDAL FOR CHITRAL CAMPAIGN GIVEN BY THE MAHARAJAH OF JUMMOO AND KASHMIR

The Maharajah of Jummoo and Kashmir presented a bronze medal to certain British officers and to the men of the native levies (irregular troops) who took part in the defence and relief of Chitral, 1895. The decoration is kidney shaped, and has on the obverse a coat of arms with two native soldiers as supporters, with, below, a native inscription on a scroll, and the words, 'JUMMOO AND KASHMIR.' The reverse has a representation of a fortress with troops in the foreground. It hangs from its ribbon by an ornamental clasp exactly similar to that of the 1895 India medal, and has a bar inscribed 'CHITRAL 1895.' The medal was not worn in uniform by British officers and men. The ribbon, in green, red and white, is moiré; but otherwise precisely the same as that of the British 'Italy Star' for the Second World War.

## 223 - KHEDIVE'S BRONZE STAR (1882–91)

The Khedive of Egypt presented a bronze star to every officer and man of the Navy and Army who had received the British war medal for the Egyptian campaigns, 1882–5. The decoration consists of a five-pointed bronze star in the centre of which is a view of the sphinx, with the desert and pyramids in the background. This is surrounded by a circular band on which are the words 'EGYPT 1882' above, and below, in Arabic, 'Khedive of Egypt 1299.' On the reverse is the Khedive's monogram surmounted by a crown. The star is suspended by a ring from an ornamental clasp in the centre of which is a star and a crescent. The star was first given for the 1882 campaign, but its issue was subsequently extended for the 1884, 1885, 1888–9 and 1890 operations. The later stars are similar in appearance to the first, but bear the words 'EGYPT 1884' or 'EGYPT 1884–6,' with the corresponding Arabic inscriptions. Stars bearing no dates were issued after 1886. Most of the troops engaged in the operations at Suakin in 1888–9, and on the Nile in 1889, had already received the decoration for the earlier campaigns, and as a second star was not issued to any one man, very few of the undated ones were issued. They are therefore rather rare. The bronze star, undated, but bearing a bronze bar with the inscription 'Tokar 1308' in Arabic, was given in 1893 to British officers and Egyptian troops who fought in the battle of that name on 19 February 1891. The officers and men of H.M.S. *Dolphin* and *Sandfly*, who were on transport duty at the time, and the troops serving at Trinkitat on the day of the battle, received the star, without bar. Queen Victoria's silver medal was not given in this case, and it is the only instance in which the star will be seen by itself.

**223 - KHEDIVE'S BRONZE STAR** (1882–91) *(Obverse)*

## 224 - KHEDIVE'S SUDAN MEDAL (1896–1908)

In 1897 the Khedive of Egypt granted a silver medal to all British and Egyptian troops, and to officers and men of the Royal Navy, who had taken part in the Dongola campaign of 1896. The medal bears on one side an oval shield charged with stars and crescents, behind which is a trophy of weapons. On the reverse there is a Turkish inscription. It hangs from its ribbon by a straight silver clasp, and the yellow ribbon, with the broad blue watered stripe down the centre, is said to typify the desert with the Blue Nile flowing through it. The medal was again given for various other expeditions between 1896 and 1905, and the following bars were awarded between those dates, though medals with no bars were also given: 'FIRKET' – To those who took part in the operations south of Akasha on 7 June 1896. 'HAFIR' – To those who took part in the operations south of Fareig on 19 September 1896. 'THE ATBARA' – For the battle of 8 April 1898. 'KHARTOUM' – For the battle of 2 September 1898. 'GEDAREF' – For the capture of Gedaref and the subsequent engagements in the neighbourhood. 'ABU-HAMED' – For the battle of 7 August 1897. 'SUDAN 1897' – To those already in possession of the medal who were at, or south of, Kerma and No. 6 station between 15 July and 6 November 1897. 'SUDAN 1899' – For services in connection with the reconquest of the Dongola province. 'GEDID' – To all who took part in the actions there on 22 and 24 November 1899. 'BAHR-EL-GHAZEL 1900-2' – For the operations resulting in the re-occupation of the province of that name. 'JEROK' – For the operations of 1904 in the Blue Nile province. 'NYAM-NYAM' – For the expedition against the tribes of this name in the Bahr-el-Ghazal province, 1905. 'TALODI' – For suppression of the Abu Rufas rising at Talodi in June 1905, 'KATFIA' – For suppression of the rising under Wad Habuba, 17 May 1908. 'NYIMA' – For operations in the Nuba Mountains, 1–21 November 1908.

## 225 - SUDAN MEDAL (1910)

This medal, awarded by the Khedive in 1911, was sanctioned by the British Government and presented to those troops who had taken part in the operations against the rebellious native tribes in the Atwot district of the Bahr-el-Ghazal province in February, March and April 1910. It was also given to those who took part in the operations against Jebel Tajoi in South Kordofan, November and December 1910, and to officers and men who took part in various punitive expeditions in the Sudan in 1911 and 1912. The medal bears on one side the cypher of the Khedive, and the date; and on the reverse a lion standing in an attitude of attention, with his fore paws resting upon a panel bearing the word 'SUDAN'. Below is an oval native shield and spears. In the background is a representation of the River Nile, with the farther bank and palm trees behind. Behind this again is the rising sun, spreading its rays across the sky. The medal hangs from a straight clasp, and bars inscribed 'ATWOT,' 'S. KORDOFAN 1910,' and 'SUDAN 1912,' in English and Arabic, were awarded with it to those who took part in the various expeditions.

(*Obverse*)

**224 - KHEDIVE'S SUDAN MEDAL** (1896–1908)
'FIRKET' 'HAFIR'
(*Reverse*)

In 1918 this medal was again granted with the new Sultan's cypher to troops, including the Sudan Government Police who were engaged in various operations in Dafur, the Zeraf Valley, against the Lokoia and Lau-nuer Tribes, in the Matong Mountains, Mongalla, and in the Bahr-el-Ghazal province between 1914–18. The following bars have been issued: 'DAFUR 1916,' 'ZERAF, 1913–14,' 'MONGALLA, 1915–16,' 'LAU-NUER,' 'ATWOT, 1918,' 'ALIAB DINKA,' 'NYALA,' 'GARJAK NUER,' 'DAFUR, 1921,' 'DAFUR, 1924,' 'FASHER,' 'MANDAL,' 'MIRI,' 'S. KORDOFAN, 1910,' 'SUDAN, 1912.'

# Sudan Defence Force

## NATIVE OFFICERS DECORATION

This decoration was instituted in 1933 to recognize long and meritorious service on the part of native officers of the Sudan Defence Force. The qualifying period is eighteen years' commissioned service on the active list of the Egyptian Army or Sudan Defence Force, half the time in the ranks being allowed to count. Recipients are entitled to use the Arabic equivalent of O.D. after their names. The decoration consists of a silver medal with the seal of the Governor-General of the Sudan on the obverse, and on the reverse a trophy of arms and the words in Arabic – 'The Sudan—For Long and Valuable Service.' The ribbon is green with broad violet edges and a thin violet stripe in the centre.

## DISTINGUISHED SERVICE MEDAL

This medal was instituted in 1933 for award to native personnel of the Sudan Defence Force, to the Police and other persons, natives of the Sudan, for gallantry in the field. Recipients are entitled to use the Arabic equivalent of D.S.M. after their names. The medal is in silver with the seal of the Governor-General on the obverse, and on the reverse the figure of a mounted camel-man with the words in Arabic – 'The Sudan—For Distinguished Service in the Field.' It is worn before war medals from a green ribbon with two narrow red stripes down the centre.

## LONG SERVICE AND GOOD CONDUCT MEDAL

This medal was established in 1933 for award to N.C.O.s and men, natives of the Sudan, who have served for eighteen years with good conduct. The medal is in bronze with the seal of the Governor-General on the obverse, and on the reverse a trophy of arms with the words in Arabic – 'The Sudan—For Long Service and Good Conduct.' The ribbon is green with broad black edges.

## GENERAL SERVICE MEDAL

The medal was instituted in 1933 for award to native personnel of the Sudan Defence Force, the Police and such other persons, natives of the Sudan, who have served in the field on such operations as may be considered worthy to warrant the award of a medal. It is in silver, with the same obverse as the others, and on the reverse a group of Sudanese soldiers with the word 'Sudan' in Arabic. The ribbon has a broad blue centre and broad black edges with narrower stripes of yellow separating the two colours.

## 226, 227 - MEDALS FOR GALLANTRY AND MERITORIOUS SERVICE
Silver medals instituted since the Second World War. When awarded for meritorious service the ribbon has a yellow centre with broad blue edges, the two colours separated by a narrow white stripe. When given for gallantry there are thin red stripes on each of the blue edges.

## 228 - INDIAN INDEPENDENCE MEDAL
In October 1949 it was announced that His Majesty King George VI had been pleased to approve the institution of this medal by the Government of India to commemorate the constitutional change which resulted in the independence of India on 15 August 1947.

The medal was granted to:

(i) All Indian nationals, male and female, on the strength of units/formations of the Indian Armed Forces on 15 August 1947, and the Ruling Princes and the State Forces of States acceding to the Dominion of India by 1 January 1948.

(ii) British officers, ratings, other ranks, and airmen, male and female –

    (a) Serving on 1 January 1948 with the Armed Forces of the Dominion of India.

    (b) Serving on 1 January 1948 on the Active List in a Government House or in Central and Provincial Governments (in civil employment).

    (c) Who proceeded on leave before 1 January 1948 pending retirement but had volunteered and were serving with the Indian Forces between 15 August 1947 and 1 January 1948.

    (d) Officers and other ranks of the Transport Squadrons and Communication Flights of the Royal Air Force which had been lent to and were serving in the Dominion of India.

The medal, which is ordered to be worn after all efficiency and long service decorations and medals and before the Service Medal of the Order of St. John, is circular and of cupro-nickel. It has on the obverse a representation of the Imperial Crown and Asoka's Chakra surrounded by the legend 'GEORGIUS VI D : G : BRITT : OMN : REX : FID : DEF :' and on the reverse the representation of

Asoka's three lions as shown on Asoka's Pillar at Sarnath, with the inscriptions 'INDIAN INDEPENDENCE' and '15TH AUGUST 1947.' The ribbon is saffron, white and green in three equal stripes, worn with saffron stripe farthest from the left shoulder.

### 229 - POLICE INDEPENDENCE MEDAL
The ribbon has a central broad stripe of orange, bordered by narrower stripes of blue, with broad red edges.

### PARAM VIR CHAKRA
This medal was established on 26 January 1950, and awarded for most outstanding bravery or valour or self-sacrifice shown in the presence of the enemy. The ribbon is deep purple.

### MAHA VIR CHAKRA
This medal was established on the same date as the above for acts of gallantry in the presence of the enemy. The ribbon is half white, half saffron.

### VIR CHAKRA
This is third highest military award for acts of gallantry, established on the same date as the two last. The ribbon is half dark blue, half saffron.

### THE GENERAL SERVICE MEDAL, 1947
This is the first campaign medal instituted by the President of India on the same date as those already mentioned and awarded with a clasp or bar indicating the operation. The medal is cupro-nickel and circular. The obverse has a representation of 'Bhavani' (Divine Sword) symbolizing justice and discrimination, and the reverse an embossed lotus flower with buds and leaves, with the words 'GENERAL SERVICE MEDAL' inside the upper rim, and '1947' below. This medal has already been authorized for the operations in Jammu and Kashmir with a bar bearing the appropriate wording. The ribbon is red, divided into six equal stripes by five vertical lines of green, the red symbolizing valour and passion and the green auspiciousness.

### THE PRESIDENT'S POLICE AND FIRE SERVICES MEDAL
This medal was established in March 1951. It is of silver, circular, with the obverse embossed with the President's flag on a shield in the centre, with the words 'PRESIDENT'S POLICE AND FIRE SERVICES MEDAL' inside the rim above, and 'INDIA' below separated by two five-pointed heraldic stars. The reverse is embossed with the State emblem in the centre and the words 'FOR GALLANTRY' or 'FOR DISTINGUISHED SERVICE,' as the case may be, along the lower edge, and a wreath joined by a plain clasp at the top along the upper edge. It is only awarded for acts of exceptional courage, or skill or conspicuous devotion to duty to members of a recognized Police Force or Fire Service within the territory of India. Bars may be

awarded for further acts of gallantry, in which case a small silver rose is added to the ribbon when it is worn alone. In the case of the medal for distinguished service the ribbon is half blue, half silver-white. When awarded for exceptional courage or gallantry the blue and white are separated by a thin red stripe.

## POLICE MEDAL

This medal was established in March 1951. It is a circular bronze medal with the obverse bearing the State emblem in the centre, the words 'POLICE MEDAL' above, and the State motto 'SATYAMEVA JAYATE' in Devnagri script below. The reverse has in the centre the words 'FOR MERITORIOUS SERVICE' or 'FOR GALLANTRY,' with 'INDIAN' above and 'POLICE' below, the whole encircled by a wreath. The medal is only awarded to members of recognized Police Forces or properly organized Fire Services within the territory of India, who have performed services of conspicuous merit or gallantry. Bars may be awarded as for the medal previously described. The ribbon is dark blue with a narrow silver stripe on either side and a broad crimson stripe in the centre when the award has been made for meritorious service. In the case of an award for gallantry the blue portions of the ribbon have a narrow silver stripe down the centre. Monetary allowances are granted when either the President's Medal or the Police Medal is awarded for gallantry, and a holder of the latter is not debarred from the subsequent award of the first named. In normal circumstances not more than forty-five President's Medals, and not more than 175 Police Medals can be awarded in any one year.

## 230 - PAKISTAN INDEPENDENCE MEDAL

This medal was instituted in 1948. It is of silver, the obverse bearing the Royal cypher 'G. VI. R.' surmounted by a crown, surrounded by the legend 'GEORGIUS VI D : G. : BR. : OMN : REX.' The reverse has the flag of Pakistan surrounded by a wreath with inscriptions in native lettering above and below. The ribbon is dark green with a narrow central stripe of white.

## 231 - DEFENCE OR GENERAL SERVICE MEDAL
(Tamgha-i-Diffa)
Established in 1947. The obverse has the slanting crescent and star of Pakistan partly surrounded by a wreath, and the reverse is plain with a smaller circle in the centre, possibly intended for an inscription. It hangs from its ribbon by a foliated clasp similar to that of the India General Service Medals of 1908 and 1936. A bar inscribed 'KASHMIR—1948' has been issued.

**230 - PAKISTAN INDEPENDENCE MEDAL**
(*Obverse*)

# REPUBLIC COMMEMORATIVE MEDAL

(Tamgha-i-Jamhuria)

On 23 March, 1956, Pakistan became an Islamic Republic still within the British Commonwealth, and issued the medal. It is a circular silver medal, with the obverse bearing the words 'THE ISLAMIC REPUBLIC OF PAKISTAN' in Arabic script surrounded by a wreath, and on the reverse the date 23 March 1956, in English, repeated in Urdu and Bengali at the top and bottom respectively. The ribbon has four equal stripes of dark green, red, black and white, from which the medal hangs by the same type of clasp as that already described.

Since becoming a Republic, Pakistan has established five Orders, each in four descending classes, and a number of Military and Civil awards. The four descending classes are as follows: '*Nishans*' (roughly comparable to the British Knights Grand Cross) incorporating the crescent and star in their design; '*Hilals*' (more or less equivalent to the British Knights Commanders) embodying the crescent; '*Sitaras*' (approximating to British Commanders or Companions in the various Orders) incorporating a star; and '*Tamghas*,' which are plain medals. To avoid repetition in the descriptions that follow, these grades are referred to as Classes I to IV.

230 - PAKISTAN INDEPENDENCE MEDAL (*Reverse*)

# THE ORDER OF PAKISTAN

Established in 1958 for services of the highest distinction to the State. *Class I* – A ten-pointed star in 22 carat gold with 'rays of glory' issuing from the central design which has the national emblem enamelled in white and green surrounded by a green circle. The badge is surmounted by the crescent and star and is worn on the left breast of the coat, accompanied in full dress by a sash 100 mm. wide, white with dark green edges, worn over the right shoulder with the bow on the left hip. The sash has no badge. *Class II* – A smaller badge of similar type in 18 carat gold surmounted by a crescent. It is worn round the neck from a ribbon 32 mm. wide, which is white with green edges and a narrower central stripe of green. *Class III* – A similar badge in 14 carat gold surmounted by a star. It also is worn round the neck from a white ribbon with green edges and two narrower central stripes of green. *Class IV* – The Medal, or Tamgha, is circular and carried out in what is officially referred to as 'tombac' bronze, which presumably means bronze gilt. It has the Pakistan emblem on the obverse, and is worn on the breast. It is suspended by a ring from a white ribbon with green edges and three narrower central stripes of green. The nearest British equivalent is stated to be the O.B.E.

# THE ORDER OF SHUJAAT

Established in 1958 for 'Acts of the greatest heroism and most conspicuous courage in circumstances of extreme danger.' It has no breast star; but is in three classes and a medal, all worn on the breast. The badges are oval. *Class I* – in 22 carat gold (stated to be the equivalent of the British George Cross) hangs from a straight clasp bearing the crescent and star. The ribbon is nominally violet. In the centre is a purple disc with the name 'SHUJAAT' in Arabic surrounded by a circular wreath of laurel. Equally spaced 'rays of glory' radiate from the inner wreath to another laurel wreath round the edge of the oval decoration. *Class II* – in 18 carat gold, has the same central design as Class I, and is hung from its ribbon by a crescent, the ribbon being violet with a narrow central stripe of white. Apart from this central design, and sprays of laurel halfway down the upper rim of the oval, the obverse is plain. *Class III* – in 14 carat gold, is the same as Class II, except that it is hung from a five-pointed star from a violet ribbon with two central stripes of white. *Class IV* – The medal, or Tamgha, is of the same design as the preceding two classes though made entirely in 'tombac' bronze. It hangs by a ring from its violet ribbon with three narrow central white stripes. The nearest British equivalent is stated to be the George Medal.

## THE ORDER OF IMTIAZ

Instituted 1958 for 'conspicuously distinguished service in literature, art, sports, medicine or science.' *Class I* – A five-pointed star with radiating beams in 22 carat gold hung from a crescent and star. A central disc of dark green enamel with the name of the Order in Arabic, surrounded by a laurel wreath in gold and a circle of pale blue enamel. The badge and sash are worn as for the Order of Pakistan, the sash being dark green with edges of pale blue. The nearest British equivalent is stated to be the Order of Merit. *Class II* – A smaller badge of similar design suspended from a crescent and worn round the neck from a 32-mm. ribbon of dark green with pale blue edges and a narrow central stripe of white. *Class III* – The same but suspended from a star. Ribbon as above with two narrow central stripes of white. *Class IV* – The medal is of 'tombac' bronze, hung from a ring. The obverse has the inscription 'IMTIAZ' in Arabic script surrounded by a laurel wreath. Ribbon, dark green with pale blue edges and three narrow white central stripes.

## THE ORDER OF QUAID-I-AZAM

Instituted in 1958 'for special merit or for eminent service in the civil, military, or any other field of national activity.' *Class I* – An eight-pointed star in gold with beams radiating from a circular disc of grey enamel bearing within a floral design the Arabic inscription 'IMAN, ITTAHED, NAZAM' surrounded by a circle of violet enamel. The badge, surmounted by the crescent and star, is worn on the breast as is the Order of Pakistan. The 100-mm. sash ribbon is grey with broad violet edges. The nearest British equivalent is quoted as the G.B.E. *Class II* – A smaller badge of the same design worn round the neck and hung by a crescent from a 32-mm. ribbon of grey with violet edges and a narrow central stripe of white. The British equivalent is quoted as the K.B.E. *Class III* – The same as Class II but hung from a star. The ribbon is also the same, but with two central narrow stripes of white. *Class IV* – The medal of 'tombac' bronze hung from a ring. On the obverse is a circular

floral design with the Arabic inscription mentioned under Class I.
The ribbon is grey, with broad purple edges and three narrow central
stripes of white. The nearest British equivalent is stated to be the
M.B.E.

## THE ORDER OF KHIDMAT

Established in its two higher classes in 1960, and the third and
fourth classes in 1958, for meritorious service. *Class I* – A plain gold
five-rayed star surmounted by a crescent and star. In the centre of
the obverse on a circular disc of white enamel is a square of scarlet
enamel with an ornamental border, the square containing the name
'KHIDMAT-I-ALA' in Arabic script. The star is worn on the breast in
the same way as the other Pakistan Orders. The sash ribbon for full
dress is 100 mm. wide; white, with broad scarlet edges. *Class II* –
The same badge but smaller, hung from a crescent, and worn round
the neck on a 32-mm. ribbon with a narrow central stripe of scarlet.
*Class III* – As for Class II and worn in the same way but hung from
a star on a white ribbon with two narrow central stripes of scarlet.
*Class IV* – The medal, 'tamgha,' worn on the breast and suspended
from a ring. It is in the normal 'tombac' bronze, and has on the
obverse the framed square containing the Arabic script as for the
preceding classes. The ribbon is white with three narrow central
stripes of scarlet.

There is also a 'Sanad-i-Khidmat,' a more junior grade, for long
and meritorious service on the part of 'Classes III and IV government servants and non-officials at the level of artisans, etc.' We
have no knowledge of its appearance or ribbon.

### MILITARY DECORATIONS

While members of the fighting services are eligible for various of the
Orders, Decorations and Medals already mentioned, there are
various other gallantry, operational and non-operational awards
made only to personnel of the Army, Navy and Air Force.

## NISHAN-I-HAIDAN

(equivalent of the British V.C.)
Awarded for gallantry in action. It is worn on the breast before any
other decorations, and ranks accordingly. It is a bronze five-pointed
star suspended by a ring from an ornamental clasp. Being a 'Nishan,'
the obverse has a centre disc with a crescent and star encircled by a
wreath. The ribbon, 38 mm. wide, is dark green, and has a small
replica of the star upon it when worn in undress.

## HILAL-I-JURAT (Moon of Bravery)

Is the equivalent of the British D.S.O. It is in gold and circular, and
like the other 'Hilals' has the crescent, on a centre disc. Around the
disc and pointing outwards towards the edge are ten equally-spaced
stylized flowers. It hangs by a ring from an ornamental clasp. The
32-mm. ribbon is red, dark green and red in equal stripes.

## SITARA-I-JURAT (Star of Bravery)

The equivalent of the British Military Cross, is a silver pentagonal figure with a large five-pointed star superimposed. The five sides have stylized flowers and rays set in semi-circles. The ribbon is white, dark green and white in equal proportions.

## TAMGHA-I-JURAT (Bravery Medal)

The equivalent of the British Distinguished Conduct Medal, is a circular medal in bronze. The obverse has a trophy of lances and pennons, swords and a field gun within a wreath, with a small central disc bearing a crescent and star. It hangs from an ornamental clasp and has a ribbon half dark green, half scarlet with narrow edges of white.

## TAMGHA-I-BASALAT

*Class I* – A circular silver medal hung from an ornamental clasp, with a star, wings and crossed swords over an anchor on the obverse. The decoration seems to be the equivalent of the British Air Force Cross, and is worn from a ribbon with a dark blue centre flanked by narrow scarlet stripes with pale blue edges. *Class II* – the equivalent of the Air Force Medal is similar; but carried out in bronze. The ribbon is like that for Class I with the two shades of blue reversed.

## TAMGHA-I-KHIDMAT

'Khidmat' means 'Services,' and the three grades of the Order and its Medal for meritorious service by civilians have already been mentioned. There is, however, a Military Division of the medal in three classes, differing in design and with different ribbons. *Class I* – Stated to be the equivalent of the old Indian Order of Merit. It consists of a gold, five-rayed faceted star bearing a white five-pointed star with crescent and star. Worn round the neck on a crimson ribbon with a white central stripe. *Class II* – the equivalent of the old Order of British India, is of the same design as Class I but in silver. The ribbon is crimson with a narrow white stripe near each edge. *Class III* – the equivalent of Meritorious Service and Long Service Medals, is carried out in bronze and worn on the breast. Ribbon is crimson, with a third narrow white stripe in the centre.

## POLICE MEDALS
## QUAID-I-AZAM POLICE MEDAL FOR GALLANTRY

Ribbon five equal stripes of white and dark blue, with a narrow green stripe in each white portion. Similar to the Queen's Police Medal for Gallantry, but with green stripes substituted for the red.

## PAKISTAN POLICE MEDAL.
## MERITORIOUS SERVICE

Ribbon the same as the old Indian Police M.S.M. but with a narrow green stripe down the centre.

## PAKISTAN POLICE MEDAL

Ribbon, as for the Quaid-i-Azam medal mentioned above but with a narrow green stripe down the central white portion only.

187

# Ceylon (Sri Lanka)

**232 - POLICE MEDAL** (for Gallantry)

**233 - POLICE MEDAL** (for Meritorious Service)
These medals were instituted on August 4, 1950. They are in silver
and circular, with the effigy of the Sovereign on the obverse, and on
the reverse an emblematic design with the words 'FOR GALLANTRY'
or 'FOR MERIT' as the case may be, circumscribed by the words
'CEYLON POLICE SERVICE.' A small silver rose is worn on the ribbon
of the Gallantry Medal, if a bar is awarded.

## CEYLON ARMED SERVICES INAUGURATION MEDAL
Established in July, 1955, for award to all ranks who served in the
Armed Services during specified periods in 1950–51, and to others
at the discretion of the Governor-General. The medal is in cupro-
nickel and circular, and has on the obverse the arms of Ceylon,
and on the reverse the legend 'Inauguration Armed Services' and
'Sri Lanka' in three languages. The ribbon is dark red with edges
from outwards of 1.5 mm. stripes of yellow, green, saffron, yellow.
It takes precedence after the Pakistan Independence Medal.

## POLICE LONG SERVICE MEDAL
## FIRE SERVICE LONG SERVICE MEDAL
Instituted on the same date as the two medals just described.
The medal is in cupro-nickel and circular with the Sovereign's
effigy on the obverse, and on the reverse an emblematic design
surrounded by the words 'CEYLON POLICE SERVICE. FOR LONG
SERVICE AND GOOD CONDUCT.' The ribbon is 35 mm. wide with
a central portion of dark blue of 16 mm., bordered on each side
by khaki stripes of 3 mm., silver stripes of 1.5 mm., with edges of
light blue of 4.5 mm. The medals differ in the ribbon, that for the
Fire Services having an additional 1.5 mm. silver stripe in the centre
of the dark blue, and 'FIRE' on the reverse instead of 'POLICE.'

# Burma

The following thirteen medals have been instituted since Burma
achieved her independence.

## 234 - AUNG SAN THURIYA
Aung San is the name of Burma's greatest national leader of modern
times who died in 1947. 'Thuriya' means 'sun.' This decoration,
the equivalent of the Victoria Cross, is a thuriya, or representation

**234 - AUNG SAN THURIYA**

**235 - THIHA THURA TAZEIT**

**236 - THURA TAZEIT**

**237 - AUNG SAN TAZEIT**

of the sun with rays, made of stainless steel and 38 mm. in diameter. The name of the recipient and year of award appear on the plain reverse. The ribbon when worn by itself carries a miniature of the decoration.

**235 - THIHA THURA TAZEIT**
(Brave like the Lion Medal)
This medal is in bronze, representing a stylized Chinthe (Lion) resting on a scroll with the words 'Thiha Thura' in Burmese.

**236 - THURA TAZEIT** (Brave or Gallantry Medal)
A silver emblem representing the Burmese conception of the rising sun emitting rays with the sun in the centre in red enamel.

**237 - AUNG SAN TAZEIT** (The Aung San Medal)
An oval-shaped medal in stainless steel, with the bust of Bogyoke Aung San in the centre surrounded by leaves and surmounted by a star.

**238 - THIHA BALA TAZEIT** (Stalwart like the Lion Medal)
This medal is similar to the Thiha Thura Tazeit, but with a different ribbon and the scroll reading 'Thiha Bala' in Burmese.

**239 - SIT HMU HTAN GAUNG TAZEIT (CLASS I)**
(Meritorious Service Medal. *First Class*)
A silver representation of a Burmese Bayet (a four-sided figure with

**238 - THIHA BALA TAZEIT**

curved edges) in three layers on steps with two embossed crossed spears in the centre of the topmost layer.

## 240 - SIT HMU HTAN GAUNG TAZEIT (CLASS II)
(Meritorious Service Medal. *Second Class*)
Similar to the medal just mentioned, but with two layers and a different ribbon.

## 241 - SIT HMU HTAN GAUNG TAZEIT (CLASS III)
(Meritorious Service Medal. *Third Class*)
Similar to the previous two medals, but in only one layer.

## 242 - A YE DAW BON TAZEIT (Emergency Medal)
In bronze in the form of a peacock as used in the A Ye Daw Bon flag.

## 243 - LUT LAT YE SI YONE HMU TAZEIT
(Independence Movement Medal)
A silver medal showing a peacock standing on a wreath.

## 244 - LUT MYAUK YE TAZEIT (Liberation Medal)
A red enamel circle, 25 mm. in diameter, with a five-pointed star in white enamel superimposed upon it.

## 245 - LUT LAT YE TAZEIT (Independence Medal)
A decagonal medal in red enamel with the edge between each point curving inwards, with a similarly shaped centrepiece in blue enamel with a five-pointed white star superimposed upon it, and a smaller white star in each of the angles.

## 246 - NAINGNGANDAW SIT HMU HTAN TAZEIT
(General Service Medal)
In silver in the shape of a triangular Burmese gong with the base extended. It has two crossed rifles in the centre over eagles' wings, with an anchor below and a sheaf of paddy above.

# South Africa

Various decorations and medals peculiar to the Defence Forces of the Union of South Africa were established in 1952, and are intended in future to replace all British decorations for which South African citizens were formerly eligible.

## 247 - THE CASTLE OF GOOD HOPE DECORATION (CASTEEL DE GOEDE HOOP-DEKORASIE)
This medal is awarded with the approval of Her Majesty for a signal act of valour in battle, and can be granted posthumously. It takes precedence over every other order, decoration or medal.

**239 - SIT HMU HTAN GAUNG TAZEIT (CLASS I)**

**240 - SIT HMU HTAN GAUNG TAZEIT (CLASS II)**

**241 - SIT HMU HTAN GAUNG TAZEIT (CLASS III)**

A gold five-pointed star represents the outline of the Castle of Good Hope surrounded by a moat, the obverse having a raised centre showing the arrival of Jan van Riebeeck in Table Bay on 6 April 1652, with Table Mountain in the background, surrounded by a wreath of protea flowers and leaves encircled by a riband with the words 'CASTEEL DE GOEDE HOOP DEKORASIE' above and 'CASTLE OF GOOD HOPE DECORATION' below. The reverse has the Royal cypher and the coat-of-arms of the Union. A recipient is entitled to use the letters C.G.H. after his name, and the decoration is worn round the neck from a ribbon of sea-green watered silk 44 mm. wide. When the ribbon alone is worn a miniature golden replica of the outline of the castle appears in the centre. A bar may be awarded for a further act of valour, and is indicated on the neck ribbon by a golden bar with a miniature replica of the castle, and with the ribbon alone by a second replica of the castle.

## 248 - THE VAN RIEBEECK DECORATION (VAN RIEBEECK-DEKORASIE)

A silver-gilt decoration in the shape of a five-pointed star represent-ing the outline of the Castle of Good Hope, awarded to officers for distinguished service against an enemy in the field. The obverse has the effigy of Jan van Riebeeck in relief against a background of three rings representing his three ships, *Drommedaris, Rijger* and *Goede Hoop*. The outer ring has the words 'UITNEMENDE DIENS – DISTINGUISHED SERVICE.' The reverse has the Royal cypher and the Union coat-of-arms. A recipient is entitled to use the letters D.V.R. after his name, and the ribbon from which the decoration is hung by a clasp of protea leaves is sky blue, 32 mm. wide. A bar, bearing a small gilt cannon, may be awarded for further distin-guished service, and is indicated by a similar gilt cannon attached to the ribbon when it is worn alone.

## 249 - THE VAN RIEBEECK MEDAL

This medal, of precisely the same pattern as the decoration but in silver, may be awarded to warrant officers, N.C.O.s and men for distinguished service in the field, with the same proviso as to bars. Holders are entitled to use the letters V.R.M. after their names. The ribbon is sky blue with a central 6 mm. stripe of white.

## 250 - THE HONORIS CRUX (CROSS OF HONOUR-EREKRUIS)

This medal is awarded for gallantry in action against the enemy. It is a silver-gilt, eight-pointed Maltese cross with the obverse enamelled green and edged gold, with, in the centre, the three colours of the flag of the Union of South Africa, surrounded by a red circle with the words 'HONORIS CRUX.' In the intersections of the cross are four eagles in gold. The reverse has the Royal cypher and the arms of the Union. The award entitles the recipient to use the letters H.C. after his name. The ribbon from which the cross is suspended by an open wreath enamelled green, is of leaf-green watered silk, 32 mm. wide, with red edges, 3 mm. wide,

separated from the green by white stripes 1.5 mm. wide. A bar
bearing a gold-embossed eagle may be awarded for further acts
and is indicated by a golden-embossed eagle on the ribbon when it
is worn alone.

### 251 - THE LOUW WEPENER DECORATION (LOUW WEPENER-DEKORASIE)

This is a circular silver medal, the award of which, subject to the
approval of Her Majesty, is confined to deeds, other than purely
military acts, of conspicuous courage or great heroism in extreme
danger in saving or endeavouring to save life on land, at sea or in
the air, or in the execution of duty. The obverse shows a mountain
peak representing Thaba Bosigo, where Louw Wepener lost his life,
at the foot of which are two horsemen with the words 'THABA
BOSIGO, 1865' immediately below. At the top are the words 'OOUW
WEPENER,' and below 'DECORATION – DEKORASIE.' The reverse
has the usual Royal cypher and arms of the Union. A recipient
can use the letters L.W.D. after his name, and the medal may be
awarded posthumously. The ribbon is 35 mm. wide with orange
and white alternating stripes each 3 mm. wide. A silver bar bearing
the letters L.W.D. on a disc may be awarded for further acts of
courage, and when the ribbon is worn alone the bar is indicated by
a disc bearing the same letters.

### 252 - THE STAR OF SOUTH AFRICA (STER VAN SUID AFRIKA)

This medal is awarded to officers, subject to the approval of Her
Majesty, for meritorious service in peace or in war, and entitles the
recipient to the letters S.S.A. after his name. The decoration consists of a series of eight superimposed five-pointed stars of differing
sizes in silver, rising to a thickness of 9.5 mm. in the centre. The size
is that of a circle, 50 mm. in diameter, described round the points
of the largest star. The reverse has the Royal cypher, and the
Union arms. The star is worn round the neck, and the ribbon,
44 mm. wide, is orange with three green stripes of 3 mm. wide in
the centre, 6 mm. apart. A silver bar bearing a star may be awarded
for further service, and is indicated by a silver star on the ribbon
when it is worn alone.

### 253 - THE JOHN CHARD DECORATION AND JOHN CHARD MEDAL (JOHN CHARD-DEKORASIE EN JOHN CHARD-MEDALJE)

The decoration is of silver and is awarded to all ranks of the Union
Defence Forces already awarded the John Chard Medal (see below)
or the Efficiency Medal for twelve years' service, and have, in addition, completed another eight years on the active list, i.e. twenty
years in all. The award entitles the holder to the letters J.C.D. after
his name. The decoration is oval, 38 mm. wide and 50 mm. long,
and has on the obverse a scene showing the house at Rorke's Drift,
with a drift and a tree in the foreground. Inscribed at the top are
the words 'JOHN CHARD,' and below 'DECORATION – DEKORASIE.'

The arm of the forces in which the recipient has served is distinguished by a silver miniature brooch on the ribbon – crossed swords for the Army, an eagle for the Air Force, and an anchor for the Navy. The reverse has the Royal cypher with the arms of the Union. When the ribbon is worn alone it has a silver button bearing the letters 'J.C.D.' A bar may be awarded for any further period of service.

The John Chard Medal, awarded for twelve years' service in the Armed Forces, is the same design as the decoration, but in bronze, and with the words 'MEDALJE – MEDAL' on the obverse. Decoration and medal may not be worn together. The ribbon of both is the same.

(The hospital at Rorke's Drift, on the Tugela, was successfully defended by Lieutenants Chard and Bromhead with a slender British force against an overwhelming horde of Zulus on 22 January 1879.)

## 254 - THE SOUTHERN CROSS MEDAL (SUIDERKRUIS MEDALJE)

This medal is awarded in peace or war for outstanding devotion to duty. The medal is circular and in silver, the obverse having a dark blue enamel centre in relief, representing the night sky, with stars of the Southern Cross in silver, the whole encircled by a wreath of silver oak leaves. The reverse is the same as for all other Union medals, and the ribbon is dark blue with two central stripes of orange and white, each 3 mm. wide, worn with the orange furthest from the left shoulder. A recipient is entitled to use the letters S.M. after his name.

## 255 - THE UNION MEDAL (UNIE-MEDALJE)

A silver medal awarded to members of the South African Permanent Forces who complete eighteen years' qualifying service, which need not be continuous, and whose character and conduct have been irreproachable. The edge of the medal is evenly scalloped, and the obverse has the design of the Union coat-of-arms embellished in coloured enamel, with the words 'UNION MEDAL' on one side, and 'UNIE-MEDALJE' on the other. The reverse is the same as before. The ribbon is 32 mm. wide, equally divided into nine stripes of orange, white and blue repeated three times, with the blue stripe nearest the left shoulder. A bar embossed with the Union coat-of-arms may be awarded for a further twelve years' service, with a miniature coat-of-arms on the ribbon when it is worn alone.

## 256 - SOUTH AFRICAN POLICE GOOD SERVICE MEDAL

This is a circular silver medal, with the arms of the Union of South Africa on the obverse and the words 'POLICE SERVICE – POLISIE-DIENS.' The reverse bears the words 'FOR FAITHFUL SERVICE – VIR TROUE DIENS.' Awarded to a policeman, other than an officer, who has served for not less than eighteen years with irreproachable character, or has performed service of a particularly gallant or distinguished nature. In the latter case a bar bearing the words 'MERIT – VERDIENSTE' is added. The ribbon has a dark blue centre edged on each side by stripes of white and green.

## KOREA MEDAL

This is a silver medal awarded to members of the Union Defence Forces in recognition of voluntary service rendered with United Nations Forces in the Korean campaign. The obverse shows in relief maps of South Africa and Korea joined by an arrow with the words 'VRYWILLGERS – VOLUNTEERS' above, with the central design surrounded by two sprays and the word 'KOREA.' The reverse has the Royal cypher and the Union coat-of-arms. The ribbon is 32 mm. wide with a central broad stripe of pale blue bordered by stripes of dark blue and edges of orange, all 3 mm. wide.

# *Botswana*

(Obverse)      (Obverse)      (Reverse)

**257 - THE ORDER OF HONOUR**      **258 - THE GALLANTRY CROSS**

*(Obverse)*

*(Obverse)*

*(Obverse)*

*(Reverse)*

*(Reverse)*

*(Reverse)*

259 -
CONSPICUOUS SERVICE
MEDAL

260 - MERITORIOUS
SERVICE MEDAL

261 - POLICE
LONG SERVICE AND GOOD
CONDUCT MEDAL

262 - PRISON SERVICE
LONG SERVICE AND GOOD
CONDUCT MEDAL

*(Obverse)*

*(Reverse)*

(*Obverse*)                    (*Reverse*)

*Brunei*

263 -
**LONG SERVICE MEDAL**

*Ghana*

264 - **REPUBLIC COMMEMORATIVE MEDAL**

(*Obverse*) .                    (*Reverse*)

(*Obverse*)                                        (*Reverse*)

**265 - LONG SERVICE AND EFFICIENCY MEDAL**

*Guyana*

**266 - INDEPENDENCE**
**COMMEMORATIVE MEDAL**          (*Obverse*)                    (*Reverse*)

# *Kenya*

**267 - THE ORDER OF THE BURNING SPEAR** *Insignia of the Third*

*(Reverse)*

*(Obverse)*

**268 - THE HARAMBEE MEDAL**

*(Obverse)*

*(Reve*

**269 - CAMPAIGN MEDAL**

*Malawi*

ar of the First Class

*Badge of the First Class*

edal of the Fourth and Fifth Class

**270 - THE ORDER OF
THE LION**
(*Shown full size*)

**MEDAL FOR BRAVERY**
The ribbon is white and green.

# *Nigeria*

## THE ORDER OF THE NIGER

(*Obverse*)        (*Obverse*)

**271 -** *The badge, Commanders*     (*Reverse*)      **272 -** *The Medal of Officers*     (*Reverse*)

**THE
ORDER OF
THE NIGER**

*(Obverse)*            *(Reverse)*

**273** - *The Medal of Members*

# *Sierra Leone*

**274 - THE
INDEPENDENCE
MEDAL**

*(Obverse)*            *(Reverse)*

# Uganda

### 275- DISTINGUISHED SERVICE ORDER

### 276 - ARMY LONG SERVICE AND GOOD CONDUCT MEDAL

### 277- POLICE JUBILEE MEDAL

*(Obverse)*

*(Obverse)*

*(Obverse)*

*(Reverse)*

*(Reverse)*

*(Reverse)*

### 278 - POLICE MEDAL FOR GALLANTRY

### 279 - CONSPICUOUS GALLANTRY MEDAL (PRISON SERVICES)

### 280 - SPECIAL CONSTABULARY SERVICE MEDAL

*(Obverse)*

*(Obverse)*

*(Obverse)*

*(Reverse)*

*(Reverse)*

*(Reverse)*

### 281 - PRISON SERVICE LONG SERVICE AND GOOD CONDUCT MEDAL

*(Obverse)*

*(Reverse)*

# The United States of America

(NOTE – These awards are not listed in their exact official order of precedence.)

## 282 - MEDAL OF HONOR

This medal was instituted by Congress in December 1861 for the Navy, and in July 1862 for the Army. It is awarded by the President in the name of Congress, to officers and enlisted men of the Army, Navy and Marine Corps for bravery in action involving actual conflict with the enemy, and then only to those who distinguish themselves conspicuously by gallantry and intrepidity above and beyond the call of duty without detriment to the mission. The grant is only made after a most searching enquiry.

In war, when the Coast Guard serves with the Navy, its members are eligible for the Medal of Honor and for all other Naval decorations.

The design of the medal varies for the two Services.

*Army.* After several alterations since the date of institution, the medal now consists of a bronze five-pointed star of the design shown in the illustration, resting upon a laurel wreath enamelled green, while on each ray of the star is a green oak leaf. The centre has the head of Minerva in a circle bearing the words 'UNITED STATES OF AMERICA.' It hangs from a bar bearing the word 'VALOR' surmounted by a spread eagle. The reverse of the bar is engraved with the words 'THE CONGRESS TO . . .' followed by the name of the recipient. In the event of a second award a bronze oak leaf cluster is worn on the ribbon.

The ribbon is light blue with thirteen white stars, and the medal was originally worn on the breast with other decorations. To show its precedence over and above all other awards it is now ordered to be worn round the neck, the complete medal being suspended by a plain blue ribbon fastened to the back of the bar above the shorter ribbon with the thirteen stars.

*Navy.* There have been various changes in the design, and for the First World War the Navy, in 1919, established a new Medal of Honor in the form of a gold cross pattée superimposed upon a laurel wreath. There was an anchor on each arm of the cross, and the centre had the Great Seal of the United States in an octagon surrounded by the words 'UNITED STATES NAVY, 1917–1918.' The cross hung from its ribbon by a ring, and at the top of the ribbon was a brooch bar bearing the word 'VALOUR,' spelt in this case with a 'u.' In August 1942 the Navy reverted to its old pattern Medal of Honor authorized in 1861. Shown in the illustration, it consists of a five-pointed bronze star tipped with trefoils, each ray containing sprays of laurel and oak. In the centre, within a circle of thirty-four stars representing the number of States in 1862, is Minerva, personifying the United States, repulsing discord. The medal hangs from its ribbon by an anchor.

**MEDAL OF HONOR (NAVY)**

In the event of a second award a gold star is worn on the ribbon, otherwise the ribbon and method of wearing the medal are the same as for the Army.

Regardless of rank, holders of the Medal of Honor over the age of sixty-five may draw ten dollars a month on formal application.

## 283 - DISTINGUISHED SERVICE CROSS (ARMY)

This decoration, confined to the Army, was instituted in January 1918 for award to any person serving in the Army who has distinguished himself or herself by extraordinary heroism against an armed enemy in circumstances which do not justify the award of the Medal of Honor.

The cross has been awarded to members of relief organizations serving with the Army within the area of actual operations, while it was made retroactive to cover conspicuous service in wars or campaigns before the First World War. In 1934 it was also authorized to be presented to those persons who had received the Certificate of Merit.

The cross is of bronze surcharged with the American spread eagle and hangs from a blue ribbon with narrow white and red stripes at either edge. The first hundred of the decorations made had the arms of the cross ornamented with oak leaves, but in subsequent issues the arms of the cross were of a more simple design as shown in the illustration. Beneath the eagle is a scroll bearing the words 'FOR VALOR.'

If a recipient is again cited for further acts of gallantry justifying the grant of the decoration, he is awarded a bronze oak cluster to be worn on the ribbon. This decoration can be granted posthumously, and to officers and men of military forces allied to the United States.

**283 - DISTINGUISHED
SERVICE CROSS (ARMY)**

## CERTIFICATE OF MERIT AND BADGE

In 1847 it was enacted by Congress that any private soldier who distinguished himself might be granted a Certificate of Merit by the President, and seven years later the award was extended to N.C.O.s. In January 1905 a medal was instituted to be worn by those granted the certificate. The award of the medal was discontinued in July 1918, and from then until 1934 those who had received it had it replaced by the Distinguished Service Medal, described later. After 1934 both these medals were replaced by the Distinguished Service Cross.

Originally awarded for distinguished service in action or otherwise, such as ... 'extraordinary exertion in the preservation of human life, or in the preservation of public property, or rescuing public property from destruction by fire or otherwise, or any hazardous service by which the Government is saved loss in men or material,' the Certificate of Merit Badge was a bronze medal with a Roman war eagle on the obverse surrounded by the inscription 'VIRTUTIS ET AUDACIAE MONUMENTUM ET PRAEMIUM.' (Virtue and Courage are their own Monument and Reward.) The reverse had the words 'FOR MERIT' within an oak wreath, in a circle of the words 'UNITED STATES ARMY' in the upper half, and thirteen stars in the lower half.

The ribbon has blue edges, with white stripes inside the blue, and in the centre two broad stripes of red narrowly divided by white.

## 284 - BREVET MEDAL (MARINE CORPS)

This medal was instituted in June 1921 for award to holders of brevet commissions issued by the President for 'distinguished service in the presence of the enemy.' Brevet commissions were awarded to twenty-three officers of the United States Marine Corps in the Mexican War, Civil War, Spanish War, Philippine Insurrection and the China hostilities of 1900.

It consists of a bronze cross with a centre medallion bearing the word 'BREVET' surrounded by a circle with the words 'UNITED STATES MARINE CORPS.' The centre of the reverse has the words 'FOR DISTINGUISHED SERVICE IN PRESENCE OF ENEMY.' The ribbon is red moiré with thirteen white stars.

## SPECIALLY MERITORIOUS MEDAL

This medal was authorized by Congress in March 1901 for award to ninety-three officers and men of the Navy or Marine Corps who rendered specially meritorious service otherwise than in action during the war with Spain. It consists of a bronze cross pattée with a medallion in the centre, bearing an anchor within a wreath of oak and laurel surrounded by the inscription 'U.S. NAVAL CAMPAIGN WEST INDIES.' The arms of the cross are inscribed 'SPECIALLY MERITORIOUS SERVICE 1898.' The ribbon is scarlet.

## 285 - NAVY CROSS

When first established in 1919, this cross could be presented by the President, but not in the name of Congress, to any one in the Naval service who, since 6 April 1917 had 'distinguished himself by extraordinary heroism or distinguished service in the line of his profession, in cases where such heroism or distinguished service is not of a character to justify the award of the Medal of Honor or Distinguished Service Medal.' In August 1942 these rules were altered, and the decoration was given precedence over the Navy Distinguished Service Medal. It was to be awarded 'to any person serving in any capacity with the Naval service of the United States who distinguished himself by extraordinary heroism in connection with military operations against an armed enemy.' It is thus given for combat action only.

The decoration consists of a dark bronze cross with points of laurel at the junction of the limbs. The centre of the obverse bears the design of a caravel, and the reverse, crossed anchors with the letters 'U.S.N.'

Further acts of gallantry are marked by a gold star worn upon the ribbon. The Navy Cross has been conferred upon officers and men of Navies allied to the United States, and a few British officers have received it.

**285 - NAVY CROSS**

### 286 - DISTINGUISHED SERVICE MEDAL (ARMY)

This medal, instituted in 1918 at the same time as the Distinguished Service Cross, is awarded by the President to any person who, while serving in any capacity with the Army, shall hereafter distinguish himself or herself by exceptionally meritorious service to the Government in a duty of great responsibility in time of war, or in connection with military operations against an armed enemy of the United States. The medal, therefore, can be awarded for exceptionally meritorious service either in the field or at any other post of duty.

If a recipient of the medal is again cited in orders for further acts that would qualify him or her for another medal, a bronze oak cluster is worn on the ribbon. The medal may be granted posthumously. The medal was awarded to a few Allied officers during the two World Wars. Admiral of the Fleet Viscount Cunningham of Hyndhope was awarded the Army D.S.M. for his services as Naval Commander of the Expeditionary Force which landed in North Africa in November 1942. His case must be unique, for he was later awarded the U.S. Navy D.S.M. also.

The Army D.S. Medal, which differs from that for the Navy, is of bronze, and bears on the obverse the coat-of-arms of the United States surrounded by a circular ribbon of blue enamel bearing the words, 'FOR DISTINGUISHED SERVICE,' and the date 'MCMXVIII.'

**286 - DISTINGUISHED SERVICE MEDAL - ARMY**

### 287 - DISTINGUISHED SERVICE MEDAL (NAVY)

This medal is awarded by the President to anyone in the Naval service who has distinguished himself by exceptionally meritorious service to the Government in a duty of great responsibility. The medal has been bestowed upon various British Naval officers.

The decoration is in gilded bronze, bearing the American eagle in the centre, surrounded by a blue-enamelled circle bearing the words shown in the illustration and a gold wave scroll border. The reverse has Neptune's trident within a laurel wreath surrounded by a blue circle with the words 'FOR DISTINGUISHED SERVICE.' The whole design is surmounted by a white-enamelled star with rays issuing from between the limbs and surcharged with a gold anchor. The ribbon of blue and yellow is symbolical of the blue uniforms and gold lace of the Navy. In the case of a recipient performing further acts to justify the award of another medal, a gold star is worn upon the ribbon.

### 288 - THE SILVER STAR

The Silver Star, which takes precedence over the Legion of Merit, is the survival of a former badge of honour, previously not a decoration, which was authorized during the First World War. Originally this was a small silver star worn on the ribbon of a campaign medal to indicate a citation in orders for gallantry in action. The award was made retrospective to include all earlier campaigns. However, the use of these small silver stars caused some confusion, as they were worn in the same manner by those who had been wounded in action. Then, following the authorization of the Purple Heart to such persons, a distinct medal, known as the 'Silver Star' decoration, was established on 8 August 1932 as a reward to those persons who, prior to 7 December 1941, had been cited in orders for gallantry in action and which citations did not warrant the award of the Medal of Honor or Distinguished Service Cross.

The star is of bronze, 32 mm. in diameter, and in the centre of the obverse bears a plain laurel wreath which encircles a small 4.5 mm. silver star. Oak leaf clusters or gold stars are worn on the ribbon by Army and Navy respectively to indicate second or subsequent awards.

**288 - THE SILVER STAR**

### 289 - LEGION OF MERIT
The Legion of Merit was established in July 1942 and is awarded as follows:

To personnel of the Armed Forces of the United States and of the Government of the Philippines, who, since 8 September 1939, shall have distinguished themselves by exceptionally meritorious conduct in the performance of outstanding services, which are officially described as: 'Services over a period of time or in the performance of a continuing duty, marked by extraordinary fidelity and a measure of efficiency conspicuously above and beyond the usual, or, a particular achievement of special note or importance. The recipient must have rendered services so outstanding as clearly to distinguish him above men of like grade or experience.' For United States personnel there is one grade only, and the decoration may be conferred upon all officers and enlisted men whose services meet the standards required. No more than one Legion of Merit may be issued to any one person; but for each succeeding achievement sufficient to justify the award a bronze oak leaf cluster is granted instead. Awards of the Legion of Merit are made in the name of the President by the War Department, or by commanders specifically authorized by the War Department to make such awards. Civilians are not eligible. Posthumous awards are authorized. The Legion of Merit takes precedence below the Distinguished Service Medal and the Silver Star.

*The badge* consists of a five-rayed cross with double points, each point tipped with a golden ball. The arms of the cross are enamelled white with red edges. In the centre is a circular plaque of blue with thirteen white stars. The cross rests upon a wreath enamelled green, each of the intervening spaces between the arms near the centre being filled in with small crossed arrows in gold.

ARMED FORCES OF FOREIGN COUNTRIES
The Legion of Merit, in four classes, is established for award to personnel of the Armed Forces of foreign nations friendly to the United States who, since 8 September 1939 shall have distinguished themselves by exceptionally meritorious conduct in the performance of outstanding services. The awards are only made with the prior approval of the President, and a very high standard is insisted upon. Civilians are not eligible.

The classes are as follows:

*Chief Commander* – The badge worn on left breast. No sash. In undress uniform chief commanders wear the small-sized ribbon with, in the centre, a miniature representation of the cross in gold on a small horizontal golden bar.

*Commander* – The badge worn round the neck. In undress, the small-sized ribbon with, in the centre, a miniature representation of the cross on a small horizontal bar, both in silver.

(NOTE – The degrees of chief commander and commander are awards for services comparable to those for which the Distinguished Service Medal is awarded to members of the United States Armed Forces.)

*Officer* – The badge worn on the left breast with a small replica in gold on the ribbon. The replica is worn on the ribbon in undress uniform.

*Legionnaire* – The badge, with plain ribbon, worn on the left breast. A plain ribbon in undress uniform.

**289 - LEGION OF MERIT**

## 290 - DISTINGUISHED FLYING CROSS

On 2 July 1926, Congress established the Distinguished Flying Cross – the only American decoration authorized for a specific branch of the Military and Naval forces — for members of the Air Corps of the Army, Navy and Marine Corps. It is also the only case wherein the identical medal is presented under like conditions by both the War and Navy Departments.

The award of the cross is confined to . . . 'any person, who, while serving in any capacity with the Air Corps of the Army, Navy and Marine Corps of the United States, including the National Guard and Organized Reserves, subsequent to 6 April 1917, has distinguished himself by heroism or extraordinary achievement while participating in an aerial flight.'

The decoration was made retroactive to include services in 1917–18.

The cross is bronze and bears the design of a four-blade propeller superimposed on a chased square.

## 291 - THE SOLDIER'S MEDAL

The Soldier's Medal was established under the same act as the Distinguished Flying Cross, and is intended as a reward for heroism during time of peace.

It may be awarded to . . . 'any member of the Army or its affiliated branches, or to members of the Navy and Marine Corps while serving with the Army of the United States who, subsequent to 2 July 1926 distinguished themselves by heroism not involving actual conflict with the enemy.' Women serving with the Army are eligible.

The Soldier's Medal is octagonal in shape and bears the design of the American eagle and fasces, with six stars on one side and seven on the other, and is in bronze.

## 292 - NAVY AND MARINE CORPS MEDAL

This medal, authorized August 1942, is the Naval equivalent of the Army 'Soldier's Medal.' It may be awarded to any person who, while serving in any capacity with the Navy or Marine Corps, including Reserves, shall have, since December 6 1941, distinguished himself or herself by heroism not involving actual conflict with the enemy, or to any person previously awarded a letter of commendation for heroism by the Secretary of the Navy, regardless of date. A gold star is awarded for a second act of heroism. The medal, octagonal in shape and of striking design, was the creation of Lieut.-Commander McClelland Barclay, U.S.N.R., a battle artist, who was reported as missing in action off New Georgia Island.

## 293 - BRONZE STAR

This star was established in February 1944 for award to any person who, while serving on or after 7 December 1941 in any capacity with the Army, Navy, Marine Corps or Coast Guard of the United States, distinguishes himself by heroic or meritorious achievement or service in connection with military operations, not involving participation in aerial flight, against an enemy of the United States. It may be awarded for acts of gallantry or meritorious service either in actual combat or in direct support of combat operations. The star is primarily intended for recognizing performance of duty beyond the ordinary, but not sufficiently outstanding to warrant the award of the Silver Star Medal or Legion of Merit.

*(Obverse)*

## 294 - COMMENDATION RIBBON (NAVY)

This is awarded by the Secretary of the Navy or the Commanders of Atlantic or Pacific Fleets for services in action of not sufficiently high a standard to warrant the award of a Silver Star. It is equivalent to a 'Mention in Despatches.' The ribbon is green with white stripes towards each edge.

*Coast Guard.* The ribbon is as for Navy with an additional narrow central stripe of white.

## 295 - COMMENDATION PENDANT (ARMY)

This is awarded in the same way to officers and men of the Army. A metal pendant is now worn from this ribbon, consisting of a bronze hexagon with an American bald eagle on the obverse and the words 'FOR MILITARY MERIT' on the reverse.

## 296 - AIR MEDAL

A sixteen-pointed bronze star with, in the centre, an eagle in flight; awarded to a pilot or a member of the crew of an aircraft who meets one of several requirements, but whose services do not warrant the award of the Distinguished Flying Cross. It can be granted for 'performing a feat which is regarded as a meritorious achievement while participating in aerial flight.' This usually applies to personnel who have taken part in missions, which, although important, have not involved actual contact with the enemy. Bomber crews

**293 - BRONZE STAR**
*(Reverse)*

can earn the medal by taking part in five combat missions, each lasting more than two and a half hours, and fighter pilots by taking part in ten sorties of less than two and a half hours, except on escort missions. The medal is also awarded to the pilot or member of a crew credited with the destruction of one enemy aeroplane. Oak leaf clusters, corresponding to the British bars, can be awarded for further acts.

## 297 - THE PURPLE HEART

The Purple Heart, the first American decoration for conspicuous military service, was instituted by George Washington, when Commander-in-Chief of the Continental Army, towards the end of the Revolutionary War.

It was not originally a medal, but the figure of a heart in purple cloth or silk, edged with narrow silver lace or binding. Not until the Civil War was the first medal – the Medal of Honor – authorized by the United States Government for individual meritorious service.

The original Purple Heart had a brief existence. With military activity virtually at a standstill at the time of its establishment, and the signing of the treaty of peace the following year, little opportunity was offered for its reward; and, according to surviving records, only three men were granted the decoration. Although never officially abolished, it appears that the Purple Heart fell into disuse or was forgotten as no further awards were made after the Revolutionary War.

**296 - AIR MEDAL**    *(Obverse)*

Finally, after a lapse of nearly a century and a half, attention was called to this rare American decoration and a movement advocating its revival was projected. As a result, the 200th anniversary of George Washington's birth was selected as the most appropriate time for its reinstitution, and on 22 February 1932 the following order was published by the War Department:

'By order of the President of the United States, the Purple Heart, established by George Washington at Newburgh, 7 August, 1782, during the War of the Revolution, is hereby revived out of respect to his memory and military achievements.'

The regulations governing the revived decoration authorize award as follows:

'For acts or services performed prior to 22 February, 1932, the Purple Heart is confined to those persons who, as members of the Army, were awarded the Meritorious Service Citation Certificate by the Commander-in-Chief, American Expeditionary Forces, and, to all officers and men who were wounded in action in any war or campaign under conditions which entitle them to wear a wound chevron.

'For acts or services performed subsequent to 22 February, 1932, the decoration is authorized to be awarded to persons who, while serving in the Army of the United States, perform any singularly meritorious act of extraordinary fidelity or essential service.'

It was announced by the War Department on 19 September 1942 that the Purple Heart would be awarded to all U.S.A. personnel, killed or wounded by enemy action during the Second World War

**297 - THE PURPLE HEART**
*(Obverse)*

without distinction of rank. The award was made posthumously to military or civilian personnel who were killed while serving in any capacity with the Army, and to all those wounded provided that their wounds required medical treatment. A further announcement in December 1942 stated that commanders of hospitals and other medical installations are authorized to award the Purple Heart and Oak Leaf Cluster to United States soldiers wounded in action. The order ensures that wounded men receive their decorations before or immediately after their arrival in a hospital. The Oak Leaf Cluster is granted to a man previously wounded who has already received the Purple Heart. Severe frostbite whilst actually engaged in combat also merits the award of this decoration.

The present decoration consists of a heart-shaped medal, its face bordered in light bronze and its centre of purple enamel. On the obverse is a relief bust of General Washington in the Uniform of a General of the Continental Army. Its reverse is bronze and bears the inscription 'FOR MILITARY MERIT.'

The Washington coat-of-arms is incorporated in the ring which attaches it to a purple ribbon, bordered with white.

## 298 - MEDAL FOR MERIT

This medal was established by President Roosevelt on 20 July 1942 for award to civilians of the United States and her Allies who, subsequent to 8 September 1939, distinguished themselves by exceptionally meritorious conduct in the performance of outstanding services. The medal might only be awarded to civilians of foreign nations for the performance of exceptionally meritorious or courageous acts in furtherance of the war efforts of the United Nations. A Board received and considered proposals for the decoration and submitted them to the President, who had the sole authority to make the final award. No Military or Naval personnel were eligible. Only one Medal of Merit could be awarded to any one person. If it was earned on a second occasion a bronze oak leaf cluster to be worn on the ribbon was awarded instead. Ribbon is bright claret as for Legion of Merit, with two central stripes of white.

*(Obverse)*

## MEDAL OF FREEDOM

This is a bronze medal for award to civilians for meritorious service in prosecution of the war. It is really a junior grade of the Medal for Merit. The ribbon is red moiré with four narrow central stripes of white.

## EXCEPTIONAL CIVILIAN SERVICE AWARDS

A small circular gilt badge may be awarded by the Department of Defense to its civilian employees for 'exceptionally meritorious service within and beyond the call of duty.' It has no ribbon.

Civilian employees of the Army and Air Force may be granted medals for the same service. The medals are of bronze and vary in design, and the Army ribbon is dark blue moiré with three narrow threaded white lines in the centre; the Air Force ribbon is the same

**MEDAL OF FREEDOM**
*(Reverse)*

colour with three narrow threaded lines of yellow. There are actually twenty-four different ribbons used in connection with these awards; but they need hardly be described here.

## MERITORIOUS CIVILIAN SERVICE - ARMY AND AIR FORCE

Small circular silver badges without ribbons may be awarded to civilian employees of the Army and Air Force for 'meritorious service within and beyond the call of duty.'

## MERCHANT MARINE DISTINGUISHED SERVICE MEDAL

This medal was established by Congress on 11 April 1943. It is awarded by the U.S. Maritime Commission to any person in the American Merchant Marine who, on or after 3 September 1939, 'has distinguished himself by outstanding conduct or service in the line of duty.' It consists of a silver compass rose of eight points each topped with a ball imposed upon a bronze compass card. It is suspended from its ribbon by an eagle in front of crossed anchors with an arch of leaves overhead. The striking ribbon has a broad red stripe in the centre flanked by narrower stripes of white, with broad edges of blue.

NOTE — For other Merchant Marine awards see at the end of United States section.

## OAK LEAF CLUSTER

This decoration corresponds to the British 'Bar,' and is a bronze twig, 1 cm. in length, comprising four oak leaves with three acorns on the stem. It is worn on the ribbon of any medal for which a second or subsequent award is made. Silver oak leaf clusters are worn on the appropriate ribbons instead of the bronze in the ratio of one to five.

## 299, 300, 301, 302 - LIFE-SAVING MEDALS

Included among the American decorations are the Treasury Life-Saving Medals, which, although not military in character, are granted to members of the Army, Navy, Marine Corps and Coast Guard, or to civilians.

These medals, one in gold and the other in silver, are awarded under the same conditions. The only difference is that the silver medal is presented for deeds not sufficiently distinguished to warrant the gold medal.

The medals are presented by the Treasury Department under a special act of Congress of 1874, and are authorized to . . . 'any persons who by extreme and heroic daring have endangered their lives in saving or endeavouring to save lives from the perils of the sea in the waters over which the United States have jurisdiction, or upon an American vessel.'

When worn with other medals, the Treasury Life-Saving Medal is placed after all other decorations, but before campaign medals. The gold and silver medals are both coin-shaped with differing designs on the obverse. The ribbons of these two medals were originally red and blue respectively; but were altered in 1947. That for the gold medal now has a gold-coloured centre with red edges, the two colours being separated by a very narrow white stripe. The ribbon for the silver medal has a silver-grey centre with bright blue edges, the two colours separated as before by a thin white striple.

## GOOD CONDUCT MEDALS, U.S.A.
In the Armed Forces of the United States medals for good conduct are ordered to be worn before war medals.

They are as follows:

### 303 - ARMY
This is a bronze medal, circular in shape, with an eagle standing on a closed book on the obverse surrounded by the words 'EFFICIENCY. HONOR. FIDELITY.' The reverse has a star and scroll with the words 'FOR GOOD CONDUCT' surrounded by two sprays of foliage tied at the bottom. The ribbon is scarlet moiré with three white stripes towards each edge. The medal was authorized in June 1941 for award to enlisted men of the Army for 'demonstrated fidelity by faithful and exact performance of duty, efficiency and behaviour deserving emulation' and who on or after 27 August 1940 had or shall have honourably completed three years of active Federal military service, or who after 7 December 1941 had or shall have honourably served one year of continuous active Federal military service while the United States is at war.

*(Obverse)*

### 304 - NAVY
A circular bronze medal with a straight bar for suspension. In the centre of the obverse, surrounded by a rope, is a full-rigged ship with the word 'CONSTITUTION' below, the whole resting upon an anchor and surrounded by a circle of chain cable. Between the rope and the cable are the words 'UNITED STATES NAVY.' In the centre of the reverse is engraved the name of the recipient and the period of his first enlistment, surrounded by the words 'FIDELITY, ZEAL. OBEDIENCE.' Bars, engraved '2ND. ENLISTMENT,' etc., are worn on the medal ribbon for further periods of service, with a numeral on the ribbon to denote the number of enlistments when it is worn alone. The ribbon is crimson. The Navy Good Conduct Medal was first authorized in 1869, and the present medal designated in 1892.

**303 - ARMY GOOD CONDUCT MEDAL**
*(Reverse)*

### 305 - MARINE CORPS
This is a circular bronze medal. In the centre, encircled by a rope, is a marine standing at the breech of a Naval gun, and below, a scroll with the words 'SEMPER FIDELIS.' This design rests on an anchor surrounded by a circle of chain cable, and between the rope and the cable are the words 'UNITED STATES MARINE CORPS.' The reverse, engraved with the name of the recipient and the period of enlistment, is the same as for the Navy, and the same rules apply as to bars for further enlistments and numerals on the service

ribbon. The medal hangs from a straight clasp formed of a rifle, and at the top of the ribbon is a rounded bar with rope edge inscribed 'U.S. MARINE CORPS.' The medal, first authorized in 1896, has a scarlet ribbon with a central stripe of blue.

## 306 - COAST GUARD

This is awarded in the same way as in the Navy. It is a bronze medal with the obverse showing a coast guard cutter within a circle of rope, surrounded by the words 'SEMPER PARATUS' with crossed oars at the bottom and with a circular length of chain cable outside. The reverse is the same as for the Navy and Marine Corps Good Conduct Medals, and the medal has a straight bar for suspension. The ribbon is claret coloured with a central stripe of white, and at the top is a bar inscribed 'U.S. COAST GUARD.' Bars bearing the name of the ship in which the recipient served are awarded for further periods of enlistment.

## 307 - NAVAL RESERVE MEDAL

This medal is granted to officers and enlisted men for ten years' honourable service, with a bronze star on the ribbon for every additional ten years. The medal is bronze and hangs from a ring. On the obverse is an eagle perched upon an anchor on a rock with rays in the background. The reverse has the words 'FAITHFUL SERVICE' surrounded by the legend 'UNITED STATES NAVAL RESERVE.' The ribbon is red, narrowly edged with stripes of yellow and blue, the blue outside.

## 308 - MARINE CORPS RESERVE MEDAL

This medal was instituted in 1939, and is awarded for four years' service. It hangs from a ring, and the obverse shows a marine and a civilian walking to the right, with the words 'FOR SERVICE' beneath and 'MARINE CORPS RESERVE' round the upper circumference. The ribbon is yellow, with a broad central stripe of scarlet, and edges of blue, white and red, the blue inside.

## NAVAL RESERVE SPECIAL COMMENDATION RIBBON

This is awarded to officers of the organized Naval Reserve who have officially commanded in a meritorious manner for a period of four years between 1 January 1930 and 7 December 1941 an organized battalion, squadron or separate division of the Naval Reserve, or a battalion or squadron of the Marine Corps Reserve, and have had a total service in the Reserve of not less than ten years. The ribbon is red with a central broad stripe of green, edged with narrow stripes of yellow and blue, the yellow inside.

## UNITED STATES WAR MEDALS

Mention has already been made of the Purple Heart, instituted by General George Washington in 1782 and revived in 1932; the Certificate of Merit, authorized in 1847, replaced by a medal in

1905 which was discontinued in 1918, and its place taken by the Distinguished Service Cross; the Medals of Honor of 1861 and 1862 for the Navy and Army, respectively; the Specially Meritorious Medal of 1901; the Life-Saving Medals of 1874; and the Good Conduct Medals authorized for the Navy in 1869, and for the Marine Corps in 1896. These are all awards for personal gallantry or faithful service.

What may be regarded as the first war medals were not authorized in the United States until June 1898, when Congress sanctioned a special award, popularly known as the 'Dewey Medal,' to commemorate the Battle of Manila Bay on 1 May that same year. In 1901, again, Congress authorized the award of the 'Sampson Medal' to officers and men of the Navy and Marine Corps who had taken part in the engagements in the West Indies in 1898.

The story of how war medals first came to be issued to officers and men of the United States Army and Navy for all the years and expeditions in which they had taken part over a period of fifty years is not without interest. The authority for the award of war medals was the prerogative of Congress, and for years efforts had been made to induce Congress to sanction their issue; but without result. It was finally brought to the notice of the President, then Theodore Roosevelt, that as Commander-in-Chief of the Army and Navy he was empowered to authorize badges to be worn as part of the uniforms of officers and men who had seen service in the various campaigns. Accordingly, in January 1905, what were known as 'Campaign Badges' with ribbons were duly authorized for the Civil War of 1861–5, the Indian wars and expeditions of 1865–91; the war with Spain, 1898; the Philippine Insurrection which started in 1899; and the operations in North China in 1900–1.

The discs of these first medals were cut, and they were struck, at the Mint in Philadelphia. They were of bronze, and the design varied for the Army and Navy, and sometimes the ribbons also. It was not until 1913 that the ribbons of the 'Campaign Badges' were made the same for both Services, as described later. They were issued gratuitously to enlisted men, and at cost price to officers.

The awards listed below are arranged as far as possible, in the chronological order of campaigns.

### 309 - CIVIL WAR (1861–65)

This medal was authorized for the Army in 1905. It has the head of President Lincoln on the obverse surrounded by the legend 'WITH MALICE TOWARD NONE, WITH CHARITY TOWARD ALL.' The reverse bears the words 'THE CIVIL WAR' with the dates '1861–65,' surrounded by a wreath of oak and olive. The first Army ribbon had red edges, with the centre divided into three stripes of grey (sometimes referred to as white), and two stripes of blue. This ribbon was discarded in 1913, when the Army adopted the Navy ribbon, half dark blue, half grey.

A medal was authorized for Navy and Marine Corps in 1908, having on the obverse a representation of the fight between the *Monitor* and the *Merrimac*, with the words 'THE CIVIL WAR,

1861–65.' The reverse has an eagle standing on an anchor and cable over the words 'FOR SERVICE' with sprays of oak and laurel beneath. Around the top circumference are the words 'UNITED STATES NAVY' or 'UNITED STATES MARINE CORPS' as the case may be. The ribbon is half dark blue, half grey as described above.

## 310 - INDIAN WARS (1865–91)

This medal was authorized for the Army in 1905. The obverse has an Indian brave on horseback in a war bonnet carrying a spear, with the words 'INDIAN WARS' above and below a wreath of arrow-heads two-thirds of the way round the lower circumference joined in the centre by a buffalo skull. On the reverse is a spread eagle on a trophy consisting of a cannon, six rifles and four standards, an Indian shield, quiver of arrows and three spears, a Cuban machete and a Sulu kris. Above are the words 'UNITED STATES ARMY,' below, the words 'FOR SERVICE' over thirteen stars.

The ribbon was originally red with borders of slightly darker red, but was later altered in 1917 to red with stripes of black towards each edge.

## 311 - BATTLE OF MANILA BAY, 1 MAY 1898
## NAVY AND MARINE CORPS

This medal was authorized by Congress on 3 June 1898 for award to all officers and men present at the battle. On the obverse is the bust of Commodore Dewey in uniform, and in the field to the right a small anchor on a laurel wreath with a star beneath it. The inscription in the field runs in ten lines – 'THE GIFT OF THE PEOPLE OF THE UNITED STATES TO THE OFFICERS AND MEN OF THE ASIATIC SQUADRON UNDER THE COMMAND OF COMMODORE GEORGE DEWEY.'

The reverse shows a half-naked gunner seated on a gun, holding a flag horizontally across his lap, and below a tablet stamped with the name of one of the seven ships which took part in the engagement. The legend runs — 'IN MEMORY OF THE VICTORY OF MANILA BAY, MAY 1, 1898.'

The medal is bronze, and is attached by two rings and a link to a clasp pin with a spread eagle in the centre resting on conventionalized waves, with a cross-handled sword to the right and a spray of olive to the left. The ribbon, 38 mm. wide, is attached to the pin and passes behind the link and the medal. It is yellow with broad edges of blue.

The sum of $10,000, 'or so much thereof as may be necessary' was voted for the supply of this medal, and 1825 specimens were delivered on the first order.

## 312 - WEST INDIES NAVAL CAMPAIGN (1898)

This medal was authorized by Congress on 3 March 1901 for award to the officers and men of the Navy and Marine Corps who had taken part in the Naval operations in the West Indies during the war with Spain. The obverse shows the bust of Admiral Sampson in uniform facing left, and in a semi-circle above, the words 'U.S. NAVAL CAMPAIGN, WEST INDIES 1898.' In the field to the left of the figure are the words 'WILLIAM T. SAMPSON,' and to the right, 'COMMANDER IN CHIEF.' The reverse has an officer, a seaman and a marine on the deck of a ship in action, and, below, a small tablet with the name and date of the engagement for which the medal was issued. It hangs from a bar bearing the name of the first engagement, and at the top of the ribbon is a brooch pin with the name of the ship. The ribbon is moiré with three equal stripes of red, blue, red.

The medal, or a separate named bar, dated on the back, was issued for forty-seven different engagements or skirmishes between 27 April and 14 August 1898, and the officers and men of sixty-eight ships received the award, some with as many as six or seven bars.

### 313 - SPANISH CAMPAIGN (1898)

This medal was authorized for the Army in January 1905 for service on shore in, or on the high seas on the way to, Cuba, Porto Rico and the Philippine Islands between certain specified dates from May to August, inclusive, 1898. The obverse has a castle with two small round towers at the corners, said to be derived from the castle that appeared on the Royal arms of Spain. The words 'WAR WITH SPAIN' are above, and below is the date '1898.' A branch of the tobacco plant and a stalk of sugar cane to right and left separate the legend and date. The reverse is the same as for the medal for the Indian wars. The first Army ribbon had a wide stripe of yellow in the centre flanked by stripes of red with narrow blue edges. This was discarded in 1913 for one officially described as blue, yellow, blue, with narrow yellow edges.

The medal was authorized for the Navy and Marine Corps in 1908 for those who served in 138 named ships on service in Cuban and Porto Rican waters between certain specified dates from April to August 1898, or on shore in Cuba, Porto Rico, the Philippines or Guam between 1 May and 16 August 1898. The medal is bronze with a view of Morro Castle, Havana, on the obverse and the legend 'SPANISH CAMPAIGN' or 'WEST INDIES CAMPAIGN' with the date '1898.' The reverse is the same as that for the Navy Civil War Medal. The Naval ribbon was originally yellow with a red stripe 3 mm. inside each edge — the Spanish colours. In 1913 this was discarded for the second Army ribbon — blue, yellow, blue with narrow edges of yellow.

### 314 - PHILIPPINE CAMPAIGN (1899–1906)

This medal was authorized for the Army in 1905 and amended in 1908. It was awarded to Army personnel for service on shore in the Philippine Islands between 4 February 1899 and 31 December 1904, as well as for operations in Jolo, April to May 1905; in Mindanao, October 1905; and against hostile Moros in Jolo, March 1906. It was re-issued for service in 1913. The obverse has a coconut palm, bearing fruit, with a pair of scales to the right and on the left a Roman lamp. Legend — 'PHILIPPINE INSURRECTION,' and below, the date '1899.' The reverse is the same as that of the medal for the Indian wars, and the ribbon is blue with broad stripes of red towards each edge, and narrow blue borders.

The medal was authorized for Navy and Marine Corps in 1908 for all officers and men who served in sixty-four ships in Philippine waters between specified dates starting in February 1899 and ending in November 1905. The obverse has a view of the old gates of the walled city of Manila, with the legend 'PHILIPPINE CAMPAIGN' above, and '1899–1903' below, the dates and inscription being separated by palm branches. The reverse is the same as for the Navy and Marine Corps Civil War Medals. The first Navy ribbon was of watered silk in three equal stripes of red, yellow, red, the Spanish man-of-war colours. This was altered in 1913 to the colours of the Army ribbon described above.

### 315 - CHINA RELIEF EXPEDITION (1900)

This medal was sanctioned for the Army in 1905. On the obverse is an Imperial five-clawed dragon, facing with the legend – 'CHINA RELIEF EXPEDITION,' and below, '1900–1901.' The reverse is as for the Civil War Medal. The ribbon is yellow with narrow blue borders.

The medal was authorized for the Navy in 1908 for personnel of eleven named ships serving in Chinese waters between April and October 1900. The obverse has the gate to the Forbidden City of Pekin with a dragon in the foreground, and the legend 'CHINA RELIEF EXPEDITION' with the date '1900' below. The reverse is the same as for previous Navy medals. The original Navy ribbon was of yellow watered silk with a narrow black stripe near each edge. This was changed in 1913 to the colours of the Army ribbon mentioned above.

### 316 - SPANISH WAR SERVICE (1898)

This medal was awarded by Congress in 1918 to all officers and men of the Army who served for ninety days during the war with Spain, otherwise than in a theatre of active operations and did not qualify for the campaign medal. The obverse has a Roman sword hanging on a tablet on which is inscribed 'FOR SERVICE IN THE SPANISH WAR.' It is surrounded by a wreath, and the sword is sheathed to indicate National Guard service in the United States, not in combat. The reverse has the coat-of-arms of the United States over a scroll surrounded by a wreath with the insignia of the infantry, artillery and cavalry.

### 317 - PHILIPPINE CONGRESSIONAL MEDAL (1899–1913)

This medal was sanctioned by Congress in 1906 for all officers and men who had volunteered for the war with Spain and served in the Philippine Islands and voluntarily remained in the Service after the term of their enlistment to help to suppress the Philippine Insurrection. The obverse has three soldiers marching to the left, the one in the centre carrying the American flag, and the legend 'PHILIPPINE INSURRECTION, 1899.' The reverse has the inscription 'FOR PATRIOTISM FORTITUDE AND LOYALTY' in five lines surrounded by a wreath of palm and pine.

The medal was confined to the Army.

**318 - ARMY OF CUBAN OCCUPATION** (1898–1902)

This medal was authorized in June 1915 for officers and men of the Army who had served in Cuba between 18 July 1898 and 20 May 1902. The obverse has a shield with the arms of Cuba resting on a *fasces* bearing the cap of Liberty, beside which are the dates '1898' and '1902.' On either side of the shield are sprays of oak and laurel. The legend round the circumference reads 'ARMY OF OCCUPATION MILITARY GOVERNMENT OF CUBA.' The reverse is the same as that of the medal for the Indian wars.

**319 - ARMY OF PORTO RICAN OCCUPATION** (1898)

This medal was authorized in June 1915 for officers and men of the Army who served in Porto Rico between 14 August and 10 December 1898. The obverse and reverse are the same as for the Army medal for the Spanish Campaign, except that the legend reads 'ARMY OF OCCUPATION PORTO RICO.'

**320 - CUBAN PACIFICATION MEDAL** (1906–09)

This medal was authorized for the Army in May 1909 for service in Cuba from 6 October 1906 to 1 April 1909. It is the usual bronze medal, with a shield bearing the arms of Cuba resting on *fasces* surmounted by the cap of Liberty with branches of oak and laurel below, and on each side of the shield a soldier with rifle at rest. The words 'CUBAN PACIFICATION' appear above, and the dates '1906–1909' below. The reverse is the same as for previous Army medals.

The medal was authorized also for the Navy and Marine Corps in 1909 who served in Cuba between the same dates as for the Army. The obverse has a figure representing America, with a sword suspended from her girdle and in her left hand the American flag, and her right hand extended and offering an olive branch to a Cuban. There is a tropical scene in the background, and above a dove of peace. The legend round the top circumference reads 'CUBAN PACIFICATION, 1908.' The reverse is the same as for previous Navy and Marine Corps medals.

**321 - NICARAGUAN CAMPAIGN**

This medal was authorized in July 1914 for all officers and men of the Navy and Marine Corps who served ashore in Nicaragua, or on board six specified ships, between 28 August and 2 November 1912, inclusive. The medal is bronze, with a tropical scene and a mountain on the obverse, with legend – 'NICARAGUAN CAMPAIGN' above, and the date '1912' below with branches of oak and laurel. The reverse is the same as for previous Navy and Marine Corps medals.

**322 - MEXICAN SERVICE MEDAL** (1911–17)

This medal was authorized in December 1917 for the Army. The obverse has a yucca shrub in flower with mountains in the background and the legend 'MEXICAN SERVICE' above and the dates '1911–1917' below. The reverse is the same as for previous Army medals.

The Navy and Marine Corps medal shows the old castle of San Juan de Ulloa at Vera Cruz on the obverse, with 'MEXICO' above and '1911–17' below, separated by branches of cactus.

The ribbon is the same for both Services.

## 323 - MEXICAN BORDER SERVICE MEDAL (1916–17)

This medal was authorized in July 1918 for service in the National Guard on the Mexican border or elsewhere in the field in 1916 or 1917, and for regular Army service in the Mexican border patrol from 1 January 1916 to 6 April 1917. The obverse is the same as for the Spanish War service Medal (No. **316**) with the inscription altered to 'FOR SERVICE ON THE MEXICAN BORDER.' The reverse is the same as for previous Army medals.

## 324 - HAITIAN CAMPAIGN MEDAL (1915)

This medal was awarded to those who took part in the joint Marine Corps and Naval expedition to Haiti between July and December 1915. The obverse has a view from the sea of the mountains of Cape Haitien with a palm tree in the left foreground. The words 'HAITIAN CAMPAIGN' appear above, with the date '1915' below. The reverse is the same as for earlier Navy and Marine Corps medals.

The same medal, but with the dates altered on the obverse to '1919–1920,' was later awarded to personnel of the Navy and Marine Corps, who served in Haiti from 1 April 1919 to 15 June 1920. Those who had already received the 1915 medal were awarded a clasp dated '1919–1920.' When the ribbon was worn alone, the clasp was represented by a bronze star.

## 325 - SANTO DOMINGO CAMPAIGN (1916)

Authorized in 1921 to commemorate services by Navy and Marine Corps in Santo Domingo (eastern part of Haiti) from May to December 1916. The obverse has a tower with the words 'DOMINICAN CAMPAIGN' and the date '1916.' The reverse is as for No. **333**, Navy Expeditionary Medal.

## 112 - VICTORY MEDAL (1917–19)

A bronze medal with the same ribbon as for the British Victory Medal was awarded to both Services for the First World War. It was granted to all members of the Army, Navy and Marine Corps whether they served overseas or not. On the obverse is the winged figure of Victory, while the reverse has the shield of the United States with the letters 'U.S.' and the names of the associated powers. The following clasps were issued:

*Army.* 'CAMBRAI,' 'SOMME DEFENSIVE,' 'LYS,' *'AISNE,' 'MONT-DIDIER-NOYON,' 'CHAMPAGNE-MARNE,' *'AISNE-MARNE,' 'SOMME OFFENSIVE,' 'OISE-AISNE,' *'YPRES-LYS,' *'ST. MIHIEL,' *'MEUSE-ARGONNE,' 'VITTORIO-VENETO,' all of which were major operations, and, with another clasp *'DEFENSIVE SECTOR,' are indicated by a small bronze star on the ribbon when it is worn alone. Five service clasps *'FRANCE,' 'ITALY,' *'SIBERIA,' *'RUSSIA' and 'ENGLAND' were also authorized for the Army; but were not awarded to persons entitled to battle clasps and do not carry the right to wear the bronze star on the service ribbon. The small silver star originally worn on the Victory ribbon to indicate a citation for gallantry in action was later replaced by the separate Silver Star Medal.

*The Navy and Marine Corps* had the following clasps in addition to those marked with an asterisk in the Army's list: 'OVERSEAS,' 'ARMED GUARD,' 'ASIATIC,' 'ATLANTIC FLEET,' 'AVIATION,' 'DESTROYER,' 'ESCORT,' 'GRAND FLEET,' 'MINE LAYING,' 'MINE SWEEPING,' 'MOBILE BASE,' 'NAVAL BATTERY,' 'PATROL,' 'SALVAGE,' 'SUB CHASER,' 'SUBMARINE,' 'TRANSPORT,' 'WEST INDIES,' 'WHITE SEA.' The Navy, too, used bronze stars on the service ribbon to indicate the possession of all clasps except those bearing the names of countries. As with the Army, the small silver star indicating a citation for gallantry in action was replaced by the Silver Star Medal, though if an officer or man had only a letter of commendation signed by the Secretary of the Navy he continued to wear a silver star on the ribbon of the actual medal as well as on the service ribbon. A small bronze Maltese cross on the ribbon indicates that its wearer served in the Marine Corps or Medical Corps, Navy, with the American Expeditionary Force in France between 6 April 1917 and 11 November 1918; but was not entitled to one or other of the battle clasps issued by the Army.

The Navy also issued the Victory Medal to men who entered the service on or after 12 November 1918 and before 30 March 1920, and served not less than ten days on shore in North Russia or Siberia or on board the ships operating in those waters.

### 326 - SECOND NICARAGUAN CAMPAIGN (1926–33)

This medal was authorized in 1929, and later given for services for operations in Nicaragua and in certain named ships between 27 August 1926 and 2 January 1933. It was awarded to Navy and Marine Corps and to those of the Army who co-operated during the period of disorder and unrest. The obverse shows Columbia in coat of mail and flowing skirt, sword in hand, protecting citizens. The legend is 'SECOND NICARAGUAN CAMPAIGN' with the dates '1926–1930' below. The reverse is as for No. **333**, Navy Expeditionary Medal.

### 327 - NC-4 MEDAL

In February 1929 Congress authorized the President to award gold medals to Commander John H. Towers for 'conceiving, organizing, and commanding the first Transatlantic flight,' and to the officers and crew of the Navy flying boat NC-4 who crossed the Atlantic with him. The original large gold medal was not intended to be worn; but in 1935 Congress authorized the grant of a bronze replica the same size as ordinary war medals worn with a ribbon. The obverse shows a gull flying over waves with the inscription 'FIRST TRANSATLANTIC FLIGHT UNITED STATES NAVY, MAY 1919,' and the reverse the words 'NEWFOUNDLAND—NC-4—PORTUGAL' in the centre, surrounded by the names of all the recipients and the words 'PRESENTED BY THE PRESIDENT OF THE UNITED STATES IN THE NAME OF CONGRESS.'

## PEARY POLAR EXPEDITION MEDAL (1908–09)

This medal was authorized by Congress in 1944 for award to the members of Admiral Peary's expedition who discovered the North Pole. The ribbon is white moiré with broad stripes of turquoise blue towards each edge.

## 328 - BYRD ANTARCTIC EXPEDITION (1928–1930)

In May 1930 Congress authorized the Secretary of the Navy to provide gold, silver and bronze medals for the officers and men of the Byrd Antarctic Expedition. The obverse shows Admiral Byrd in winter clothing holding a ski-pole, surrounded by the words 'BYRD ANTARCTIC EXPEDITION 1928–1930.' The reverse shows Byrd's ship above a panel inscribed – 'PRESENTED TO OFFICERS AND MEN OF THE BYRD ANTARCTIC EXPEDITION TO EXPRESS THE HIGH ADMIRATION IN WHICH CONGRESS AND THE AMERICAN PEOPLE HOLD THEIR HEROIC AND UNDAUNTED SERVICES IN CONNECTION WITH THE SCIENTIFIC INVESTIGATIONS AND EXTRAORDINARY AERIAL EXPLORATION OF THE ANTARCTIC CONTINENT.' Beneath the inscription is an aeroplane.

## 329 - SECOND BYRD ANTARCTIC EXPEDITION (1933–35)

A silver medal was authorized by Congress in June 1936 for award to 'deserving personnel' of the expedition. The obverse shows Admiral Byrd with an Eskimo dog with the words 'BYRD ANTARCTIC EXPEDITION 1933–1935.' The reverse has a panel inscribed – 'PRESENTED TO THE OFFICERS AND MEN OF THE SECOND BYRD ANTARCTIC EXPEDITION TO EXPRESS THE VERY HIGH ADMIRATION IN WHICH CONGRESS AND THE AMERICAN PEOPLE HOLD THEIR HEROIC AND UNDAUNTED ACCOMPLISHMENTS FOR SCIENCE UNEQUALLED IN THE HISTORY OF POLAR EXPLORATION.'

There is an aeroplane above the panel, a sledge and dog team below, and on either side the radio towers at 'Little America' and Admiral Byrd's ship.

## 330 - UNITED STATES ANTARCTIC EXPEDITION (1939–41)

This medal was authorized by Congress in 1945 for award to members of the expedition in recognition of their valuable services to the nation in the field of polar exploration and science.

## 331 - YANGTSE SERVICE

This medal was authorized in 1930 for officers and men of the Navy and Marine Corps who served at Shanghai or in the valley of the Yangtse from 3 September 1926 to 21 October 1927, and from 1 March 1930 to 31 December 1932. The obverse has a Chinese junk under sail with the words 'YANGTSE SERVICE.' The reverse is the same as that of No. 333.

## 332 - CHINA SERVICE

This medal was authorized in August 1940 for award to Navy and Marine Corps for services in China from 7 July 1937 to 7 September 1939. The obverse has a Chinese junk resting on waves, and the words 'CHINA SERVICE.' The reverse is as before.

### 333 - NAVY EXPEDITIONARY MEDAL

This medal was issued to all officers and men of the Navy who served in the various campaigns not already covered by a specific campaign medal, viz.: Panama 1873, 1885, 1901, 1903, 1904; Hawaiian Islands, 1874; Samoa, 1888, 1889, 1899; Korea, 1894; China, 1895; Cuba, 1912, 1917; Honduras, 1907, 1924; Nicaragua, 1926. The obverse has a sailor beaching a boat containing an officer and marines with flag of the United States, with the legend 'EXPEDITIONS' above. The reverse has an eagle perched on an anchor and branches with the legend 'UNITED STATES NAVY' and the words 'FOR SERVICE.' The ribbon is blue with broad stripes of old gold towards each edge.

### 334 - MARINE CORPS EXPEDITIONARY MEDAL

This was issued in the same way as the preceding medal for services in Hawaiian Islands, 1874, 1889, 1893; Egypt, 1882; Columbia, 1885, 1895, 1901-2-3-4-5; Korea, 1888, 1894-5-6, 1904-5; Argentina, 1890; Haiti, 1891, 1914-15-16-17-18-19-20, 1924; China, 1894-5, 1911-14, 1924-34; Samoa, 1899; Syria, 1903; Honduras, 1903-7, 1924; Dominican Republic, 1903-4, 1914-16-17-18-24; Abyssinia, 1903; Russia, 1905-7; Nicaragua, 1910-12-17-18-25-26; Cuba, 1912, 1917, 1920-2; Panama, 1885, 1895, 1903-4; Chile, 1891; Siberia, 1920-2. The obverse shows a marine with full pack charging with fixed bayonet, with wave scrolls at base to indicate Naval phase of Marines' duties. The word 'EXPEDITIONS' appears above. The ribbon is khaki colour with narrow red edges and a broad central stripe of red. Bronze stars are worn on the ribbons of medals Nos. 333 and 334 for each expedition after the first. Navy and Marine Corps personnel who served in the defence of Wake Island – 7 December to 22 December 1941 — wear a silver 'W' on the service ribbon.

*(Obverse)*

### 335 - ARMY OF OCCUPATION (GERMANY) (1918-1923)

This medal was authorized by Congress in November 1941 for all members of the U.S. Army, Navy, Marine Corps or Coast Guard who served in Germany or Austria-Hungary from 12 November 1918 to 11 July 1923. The obverse has General Pershing's profile with a general's four stars above. To the left, in small letters, are the words 'GENERAL JOHN J. PERSHING,' and to the right an unsheathed sword within a laurel wreath and the dates '1918' and '1923.' The reverse has the American eagle standing on a castle and the inscription 'U.S. ARMY OF OCCUPATION OF GERMANY' and three stars.

### 336 - AMERICAN TYPHUS COMMISSION

This is a medal instituted in December 1942 and awarded by the President for meritorious service in connection with the work of the Typhus Control Commission.

### 337 - WOMEN'S ARMY CORPS SERVICE MEDAL

This is a bronze medal worn from a ribbon of dull olive green with edges of old gold awarded to members of the Women's Army Corps who belonged to the former Women's Army Auxiliary Corps. The

**338 - AMERICAN DEFENSE SERVICE MEDAL** *(Reverse)*

obverse has a helmeted female head on two branches of palm with
the words 'WOMEN'S ARMY CORPS.'

## MEDALS OF THE SECOND WORLD WAR
## AND LATER

### 338 - AMERICAN DEFENSE SERVICE MEDAL

This medal was established in June 1941 for award to personnel
of the Army, Navy, Marine Corps and Coast Guard serving during
the limited emergency proclaimed on 8 September 1939, or the
unlimited emergency proclaimed on 27 May 1941. The obverse
shows Liberty in an attitude of defence holding a shield and sword,
standing on live oak with branches terminating in four leaves
representing the Army, Navy, Marine Corps and Coast Guard.
The reverse has an inscription. Clasps, or bars were awarded to
those who served at sea or beyond the continental limit of the
United States. That for the Army has the words 'FOREIGN
SERVICE,' and those for the Navy 'FLEET' or 'BASE.' A small bronze
star is worn on the service ribbon to indicate the award of a bar,
while those in certain designated vessels of the Atlantic Fleet
between 22 June and 7 December 1941 had a bronze 'A.'

The limiting dates for the award of this medal were 8 September
1939 to 7 December 1941, the date of the Japanese attack on Pearl
Harbour and the official entry of the United States into the war.

(*Obverse*)

### 339 - EUROPEAN – AFRICAN — MIDDLE EASTERN CAMPAIGN MEDAL

This medal was instituted in 1942, and the ribbon was automatically
awarded to personnel on arrival in a theatre of war under permanent
change of station orders. Anyone not permanently in the theatre
was entitled if he served in combat operations, if he served for more
than thirty consecutive days, or a total of sixty days not necessarily
consecutive. The medal, in bronze, shows an L.S.T. and landing
craft with troops landing under fire, and an aeroplane in the background. The title of the medal appears below. The reverse shows an
American eagle between the dates '1941' and '1945.' and the words
'UNITED STATES OF AMERICA.' The ribbon is green with brown
edges, the green representing the forests and pastures of Europe
and the brown the arid hills of Africa. In the centre of the green is
a narrow stripe of blue, white and red, the colours of the United
States; to the left, separating the green from the brown, is a stripe
of green, white and red, for Italy; to the right a stripe of white, black,
white, for Germany.

### 339 - EUROPEAN – AFRICAN — MIDDLE EASTERN CAMPAIGN MEDAL (*Reverse*)

### 340 - ASIATIC – PACIFIC CAMPAIGN MEDAL

This medal was instituted in 1942, and the ribbon was automatically
awarded in the same manner as that just described. The medal is
bronze, and the obverse shows a tropical landing scene with a
battleship, aircraft carrier, submarine, and aeroplane in the background, with palm trees and troops landing in the foreground.
The title of the campaign appears above, and the reverse is the same

as that of the previous medal. The ribbon is orange, with a stripe of blue, white and red in the centre, and towards each edge a stripe of white, red, white, representing Japan.

### 341 - AMERICAN CAMPAIGN MEDAL

This medal was established in 1942, and the ribbon was granted to those who were certified to have taken part in combat operations; who were permanently transferred to a place of duty in the American theatre beyond the continental limits of the United States, or who served for thirty consecutive days at sea, or in aircraft making regular and frequent trips beyond the limits of the United States. It is the usual bronze medal, with, on the obverse, a warship at full speed with a B-24 bomber aircraft overhead. In the foreground is a sinking enemy submarine over three wave symbols; in the background a few buildings representing the arsenal of democracy, with the title above. The reverse is the same as for the two previous medals. The ribbon is bright azure blue, with a stripe of darker blue, white and red in the centre, and on each side, half-way to the edge, stripes of white, red, black, and white, representing Japan and Germany.

*Emblems on Ribbons.* Small bronze stars are worn on the service ribbons of all these last three medals to indicate 'battles' and 'campaigns' as specified in general orders, five bronze stars being replaced by one in silver.

A small bronze arrow-head, worn point up, indicates participation in a combat parachute jump, a combat glider landing, or an amphibious assault.

340 - ASIATIC – PACIFIC CAMPAIGN MEDAL *(Obverse)*

### 342 - WORLD WAR II VICTORY MEDAL

This bronze medal was authorized on 6 July 1945. On the obverse is the figure of Liberty standing full length with head turned to the left looking towards the dawn of a new day. Her right foot rests on a war god's helmet, and in her right hand she carries the hilt of a broken sword, with the blade in her left. The inscription 'WORLD WAR II' appears below. On the reverse are the inscriptions 'FREEDOM FROM FEAR AND WANT,' and 'FREEDOM OF SPEECH AND RELIGION,' separated by a palm branch, all within a circle composed of the words 'UNITED STATES OF AMERICA—1941–1945.' The ribbon is red, with a double rainbow (as for the World War I Victory Medal), at each edge, separated from the red by a narrow stripe of white.

### 343 - ARMY OF OCCUPATION MEDAL (1946)

This is a bronze medal with, on the obverse, the Remagen Bridge, and, below, the words 'ARMY OF OCCUPATION.' On the reverse is the mountain of Fujiyama, a cloud, two Japanese junks and the date '1945.' The ribbon is half black, half red, with white edges. Clasps with the words 'GERMANY' or 'JAPAN' indicate where the recipient served.

For a period a gilt aeroplane was worn with this medal to indicate service in the Berlin air lift. This symbol was abolished on the institution of the special medal mentioned below.

341 - AMERICAN CAMPAIGN MEDAL *(Obverse)*

### 344 - MEDAL FOR HUMANE ACTION

This medal was instituted in 1949 for service of at least 120 days during the period 26 June 1948 to 30 September 1949, within the boundaries of the Berlin air lift operations. The medal is in bronze, and bears on the obverse a C-54 transport aircraft within a wreath of wheat centering at the bottom in the coat-of-arms of Berlin. The reverse has the eagle shield and arrows from the seal of the U.S. Department of Defense beneath the words 'FOR HUMANE ACTION.' Above are the words 'TO SUPPLY NECESSITIES OF LIFE TO THE PEOPLE OF BERLIN, GERMANY.' The ribbon is light blue with black edges separated from the blue by narrow white stripes. In the centre of the blue are narrow stripes of white, red, white.

### NATIONAL DEFENSE SERVICE MEDAL

Established in August, 1953, for honourable active service for any period between 27 June, 1950, and 27 July, 1954. Reserve personnel on short tours of duty to fulfil training obligations under 'an inactive training programme' are not eligible. The obverse has an eagle and the words 'NATIONAL DEFENSE,' and the reverse the shield of the United States. Ribbon is red with a yellow centre, the yellow edged with narrow stripes of red, white and blue.

*(Obverse)*

### 345 - MEDAL FOR KOREA (1950)

Authorized in 1951. Obverse, the Korean taejuk (a circle divided into halves by a wavy line); reverse, a temple gateway (two uprights and a lintel) and the words 'KOREAN SERVICE.'

### MEDAL FOR VIETNAM

### 346 - ARMED FORCES RESERVE MEDAL

This medal is granted for periods of ten years' service for which one of the other reserve medals is not awarded. The ribbon has a background of deep cream on which are seven blue stripes, three on the left, one in the centre, and three on the right.

### UNIT CITATIONS

In February 1942 a system of unit citations was adopted for the Army and Navy of the United States, including, of course, the U.S. Marine Corps. In both services a very high standard is required before recommendations for citations can be forwarded, and the award is only made when the ship or unit has performed in action with such extraordinary heroism in unusually difficult and hazardous conditions as to set it apart and above other units engaged in the same or similar actions.

**NATIONAL DEFENSE SERVICE MEDAL**    *(Reverse)*

### 347 - ARMY

In the case of the army, streamers of blue gold, and red are provided for the distinguishing flags, colours, or guidons of units 'cited' in War Department general orders. If a unit is twice cited, its personnel are allowed to wear the '*Individual Decoration*,' which consists of a blue ribbon set in a gold-coloured frame of laurel leaves worn on the *right* breast above the pocket. After the second citation, all officers and men who were attached or assigned to the unit on any one of the occasions for which it was cited may wear the Individual Decoration permanently, and may add an oak leaf cluster each time their unit is again cited. Officers and men joining a cited unit, but who were not serving with it on the occasion for which an award was made, may only wear the Individual Decoration while actually assigned or attached.

## NAVY

In the Navy, the 'Presidential Unit Citation' may similarly be awarded to any ship, aircraft or Naval unit, or any Marine Corps aircraft, detachment or higher unit, for outstanding performance in action. For a ship the insignia consists of a burgee pendant design in blue, gold (yellow) and scarlet, and is ordered to be worn in peacetime at some place visible to other units. Individual aircraft, tanks, etc., of a cited unit may paint the design in any appropriate place. For ships, aircraft units, tank units, etc., there is also a bronze plaque bearing the citation insignia, with the citation engraved beneath.

If a ship or unit is cited more than once, a blue star is added for each further citation up to a total of five, and is displayed on the gold part of the insignia.

If a ship is lost, her namesake displays the bronze plaque.

After any Naval unit has been cited, the insignia becomes part of the uniform of such unit. It consists of a ribbon of 38 x 12 mm., worn as a medal ribbon, with three horizontal stripes – narrow blue at the top, narrow scarlet at the bottom, with a wider gold stripe in between. When ribbons alone are worn in service dress it appears on the left breast between personal decoration ribbons and service medal ribbons. When medals are worn it is carried on the right breast. Bronze citation stars are displayed on the gold part of the ribbon.

    (i) Personnel attached to the ship or unit on one or more occasions for which the citation was awarded wear the ribbon with one star permanently, regardless of station assignment.

    (ii) Personnel attached to the ship or unit on two or more occasions for which citations were awarded shall wear the ribbon with two stars to denote two citations, and an additional star up to a total of five for each additional citation. The ribbon and stars are worn permanently, regardless of station assignment.

    (iii) Personnel later joining a ship or unit which has been cited wear the plain citation ribbon without star only while serving in the ship or unit.

The citation was awarded to the U.S. Submarine *Nautilus* for her notable voyage from the Pacific to the Atlantic under the ice of the North Pole in 1958, and all her crew wear the ribbon with a special gold 'N.' In addition, her captain, Commander William R. Anderson, was awarded the Legion of Merit.

*(Obverse)*

**MEDAL FOR VIETNAM**
*(Reverse)*

## 348 - NAVY UNIT COMMENDATION

This medal is awarded by the Secretary of the Navy to any ships, aircraft, detachment or other unit of the U.S.N. for outstanding heroism in action against the enemy, or for extremely meritorious service not in combat, but in support of military operations, not sufficient to justify the award of the Presidential Unit Citation.

## MERCHANT MARINE DEFENSE BAR

This is the Merchant Marine counterpart of the Defense Medal. The ribbon is white with green edges. In the centre is a black stripe shading outwards into red, orange and white.

## 349 - MERCHANT MARINE COMBAT BAR

This is not a medal, but a ribbon half dark and half light blue with a narrow stripe of scarlet, edges white, in the centre. It was issued to the men of any merchant vessel attacked by the enemy, and those forced to abandon their ship were awarded a small silver star to be worn on the ribbon.

## 350 - MERCHANT MARINE (ATLANTIC WAR ZONE SERVICE BAR)

This is not a medal, but a ribbon awarded to merchant seamen, as was the campaign medal to officers and men of the Navy. The ribbon has a central stripe of darkish red edged white, shading to bright red at each border.

## 351 - MERCHANT MARINE (PACIFIC WAR ZONE BAR)

This is a bar as for the above for service in the Pacific. The ribbon has a dark red centre stripe flanked by narrow stripes of white and blue, flanked by red, shading into orange and yellow at each edge.

## 352 - MERCHANT MARINE (MEDITERRANEAN AND MIDDLE EAST BAR)

This is a bar, as above, for services indicated in the title. The ribbon is yellow with stripes of green, white, green in the centre, and of red, white and blue at each edge.

## MERCHANT MARINE (MARINER'S MEDAL)

This medal is awarded only to merchant seamen wounded in action, or who suffered physical injury, or through dangerous exposure through an act of the enemy, and to the relatives of those killed. The medal is in the shape of an eight-pointed bronze star with a large central circle bearing an eagle and an anchor. The ribbon is half red, half blue with a white stripe down the centre.

## MERCHANT MARINE (MERITORIOUS SERVICE MEDAL)

This is a bronze medal with an eagle perched on the flukes of an anchor. The ribbon is of medium blue, in the centre of which is a stripe of dark blue flanked, towards each edge, by stripes of white, red and yellow.

*Abu Dhabi*

**353- UNION DEFENCE FORCE LOYAL SERVICE MEDAL** *(Original Medal)*

**353 - UNION DEFENCE FORCE LOYAL SERVICE MEDAL**

**354 - GOOD SERVICE MEDAL WITH LONG SERVICE BAR**

*Austria*

The Republic of Austria is divided into nine provinces each of which supports a full range of civic, social, academic and sporting awards, most of which incorporate the provincial coats of arms and individual ribbon designs. Many are awarded in ascending grades. Because of the multiplicity of these awards it is only possible here to summarise the federal Orders and Decorations.

**DECORATION OF HONOUR FOR MERIT**
Characterised by one of the most attractive and colourful badges in Europe, this Order is bestowed in five classes according to the rank, status or position of the individual, rather than as the result of a strict assessment of the services rendered. The five classes conform to the conventional European divisions, but are uniquely subdivided into further grades. Instituted on 2 April 1952, the Order is bestowed upon Austrian nationals and foreigners, men or women alike, who have rendered exceptional services to the Republic or achieved outstanding merit.
i. *Grand Star*, wears the Badge in gold on a sash, and the Star in solid gold on the breast. This class is divided into the *Grand*

*Decoration of Honour in Gold with Sash* and the *Grand Decoration of Honour in Silver with Sash*. The class is applicable only to the Federal President and foreign heads of state.

ii. *Grand Decoration of Honour in Gold with Star*. In this instance the Badge in gold is worn suspended from a neck ribbon of white with a scarlet stripe near each edge. A smaller breast star in gold is worn. The second division is the *Grand Decoration of Honour in Silver with Star*.

iii. *Grand Decoration of Honour in Gold* wears the Badge in gold suspended from the neck. The second division is the *Grand Decoration of Honour in Silver*.

iv. *Grand Decoration of Honour*. In this class a slightly larger Badge in silver is worn as a breast star without ribbon.

v. *Decoration of Honour in Gold*. This consists of a smaller Badge in gold and enamel worn suspended from a chest ribbon of scarlet with a single central white stripe; the ribbon is worn crossover fashion. The second division is the *Decoration of Honour in Silver*.

The *Badge* of the Order is a gold or silver Maltese cross, enamelled red, with an inset white Greek cross; above this, and forming the suspension is an Austrian eagle in gold or silver in a semi-circle of the nine provincial coats of arms enamelled in their full colours. The *Star* of the Order omits the Maltese and Greek crosses and consists of the Federal coat of arms superimposed upon an eight-pointed gold or silver star of plain fluted rays.

Associated with the Order is the *Decoration of Merit*, awarded in either gold or silver; this is a chest decoration similar to the insignia of Class (v) above, but not enamelled; the ribbon is white with red borders. The *Medal of Merit*, awarded in gold, silver or bronze, is a circular medallion on which is a representation of the badge on the obverse, and on the reverse the inscription 'FUR VERDIENSTE UM DIE REPUBLIK OSTERREICH' – For Services to the Austrian Republic; its ribbon is scarlet with a single central white stripe.

## DECORATION OF HONOUR FOR SCIENCE AND ART
Instituted on 25 May 1955 this decoration is awarded in a single class to Austrians (limited to 36) and foreigners (also limited to 36) who have won international repute for their work in science and the arts. The Badge, which is worn suspended from a neck ribbon of plain red, consists of a narrow-limbed, white-enamelled Maltese cross superimposed on a broad-limbed, red-enamelled Maltese cross. A centre convexed medallion in gold is inscribed 'LITTERIS ET ARTIBUS' – For Science and the Arts. The suspension is formed by two stylized laurel sprigs in gold.

## CROSS OF HONOUR FOR SCIENCE AND ART
Instituted at the same time as the above decoration, the Cross is, in effect, a lower class of the Decoration. It is itself awarded in two classes, in the 1st Class of which the Badge (described above) is worn as a breast star without ribbon, and in the 2nd Class it is worn suspended from a plain red ribbon, mounted crossover fashion, on the chest.

# *Belgium*

*(Obverse)*

## 355 - ORDER OF LEOPOLD

Instituted in 1832 by Leopold I in five classes, and may be conferred upon officers for gallantry in the field and long service, and upon N.C.O.s and men for war service. The badge is carried out in white enamel, with the Belgian lion in the centre on a black ground surrounded by a crimson circular riband bearing the motto. The cross rests on a wreath of oak and laurel enamelled green, and is surmounted by a crown. The badges of the first four classes are in gold and enamel, and that of the fifth class in silver and enamel. When awarded to officers for service in the field there are crossed swords beneath the crown, while civilian badges are without the swords. When granted '*au titre maritime*,' the swords are replaced by crossed anchors. The ribbon is a deep violet colour, though officially described as 'poppy red.' When awarded to civilians who particularly distinguished themselves during the First and Second World Wars, a gold stripe near each edge or in the centre may be added to the ribbon.

## 356 - ORDER OF THE CROWN

Originally an Order of the Independent Congo State, this was instituted in 1897, and primarily designed for honouring those who 'distinguished themselves in artistic, literary or scientific work; in industrial or commercial activity; or by their devotion in works of African civilization.' There are five classes. The badge consists of a five-pointed star with V-shaped extremities enamelled white and edged gold. Between the limbs of the star are golden rays. In the centre, on a blue enamelled plaque edged gold, is the Royal Crown in gold. A laurel wreath enamelled green attaches the badge to its ribbon. The decoration of the lowest class of the Order, except for the device in the centre, is worked in silver. The ribbon is dark maroon, moiré.

Lower classes of the Order comprise gold and silver palms, and gold, silver and bronze medals, worn from the same ribbon with a white stripe near each edge. No. **357**.

In the first five classes gold stripes may be added as for the Order of Leopold.

## 358 - ORDER OF LEOPOLD II

This Order was established in 1900 in five classes, and was primarily intended 'for rewarding services rendered to the King or for marking his personal approbation.' The badge, in metal with the Belgian lion on a black background in the centre surrounded by the motto, is surmounted by a crown and is very similar to that of the Order of Leopold. The badge of the fifth class is in silver, and the higher classes in gold. Gold, silver and bronze medals are attached to the Order. The ribbon for all classes and medals is identical.

**355 - ORDER OF LEOPOLD**
*Insignia of the Fifth Class (Reverse)*

**356 - ORDER OF THE CROWN**  *Star of the Second Class*
(*Shown full size*)

(*Obverse*)

## 359 - ORDER OF THE AFRICAN STAR

This Order was created in 1888 in the usual five classes, with three medals in gold, silver or bronze, for rewarding services rendered to the Congo State and to African civilization. It is a five-pointed star, enamelled white, edged blue, with the centre of the obverse containing a small five-pointed star on a blue ground surrounded by the motto 'TRAVAIL ET PROGRÉS.' The badge rests upon a wreath enamelled green, that for the fifth class being in silver and the others gold. The ribbon, pale blue moiré with a central stripe of pale yellow, is the same for all grades and medals.

## 360 - ROYAL ORDER OF THE LION

This Order was founded in 1891 in five classes, with three medals, for rewarding merit and service in the Congo. The badge, in silver for the lowest and gold for the higher classes, is a cross pattée with white enamel limbs, edged with metal and blue enamel, the limbs separated by two Cs interlaced. The centre has a gold, crowned lion on a blue ground surrounded by the motto of the Congo, 'TRAVAIL ET PROGRÉS.' Around the centre is a second wavy circle of gold, edged blue. The reverse has a monogram and crown, and the decoration is surmounted by a crown. The ribbon, of deep violet with narrow edges of pale blue, yellow, pale blue, is a combination of the Orders of Leopold and the African Star.

**358 - ORDER OF LEOPOLD II**
*Insignia of the Fifth Class*  (*Reverse*)

233

### 361 - MILITARY CROSS

This cross was created in 1885 in two classes. The first is for rewarding officers who have completed twenty-five years' good and loyal service as officers, and the second for twenty-five years' military service. The decoration is worked entirely in gold, except that the arms of the cross are enamelled black. There is a rosette on the ribbon of the first class. The ribbon is green with a red stripe near each edge.

### 362, 363 - MILITARY DECORATION

This decoration was established in 1902 for rewarding N.C.O.s and men of the Army who by their 'conduct and service have deserved some special distinction.' There are two classes, the first for N.C.O.s with fifteen years' service, and the second for soldiers with ten years. It can be conferred, irrespective of length of service, for acts of courage and devotion. The design is carried out in gilt. If awarded for distinguished service, the ribbon is scarlet, moiré, with edges of black, yellow, red, reading outwards. For long service, the ribbon has narrow stripes of red, yellow, and black, arranged as shown in the coloured plate.

### 364 - CROIX DE GUERRE (1914–18)

This decoration was established in 1915 for those mentioned in despatches, in much the same way as its French counterpart, for acts of courage on the field of battle; or for long service at the front. It is similar to the Military Cross, but worked entirely in bronze. Circular bronze or silver emblems bearing the Belgion lion, or palms, are worn on the ribbon to indicate further 'mentions.'

### YSER MEDAL AND CROSS

This was established in 1918 for all those who took part in the battles on the Yser between 17 October and 31 October 1914. It was originally a medal, with the obverse bearing a symbolic figure and the reverse a lion above the word 'YSER.' It hung from a medallion also bearing the word 'YSER.' In 1934 four arms were added, transforming it into a cross. The badge is in greenish bronze, the ribbon being fire-red with broad black edges.

### CROIX DU FEU (1914–18)

This decoration was established in 1934 for award to all who served at the front during the First World War. The badge is bronze and consists of two oblongs placed crosswise, the upright one bearing at the foot a steel helmet on a bayonet. The ribbon is red with three narrow stripes of pale blue, one at each edge and one in the centre.

### MARITIME DECORATIONS (1914–18)

These were established in 1918 for award to seamen for devotion to the country during the First World War. There were two crosses, first and second class, in gold and silver and white enamel, with swords in the angles and the monogram 'A' in the centre, and medals in gold, silver and bronze, with crossed swords at the top.

*(Obverse)*

**363 - MILITARY DECORATION** *(Reverse)*

The ribbon for all classes is sea-green, with two groups of five narrow stripes of red, yellow, black, yellow, red. Crossed anchors in the same metal as the cross or medal are worn on the ribbon.

### CIVIC DECORATIONS (1914–18)
These are similar to the above, but without anchors and worn from a different ribbon, which is pale green with edges of red, yellow and black. With the crosses a gold stripe is worn in the centre of the ribbon. A bar of the same metal as the badge with the dates '1914–18' is worn on the ribbon.

### MEDAL OF KING ALBERT (1914–18)
This medal was established in 1919 for rewarding Belgians and foreigners who had organized, promoted or administered works of charity or humanity in aid of necessitous Belgians during the First World War. The medal is bronze, patiné, with the effigy and name of the King on the obverse. The ribbon is a purple colour, and usually has a narrow central stripe of the national colours, black, red, and yellow. If awarded for the revictualling of Belgium in 1918–19, it has two sets of the national colours cutting it into thirds.

### 365 - MEDAL 'DE LA REINE ELISABETH'
This medal was instituted in 1916 for award to women, without regard to rank or class, who distinguished themselves by personal help given to Belgian civilians or soldiers during the First World War. The medal is in dull gilt. When awarded for services to wounded or invalided soldiers it had a red enamel cross inside the laurel wreath.

### MEDAL FOR VOLUNTEERS (1914–18)
This is a bronze, oval medal with two heads facing left, one representing 1830 and the other 1914–18. The reverse has the inscription 'VOLUNTARIIS 1914/18 PATRIA MEMOR.' The ribbon is dark blue.

*(Obverse)*

YSER MEDAL      *(Reverse)*

*(Obverse)*      *(Reverse)*

365 - MEDAL 'DE LA REINE ELISABETH'

MEDAL OF KING ALBERT
*(Obverse)*

## VICTORY MEDAL (1914–18)

This medal is of the usual type adopted by all the Allies for the First World War, with the rainbow ribbon and the winged figure of Victory on the obverse, and on the reverse the coats-of-arms of the Allies and the words 'The Great War for Civilisation' in French.

## COMMEMORATIVE WAR MEDAL (1914–18)

This medal was awarded to all who served in the Belgian Army in the First World War. It is a bronze, oblong-shaped medal with the upper angles running up to a ring, and has on the obverse the head of a soldier in a steel helmet. The reverse has an inscription. The ribbon has a broad central stripe of yellow, bordered by narrow stripes of black and wider red edges. Emblems were worn on the ribbon as follows – a gilt crown for volunteers; small bars in gold or silver to denote service at the front; a small red cross to denote a wound; and a silver star for those who were disabled through wounds or sickness in war.

*(Obverse)*

## 366 - MEDAL FOR POLITICAL PRISONERS (1914–18)

This is a bronze medal instituted in 1930 for those who were imprisoned by the Germans for a month or more during the occupation.

## 367 - CROSS FOR THOSE DEPORTED (1914–18)

This is a plain Maltese cross in bronze with the dates '1914–1918' instituted in 1922 for award to persons deported from Belgium to Germany for refusal to work for the occupying power.

## MEDAL FOR CAMPAIGN IN AFRICA (1914–17)

This medal is in silver for Europeans or bronze for natives, the obverse bearing a lion with its paws resting on a rock, with a crown above. The reverse has the dates '1914–16' and the names of the principal places where fighting occurred. One bar, 'MAHENGE,' was authorized. The ribbon is pale blue with narrow yellow edges.

## COLONIAL COMMEMORATIVE MEDAL (1914–18)

This medal was instituted in 1935 for award to those whose civilian duties prevented them from participating in the fighting forces during the First World War. It is of gilt and bears a five-pointed star with tracery in the angles and a rampant lion in the centre. The ribbon is bright blue with narrow edges of the national colours.

**COMMEMORATIVE WAR MEDAL** (1914–18)    *(Reverse)*

## MEDAL FOR NATIONAL RESTORATION

This medal was awarded to those who helped the Government in the task of restoring Belgium after the First World War. It is of gilt and worn from a scarlet ribbon with a pale blue stripe near each edge.

## COMMEMORATIVE MEDAL OF THE NATIONAL COMMITTEE FOR HELP AND 'ALIMENTATION' (1914–18)

This was awarded in four classes to those who participated in the work of assistance and distribution of food during the war. The ribbon is red with white edges, and holders of the first class had a rosette.

## DECORATIONS CREATED FOR THE SECOND WORLD WAR

### 368 - CROIX DE GUERRE
This decoration was instituted in 1941 by the Belgian Government in England. The design is the same as for the Croix de Guerre of 1914–18, except that the Royal monogram on the reverse is altered from 'A' to 'L' and there is an alteration in the ribbon. Citations in various 'Orders of the Day' are indicated by the previous emblems.

### 369 - CROIX DES ÉVADÉS
This decoration was instituted by the Belgian Government in London in March 1944 in recognition of the courage and civic spirit of Belgians who, with patriotic motives and in the face of grave danger, escaped from their occupied country. It was also awarded to persons who gave evidence of a patriotic attitude during the war; who had taken part in clandestine work in occupied terri-roty; who had been detained by the enemy for not less than three months; or had travelled secretly to Belgium to take part in war activities. It could also be conferred upon those who had escaped from an enemy prison camp. The badge is bronze, and the reverse is quite plain.

### 370 - CROSS FOR POLITICAL PRISONERS (1940–45)
This is a silver Maltese cross with a large circle in the centre within which is a red triangle standing on one point and bearing the letter 'B' in black. A silver star for each six months of captivity is worn on a bar placed across the ribbon, four stars being the maximum on any one bar.

### 371 - RESISTANCE MEDAL (1940–45)
This medal was for award to those who served in or assisted the armed resistance movement during the German occupation. The reverse has a laurel wreath, the word 'RÉSISTANCE' and the dates '1940' and '1945.' The medal is in bronze.

### 372 - MEDAL FOR VOLUNTEERS (1940–45)
This is a bronze medal with, on the reverse, the word 'VOLUNTARIIS' and the dates '1940–45.'

### 373 - WAR MEDAL (1940–45)
This is a bronze medal with an inscription on the reverse. Devices are worn on the ribbon to denote certain activities – crossed swords, for those who took part in the campaign of May 1940; a red cross, for those wounded; two forks of lightning, for the service of information and action; a bronze bar, for prisoners; crossed anchors, for those who served at sea; a gold star, for those serving in the colonial public services.

### 374 - MEDAL FOR PRISONERS OF WAR (1940–45)

*(Obverse)*

**372 - MEDAL FOR VOLUNTEERS** (1940–45)
*(Reverse)*

### 375 - MARITIME MEDAL (1940–45)
This is a bronze medal instituted by the Belgian Government in England in 1941 for rewarding acts of courage in saving lives or ships endangered by the enemy. The obverse is shown in the illustration, and the Royal monogram appears on the reverse. Crossed anchors are worn on the ribbon.

### 376 - CIVIC DECORATIONS AND MEDALS (1940–45)
The decorations consist of crosses in gold and silver with the arms in white enamel, and the angles filled in with torches. The medals, in gold, bronze and silver, are of similar design with the spaces between the cross filled in with metal.

### 377 - MEDAL 'DU RÉFRACTAIRE' (1940–45)
This is a bronze medal instituted in 1951. There are three ribbons, all green moiré with two stripes of yellow, or white, or red, equally spaced across it.

### 378 - MEDAL FOR CIVIL RESISTANCE (1940–45)
This is another bronze medal.

### 379 - MEDAL OF BELGIAN RECOGNITION (1940–45)
This is an octagonal medal in gold, silver, or bronze awarded for charitable and similar work during the war. The obverse has the face of a woman representing Belgium, with an upright sword held in salute. When the medal is awarded for service to the sick or wounded there is a red cross in the wreath. The reverse has the inscription 'PATRIA GRATA. 1940–1945.'

### 380 - ABYSSINIAN CAMPAIGN (1941)
This bronze medal was awarded to those who served in Abyssinia between 6 March and 3 July 1941. The reverse has the names of engagements, 'SAYO, GAMBELA, ASOSA.' One bar, 'ABYSSINIE,' was awarded.

### 381 - AFRICAN WAR MEDAL (1940–45)
This is a bronze medal with bars showing where the recipient served.

### 382 - MEDAL FOR THE COLONIAL WAR EFFORT (1940–45)

### 383 - KOREA (1950)
This is a bronze medal entitled 'Medal commemorating foreign theatres of war' instituted by King Baudouin in September 1951. It is circular, the obverse bearing the Royal Arms in the centre surrounded by the sixteen points of a star showing a wreath of laurel between them. The reverse has the badge of the United Nations within a wreath. The award is intended as a general service medal with bars denoting the particular campaign, and the first one issued has the words 'COREE – KOREA.' In common with many Belgian awards the medal is not provided by the Government, but must be purchased by the recipient.

## MEDAL FOR WAR VOLUNTEERS
This is a bronze medal instituted in 1952 and of a different design to the Medal for Volunteers, 1940–45; but worn from the same ribbon.

## MEDAL FOR FRANCO-PRUSSIAN WAR OF 1870–71
This medal was issued in 1911, following the example of the French, to all who served in the Belgian Army or were called up for service between 15 July 1870 and 5 March 1871. The medal is in bronze and circular, and has on the obverse a crown above a shield with the lion, and on the reverse the letter 'A' and the dates '1870–1871.' The ribbon is of seven equal stripes of black, yellow, red, yellow, red, yellow, black.

## CENTENARY MEDAL (1930)
This is a silvered, octagonal medal bearing the profiles of the three Kings, Leopold I, Leopold II and Albert, issued to commemorate the centenary of independence, 1830–1930. The ribbon is white with narrow edges of the national colours.

## OTHER BELGIAN AWARDS
It is impossible to give details of numerous other Belgian decorations and medals, among which are:

The *Civic Decoration* for long service and acts of courage. There are two crosses in white enamel edged gold or silver, worn from a red moiré ribbon with three black stripes, and three medals, in gilt, silver, and bronze, with a ribbon of red with two broader black stripes narrowly edged with yellow.

There are also in existence *Industrial and Agricultural Decorations* of varying design, as well as *Special Decorations* for persons managing mutual, co-operative and agricultural societies, professional unions and provident institutions, etc. The ribbon in all cases has equal thirds of black, yellow and red, with a rosette for the first class.

*Service Stars* also exist for award to Europeans serving in the Congo, and *Service Medals* for native N.C.O.s and men, police, and native workers in agriculture, industry, etc. The ribbon for the star, and the medal for native soldiers and police is blue, and that for native workers yellow with pale blue edges and a central stripe of black, yellow, red.

# Brazil

## ORDER OF THE SOUTHERN CROSS
This Order was established in 1822 with five classes. The badge is a five-armed, white-enamelled star, edged gold, resting on a green wreath. In the centre, on a pale blue ground, are the five stars of the Southern Cross, surrounded by a garter with an inscription. The centre of the reverse has a gold female head surrounded by the

legend, 'ESTADOS UNIDOS DO BRASIL.' The decoration is surmounted by a red star with rays in the angles placed on a green
wreath. The ribbon is pale blue.

### 384 - ORDER OF MILITARY MERIT

This Order has five classes. The badge consists of a white-enamelled,
gold-edged cross with ornamental ends, with a female head on the
obverse with the words 'MERITO MILITAR.' The reverse has three
circles of gold, green and yellow, and on the outer gold circle are
the words 'REPUBLICA DOS ESTADOS UNIDOS DO BRASIL 1934.'

### 385 - ORDER OF NAVAL MERIT

### ORDER OF AERONAUTICAL MERIT

The ribbon is pale blue with three narrow white stripes equally
spaced.

———————

Four decorations were authorized for members of the Brazilian
Expeditionary Force who served in Italy in 1944:

### COMBAT CROSS

This cross is in gilt (*First Class*) or silver (*Second Class*). It consists
of a four-armed cross with ball points and rays in the angles, and
in the centre a wreath round the five stars of the Southern Cross.
The decoration hangs from a trophy of a globe with the letters
'FEB' ('Forca Expedicionaria Brasileria') resting upon an anchor,
a gun and several flags. The ribbon is red with very narrow green
edges, and when worn alone bears a small plain replica of the cross
in gilt or silver according to class.

### ORDER OF THE SOUTHERN CROSS
*Star of the Second Class      Badge of the Second Class (Reverse)*

## WAR MEDAL

This is an elaborate cross with concave ends and convex sides, with the arms enamelled yellow edged with green. In the centre is a blue circle with the five stars of the Southern Cross in gold, surrounded by a garter bearing the words 'ESTADOS UNIDOS DO BRASIL.' The cross rests upon a gilt wreath, and the reverse has the words 'MEDALHA DE GUERRA 22-VIII-1942.' The ribbon is yellow with narrow green edges.

## CAMPAIGN MEDAL

A small bronze cross with the words 'BRASIL 16-VII-1944' on the arms, and in the centre a wreath round the letters 'FEB.' The ribbon is green, red, green, and has a perforated bar with the letters 'FEB.'

## SANGUE DO BRASIL

This is an oval-shaped bronze medal awarded to those wounded in action. It has three red stars in the centre, and below a sword, point up, crossed by a scroll with the words 'SANGUE DO BRASIL.' The edge of the medal consists of an oval chaplet of leaves, and the reverse shows the heavens with the five stars of the Southern Cross, and a band bearing the words 'ORDEM E PROGRESSO.' The ribbon is red with narrow centre stripes of yellow, green, yellow.

## NAVAL MEDAL FOR WAR SERVICE

The ribbon is dark blue with a pale blue centre stripe and a narrow pale blue stripe near each edge.

## NAVY DISTINGUISHED SERVICE MEDAL

The ribbon is yellow with two narrow green stripes towards each edge, and a centre stripe of white, dark blue, white.

## NAVY CROSS

The ribbon is scarlet with a central stripe of golden yellow and a narrow white stripe near each edge.

# Czechoslovakia

## 386 - MILITARY ORDER OF THE WHITE LION 'FOR VICTORY'

This Order was instituted in February 1945 as an award for Czechoslovak citizens and foreigners for outstanding military achievements which benefited the Czechoslovak State and contributed to its victory, and also for personal gallantry in action. The Order has stars of the *First* and *Second Class*, a cross, and medals in gold and silver. The ribbon when worn alone has a miniature star or other emblem.

## 386 - THE ORDER OF THE WHITE LION

This Order is awarded only to foreigners. It is in five classes, with a chain primarily for Heads for States who are also Grand Commanders, and medals in gold and silver.

The *star* worn by members of the two highest classes has a silver lion in the centre on a coloured enamel background, surrounded by a double circle with the motto 'Pravda Vítězí' ('Truth Prevails') and two linden leaves.

The *badge* consists of a star with five rays each split into three points terminating in small globes. The rays are enamelled red and are joined by linden leaves. In the centre, within a circle, is an upright silver lion. The reverse has a centre of red enamel bearing a golden monogram surrounded by a circle of white enamel bearing the motto. The five rays of red enamel are each engraved with the arms of one of the provinces: Bohemia, Moravia, Silesia, Slovakia and Carpathian-Ruthenia. The badge hangs from its ribbon by means of an oval garland of linden leaves, crossed by two swords if awarded for military services, and by palm leaves if given for civilian achievements.

## 387 - REVOLUTIONARY CROSS (1918)

This decoration is a commemorative award granted in 1918 to all who had served in the Czecho-Slovak Legions co-operating with the French, Italian and Russian Armies and who had fought for the independence of Czecho-Slovakia. The ornate bronze cross has on the obverse the Angel of Peace trampling serpents underfoot and holding a scroll with the words 'For Freedom' in Czech. The reverse shows a man holding a flag and mounted on a winged horse, and the words as a circle joining the four arms of the cross read – 'Be on your guard. Free Nations!' The following bars may be worn on the ribbon: 'L.E.' ('Légion Étrangère'); 'Alsace'; 'Argonne'; 'Bachmatch'; 'Doss Alto'; 'Sibérie'; 'Zborov.'

## 388 - WAR CROSS (1918)

This decoration was instituted in 1918 and awarded in much the same way as the French Croix de Guerre, with emblems on the ribbon. It was superseded by the War Cross of 1939.

## 389 - THE WAR CROSS (1939)

This decoration was awarded to Czechoslovak citizens at home and to members of the Czechoslovak Army abroad who took part in the Second World War and performed some gallant act which endangered their own lives. Bronze clasps could be added to the ribbon for further acts of gallantry. The centre of the obverse has a shield bearing a lion rampant. The reverse has a shield with the Bohemian lion and the date '1939' in the centre, and on the four arms the emblems of Slovakia, Moravia, Silesia and Ruthenia.

## 390 - MEDAL FOR VALOUR

This medal was instituted in October 1940 as an award for personal gallantry in the face of the enemy. A circular bronze medal. The inscription on the obverse means 'For Valour!' The reverse has two sprays of linden and the words 'PRAVDA VÍTĚZÍ' ('Truth Prevails'), with the date '1939.'

### 391 - MILITARY MEDAL OF MERIT
This medal was awarded in two classes, silver and bronze, as a military distinction in recognition of outstanding merit during war. The obverse has three helmeted heads below the words 'ZA ZASLUHY' ('For Merit'), with the letters 'C.S.R.' beneath. The silver medal has a silver star on the ribbon.

### MEDAL OF THE SLOVAK NATIONAL RISING
This is a circular bronze medal, the obverse showing a figure playing a musical instrument surrounded by the inscription 'SLOVENSKE NARODNI POVSTANIE 29-VIII-1944.' The ribbon is dark blue with a central stripe of white, narrowly edged with red.

### COMMEMORATION MEDAL OF THE WAR OF 1939–45
This medal consists of a circular bronze wreath enclosing a sword, point down, with the Czech lion covering the point. The medal hangs from the hilt of the weapon, and the ribbon is red with a black stripe near each edge.

### COMMEMORATION MEDAL FOR VOLUNTEERS OF 1918–19
This medal consists of a plain bronze cross pattée with the Czech lion on a shield in the centre. The ribbon is pale blue with a red, white-bordered stripe near each edge.

(*Obverse*)

### ZBOROV MEMORIAL MEDAL (1947)
This is a bronze medal bearing a moustached head in a military cap facing left, and the inscription 'PRAVDA VÍTĚZÍ.' The ribbon is red with three black and two orange stripes in the centre, separated from the red on each side by a narrow white line. The ribbon has narrow black edges.

### 392 - ORDER OF THE CZECHOSLOVAK REPUBLIC (RAD REPUBLIKY)
This Order was established in 1951 and awarded for exceptional services in respect of the advancement of the State, in particular for constructive efforts in output, cultural or scientific activity, or promoting the defensive capacity of the country. The obverse has two linden branches beneath the hammer and sickle on a background representing a brick wall. Above are two flags enamelled in colour, that of Czechoslovakia in front and the Red flag behind. The badge is silver, with the linden branches, hammer and sickle, and the two linden branches for suspension in gilt. The reverse has two branches of laurel, the letters 'Č.S.R.' and the registration number. The badge is worn on the breast from a ribbon of blue, red, blue, the blue representing the colour of working dress.

### 390 - MEDAL FOR VALOUR
(*Reverse*)

### GOLD STAR OF A HERO OF LABOUR (ZLATÁ HVĚZDA HRDINY PRÁCE)

This is a gold, five-pointed star with two smaller rays between each of the limbs. The ribbon is of scarlet moiré with a gold star at the top.

### ORDER FOR SOCIALISM (RÁD SOCIALISMU)

This Order consists of a circular wreath in gold resting on five rays in gold divided by four rays in red enamel, rising from a building on a plain. On the centre ray is a red star, while the twenty small circles around the circumference are also in red enamel. The ribbon is blue moiré with a broad central stripe of red.

### ORDER FOR LABOUR (RÁD PRÁCE)

This Order consists of a red star with gold edges upon a wreath composed of ears of corn set on a cog-wheel. The centre has a circular plaque in gold with a sun-burst over two linden branches, and the words 'C Esr Praci' above. The ribbon is red with broad blue edges.

### MEDAL FOR MERIT IN CONSTRUCTION (ZA ZÁSLUHY O VYSTAVBU)

This is a circular medal, the obverse showing a red star charged with the hammer and sickle, the Czech and Red flags, two branches of linden and the letters 'Č.S.R.' below. The ribbon is scarlet moiré with two narrow central stripes of blue.

### MEDAL FOR BRAVERY

This is a circular medal, the obverse bearing two branches of linden bound together with a scroll bearing the words 'Za Statečnost,' ('For bravery'). The ribbon is blue with narrow stripes of white, blue, red in the centre.

### MEDAL FOR A PROMINENT LABOURER

This is a circular medal, the obverse bearing the hammer and sickle on a background of linden leaves with a scroll with the words 'Za Vynikajiei Práci' ('For distinguished labour'), below. The ribbon is blue with two narrow central stripes of red.

# *Denmark*

### ORDER OF THE ELEPHANT

This is the premier Order of Denmark, founded in 1462 and re-constituted by King Christian V on 1 December 1693. The insignia consists of an elephant in gold, enamelled white, with blue harness and a blue carpet on its back on which is a tower. In front of the tower sits a Moor dressed in purple with a gold spear in his hand. On one side of the elephant is a cross of five table diamonds, while the animal has another diamond on its forehead and brilliants for eyes. The star has eight points, four longer and four shorter, with five rays between the points. In the round centre on a red background is a cross surrounded by a laurel wreath. The sky-blue watered ribbon, 102 mm. wide, is worn over the left shoulder with the badge on the right hip.

## 393 - THE ORDER OF DANNEBROG

This Order is believed to have been founded by King Waldemar II in 1219, and is one of the oldest in existence. It was revived in 1671. The statutes were laid down by King Christian V in 1693, and were modified in 1808 and 1842, and again in 1952 by King Frederick IX.

The Order, which can be conferred upon ladies, is divided into what are really six classes, with a seventh class known as the 'Badge of Honour of the Dannebrog Order' in silver.

The badge consists of an oblong cross, enamelled white with red edges with a golden crown between each of the limbs, the initial and crown of Christian V in the centre, the whole surmounted by the cypher and crown of the reigning sovereign. The words 'GUD OG KONGEN' (God and the King) are on the four arms of the cross. The reverse has the dates '1219,' '1671' and '1808' in gold lettering on the white enamel, together with the initials 'W' and 'FR. VI.'

*Grand Commanders*, who consist of Royal personages only, wear the badge from a collar, with the white enamel of the cross filled in with table diamonds.

*Knights Grand Cross* wear the badge on the left hip from a sash, 102 mm. wide, passing over the right shoulder, and on the left breast a silver star charged with the cross.
(The sash for ladies is 56 mm. wide.)

*Commanders of the First Degree* wear the cross round the neck from a ribbon, 38 mm. wide, and on the left breast the cross in frosted silver edged with red enamel.

*Commanders* have the cross round the neck only.

*Knights of the First Degree* wear the badge on the breast from a folded ribbon with a rosette, and ladies from the ribbon tied in a bow with a rosette in the centre.

*Knights* wear the badge in the same way, but it is worked in silver and enamel instead of gold.

*The Badge of Honour* is of silver and is unenamelled.

The ribbon of all classes is white moiré with narrow scarlet edges.

The Order of Dannebrog, Grand Commander, was worn by the late King George VI, while the Grand Cross and junior grades were awarded to various British officers for their services during the Second World War.

**ORDER OF THE ELEPHANT**

## 394 - THE SLESVIG MEDAL

This medal was instituted in 1920 for award to the Allied forces who took part in the occupation of Slesvig during the voting before the reunion of Northern Slesvig with Denmark. It is a circular silver medal 27 mm. in diameter with the effigy of Christian X on the obverse with a legend. On the reverse are the words 'SLESVIG. 1920,' surrounded by a wreath. The medal is worn from a moiré ribbon, 27 mm. wide, of scarlet, white, scarlet in equal stripes.

### 394 - THE MEDAL OF LIBERTY

This silver medal was instituted in 1946 for foreigners and Danes living abroad who during the German occupation of Denmark rendered special service to that country. The ribbon is the same as that of the Slesvig Medal.

### 395 - MEDAL FOR PARTICIPATION IN THE WAR OF 1940-45

This silver medal (38 mm. diameter) was instituted in 1946 for award to Danish men and women who took part in the war in Allied forces.

### 396 - ROYAL MEDAL OF RECOMPENSE

This medal was instituted in 1865. It has two classes, gilt and silver, and each class is issued with or without the crown above it. On the obverse is the effigy of the reigning sovereign surrounded by his name in latin and the words 'REX DANIAE.'

### MEDAL FOR FORCES SERVING WITH THE U.N. CONTINGENT IN KOREA, 1951-53

# Egypt

NOTE – Early in 1954 the Council of Ministers approved a law creating seventeen new civil decorations and medals and regulating their wear. All the civil decorations and medals of the old régime were abolished, and those conferred before 23 July 1952 are no longer allowed to be worn. The new distinctions are to be conferred by the President on the recommendation of the Minister responsible. A list of the new awards appears at the end of this Egyptian section.

The following Orders, Decorations and Medals were in existence during the period of the monarchy:

### 397 - ORDER OF MOHAMMED ALI

This was formerly the highest award for special merit or eminent service to the country and was very rarely conferred. It comprised a collar, worn round the neck, which, with the insignia of 'Grand Cordon,' was conferred upon Royal personages or the heads of foreign states.

Otherwise there were two classes: *Grand Cordons*, with star on the left breast and broad ribbon passing over the right shoulder with badge on the left hip; *Commanders*, with smaller star on the right breast and badge worn round the neck from a narrower ribbon.

There were two medals of the Order, in gold and silver, awarded to all ranks of the Army and Navy for deeds of valour.

### THE COLLAR OF FOUAD I

This was founded in 1936, and ranked between the Collar and the Grand Cordon of Mohammed Ali. It was awarded to crowned heads, heads of foreign states and other eminent personages. There

**398 - ORDER OF THE NILE**     *Star of the Second Class*
*(Shown full size)*

*Badge of the Second Class*
*(Shown full size)*

was one class only which consisted of a double chain in gold with twelve motifs worn round the neck from which hung the monogram of Fouad I. There was no ribbon.

### 398 - ORDER OF THE NILE

This was instituted in 1915 by the Sultan of Egypt for rewarding persons who had rendered useful service to the country.

*Grand Cordon.* A star on left breast with badge on left hip from a broad ribbon passing over right shoulder.

*Grand Officer.* Smaller star on right breast with badge worn round the neck from a narrower ribbon.

*Commander.* Badge round the neck.

*Officers and Chevaliers* (Knights). Badge on left breast from a still narrower ribbon, the former having a rosette.

*The Star* in its original form was of ten points with alternate rays of gold and silver, having in its centre a five-pointed star of white enamel with a crown in gold between its two upper rays. In the centre, on azure enamel, was an Egyptian inscription meaning: 'What benefits Egypt owes to the Nile, her source of prosperity and happiness!'

The original *badge*, shown in the illustration, was similar to the star, but smaller, and was hung from its ribbon by a crown.

The various grades of the Order were conferred upon Naval and Military officers according to rank, and upon civil officials according to their salaries; and upon many British officers serving in Egypt.

247

## 399 - ORDER OF ISMAIL (presumably obsolete)

This Order was awarded in five classes, as for the Order of the Nile, for civil merit. The badge was an ornamental five-pointed star with ball tips with a circular plaque in the centre bearing an inscription in Arabic. It was suspended from a crown. The star for the *First* and *Second Classes* had a replica of the badge set upon faceted rays appearing between the five arms.

## ORDER OF EL KEMAL

This Order was instituted in 1915 exclusively for ladies and in three classes. *First Class.* Star on the left side, and a broad ribbon of light grey moiré, with a thick edging of gold tissue, passing over the right shoulder with the badge hung therefrom. *Second* and *Third Classes.* Badge on left side from a bow of narrower ribbon, the *Second Class* with a rosette. *The Star* is gold and formed of ten ornamental flowers enamelled alternately in blue and white, and, in the centre, on a ground of white enamel, the inscription 'El Kemal' in Kufic, azure lettering. In certain of the spaces between the flowers, in white enamel in high relief, are inscriptions in Kufic characters signifying 'Charity,' 'Duty,' 'Devotion,' 'Nobility,' 'Pity.'

*The Badge*, the original design of which is shown in the illustration, is similar to the star but without the Kufic characters between the flowers.

## 400 - MILITARY STAR OF FOUAD I

This decoration was instituted in 1919 for award to officers of the Egyptian Army, and attached foreign officers, mentioned in despatches for merit or distinguished services in the field or before the enemy. It consists of a five-rayed star, enamelled white, bordered gilt, with a gilt fillet down the centre of each ray, hung from a straight clasp. The centre is enamelled blue, with two crossed swords in gilt, and is surrounded by a garland of laurel in gilt on a circular red riband, with a gilt crown above. Bars may be awarded for further services. It is worn on the breast after the Order of the Nile and before all other decorations.

## MEDAL FOR BRAVERY

This is a silver medal established in 1913 for rewarding N.C.O.s and men of the Egyptian Army for gallantry in action. It corresponds to the British D.C.M. and the ribbon is pale blue.

## MEDAL FOR MERITORIOUS ACTS

This medal was established in 1917 in silver and bronze for rewarding persons, irrespective of sex or nationality, who distinguished themselves by meritorious services to the state, special acts of gallantry, saving life, or for long and loyal service to the country in any profession. Bars could be added each time a recipient merited a new distinction. It is worn on the left breast after war medals from a ribbon of purple moiré.

## MEDAL FOR DEVOTION TO DUTY
This is a similar medal to that just described and was instituted in 1920. The ribbon is a medium blue.

## 401 - ORDER OF AGRICULTURE

## 402 - ORDER FOR PUBLIC INSTRUCTION (EL MAAREF)

## 403 - ORDER FOR INDUSTRY AND COMMERCE
Each of these three Orders is in three classes.

## 404 - PALESTINE MEDAL (1948)
This is a dark bronze, seven-sided medal of irregular shape measuring 36 x 45 mm., the obverse showing Farouk in Field-Marshal's uniform, hatless, facing left. To the left is the Parliament building, to the right a mosque. At the top are the Arabic words 'Medalyen Falasteen.' The reverse shows three uniformed figures representing the three services, with Arabs, presumably refugees, in the foreground, and in the background, a village. It is dated '1948' in Arabic numerals.

## 405 - MEDAL OF MOHAMMED ALI
This medal was issued in November 1949 to all officers and men of the Egyptian Army, Navy and Air Force who served between the 19th and 26th of that month. It is not to be confused with the medals of the Order of Mohammed Ali described earlier.

## 406 - LIBERATION STAR (ARMY)
This star was issued in 1952 with a ribbon in three equal stripes of red, white and black – the red to symbolize the Army's revolution; the white, the liberation achieved through its political purges; the black, the corruption that has been abolished.

---

### EGYPT - ORDERS, DECORATIONS AND MEDALS NOW AUTHORIZED
**Order of the Nile.** In five classes, with a Collar. Ribbon 398. (See above.)

**Order of the Republic.** In five classes, with a Collar. The ribbon has a broad green centre, flanked by stripes of old gold, with narrower edges of red.

**Order of Merit.** In four classes. Ribbon deep red flanked by stripes of white with narrower edges of black.

**Order of Agriculture.** Presumably No. 401. (See above.) It is believed to have three classes.

**Order for Public Instruction (El Maaref).** Presumably No. 402. (See above.) Three classes.

**Order for Industry and Commerce.** Presumably No. 403. (See above.) Three classes.

**Order of Sports.** Three classes. The ribbon is white with green edges.

**Order of El Kemal.** In three classes. Presumably that described above after No. 399.

**Liberation Star (Army).** No. **406**. (See above.)

**Liberation Star (Police).** Ribbon green moiré, bordered from centre to edge with stripes of red, white and black.

**Military Star.** Presumably an adaptation of No. **400**. (See above.) The ribbon is moiré with five approximately equal stripes of bright blue, yellow, black, yellow, bright blue, with very narrow edge of yellow.

**Mobilisation Medal.** The ribbon has six equal stripes of blue, green, red, white, pale buff, and black.

**Shooting Medal.** Ribbon has a broad white centre with broad deep red edges and a black stripe down each red edge.

**Bravery Medal (Military).** Ribbon deep red with two broad black stripes towards the centre.

**Bravery Medal (Civil).** Ribbon as that just described with the central red stripe replaced by green.

**Medal of the Republic.** The ribbon has a broad green centre with edges of deep red, the two colours being divided by a stripe of white.

**Medal of Merit.** The ribbon is white with a broad central stripe of deep red and narrow edges of black.

**Evacuation Medal.** The ribbon is green, with central stripes of red, white and black, conjoined.

**Medal for Devotion to Duty (Military).** Ribbon is bright blue, moiré. (This is apparently the medal mentioned above before No. **401**.)

**Medal for Devotion to Duty (Civil).** Similar to that just mentioned, but ribbon has a narrow red stripe towards each edge.

**Good Conduct Medal.** The ribbon is bright blue with a broad central stripe of pale orange.

**Special Promotion.** The ribbon is moiré, half black, half crimson.

# Eire
## (Republic of Ireland)

## 407 - THE 1916 MEDAL

This medal was established by the Eire Government in August 1942 to commemorate the Easter Rising of 1916. It was mainly awarded to members of the Dublin Brigade, I.R.A. It takes precedence over all other Irish medals, and consists of a bronze star-shaped reproduction of the Army cap badge, with the letters in the centre replaced by a replica in low relief of a statue erected as a 1916 memorial in the Dublin General Post Office. There is a chased bar at the top of the ribbon, which is half orange, half green. Recipients are entitled to a pension of £10 to £15 a year, and special Government grants may be awarded in cases of financial hardship.

### 408 - THE GENERAL SERVICE MEDAL (1916–21)

This medal was awarded to all those who took part in the war which was fought intermittently throughout the country from 1916 to the signature of the treaty with Britain in 1922. It was far more freely granted than the 1916 medal. The same conditions apply as to pensions and grants in cases of financial hardship. The medal, which is of very rough design, has an armed Irish soldier on the obverse, with four crests in frames, an inscription below, and the word 'Eire' across the centre.

### THE MILITARY MEDAL FOR GALLANTRY

This medal was authorized in July 1948 for award to members of the defence forces who perform outstanding acts of gallantry in the course of their military duty, though not in war, which endanger their own life and limb. A bar may be awarded for further acts. The ribbon is green with crimson edges.

### 409 - THE GOLD MEDAL FOR VALOUR

### 410 - THE BRONZE MEDAL FOR VALOUR

Gold and bronze medals are awarded by the Department of Justice, and are the civil equivalents of the Military Medal for Gallantry. The gold medal is mainly granted for saving life at extreme personal risk. The bronze medal is awarded to civilians for brave deeds not justifying the award of the gold medal. The design of both medals is the same, the obverse bearing a winged figure with a flaming sword and shield standing upon the recumbent winged figure of death and a scythe with a semicircular inscription in Erse below. The reverse bears another inscription in Erse, together with the inscribed name of the recipient and a spray of laurel.

### 411 - THE SCOTT MEDAL FOR VALOUR

This medal is awarded to members of the Police Forces for acts of bravery in the course of their duty.

The obverse consists of four panels – the top panel bears the inscription 'WALTER SCOTT MEDAL' and the lower panel 'FOR VALOR'; on the left and right panels respectively are the American eagle and the Irish harp and sunburst. On the reverse are the arms of the Four Provinces with the inscription 'GÁRDA SIOCHÁNA NA H-EIREANN.' The name of the recipient is engraved on the top clasp. The medal takes the form of the Garda Siochana badge.

### 412, 413 - THE EMERGENCY SERVICE MEDAL

Though Eire declared her neutrality during the Second World War she took defence measures involving a very great expansion in her armed forces, and in the raising of a number of emergency services. The Army was expanded from 4,000 to nearly 50,000 in twelve months. All those who served with satisfactory conduct for the qualifying period in any of these services were eligible for the award of the 'Emergency Service Medal.'

For the Army, Navy and Air Corps the qualifying period was not

(*Obverse*)

**THE EMERGENCY SERVICE MEDAL**    (*Reverse*)

less than 365 days between the dates 3 September 1939 and 31 March 1946. For every 730 days in excess of this, recipients were entitled to a bar to their medal.

In the case of the Emergency Services, which consisted of the Local Defence and Security Forces; the Air Raid Precautions Service; the Voluntary Aid Division of the Irish Red Cross Society; and the First Aid Organization in the Air Raid Precautionary Service, the minimum qualifying period was two years, with a bar to the medal for every two years thereafter.

The medal is in bronze and circular, and is surmounted by two bronze bars – the upper bearing the inscription 'SEIRBHIS NAISIUNTA,' and the lower the dates '1939–1946.'

The obverse has the inscription 'RE NA PRAINNE' and shows the traditional figure of Eire with a sword in her right hand and holding an Irish wolfhound on a leash. The reverse has a spray of laurel, and is inscribed with the name of the service (Army, L.D.F., L.S.F., A.R.P.S., etc.), in which the recipient qualified for the award.

For the Armed Forces the ribbon is scarlet with two white central stripes; and for the Emergency Services, three equal stripes of scarlet, white, scarlet.

Those who received the medal for service in the Armed Forces and later became eligible for the award in the Emergency Services were awarded both medals.

*(Obverse)*

### 414 - THE MERCHANT SERVICE MEDAL

This medal was awarded to officers and men of Irish merchant vessels for service during the Second World War, the qualifying period being six months *at sea*, with a bar for every two years in excess of six months. The medal has the same obverse as that just described, and on the reverse is a steamship, an inscription, with a spray of laurel and the dates '1939–1946.'

### 415, 416 - THE SERVICE MEDAL

This medal is awarded to members of the Defence Forces below commissioned rank for ten years' service with good conduct. A bar is added after another five years. The ribbon is plain blue for the ten-year award, and blue with a central stripe of gold when the bar is awarded.

**THE SERVICE MEDAL**
*(Reverse)*

### 417 - THE IRISH RED CROSS MEDAL

This medal is awarded for long service or outstanding work 'in the cause of suffering humanity.'

# *Finland*

## ORDER OF THE CROSS OF LIBERTY

Originally instituted on the recommendation of the then Commander-in-Chief, Baron Carl Gustav Mannerheim, on 4 March 1918, the Order of the Cross of Liberty was subject to new Statutes for the so-called Winter War of 1939–40, and in December 1940 was re-instituted as a permanent Order and as such is now regarded as the nation's premier award. The present statutes were promulgated on 18th August 1944. The Order is conferred in both military and civil divisions for services by subjects and foreigners in the interests of the security of the state.

The Order is conferred in four classes: *The Grand Cross of the Cross of Liberty*, and *The Cross of Liberty, 1st Class*. The insignia is a large Badge, with or without oakleaves, on a sash, and the Star of the Order.

*The Cross of Liberty, 2nd Class*, of which the insignia is a smaller Badge, with or without oakleaves, suspended from a chest ribbon.

*The Cross of Liberty, 3rd Class*, of which the insignia is a yet smaller Badge, without oakleaves, suspended from a chest ribbon.

*The Cross of Liberty, 4th Class*, of which the insignia is a silver Badge suspended from a chest ribbon.

The *Star* consists of a circular gold medallion mounted on a five-pointed silver star of faceted rays, the five points being three rays of equal length. If awarded for military services there are crossed swords with hilts below the medallion. In the centre of the medallion is a white rose on a stylized swastika on a black-enamelled ground surrounded by the inscription 'ISÄNMAAN PUOLESTA' – For the Fatherland. The Badge of the 1st Class is a white-enamelled Cross of St. George with a superimposed stylized swastika on its arms, in the centre a white rose on a black circular ground, the badge being suspended by a wreath and oakleaves (if awarded) from a scarlet ribbon with narrow white stripes near the edges. The Badge of the 3rd Class is a smaller variation of the above, the cross being enamelled in black and the rose fashioned in gold. The Badge of the 4th Class is similar in size to that of the 4th Class, but is of blue-enamelled silver and is suspended from a yellow ribbon with two narrow scarlet stripes near the centre.

*The Mannerheim Cross of the Cross of Liberty* is an associated award made for outstanding bravery and meritorious actions in war, and is conferred upon members of the armed forces irrespective of rank in two classes. The insignia of the 1st Class is a large variation of the black-enamelled Cross with a white central rose, worn suspended from a neck ribbon of scarlet with white stripes

253

near the edges, and the insignia of the 2nd Class is a smaller variation of this, worn on the chest without ribbon. In the event of a
second award, crossed field marshal's batons in black, tipped with
gold, are worn.

The *Medal of Liberty* is awarded to the armed forces in two
classes, of which the 1st Class, if awarded with a rosette, is the
highest military decoration. The medal of the 1st Class is a circular
silver medal with the Finnish lion in the centre, surrounded by the
inscription 'URHEUDESTA – FÖR TAPPERHET,' meaning From the
People of Finland – For Bravery. The ribbon is of bright blue with
a narrow white stripe near each border. The medal of the 2nd Class
is similar but in bronze, and is suspended from a scarlet ribbon
with broad yellow stripes near the borders.

Also associated with the *Cross of Liberty* are the *Cross of Liberty
3rd and 4th Classes with Red Cross* (in which a Geneva Red Cross
replaces the central white rose on the badges), and the *Cross* and
*Medal of Mourning of the Cross of Liberty* awarded to the nearest
relatives to the fallen in each relevant instance. In each instance
the chest ribbon is in black.

It is said that there are more than 40 variations of award in the
Order of the Cross of Liberty. When awarded to foreigners, the
insignia is to be returned to the state by the relatives of a deceased
recipient.

## ORDER OF THE WHITE ROSE

Instituted by Baron Mannerheim on 28 January 1919, the Order
of the White Rose may be conferred, in any of five classes, in times
of peace or war, to Finnish subjects or foreigners for services to
Finland. It may also be awarded for bravery in the field. The five
classes are:

*Commander Grand Cross*, of which the insignia consists of the
Badge, worn on a collar or sash, and the Star of the Order.

*Commander 1st Class*, in which the Badge is worn suspended
from a neck ribbon, and a slightly smaller variation of the Star.

*Commander*, in which only the Badge is worn, suspended from a
neck ribbon.

*Knight* or *Member 1st Class*, in which the Badge in gold is worn
suspended from a ribbon on the chest.

*Knight or Member*, in which the Badge, in silver, is worn suspended from a ribbon with rosette on the chest.

The *Collar* consists of gold swastikas interspersed with white
roses, linked by a double gold chain, and is reserved for bestowal
upon the Grand Master of the Order (the President of Finland)
and, as a mark of courtesy, upon certain other heads of state. The
*Badge* is a Cross of St. George, enamelled white (except in the
Knight or Member class, and in the Medal, when the cross is in
silver and gold respectively), with a white rose in a central medallion. Between the arms of the cross are Finnish lions. The *Star*
consists of a five-pointed silver-faceted star, the points being of
three rays of equal length. In the instance of the star worn by the
Commander Grand Cross the three central rays between the points

**ORDER OF THE WHITE ROSE**       *Star of the First Class*                *Badge of the Second Class*
                                          *(Shown full size)*                         *(Shown full size)*

are in gold, but otherwise the entire star is in silver. In the centre of the star is a medallion, in the centre of which is a white rose on a blue ground, surrounded by the inscription 'ISÄNMAAN HYVÄKSI' (For the Good of the Fatherland) in gold on a black circlet. All classes of the Order may be bestowed 'with diamonds,' in which case the diamonds are mounted upon the central rose, and in the case of the two senior classes on the star around the central medallion as well.

The *Badge of the White Rose* may be awarded in bronze with crossed swords for gallantry in war.

The *Medal of the White Rose* may be awarded in three classes: *1st Class with Gold Cross, 1st Class* in silver and *2nd Class* in bronze. The medal is a representation of the Badge on a circular medallion and is suspended from a chest ribbon. The ribbon of the Order is plain royal blue.

(NOTE. A redesign of the *Collar* has recently been undertaken, replacing the swastikas of the chain by a form of stylized spruce branches in the geometric form of a chamfered and faceted cross.)

## ORDER OF THE LION OF FINLAND

This Order was instituted on 11 September 1942 and may be conferred both upon Finns and foreigners for civic and military services to the state. It has five classes:

*Commander Grand Cross*, in which the Badge is worn from a sash and the Star on the breast.

*Commander 1st Class*, in which the Badge is worn suspended from a neck ribbon (with swords, when conferred), and a small Star on the breast.

*Commander*, in which the Badge only is worn suspended from a neck ribbon (with swords, when conferred).

*Knight, 1st Class*, in which the Badge is worn on a chest ribbon with rosette (with swords, when conferred).

*Knight*, in which the Badge is worn on a chest ribbon without rosette.

The *Badge* is a white-enamelled Cross of St. George (in gold for the first three classes, and in silver for Knights) with a central medallion bearing the Finnish lion in gold on a red ground, surrounded by a gold circlet. When awarded 'with swords,' the hilts appear below the horizontal arms of the cross, the points above. The *Star* is a five-pointed star of faceted rays, in gold and silver for the Commander Grand Cross, and in silver only for the Commander 1st Class. The ribbon of the Order is plain scarlet.

Associated with the Order are the *Cross of Merit of the Order of the Lion of Finland*, awarded to civilians in government service and non-commissioned officers. This is a silver representation of the Cross, suspended from a decorative ring and a chest ribbon. The *Pro-Finlandia Medal*, also associated with the Order, is a silver-gilt, circular medal bearing, on the obverse the Finnish lion, and on the reverse the inscription 'PRO FINLANDIA' and the recipient's name. The medal, which is also worn suspended from the scarlet ribbon on the chest, is awarded for services to the Arts.

## ORDER OF THE HOLY LAMB

Instituted by the Greek Orthodox Catholic Church of Finland on 20 June 1935, this Order is conferred irrespective of the recipient's creed and nationality. Its Grand Master is the Greek Orthodox Archbishop of Finland, and it is conferred in five classes:

*Commander Grand Cross*, in which the insignia is the Badge, worn from a sash of pale blue with narrow white stripes near the borders, and the Star of the Order on the breast.

*Commander, 1st Class*, in which the Badge is worn suspended from a neck ribbon, and the Star of the Order on the breast.

*Commander, 2nd Class*, as above but without the Star.

*Knight*, or *Member 1st Class*, in which the Badge, in gold, is worn suspended from a chest ribbon.

*Knight*, or *Member 2nd Class*, in which the Badge, in silver, is worn suspended from a chest ribbon.

The *Badge* is a narrow-armed cross enamelled blue with a central medallion bearing the Lamb of God (*Agnus Dei*) in gold on a white ground. Between the arms of the cross are stylized seraphims with outstretched wings in gold. The *Star* of the Order is an enlarged variation of this design; in the centre of the cross is an enlarged medallion bearing the Lamb of God with a circlet carrying the inscription 'KIRKON HYVÄKSI' (For the Benefit of the Church) on a black ground. The seraphims between the arms of the cross are enlarged so that the tip of their wings form the points of an eight-pointed star; they are in gold for the Commander Grand Cross, and in silver for the class of Commander.

Associated with this Order is the *Medal of the Holy Lamb,* in *gold* and *silver,* this medal being a miniature representation of the Badge upon a circular medallion and is worn on the chest, suspended from the ribbon of the Order which is pale blue with a white stripe near the borders.

# *France*

*Badge of the First Class (Obverse)*          *Badge of the First Class (Reverse)*

### 418 - THE LEGION OF HONOUR

### 418 - THE LEGION OF HONOUR
The 'Légion d'Honneur' was instituted by Napoleon I on 19 May 1802 for rewarding distinguished military and civil services. Before this date there was no special award which could be bestowed upon civilians, though swords of honour, muskets of honour and other

weapons could be granted to soldiers and sailors for gallantry in war. The original cross was a white-enamelled gold badge, with five rays with double points. Between the arms of the cross appeared a green enamel wreath of oak and laurel, while in the centre of the obverse, on a silver gilt ground, was the effigy of Napoleon, surrounded by a riband of blue enamel, with the inscription 'NAPOLÉON, EMP. DES FRANÇAIS' in gold lettering. The reverse was similar but bore the Imperial eagle in the centre, with the words 'HONNEUR ET PATRIE' on the blue riband. The badge after 1806 was surmounted by an Imperial Crown for suspension. The present badge is much the same, but has on the obverse the female head symbolic of the Republic, surrounded by the blue riband bearing the words 'RÉPUBLIQUE FRANÇAISE.' (The date '1870' was recently removed.) The reverse has two crossed tricolor flags with the wording 'HONNEUR ET PATRIE.' A green enamel wreath is provided for suspension in place of the crown. The Order is divided into five grades, 'Grands Croix,' 'Grands Officiers,' 'Commandeurs,' 'Officiers' and 'Chevaliers.'

*Grands Croix* wear a gold badge suspended on the left hip by a broad scarlet watered ribbon passing over the right shoulder and on the left breast a silver star.

*Grands Officiers* wear the badge in gold on the left breast and on the right breast a silver star similar to that of a Grand Croix.

*Commandeurs* wear the badge round the neck on a scarlet ribbon.

*Officiers* wear the badge on the left breast suspended from a scarlet ribbon with a rosette in the centre.

*Chevaliers* wear a similar badge in the same place but without the rosette. The badge for Chevaliers is white enamel on silver, but all superior grades have it white enamel on gold.

The Legion of Honour is the premier order of the French Republic and is only conferred for gallantry in action or for twenty years' distinguished military or civilian service in peace. The Order can be bestowed upon foreigners. When given for war services it carries with it the automatic award of the Croix de Guerre with palm.

**418 - THE LEGION OF HONOUR**
*Badge of the Second Class*

### 419 - MÉDAILLE MILITAIRE

This is the French counterpart of the Distinguished Conduct Medal, established in 1852. It is awarded only to general officers in command of Armies or admirals in command of Fleets, and to non-commissioned officers of the Army and Navy who specially distinguish themselves in war. The decoration has a silver rim formed of a wreath of laurel leaves tied at top and bottom with narrow gilt ribbons. In the centre of the obverse is a gilt female head symbolic of the Republic on a roughened gilt ground, the whole being surrounded by a narrow riband of blue enamel bearing the words 'RÉPUBLIQUE FRANÇAISE.' (The date '1870' was recently removed.) The centre of the reverse has the words 'VALEUR ET DISCIPLINE.' Above the medal is a trophy of arms consisting of crossed cannons, a cuirass, anchor, swords and muskets and above this is the ring through which the yellow, green-edged ribbon passes.

*(Original Medal)*
**419 - MÉDAILLE MILITAIRE**

### 420 - CROIX DE GUERRE

This decoration was established on 8 April 1915 to commemorate individual mentions in despatches. The cross is awarded to soldiers or sailors of all ranks, officers included, and also to officers and men of Allied Forces, mentioned in French despatches, for an individual feat of arms mentioned in a despatch from the general officer commanding an Army, Army Corps, Division, Brigade, or the C.O. of a regiment, or the corresponding units of Naval forces. The different classes of despatches for which a recipient was awarded the cross may be recognized by the following emblems on the ribbon: Army Despatch – small bronze laurel branch (Palme en bronze); Army Corps Despatch – silver gilt star; Divisional Despatch – silver star; Brigade, Regimental or similar Unit Despatch – bronze star.

Every mention is represented by its emblem, thus a man can wear the cross with say the silver star and the bronze palm. When a recipient has been awarded five bronze palms, he wears instead of them a silver palm.

In the 1939–45 campaigns a different ribbon, No. **421**, was adopted and in certain cases the Head of the Republic was replaced by crossed tricolors.

### 422 - CROIX DE GUERRE DES THÉATRES D'OPÉRATIONS EXTÉRIEURS

The original Croix de Guerre was intended only for award for services in Metropolitan France. In 1921 a similar decoration, but hung from a different ribbon, was instituted for award to French and Colonial troops serving abroad. The obverse is the same, but the reverse bears the words 'THÉATRE D'OPÉRATIONS EXTÉRIEURS' instead of year dates.

*(Obverse)*

*(Obverse)*                         *(Reverse)*

**422 - CROIX DE GUERRE DES THÉATRES D'OPÉRATIONS EXTÉRIEURS**

*(Reverse)*

**420 - CROIX DE GUERRE**

### 420 - ST. HELENA MEDAL

This medal was granted in 1857 to all soldiers and sailors who had taken part in the wars lasting from 1792 to 1815. It is of bronze and bears on one side the effigy of Napoleon I and on the other, in embossed letters 'CAMPAGNES DE 1792–1815 À SES COMPAGNONS DE GLOIRE, SA DERNIÈRE PENSEE. SAINT HÉLÈNE 5 MAI 1821.' The ribbon of this medal was reissued with the Croix de Guerre in 1915.

### 423 - MEDAL FOR ITALY (1859)

This is a silver medal granted to all those in the French Forces who took part in the war in Italy against Austria in 1859. The obverse consists of a wreath surrounding the head of Napoleon III and the reverse bears the names of the following battles: 'MONTEBELLO, PALESTRO, TURBIGO, MAGENTA, MARIGNAN, SOLFERINO,' with the legend 'CAMPAGNE D'ITALIE 1859.' The medal was also awarded to the Sardinian troops who were allied to the French.

### CRIMEAN AND BALTIC MEDALS (1854–5)

French soldiers and sailors who took part in the Crimean War and the expedition to the Baltic were presented by Queen Victoria with the British medals for these campaigns. Unofficial bars were struck in France for the Crimea medal – 'TRACKTIR. KINBURN. MAMELON VERT. MALAKOFF.'

### CHINA MEDAL (1861)

This silver medal was granted to those who took part in the Anglo-French China Expedition of 1860. The obverse is the same as that of the Italy Medal, while the reverse has the names 'TA-KOU. CHANG-KIA-WAN. PA-LI-KAO. PE-KING.' Also the legend 'EXPÉDITION DE CHINE 1860.' The ribbon is yellow with the two Chinese characters Pe Kin, in blue.

### MEXICO MEDAL

This medal was awarded in 1863 to those who took part in the expedition to Mexico in 1862–3. It is silver with the same obverse as before while the reverse bears the legend 'EXPÉDITION DU MEXIQUE 1862–3' and the names 'CUMBRES. CERRO-BORREGO. SAN LORENZO. PUEBLA. MEXICO.' The ribbon is white with the Mexican eagle in black holding a green snake in its mouth, upon a saltire of red and green.

### PONTIFICAL CROSS

This medal was awarded by Pope Pius IX to all members of the French Expeditionary Force, but more particularly to the Papal Zouaves who took part in the defence of Rome in 1867 and who actually landed in the Pontifical States up to 3 November 1867. It is a small, silver four-armed cross with a large circular centre bearing the Papal arms, and the reverse bears the words 'PIUS IX 1867' and the motto 'HINC VICTORIA.' The decoration was worn from a ribbon of five equal stripes of white, blue, white, blue, white, or of yellow moiré with broad white edges. A similar decoration was later awarded by Pope Leo XIII with a ribbon of three pale blue stripes and two white.

**420 - ST. HELENA MEDAL**
(*Obverse*)

**424- CHINA MEDAL** (1900–1)

**424 - TONKIN MEDAL**
'CAU GIAI'          (*Reverse*)

**424 - TONKIN MEDAL**
*(Obverse)*

*(Obverse)*

*(Reverse)*

**426 - DAHOMEY MEDAL**

*Bar:* 'DAHOMEY'

*(Obverse)*

### 424 - TONKIN MEDAL (1883–93)

This silver medal was instituted in 1895 and granted to all those who took part in the operations against China and Annam between 1883 and 1885 and also for the operations after 1885 in Tonkin, Annam, Cambodia, Siam and Mekong. The obverse bears the female head of the Republic in an ornamental border, and on the reverse the legend. 'TONKIN CHINE ANNAM 1883–1885,' and an inscription 'SONTAY. BAC-NINH. FOU-TCHÉOU. FORMOSE. TUYEN-QUAN. PESCADORES.' The Naval medal also had the inscription 'CAU GIAI' in addition to the above. The same ribbon was afterwards used for the China Medal of 1900–1.

### 425 - MADAGASCAR MEDAL (1885, 1894–95)

A silver medal authorized in 1886 and granted to those who had taken part in the Madagascar Campaign of 1885. The obverse is the same as that of the Tonkin Medal, while the reverse bears the words 'MADAGASCAR 1885–6.' The second medal, granted to all those who took part in the expedition of 1894–5, had the same ribbon bearing an ornate bar with date '1895.'

### 426 - DAHOMEY MEDAL

This is a silver medal granted in 1892 to those who had taken part in the Dahomey and Soudan campaigns in previous years. The obverse is the same as for the Tonkin Medal, while the reverse bears the word 'DAHOMEY.'

### 427 - COLONIAL MEDAL

This is a silver medal established in 1893 and granted to those who have taken part in wars, operations or expeditions in the French colonies or protectorates. It corresponds to our 'general service' medals. On the obverse appears the usual head of the Republic and on the reverse the terrestrial globe on a trophy of flags with

**427 - COLONIAL MEDAL**
*(Reverse)*

the legend 'MÉDAILLE COLONIALE.' A bar is always seen on the ribbon stating the service for which the decoration has been awarded, and they were granted retrospectively for colonial expeditions as far back as 1830. The following gold bars have been issued: 'DE L'ATLANTIQUE À LA MER ROUGE' for the Marchand Expedition, 'MISSION SAHARIENNE,' 'GABON CONGO,' 'CENTRE AFRICAIN,' while there are more than thirty silver bars up to post-1945 ones for 'EXTRÊME-ORIENT' and 'INDOCHINE.'

### 428 - MOROCCO MEDAL

This, a silver medal, was granted in 1909 as a general service medal for operations in Morocco. The obverse bears the female head symbolic of the Republic, and the reverse a military design with the word 'MAROC.' It hangs from its ribbon by means of two branches of laurel and a crescent. Various bars have been awarded with it among which are those lettered 'CASABLANCA,' 'OUDJDA,' 'HAUT-GUIR' and 'MAROC.'

### 429 - MEDAL FOR THE WAR OF 1870-1871

This bronze medal was awarded in 1911 to all the old combatants of the war of 1870–1 who served in France and Algeria between the months of July 1870 and February 1871, inclusive. The obverse bears the head of the Republic and the reverse the dates and a trophy of arms and flags. Volunteers received a silver bar with the words 'ENGAGÉ VOLONTAIRE.'

### GENEVA CROSS (1870–71)

This decoration, recognized by the British Government, was awarded by the French Society for Succouring the Wounded, to many people who assisted in this work during the Franco-Prussian War. It was bestowed upon the Prince of Wales (later King Edward VII), various British doctors, nurses and civilians, and was issued in silver and bronze. The decoration is in the form of a Roman cross with a raised edge. The ground of the obverse is lined perpendicularly and bears, in raised characters, '1870' on the upper limb and '1871' on the lower. Running across the transverse limbs is the inscription 'SOCIÉTÉ FRANÇAISE DE SECOURS AUX BLESSÉS DES ARMÉES DE TERRE ET DE MER.' The reverse is plain but sometimes has the name of the recipient engraved upon it. The decoration hangs by means of a ring from a white unwatered ribbon with a red cross in the centre.

### 430 - SPECIAL RIBBON FOR THOSE WOUNDED (INSIGNE DES BLESSÉS MILITAIRES)

This ribbon was adopted in 1916 as the special distinguishing mark of those men of the French Army and Navy who were wounded during the First World War, or who were invalided through wounds or illnesses contracted or aggravated on service. The ribbon is of watered silk with blue, white and yellow stripes with a narrow red stripe in the centre. A small metal five-pointed star, enamelled crimson, is worn on the central red stripe. The medal is a red-enamelled star on a gilt wreath.

**GENEVA CROSS** (1870–71)
(*Obverse*)

**430-INSIGNE DES BLESSÉS MILITAIRES**                          (*Obverse*)

## 431 - MÉDAILLE DE LA RECONNAISSANCE FRANÇAISE

This medal, established by the French Government in 1917, was designed for the purpose of rewarding and distinguishing those persons who performed acts of devotion in the public interest in war. The award is selective and is not granted for the accomplishment of ordinary military duties, for simple liberality or for occasional participation in the various works of benevolence or assistance. Conferred by decree it has three classes; silver-gilt, silver and bronze. The ribbon of the silver-gilt medal has a rosette, the silver a blue star. An alternative obverse is a woman facing left, holding a branch in both hands. The medal was conferred upon various British subjects in both World Wars.

## 432 - COMMEMORATIVE MEDAL OF THE GREAT WAR (1914–18) (MÉDAILLE COMMÉMORATIVE DE LA GRANDE GUERRE)

This was the first medal instituted after the First World War. Authorized by a law of 23 June 1920 it was conferred on all soldiers and sailors mobilized between 2 August 1914 and 11 November 1918. Male nurses, doctors, chemists, welfare workers, nurses, police, civil guards, and firemen of the towns that had been bombarded could claim it. Women drivers, telephonists and secretaries in the Army were also entitled provided they were employed for at least six months. Volunteers received a bar 'ENGAGÉ VOLONTAIRE.'

## 433 - MEDAL FOR VICTIMS OF THE INVASION (MÉDAILLE DES VICTIMES DE L'INVASION)

This medal was authorized in June 1921 for hostages of the First World War, persons deported out of France, imprisoned by the enemy or condemned to hard labour. There were three classes – bronze, silver and silver-gilt. The two bars awarded with this medal were 'OTAGE DE GUERRE' and 'PRISONNIER POLITIQUE.'

## MEDAL OF SYRIA AND CILICIA MÉDAILLE DU LEVANT

This medal was authorized in July 1922 for soldiers belonging to the Army of the Levant and to Naval officers and men who had operated on the Syrian-Cilician coast between 11 November 1918 and 20 October 1921, and to those who after this date took part in certain other battles. It was awarded by the Vichy Government for the campaigns in 1941 and bore a bar 'LEVANT 1941.' The ribbon is in horizontal wavy stripes of pale blue and white.

## INTERALLIED VICTORY MEDAL (MÉDAILLE INTERALLIÉE DITE 'DE LA VICTOIRE')

This medal was authorized in July 1922. The ribbon is the same as for the British Victory Medal. It was awarded to a large variety of applicants, including civilian nurses and all combatants.

## MÉDAILLE COMMÉMORATIVE DU LIBAN

This medal was instituted in 1926 for French troops who repelled invasion of Libanese territory. The obverse bears an upright palm

*(Obverse)*

**431 - MÉDAILLE DE LA RECONNAISSANCE FRANÇAISE** *(Reverse)*

**432 - MÉDAILLE COMMÉMORATIVE DE LA GRANDE GUERRE** *(Obverse)*

*(Obverse)*     *(Reverse)*         *(Obverse)*     *(Reverse)*

**434 - MEDAL OF THE ORIENT**     **435 - MEDAL OF THE DARDANELLES**

branch with crossed swords at foot, and the reverse a mountain scene with setting sun. The ribbon is red with six blue stripes.

### MÉDAILLE DU MÉRITE LIBANAIS

This is a bronze medal with a native figure defying a raging lion, and a castle in the background. The ribbon is blue-white-red with an embroidered cedar tree in the centre of the white.

### 434 - MEDAL OF THE ORIENT
### (MÉDAILLE D'ORIENT)

### 435 - MEDAL OF THE DARDANELLES
### (MÉDAILLE DES DARDANELLES)

This medal was instituted in June 1926 for award to military and civil persons who embarked before 11 November 1918 for one of the units or services of the French Expeditionary Force in the Dardanelles or the French Army of the East.

At the request of the ex-servicemen of the Dardanelles, two medals were created with ribbons of different colours, white with five green stripes for the Dardanelles and pale blue with yellow centre and narrow yellow stripes near the edges for the Orient.

### 436 - MEDAL FOR ESCAPED PRISONERS
### (MÉDAILLE DES ÉVADÉS)

This medal was created by decree of 20 August 1926 to commemorate escapes accomplished by prisoners of war during 1914–18, and later extended to cover 1939–45. Soldiers or sailors killed or deceased as a result of injuries received during an escape have a posthumous title to this decoration.

### 437 - COMBATTANT VOLONTAIRE

This is a cross awarded to those who volunteered for combatant service in any war.

*(Obverse)*

**436 -**     *(Reverse)*
**MÉDAILLE DES ÉVADÉS**

### 438 - COMBATANTS' CROSS (CROIX DU COMBATTANT)
This decoration was created by decree of 24 August 1940 and granted to those who have the combatants' card.

### 439, 439A- VOLUNTARY MILITARY SERVICES (SERVICES MILITAIRES VOLONTAIRES)
This is an ornamental cross awarded for services indicated by the title. There are three classes; first, which has a rosette on the ribbon which has three equal-sized stripes of bright blue, scarlet, blue with narrow white stripes near the edges; second, the same without rosette; third, the same without rosette and a ribbon without white edges.

### 440 - ORDRE DE LA LIBÉRATION
This Order was created by General de Gaulle in November 1940 to reward distinguished services rendered to the cause of the liberation of France. It could be bestowed upon civilians as well as upon soldiers, sailors and airmen. Holders are styled 'Compagnons de la Libération.' The decoration, known as the Liberation Cross, has a sword on a square shield with a black Lorraine cross upon it. The reverse has the inscription 'PATRIAM SERVANDO VICTORIAM TULIT.' The ribbon is green with black edges and two narrow black stripes in the centre, which symbolized France's mourning and hope.

### 441 - MÉDAILLE DE LA RÉSISTANCE FRANÇAISE
On 9 February 1943 General de Gaulle created a new decoration to be given to those whose actions in active resistance to the enemy merited such award. The medal was meant to be more widely awarded than the Croix de la Libération. It is circular and inside a raised rim shows a cross of Lorraine.

*(Obverse)*

438 - *(Reverse)*
**CROIX DES COMBATTANTS**

*(Obverse)*     *(Reverse)*
**439 - SERVICES MILITAIRES VOLONTAIRES**

### FREE FRENCH FORCES MEDAL (MÉDAILLE DES FORCES FRANÇAISES LIBRES)

This is a double silver cross hanging from a dark blue ribbon with narrow red diagonal stripes and bearing the words 'FRANCE LIBRE.'

### MEDAL FOR VOLUNTEERS (MÉDAILLE DES ENGAGÉS VOLONTAIRES)

This is a bronze medal bearing a helmeted head. On the reverse is a trophy of arms and the words 'HONNEUR ET PATRIE.' The ribbon is green with yellow edges. There is a bar with the words 'ENGAGÉ VOLONTAIRE.'

### MEDAL FOR PRISONERS (MÉDAILLE DES PRISONNIERS)

This is a bronze medal bearing an erect female figure with a bowed head. The ribbon is red with narrow green edges with a blue stripe in the centre narrowly edged with white.

### MEDAL OF LIBERATED FRANCE (RECONNAISSANCE DE LA FRANCE LIBÉRÉE)

This medal was authorized in 1947 to commemorate the liberation of France and awarded to French nationals or allies who made a notable contribution to the Liberation. It bears a map of France surrounded by a chain broken in the top left and lower right corners. The ribbon is two rainbows from red on either edge to purple in the centre.

### 442 - COMMEMORATIVE MEDAL OF THE SECOND WORLD WAR

This is a bronze, hexagonal medal bearing on the face a Gallic cock on a Lorraine cross and on the reverse the words 'RÉPUBLIQUE FRANÇAISE, GUERRE 1939/45.' Numerous bars were granted.

### CAMPAIGN AGAINST ITALY

A medal has recently been authorized for award to those who took part in the fighting against Italy during the Second World War. Ribbon, seven red, six white equal stripes.

### MEDAL FOR INDO-CHINA

Authorized in 1953. Ribbon, green with four yellow stripes.

### MEDAL FOR CIVILIAN WOUNDED

This medal consists of a white-enamelled star on a gilt wreath with a grey ribbon having a broad centre stripe and two narrow edge stripes of yellow. When the medal is not worn a silver star is worn on the ribbon.

### 443, 444 - MEDAL FOR THOSE DEPORTED OR INTERNED DURING THE RESISTANCE (1939–45)

This medal has five sides, depending from one of the flat sides.

**BARS TO COMMEMORA-
TIVE MEDAL OF THE
SECOND WORLD WAR**

**CAMPAIGN AGAINST ITALY**
*(Obverse)*

The obverse bears two hands crossed and chained at the wrists with flames in the rear.

### 445 - MEDAL FOR KOREA
This is a bronze medal authorized in January 1952 bearing a Korean symbol surrounded by a wreath; above is an urn with flame, by which the medal is suspended from a temple.

### 446 - MÉDAILLE COMMEMORATIVE DE RHÉNANIE

### 447 - MÉDAILLE DE HAUTE SILESIE

### 448 - MÉRITE MARITIME
This Order is divided into three grades, Commandeur, Officier and Chevalier. The badge consists of an eight-pointed star in white enamel, divided by eight smaller points in gold. On the obverse within a blue enamel circle, pierced by a silver anchor, are the words 'RÉPUBLIQUE FRANÇAISE' surrounding a full-faced female head in gold symbolic of the Republic. The reverse is similar except for the words 'MARINE MARCHANDE' on the blue circle and the words 'MÉRITE MARITIME' in place of the head in the centre gold circle.

### 449 - PALMES UNIVERSITAIRES
Instituted in 1808, in two classes, 'Officier de l'Instruction Publique' and 'Officier d'Académie,' and awarded on the recommendation of the Minister of Education to those who have specially distinguished themselves by eminent services in connection with teaching, and to learned, literary and scientific men who have done particularly brilliant work. 'Officiers de l'Instruction Publique' wear the decoration in gold with a rosette on the ribbon, while 'Officiers d'Académie' have it in silver without rosette. At least five years must be spent in the lower grade. A higher class, that of 'Commandeur,' with the decoration worn round the neck, has been instituted since 1945.

### 450 - MÉRITE NATIONALE

### 451 - ORDER OF AGRICULTURAL MERIT (ORDRE DU MÉRITE AGRICOLE)
This Order was instituted in 1883 for rewarding those who have rendered eminent services to the cause of agriculture. There are three classes: Commandeur, Officier and Chevalier. The decoration consists of a six-pointed star enamelled white resting on a wreath of oak and Indian corn. The centre of the obverse has the effigy of the Republic surrounded by a riband of blue enamel bearing the legend 'RÉPUBLIQUE FRANÇAISE,' and the reverse 'MÉRITE AGRICOLE. 1883.' The decoration hangs from its ribbon by means of a wreath of olive and oak, above which is a ring. The badge for Chevaliers is of silver and enamel and is worn on the left breast. Officiers have the decoration in gold and wear it on the left breast with a rosette on the ribbon, while Commandeurs wear the star round the neck.

**445 - MEDAL FOR KOREA**
*(Obverse)*

**449 - PALMES UNIVERSITAIRES**
*Insignia of the First Class*

## ORDER OF COMMERCIAL MERIT
## (ORDRE DU MÉRITE COMMERCIAL)

This is a bronze six-pointed star hanging from an eagle with out-spread wings. The ribbon is grey with a gold stripe at each edge.

## 452 - ORDER OF SOCIAL MERIT
## (ORDRE DU MÉRITE SOCIAL)

This is a seven-pointed blue star on a silver wreath. It has a silver centre with the usual head.

## 453 - MEDALS OF HONOUR FOR SAVING LIFE,
## AND FOR DEEDS OF COURAGE AND DEVOTION

These are awarded in Metropolitan France by the Minister of the Interior for saving life or for acts of courage on land or in inland waters. The medals are in five classes, awarded according to the degree of bravery displayed: *Gold medal*, with the wreath of olive and oak in gold, and a rosette on the ribbon; *Silver-gilt*, with silver-gilt wreath and plain ribbon; *Silver, First Class*, with silver-gilt wreath and plain ribbon; *Silver, Second Class*, with silver wreath and plain ribbon; *Bronze*, with bronze wreath and plain ribbon.

Similar medals are awarded by the Minister of Foreign Affairs or the Minister of the Colonies for acts of bravery in French colonies and protectorates, and also in Algeria.

The ribbon for all these medals is in three equal stripes of blue, white and red.

The Minister of Marine can also award medals in five classes to persons who save life at sea, or in the maritime portions of rivers. They hang from their ribbons by means of an oak wreath or ring, according to class, from a ribbon of blue, white and red, as follows: *Gold medal, First Class*, gold wreath and gold anchor on white portion of ribbon; *Gold, Second Class*, no wreath but gold anchor; *Silver, First Class*, silver wreath with red anchor on ribbon; *Silver, Second Class*, no wreath and red anchor; *Bronze*, no wreath and red anchor.

Similar medals with the same ribbons are bestowed upon officers and men of the French Navy for saving life at sea.

## MÉDAILLE DE LA FAMILLE FRANÇAISE

On 28 May 1920 a decree signed by the Minister of Public Health authorized a medal for award to the mothers of French families who have reared a number of children and thus become entitled to recognition by the nation. The medal is issued in three classes. The first is in bronze, for mothers of five legitimate children, the youngest to be at least a year old. For eight children the medal is silver, and for ten in silver-gilt, bearing the name of the Gold Medal. Holders are authorized to wear the medal or medal-ribbon on all occasions. The ribbon is red, green, red in equal stripes.

## MERCHANT MARINE LONG SERVICE MEDAL

This medal has a ribbon of blue, white and red horizontal with a blue anchor on the white portion. The medal for non-military persons employed by the Navy has a similar ribbon with a large black anchor.

*(Obverse)*

**451 - ORDRE DU MERITE AGRICOLE**
*Insignia of the Third Class (Reverse)*

## 454 - MUNICIPAL AND RURAL POLICE LONG SERVICE MEDAL

This medal is of silver, bearing two figures, one standing, one kneeling. It hangs from a semicircular branch.

## 455 - FIREMEN'S MEDAL OF HONOUR (MÉDAILLE D'HONNEUR DES SAPEURS POMPIERS)

This silver medal was instituted in 1900 and awarded to firemen and those connected with fire brigades who have specially distinguished themselves by acts of courage or who have thirty years of irreproachable service. With a special device on it, the medal was also awarded in Algeria. Ribbon, yellow, with blue, white, red edges, and two stripes of blue, white, red dividing the yellow into three.

(*Obverse*)

### CIVIL AWARDS

There are decorations and medals for award to practically every branch of the civil services in France and the colonies, as well as to private citizens in many walks of life who excel in their various professions, and for long and faithful service. Among them are the following:

**Order for 'Mérite Artisanale.'** The ribbon is blue with four grey stripes grouped in the centre.

**Order of 'Tourist Merit.'** The ribbon is pale blue with red, outer, and green, inner, conjoint stripes at the edges.

**456 - Order for Public Health.** The ribbon is dark blue.

**Orders of Combatant Merit** and **For Postal Merit** were established in 1953, and an **Order of National Economy** in 1954. Ribbons, respectively, dark green with narrow yellow diagonal stripes; orange, with two narrow black stripes towards each edge; plain yellow.

And the following medals, with the colours of their ribbons:

**457, 457A - Physical Education.** Gold and silver medals – pale blue with gold edges; bronze medal – pale blue.

**Departmental and Communal Workers.** Three equal stripes of green, white, green.

**Teachers.** Silver and bronze medals, the first with a purple ribbon with yellow edges.

**Forrestry Officials.** Green with orange edges and five narrow orange stripes on the green.

**Prison Officials.** Green with purple chevrons, pointing downwards.

**Colonial Prison Officials.** Pale blue with narrow edges of blue, white, red.

**Members of Musical Societies.** Maroon with green edges and central stripe of green.

**Posts and Telegraphs.** Six conjoint stripes of blue, white, red.

**Railway Employees.** Blue, white, red, white, blue, white red, with a silver railway engine thereon.

**Highways Officials.** As above, omitting engine.

**455 - MÉDAILLE D'HONNEUR DES SAPEURS POMPIERS**      (*Reverse*)

**Taxation Officials.** Green with white edges and five narrow white stripes on the green.

**Customs Officials.** Green with red edges and five narrow white stripes on the green.

**Encouragement to Devotion.** Green with red, outer, and yellow, inner, edges.

**Encouragement to Good.** Green with a black stripe at each edge.

**Nurses.** White with a red cross at the junction of two horizontal branches of laurel.

**Public Assistance.** Gold and silver medals – four yellow and three white stripes, with red edges; bronze medal – the same without the red edges.

**City of Metz, 1944.** Half black, half white.

**Gendarmerie.** Blue, yellow, blue separated by narrow white stripes with narrow red outside edges. When the medal is worn the ribbon has a silver grenade; when worn alone, ribbon has a smaller bronze grenade.

**Epidemics.** Blue, white, red. The Naval gold medal has a gold wreath and gold anchor; the silver, a woven yellow anchor.

**Octroi** (Local Customs) **Officials.** Yellow with red, white, blue edges, and a blue mural crown on the yellow.

**Mutual Help Societies** (Sécours Mutuels). Bronze medal – black with pale blue stripe near each edge; silver medal – silver stripes inside the blue; gold medal – gold stripes inside the blue.

**Savings Bank Employees** (Prévoyance Sociale). Bronze medal – orange with white edges; silver medal – an orange stripe in the centre of the white; gold medal – a gold stripe in the centre of the white.

**Social Assurance Officials.** Bronze medal – pale blue with an orange centre stripe; silver medal – an additional narrow orange stripe at each edge; gold medal – a rosette.

**Education Surveillé.** Purple with green chevrons, pointing downwards.

**Médaille Aeronautique.** Blue. The gold medal has a pair of gilt outspread wings.

**A Medal for Service in the Mines,** of which we have no details was instituted in 1953. Ribbon black with orange chevrons.

### FRENCH COLONIAL ORDERS

Detailed descriptions of the various French Colonial Orders which are awarded to officers and civilians alike for long and distinguished services in French colonies or protectorates abroad, are not possible within the limits of this work.

The five Orders mentioned below are recognized by the French Government and are bestowed by the President on the recommendation of the Colonial Minister:

**The Order of the Dragon of Annam.** Green ribbon with orange edges; when awarded to Annamese, red with yellow edges.

**The Royal Order of Cambodia.** White ribbon with orange edges; when awarded to Cambodians, red with green edges.

**The Order of the Black Star (Dahomey).** Light blue ribbon.

*(Obverse)*

**459 - ORDER OF OUISSAM ALAOUITE - MOROCCO**
*Insignia of the Third Class* (*Reverse*)

## ORDER OF
## THE BLACK STAR - DAHOMEY *Star of the First Class*

**The Order of Nichan-el-Anouar (Tadjourah), Gulf of Aden.** Ribbon dark blue, white, dark blue, equal.

**The Order of the Star of Anjouan, Comoro Islands.** Ribbon light blue with two narrow orange stripes near each edge. These Orders all have the same five classes as the Legion of Honour.

### OTHER ORDERS AND MEDALS OF
### FRENCH COLONIES AND PROTECTORATES

The following, though not actually awarded by the French Government, are frequently bestowed on French officers and civilians for services abroad, and also upon foreigners:

**458 - Order of Nichan-Iftikhar (Tunis).** Founded in 1837 by the reigning Bey, this Order has developed into the principal Tunisian Order, having six classes from Grand Cordon to Chevalier, *Second Class*. The basic insignia for all classes is a silver star of ten points with rays in the angles, and in the centre the Bey's name in arabic characters.

**Medal for Customs Officials, Tunis.** Pale green with a red stripe in the centre and a narrow red stripe at each side.

**Police Medal, Tunis.** Three pale green and two red equal stripes.

**459 - Order of Ouissam Alaouite, Morocco.** This Order takes a similar place in Morocco to the Nichan-Iftikhar in Tunis, and has five classes. The insignia is a white-enamelled five-pointed star with leaves in the angles and bearing in the centre and on the arms inscriptions in arabic. It hangs by a wreath.

271

'**Dahir de Satisfaction,' Morocco.** Ribbon orange with three narrow white centre stripes.

**Medal for Customs Officials, Morocco.** Ribbon orange with four green stripes.

**Firemen's Medal, Morocco.** Orange with two white stripes equally spaced across it.

**Police Medal, Morocco.** Three orange and two green stripes of equal width.

**Order of Ranavalo, Madagascar.** White with a red rhomboid on the right half.

**Order of Merit, Madagascar.** White with a blue stripe each side.

**Order of Radama, Madagascar.** Red with two narrow white stripes near each edge.

**Medal of Honour for Labour, Madagascar.** Maroon with yellow edges.

**Order of Kim-Kanh, Annam.** Half red, half yellow.

**Order of Kin-Tien, Annam.** Yellow with a red stripe near each edge and one in the centre.

**Order of Kim-Boi, Annam.** Same but green instead of red.

**Order of Agricultural Merit, Annam.** Green-gold-green.

**Medal of the Federation TAIH – Military.** Pale blue with black edges.

**Medal of the Federation TAIH – Civil.** Black with a gold centre and a narrow gold stripe just right and left of the centre.

**Order of the Hundred Million Elephants, Laos.** Red with two narrow yellow stripes near each edge and on the inner side of the inner yellow stripe an arabesque design in yellow.

**Royal Order of Luang Prabang, Laos.** Yellow with red edges.

**Order for Civil Merit, Laos.** Orange with three white stripes.

**Croix de Guerre, Laos.** White with three orange stripes.

**The National Order of Viet Namh.** Red with yellow edges.

**Cross for Valour, Viet Namh.** Yellow with broad red edges; on the yellow part are eight pairs of very fine red lines.

**Military Medal, Indo-China.** Yellow with blue edges and a black ideograph in the centre.

**Police Medal, Indo-China.** Horizontal stripes of green, yellow and red.

**Customs Medal, Indo-China.** Horizontal stripes of green, black and red.

**Royal Order of Muniseraphon, Cambodia.** Yellow.

**Royal Order of Sahametrei, Cambodia.** Red with broad blue edges divided in half by a narrow yellow stripe.

**Medal of National Merit, Cambodia.** Plain dark blue.

**Medal of National Defence, Cambodia.** Red, blue edges and three blue stripes on the red.

**Medal of the Crown or Royal Recognition, Cambodia.** Six yellow stripes each edged blue; between the blue stripes are five purple stripes.

**Medal of Sena Jayassedh, Cambodia.** A blue centre with red edges; on the red edges are two series of yellow squares, large down the centre and very small on the inner side.

## AWARDS OF THE VICHY GOVERNMENT, 1940–44

### 460 - CROIX DE GUERRE

This decoration was instituted by Marshal Pétain on 28 March 1941. It is in the usual forn with the Republican head on the obverse, and on the reverse the dates '1939–40.'

### 461 - CROIX DES COMBATTANTS

This decoration was instituted on the same day as the Croix de Guerre. It is of the usual design, but has the dates '1939–40' on the reverse.

### FRANCISQUE GALLIQUE

This was first awarded on 26 May 1941. It is a small badge pinned on the lapel of civilian clothes or above the pocket in uniform and takes the form of a double-headed axe protruding from a marshal's baton enamelled in blue, white and red. It was awarded 'for acts in promotion of the National Revolution,' and had no ribbon.

### MÉDAILLE DE MÉRITE DE L'AFRIQUE NOIRE

This medal was authorized by the Vichy Government on 26 June 1941 for award to native troops in French Equatorial Africa, French Somaliland and Madagascar. It is bronze and has on the obverse a map of Africa in relief with a native sword hilt superimposed. The reverse has an anchor with native hieroglyphics. The ribbon is pale blue with narrow stripes of green and red at each side.

### CROIX DE GUERRE L.V.F. (LÉGION VOLONTAIRE FRANÇAISE)

This decoration was authorized on 18 July 1942 for award to the division recruited in France to help Germany in the war against Russia. It is in bronze, and it is of interest to note the French shield superimposed upon the Nazi eagle. The reverse has the words 'CROIX DE GUERRE LÉGIONNAIRE.' It is believed that no more than 400 of these crosses were ever awarded. The ribbon is green with black edges and seven narrow black stripes in the centre.

### ORDRE NATIONAL DU TRAVAIL

This Order was instituted on 1 April 1942 by Marshal Pétain. It was to have consisted of three classes – Commandeur, Officier, and Chevalier. In fact no more than 200 Chevaliers were ever appointed.

The badge was a four-armed cross in gilt and blue enamel, with a centre shield on the obverse bearing the head of the Marshal surrounded by the words 'PH. PÉTAIN MAL. DE FR, CHEF DE L'ETAT,' and again surrounded by a wreath of laurel. The reverse has the 'Francisque Gallique' badge encircled by the words 'ORDRE NATIONAL DU TRAVAIL.' The ribbon was blue with a red stripe near each edge.

#### OTHER VICHY AWARDS

The Vichy Government sanctioned a bar 'LEVANT. 1940–41' with the French Oriental Medal; and a bar '1940 – COTE DES SOMALIS – 1941' for the usual Colonial Medal.

# Germany

Many queries having been received about German Orders, Decorations and Medals, the following notes may be of interest. It is impossible to include the many awards of Bavaria, Saxony, Wurtemberg, Baden, Hesse, Mecklenburg, Oldenburg, Brunswick and other German states, all of which at one time had their complete ranges of Orders, Decorations and Medals.

### 462 - POUR LE MÉRITE

This Prussian Order was founded by Prince Frederick, later Frederick I of Prussia, in about 1667, as the 'Order of Generosity.' It became the Order of Merit in 1740, and was granted for civil and military distinction by Frederick the Great. In 1810 it was made an award for military merit against an enemy in the field exclusively; but some thirty years later Frederick William IV added a civil class, with a different badge, for distinction in science and art. The number of awards was strictly limited.

In the Franco-German and First World Wars the Order was the highest reward for individual gallantry in action, and as such was bestowed upon Göring for his services as an airman. It was not awarded after the defeat of Germany in 1918. The decoration, worn round the neck from a black ribbon with stripes of white interwoven with silver towards each edge, was a Maltese cross in blue enamel, edged gold, with four golden eagles between the limbs. On the upper arm of the cross was the letter 'F' in gold surmounted by a crown, and on the three other arms 'Pour – le Me – rite.'

There was a higher class of the Order with a spray of three golden oakleaves worn on the ring for suspension, in which case the ribbon had an additional central stripe of silver.

462 - POUR LE MÉRITE

### 463, 464 - THE IRON CROSS

This decoration was established by Frederick William III in 1813 as an award for gallantry in action. It had two classes, together with a Grand Cross, which latter was awarded only nineteen times up till the end of the First World War. A special class, the Grand Cross on a radiant star, was created for Blücher after the battle of Waterloo. It was only once again awarded, to Field-Marshal Von Hindenburg in 1918.

The Iron Crosses of the *First* and *Second Classes* were revived for the Franco-German War of 1870–1, and the First World War. Some 219,300 awards were made of the *First Class*, and 5,500,000 of the *Second Class*, from 1813 up till the end of the First World War in November 1918, so it was far more freely granted than any British decoration or medal given for bravery in action. The decoration consisted of a cross patée in black iron edged with silver,

463 - THE IRON CROSS - 1813

having in the centre a spray of oakleaves. The crown and Royal cypher appeared on the upper limb, and the dates '1813,' '1870,' or '1914' on the lower limb. The cross of the *First Class* was pinned to the tunic like the star of an Order. That of the *Second Class* was worn on the breast from a black ribbon with white stripes towards each edge.

There was an Iron Cross for non-combatant services of exactly the same design as that described, worn from a white ribbon with black stripes towards each edge.

On 2 September 1939 Hitler reinstituted the Iron Cross for the Second World War. The general design remained the same as before, with the swastika in the centre and the date '1939' on the lower limb. The ribbon was altered to red, with stripes of white and black at each edge. Holders of the Iron Cross for the First World War were permitted to wear the old ribbon. If awarded Hitler's Iron Cross in addition they wore a bar of the design illustrated.

There were various classes of the Iron Cross. Starting with the lowest:

*Second Class* – A small cross worn on the breast from a ribbon. Those awarded the 1914 cross and that for 1939–45 wore a bar consisting of a silver Nazi eagle and swastika on the 1914 ribbon.

*First Class* – A similar cross worn on the breast, but without ribbon, like the star of an Order. Those awarded the First Class of 1914 and that for 1939–45 wore a bar similar to that mentioned welded above the First Class cross of 1914 design.

*Knight's Cross* – A slightly larger cross worn round the neck from a wider ribbon of the same colouring as for the *Second Class*. It could be awarded both to officers and to men.

*Knight's Cross, with Oakleaves* – A higher award than the last; but of exactly the same design with the addition of three silver oakleaves above the cross. About 862 were awarded during the period of the Third Reich, including four to Romanian officers, two to Japanese and one to each of Finland, Spain and Belgium.

Still higher awards were:

*Knight's Cross, with Oakleaves and Swords* – About 151 were awarded during the period of the Third Reich, including one to the Japanese Admiral Isoroku Yamamato.

*Knight's Cross, with Oakleaves, Swords and Diamonds* – Twenty-seven were awarded during the period of the Third Reich, all to German nationals.

*Knight's Cross, with Golden Oakleaves and Diamonds* – A higher grade than the last with the oakleaves embellished with brilliants. This was only once awarded, to Oberst Hans-Ulrich Rudel, a ground-attack pilot of the *Luftwaffe* during the Second World War.

*Grand Cross* – A still larger cross worn round the neck from a wider ribbon. Awarded only for activities having a decisive influence upon the course of the war. It was only granted once during the Second World War, to Göring after the surrender of France in 1940.

463 - THE IRON CROSS - 1914

464 - THE IRON CROSS
1939

BAR TO IRON CROSS

## GERMAN WAR SERVICE MEDAL (1914–18)

## ACTIVE WAR SERVICE CROSS (1914–18)

## 465 - CROSS OF HONOUR

This decoration was instituted by President Von Hindenburg in July 1934 'to the memory of the imperishable deeds of the German people' during the First World War 'for all participants as well as for the widows and parents of those who fell or died of wounds or as prisoners of war, or were reported missing and have not since been traced.'

The cross for those who had fought was made of iron, bronzed. The obverse has a shield with the dates '1914–1918' and a garland of laurel. Through the shield pass two swords. The swords were omitted in the crosses awarded to non-combatants and the garland was of oak instead of laurel. The crosses for widows and parents was of lacquered iron.

The Crosses of Honour were only granted on application, and the necessary enquiries into claims involved a very heavy burden not only for the Naval and Military departments, but also for the police and local authorities who had to make investigations. A document of identification was presented with each cross, which was conferred in the name of the President.

## 466 - ORDER OF MERIT OF THE GERMAN EAGLE

This Order was founded by Hitler on 1 May 1937 in five classes with a medal of merit, and intended only for award to foreigners, except that on official occasions the Grand Cross could be worn by the German Foreign Minister.

The badge was an eight-pointed, white-enamelled, gold-edged cross, in the corners of which were eagles standing on a swastika in a wreath.

The five classes followed the usual German style:

*Grand Cross* – Sash over the right shoulder with badge on the left hip, with eight-pointed star on left breast.

*Cross of Merit with Star* – Badge round neck and a smaller six-pointed star on the breast.

*Cross of Merit. First Class* – Badge round the neck.

*Cross of Merit. Second Class* – Badge worn on left side like a star, without ribbon.

*Cross of Merit. Third Class* – Badge worn on left breast from a narrower ribbon.

The medal was in silver with the badge of the Order on the obverse, and the words 'DEUTSCHE VERDIENSTMEDAILLE' on the reverse.

Two additional classes appear to have been instituted during the Second World War as there are in existence a Grand Cross ribbon and a narrow ribbon of the ordinary type both with an additional white stripe in the centre. They were presumably intended as a *First Class* ranking immediately below the Grand Cross, and for a bronze medal.

On the occasion of Hitler's visit to Rome in 1937 he presented Mussolini with a Grand Cross in gold which hung from a unique sash ribbon of scarlet with two sets of narrow white, black, white stripes equally spaced across it.

GERMAN WAR SERVICE MEDAL (1914–18)    (*Obverse*)

ACTIVE WAR SERVICE MEDAL (1914–18)    (*Obverse*)

(WITH SWORDS)

### 467 - SERVICE MEDAL (DIENSTAUSZEICHNUNG)

This medal was established by Hitler in March 1936 when compulsory military service was reintroduced, for all members of the armed forces who were of good conduct and had served their full term of service on 16 March 1935 or later. A medal in frosted silver was awarded for four years' service; a bronze medal for twelve years'; a silver cross for eighteen years'; and a gold cross for twenty-five years'. Officers were eligible as well as men, and the ribbon was cornflower blue, always popular in Prussia as the favourite flower of William I. These awards, which were not very greatly valued, correspond to the British Long Service and Good Conduct Medals.

### GOLD PARTY BADGE

This badge might be worn in uniform if awarded to those who were members of the Nazi Party before its accession to power on 30 January 1933. It consists of a circular badge surrounded by gold laurel leaves. In the centre is a white circle bearing a black swastika, and around this is a red circle on which in white letters appears the inscription: 'NATIONAL SOZIALISTICHE D.A.P.' The gold laurel leaves denote membership of the party before 30 January 1933, and the central design the ordinary party badge, which was not worn in uniform.

### BLOOD ORDER

This is a circular medal with a ribbon practically the same as that of the Iron Cross, granted to those who took part in the unsuccessful 'putsch' in Munich in 1923. The obverse has an eagle, and at the bottom a wreath in which appears '9 Nov.' To the right are the words 'MUNCHEN. 1923–1933.' The reverse shows the Feldherrnhalle in Munich, and above a swastika emitting rays. Near the upper circumference are the words 'UND IHR HABT DOCH GESIEGT' – 'And yet you have conquered!'

### NAZI PARTY LONG SERVICE CROSSES

A cross in bronze and white enamel was awarded for ten years' service, and was worn from a brown ribbon with two narrow white stripes near edge. A cross in silver and blue enamel was given for fifteen years', with a ribbon of blue with two narrow silver stripes near each edge. A further award in gold, for twenty-four years' service, was designed but cannot have been issued.

### DEUTSCHES KREUZ

This is the highest German Order awarded by Hitler during the Second World War. It was in three classes, gold with brilliants, gold, and silver; the gold being awarded for courage in the face of the enemy, and the silver for 'leadership of men,' not in the face of the enemy. There was no ribbon, and the badge, worn on the right side like the star of an Order, was a large star with a swastika in the centre surrounded by rays.

### 468 - WAR MERIT CROSS

This decoration was instituted during the Second World War as an inferior award to the Iron Cross. It could be awarded with or

(*Obverse*)

**NAZI SOCIAL SERVICE MEDAL** (*Reverse*)

**S.S. LONG SERVICE CROSS**

**468 - WAR MERIT CROSS**
*(Obverse)*

**468 - WAR MERIT CROSS
(WITH SWORDS)** *(Reverse)*

**471 - MEDAL FOR
CAMPAIGN AGAINST
RUSSIA** (1941–2) *(Obverse)*

without 'swords' according to whether the services rendered were in action or otherwise. The cross was struck in silver and bronze and had a swastika in the centre surrounded by a wreath of oak leaves. When awarded with 'swords' there were crossed swords with the points and hilts showing between the arms of the cross, while small crossed swords were worn on the ribbon when it was worn alone. The ribbon is the reverse of that for the Iron Cross, i.e., a black centre bordered by red and white. There was also a medal worn from a similar ribbon with a narrow red stripe down the centre, No. **469**.

### CROSS OF HONOUR FOR THE SPANISH CAMPAIGN

This decoration has a design very similar to the War Merit Cross, and it also was issued with and without 'swords.' It had no ribbon, but was worn on the breast like the star of an Order. There were four classes – gold with brilliants, gold, silver, and bronze awarded according to the rank and services of the recipient.

### WOUND BADGES

These had no ribbons; but were worn on the breast like the star of an Order. They were issued in black metal for one or two wounds; in silver for three or four; and in gold for five or more. The Army badge was an oval with crossed swords surmounted by a steel helmet bearing a swastika, the whole surrounded by a wreath of laurel. The Navy badge was similar in shape with crossed swords superimposed on an anchor, the whole surrounded by an oval of chain cable.

### ANSCHLUSS MEDAL

This medal, officially known as 'The Medal in remembrance of 13 March, 1938,' was given for the occupation of Austria. It is circular and on the obverse are two allegorical male figures in the nude

*(Obverse)*

**472 - THE WEST WALL
MEDAL**      *(Reverse)*

moving to the left. The larger (Germany), grasping a furled banner, is assisting the smaller figure (Austria) to ascend a tower. The ribbon is bright red, with edges of black, bordered each side by narrower stripes of white, almost exactly the same as that of the Order of Merit and the German Eagle.

## 470 - SUDETENLAND MEDAL

This medal, officially known as 'The Medal in remembrance of 1 October, 1938,' was given for the occupation of the 'Sudetenland.'

The design is precisely the same as the Anschluss Medal; but the ribbon is black, red, black in equal proportions, with very narrow white edges.

## PROTECTORATE MEDAL

This is the same as the Sudetenland Medal, but is worn with a clasp, the official name of which is 'Clasp to the medal commemorating 1 October, 1938, for participation in the occupation of Bohemia and Moravia in March and April, 1939.'

CROSS OF HONOUR FOR
THE SPANISH CAMPAIGN

## 471 - MEDAL FOR CAMPAIGN AGAINST RUSSIA
(1941–2)

This is a medal of dull silver metal with, on the obverse, the Nazi eagle on a swastika, and a steel helmet and hand grenade above. The reverse has the inscription 'WINTERSCHLACHT IM OSTEN. 1941/2,' with a crossed sword and laurel branch.

## 472 - THE WEST WALL MEDAL

This medal was issued to those who assisted in building the 'Siegfried Line.' It is oval with, on the obverse, an eagle and swastika, crossed sword and spade, and a fortification. On the reverse is the inscription 'FÜR ARBEIT ZUM SCHUTZE DEUTSCHLANDS' ('For work in the defence of Germany.')

## 473 - MEDAL COMMEMORATING RETURN
OF MEMEL

This is a bronze medal, like those for the Anschluss and Sudetenland, in remembrance of the return of Memel to Germany on 22 March 1939. The reverse has a suitable inscription.

WOUND BADGE

## THE LUFTSCHUTZ MEDAL

This medal was awarded in two classes, a cross and a medal, to those in the air-raid precautions services. The ribbon is mauve, with edges of black, white and red.

## 474 - VOLUNTEERS FROM EASTERN COUNTRIES
MEDALS FOR BRAVERY

These awards had five classes and two divisions, with and without swords. The first two classes were small 'pin-on' stars in gilt and silver with a flower design in the centre. The awards of the other three classes were smaller stars of the same design in gilt, silver or bronze worn with ribbons. The gilt star had a ribbon of light green with a red stripe near each edge; the silver, a medium green with a white stripe near each edge; the bronze, a plain, dark green ribbon.

## 475 - DECORATION OF HONOUR FOR NATIONAL WELFARE

This was formerly the German Red Cross decoration, and was a plain white-enamelled cross with an eagle in black in the centre.

## THE FEDERAL REPUBLIC OF GERMANY

### 476 - ORDER OF MERIT OF THE FEDERAL GERMAN REPUBLIC

A new Order in eight classes was instituted by the Federal German Government in September 1951. The ribbon is scarlet, with edges of gold, black, gold. In the sash of the three highest classes small eagles of a slightly darker colour are woven into the red of the ribbon.

The various classes are:

1. *Grand Cross* with laurel leaves. Eagles on sash.
2. *Grand Cross* with eight-pointed star. Eagles on sash.
3. *Grand Cross* with six-pointed star. Eagles on sash.
4. *Large Merit Cross* with four-pointed star. Plain sash.
5. *Large Merit Cross* with four-pointed star.
6. *Large Merit Cross* worn round the neck.
7. *Merit Cross* worn pinned to breast.
8. *Merit Cross* worn on breast from a ribbon.

### ORDER 'POUR LE MÉRITE' FOR THE ARTS AND SCIENCES

Following a period of lapse after 1935, the Order *Pour le Merite* was reinstituted on 31st May 1952 by the Federal Republic as an Order recognising the free association of artists and scientists under the Protectorship of the Federal President. The Order is conferred in one class only, administered by the Chancellor of the Order who is elected by its members.

The total number of members of the Order is strictly limited to 30 German subjects, of whom a maximum of ten may be artists, ten in the field of scientific philosophy and ten in the field of natural science. A further 30 foreigners may be appointed members of the Order.

The *Badge* of the Order is of unusual design and consists of a gold medallion displaying the Prussian Eagle; a blue-enamelled scroll surrounding the medallion carries the inscription 'POUR LE MERITE' in gold, and in open-worked gold between the medallion and scroll are four pairs of 'Fs,' monogrammed back-to-back, interspersed with four 'IIs,' this being representative of King Frederick II of Prussia. Outside the scroll are four small Prussian crowns. The Badge is worn at the throat suspended from a ribbon of black with silver-white borders, the traditional position of the Pour le Mérite The insignia remains the property of the Order and is to be returned on the death of a Member.

*(Obverse)*

**476 - ORDER OF MERIT OF THE FEDERAL GERMAN REPUBLIC**
*Badge of the Merit Cross*
*(Reverse)*

*Star of the Grand Cross*

*Badge of the Large Merit Cross*

**476 - ORDER OF MERIT OF THE
FEDERAL GERMAN REPUBLIC**

*Star of the Large Merit Cross*

# *Greece*

### 477 - ORDER OF THE REDEEMER

This Order was instituted in 1829 in five classes. It consists of a white-enamelled cross resting upon a wreath of oak and laurel enamelled green. The first four classes are in gold, and the fifth class in silver.

### 478 - ROYAL ORDER OF GEORGE I

This Order was instituted in 1912. It comprises a gold collar, for award to Royal personages only, with five classes and a sixth class consisting of the cross in bronze. The cross is enamelled white and rests upon a wreath of green enamel. The badge is in gold for the first four classes, and in silver and enamel for the fifth. The Order has a military and civil division, and in the first case is awarded 'with swords' which appear crosswise between the limbs of the cross.

### 479 - ROYAL ORDER OF THE PHOENIX

This Order was founded in 1936 in five classes in military and civil divisions, with and without swords placed crosswise between the limbs of the cross. The design is shown in the illustration, the crosses of the first four classes being enamelled white, edged gold, with the phoenix in the centre in proper colours, and the badge of the fifth class being in silver and enamel. The ribbon, formerly orange moiré with black edges, is now issued in the same colours but unwatered.

### ROYAL FAMILY ORDER (MEN)
### 480 - ORDER OF ST. GEORGE AND ST. CONSTANTINE

This Order has a chain and five classes, with medals in silver-gilt, silver, and bronze.

*The Chain*, in silver-gilt, consists of eight lions, each one separated by a Greek letter, from which is suspended the badge, which is in the form of a cross in white enamel, edged red, in the centre of which are the enamelled miniatures of the two Saints surrounded by a garter of lions and hearts in silver-gilt. It is surmounted by a crown. The breast star is similar to the badge but larger, and has a Greek inscription on a blue enamel garter instead of the hearts and lions.

*First Class.* An eight-pointed silver star on the breast with a smaller badge superimposed, and a 102-mm. sash worn over the right shoulder with the badge on the left hip.

*Second Class.* A smaller breast star with faceted rays with the badge in the centre, and badge worn round the neck from the ribbon.

*Third Class.* As for *Second Class*, but without the breast star.

*Fourth Class.* A slightly smaller badge in silver-gilt and enamel

**477 - ORDER OF THE REDEEM[**
*Badge of the First Class*     *(Obver*

**477 - ORDER OF THE REDEEMF**
*Badge of the Fourth Class*     *(Rever*

worn on the breast from a ribbon.

*Fifth Class.* As for *Fourth Class,* but with the badge in silver and enamel.

The Order is awarded in a military division, with swords, in which case the hilts and blades of swords appear in the angles of the cross both on the badges and stars. There are no swords in the badges of the civil division.

*Medals.* These are in silver-gilt, silver, and bronze. When awarded for military service crossed swords are worn on the ribbon.

The ribbon in all cases is dark blue, with short horizontal stripes of alternate red, blue and white at the edges.

## ROYAL FAMILY ORDER (LADIES)
### 481 - ORDER OF ST. OLGA AND ST. SOPHIA
In four classes.

*First Class.* A four-pointed star worn on the breast with, in the centre, the enamelled miniatures of the two Saints surrounded by a circular garter with a Greek inscription. A sash, 63 mm. wide, is worn over the right shoulder, with the same badge as that in the centre of the star.

*Second Class.* Breast star as for *First Class,* and the badge worn on the breast from the ribbon tied in a bow.

*Third Class.* A circular breast badge worn from a bow of the ribbon. The badge, in silver-gilt, has the Greek inscription on the

**478 - ROYAL ORDER OF GEORGE I** *Badge of the First Class*

**479 - ROYAL ORDER OF THE PHOENIX**
*Insignia of the First Class*

283

lower half, and alternate hearts and lions above with a saw-pierced central cross and the enamel portraits of the two Saints. The whole is surmounted by a crown.

*Fourth Class.* As for *Third Class*, but the badge is in silver instead of silver-gilt.

The ribbon for all classes is dark blue with narrow white horizontal lines at each edge.

## 482 - THE WELFARE ORDER

This Order is awarded to ladies only. It is in five classes.

*First Class.* A silver eight-pointed star worn on the breast with the badge in the centre, and a sash worn over the right shoulder with another badge on the left hip.

The badge is a five-petalled, rose-shaped flower enamelled pale blue, with the turned over extremities of the petals enamelled pale yellow, with green-enamelled leaves between each of the petals. The centre has an embossed representation of the Virgin and Child in silver-gilt, surrounded by a white-enamelled circle with the gilt letters 'Ευττοιια.' (In appearance it is much like the badge of the Order of the Indian Empire.)

*Second Class.* A similar star as that for the *First Class*, but smaller, and the badge worn on the breast from a narrower ribbon tied in a bow.

*Third Class.* As for *Second Class*, but without star.

*Fourth Class.* A smaller silver-gilt badge worn on the breast.

*Fifth Class.* As for *Fourth Class* with badge in silver.

## 483 - WAR CROSS (1914–18) (now obsolete)

This decoration, sometimes known as the Military Cross, was instituted in 1917 by M. Venizelos for award to the Greek Nationalist troops, but was later officially recognized. It was first awarded solely for bravery in the field, but was afterwards granted for war service in general. The medal is in dull silver and consists of a wreath of laurel upon a horizontal tablet worded as shown, with a broad-bladed sword, point upwards. The reverse bears the inscription 'ΕΛΛΑε, 1916–1917.' There are three classes of the cross, awarded entirely according to merit, and not by rank. The *First Class* has a gold wreath on the ribbon; the *Second Class*, a silver wreath; and the *Third Class*, the plain ribbon.

483 - WAR CROSS (1914–18)

After having received the cross each mention in despatches was designated by a five-pointed star attached to the ribbon.

## 484 - MEDAL OF MILITARY MERIT (now obsolete)

This medal was also instituted by M. Venizelos in 1917 and was later officially recognized. It was awarded to officers of the Army, Navy, Red Cross and other organizations for services in war, though not necessarily under fire. The medal is a round plaque of bronze, edged with a wreath of laurel, superimposed upon a Greek cross with inscribed arms and a phoenix in the centre, with two swords placed saltire-wise under the cross. The reverse has the inscription 'ΕΛΛΑε, 1916–1917.'

The medal was awarded by rank, as follows:

*First Class.* Gold wreath on ribbon. Senior general officers.
*Second Class.* Silver wreath on ribbon. Junior general officers.
*Third Class.* Bronze wreath on ribbon. Colonels and majors.
*Fourth Class.* Plain ribbon. Captains and junior officers.

The ribbon was orange moiré with a black stripe towards each edge.

This same medal, apparently in one class only, was reinstituted in 1940 with an unwatered ribbon of the same colours and with a gold bar with the date '1940' worn on the ribbon. Known as the 'Medal for outstanding Acts' or the 'Distinguished Conduct Medal' it was awarded to civilians as well as to members of the fighting services.

Both these awards have now been superseded by another medal in bronze of very similar design with the Royal cypher and crown in the middle of the cross, and another crown below the ring for suspension.

### 485 - CROSS OF VALOUR
This decoration, in three classes, was instituted during the Second World War. It is issued in gold, silver, and bronze. The badge consists of a cross, with the lower limb longer than the others, enamelled white, edged blue, both colours narrowly edged with the appropriate metal. In the centre, on a white ground and surrounded by a wreath of laurel, is a representation of St. George fighting the dragon.

### 486 - WAR CROSS (1940–45)
This is a plain bronze cross of the same shape as the French Croix de Guerre with the hilts and points of swords appearing between the limbs. It is surmounted by a crown, and carries a crown and Royal cypher in the centre. It was established in three classes during the Second World War, and apparently worn with different emblems on the ribbon.

### 487 - NAVY CROSS (1940–45)
This is a bronze cross instituted during the Second World War. Stars are worn on the ribbon to denote bars for further awards.

### 488 - MERCHANT NAVY CROSS (1940–45)
This is a bronze cross worn from a ribbon of dark blue with narrow yellow edges and a central stripe of the same colour.

### DISTINGUISHED FLYING CROSS, AND MEDAL
### 489 - AIR FORCE CROSS, AND MEDAL
These four ribbons were issued during the Second World War, that for the D.F.C. having broad stripes of dark blue and grey running diagonally downwards from right to left and the D.F.M. narrower diagonal stripes in the same colours.

The A.F.C. and A.F.M. had similar ribbons with diagonal stripes of white and grey.

The present **Distinguished Flying Cross, No. 490,** is a gold cross composed of four wings suspended from a crown. The reverse is dated 1948. The ribbon has diagonal stripes of scarlet and yellow running downwards from left to right, with very narrow scarlet borders.

The **Air Force Cross, No. 491,** is in bronze, the upper and lower arms consisting of propeller blades, and the transverse limbs of eagle's wings. In the centre is a small St. George's cross with a small crown at each extremity. The whole is surmounted by a crown, and the ribbon is scarlet with a yellow stripe towards each edge.

The **Distinguished Flying Medal,** which is awarded to non-commissioned officers, has a ribbon with alternate narrow stripes of dark blue and light blue running diagonally downwards from left to right, and the **Air Force Medal** has a similar ribbon with stripes of dark blue and white.

There is also a **Distinguished Service Medal,** believed to be Naval, worn on a yellow ribbon with a scarlet stripe towards each edge.

## ORDER OF NAVAL COMMANDOS

This Order was created by Royal Decree of 3 March 1948 in recognition of the Royal appreciation of the conduct of those officers, petty officers and men who on the night of 22 April to 23 April 1944, in Alexandria, boarded ships of the Royal Hellenic Navy whose crews had mutinied and brought them back to duty. The bronze badge, which has no ribbon, is worn on the left side a few inches above the belt.

## 492 - MEDALS FOR FIRST BALKAN WAR (1912)
## v. TURKEY

The ribbon was pale blue, with white stripes near each edge, and in the centre a stripe of scarlet narrowly edged with white. The Red Cross Medal for the same war was white with stripes of pale blue near each edge, and in the centre a narrow stripe of scarlet.

## MEDALS FOR SECOND BALKAN WAR (1913)
## v. BULGARIA

The ribbons were the same as those just described except that the central stripes were green.

## NAVY MEDAL (SECOND WORLD WAR)

The ribbon is 32 mm. wide in three equal stripes of dark blue, white, dark blue.

## WAR MEDAL (1940–41)

This is a bronze medal awarded for service in the Epirus, Albania, Macedonia, Crete, etc. It has the King's effigy on the obverse surrounded by a wreath of laurel joined together at the top by a crown. The reverse has the date '1940–41' and the theatres of war for which it was awarded. The ribbon is pale blue with a stripe of dark blue towards each edge.

## STAR FOR 1941–45

This is a six-pointed bronze star with a crown on the top ray, crossed swords, and a wreath of laurel. The reverse has the date '1941–45,' and the theatres of war for which it was granted. It was awarded for service in North Africa, the Aegean and Italy. The ribbon is in three equal stripes of red, blue, and green.

(*Obverse*)

**MEDAL FOR SECOND BALKAN WAR** (1913)
**v. BULGARIA** (*Reverse*)

## WAR MEDAL

Another war medal exists with a ribbon of blue with three broad stripes of yellow. It is said to have been awarded to the Navy and Merchant Navy.

## RED CROSS MEDAL (1940–41)

This is a bronze medal with an inscription on the obverse surrounding a cross in red enamel superimposed upon a wreath of laurel enamelled green. The date '1940–41' appears on the reverse. The ribbon is white, with two narrow stripes of scarlet towards each edge.

## LIBERATION OF GREECE, etc.

Two decorations were apparently awarded for the fighting that followed the liberation of Greece by the Allies in 1944. They are both crosses in dull silver metal, of the same shape as the cross of the Order of the Redeemer, with a crown over the upper limb. Both have a central device with the Greek cross on a shield surrounded by an inscription. One, with a wreath of laurel appearing between the arms and the date '1946' beneath, has a ribbon of three equal stripes of orange, black, orange. This has been described as the Police Cross.

The second has rays issuing between the limbs of the cross, and a red ribbon with a central stripe of blue, and has been described as the Police Valour Medal.

NOTE: Awards of many of the above decorations and medals are believed to have lapsed during the King's exile in recent years, and it is anticipated that a new series of awards will be instituted by the Republic.

# Hashemite Kingdom of the Jordan

## THE ORDER OF MILITARY GALLANTRY (OUISAM AL IKDAM AL ASKARI)

Awarded to all ranks of the Arab Legion for gallantry on the battlefield only. The obverse has the head of King Abdullah and the reverse a reproduction of the Aksa mosque taken from the former Palestine pound note. The medal is in bronze, and the ribbon is green moiré, exactly similar to the Italian order of St. Maurice and St. Lazarus, No. **508**. It is worn before all other decorations.

## 493 - ORDER OF AN NAHADA (OUISAM AN NAHADA)

This Order was instituted by Ali Hussain, King of the Hedjaz, after the First World War to commemorate the renaissance of the Arab kingdom, but it is now granted for distinguished service. It has five classes, the first two having a sash and breast star, and the others the badge worn on the breast from the ribbon. The badge is an

287

elaborate six-pointed star in tracery and green enamel. In the centre are crossed flags in colour on a gold ground surrounded by an Arabic inscription in gold on a red-enamelled circle. The green of the ribbon represents the colours of the Prophet's banner; the white that of the Amawi tribe; the black, that of the Abassi; and the red, that of the Hashimi.

### 494 - ORDER OF ISTIQLAL (INDEPENDENCE) (OUISAM AL ISTIQLAL)
This order was also founded by Ali Hussain in five classes. It is a ten-pointed star with a smaller five-pointed star in white enamel in the centre mounted on a wreath. The centre medallion has an Arabic inscription. There is also a medal for rewarding junior officials and members of the Arab Legion.

### 495 - THE ORDER OF KAWKAB (THE JORDAN STAR) (OUISAM AL KAWKAB AL URDANIYE)
This Order, which is actually senior to the Order of Istiqlal, also has five classes.

### THE ORDER OF PRIDE (OUISAM AL IFTIQHAR AL ASKARI)
Has no ribbon, but is a costly star studded with diamonds. Only two have been awarded, one to Glubb Pasha.

### 496 - LOYAL SERVICE MEDAL
The medal is awarded to warrant officers who complete 15 years' service without punishment, and to officers for 20 years' service without court martial or conviction by a civil court.

### 497 - MAAN MEDAL (1918)
This medal was awarded after the First World War for general service.

### 498 - CAMPAIGNS IN IRAQ AND SYRIA (1942)

### 499 - WAR MEDAL (1939–45)

### 500 - PALESTINE WAR SERVICE (1947)

### 501 - NATIONAL GUARD MEDAL

# The Kingdom of Hawaii

During the nineteenth century the independent kingdom of Hawaii instituted a number of Orders for bestowal upon Hawaiian nationals and foreign dignitaries. As British and American subjects were thus eligible for some of these awards, brief details are included here. Membership was strictly limited to a relatively small number so that the insignia is amongst the rarest in the world today.

## ROYAL ORDER OF KAMEHAMEHA I

Instituted by King Kamehameha V on 11 April 1865 to commemorate the first Kamehameha who founded the kingdom of
Hawaii, this Order was conferred upon subjects and foreigners who
rendered high services to the dynasty. It was divided into three
classes.

*Knights Grand Cross.* The insignia was an eight-pointed star of
gold radiating rays with a white-enamelled gold cross superimposed
in the centre. In the centre of the cross was a circular shield round
which was the name 'KAMEHAMEHA I' and on which was the
stylized letter 'K.' The star was worn on the breast, and in addition
there was a sash of red ribbon bordered by a thin white stripe; the
pendant cross of the Knights Commander class (see below) was
suspended under the bow of this sash.

Membership of this class was limited to ten subjects of the
kingdom plus a small number of foreigners, and a total of 40 such
appointments and promotions from lower classes were made.
The instituting statute provided for the post-nominal letters
K.C.C.K. to be used.

In addition, the Grand Master could direct the wearing of the
Knights Commander cross from a gold collar or chain, and this
chain was only bestowed twice – upon Queen Victoria and Emperor
Mutsuhito of Japan.

*Knights Commander.* The insignia consisted of the same circular
shield as on the star, but surmounting an eight-pointed cross of
gold, enamelled white; there were radiating rays of gold between
the arms of the cross. On the reverse of the shield were the words
'E HOOKANAKA,' meaning 'the Order.' The cross, surmounted by a
crown, was worn suspended from the neck with a ribbon of
alternating red and white stripes.

The class was conferred upon a total of 56 subjects and foreigners
and the post-nominal letters K.C.K. were authorised in the
statute.

*Knights Companion.* The insignia was similar to that of the
Knights Commander but smaller, in gold or silver. It was worn
suspended from a ribbon of alternating red and white stripes on
the left breast. This class was bestowed upon 43 subjects and
foreigners who were permitted the use of post-nominal letters C.K.
Appointments to the Order of Kamehameha were discontinued in
1886.

## ROYAL ORDER OF KALAKAUA I

Created on 28th September 1875 by King Kalakaua to commemorate his election to the throne of Hawaii, the Order was
awarded for services of merit rendered to the sovereign or state.
There were four classes.

*Knights Grand Cross.* The insignia was a silver eight-pointed star
on the centre of which was a gold eight-pointed cross, enamelled
in blue and white. Between the arms of the cross was a golden
wreath with a puloulou – a staff tipped with a golden globe used
to depict the presence of royalty. A central circular shield enamelled

**ROYAL ORDER OF KALAKAUA I**
*Badge of the Knights Commander*
*(Shown full size)*

in blue and white was surrounded by the inscription 'KALAKAUA FEBRUARY 12TH 1874' (the date of King Kalakaua's election to the throne) and in the centre was a kahili – a ritual staff, denoting nobility, topped by a cylindrical device fashioned in feathers. In addition to the star was worn a sash of blue ribbon under the bow of which was suspended the pendant cross of the Knights Commander. This class was conferred upon 38 subjects and foreigners.

In addition, the Grand Master could confer a gold chain or collar fashioned with ornamental letters K.I.K. interspaced with red and yellow kahili staff, and fronted by a gold wreath supporting the monogram K.I.K. The collar was only bestowed twice – upon King Kalakaua himself and upon the Prince of Wales, later King Edward VII.

*Knights Grand Officer*. This was similar to, but smaller than, the star of the Knights Grand Cross; round the central shield was the word 'KEOLA' on the reverse, meaning 'eternal life.' In 1879 the size of the badge was reduced to a width of approximately 70 mm. This class did not include the cordon sash or pendant cross, and there was a total of 49 awards.

*Knights Commander*. The insignia consisted of the cross and wreath (with puloulous) of the Knights Grand Cross, but without the silver star. This pendant cross, surmounted by a crown, was worn from the neck suspended from a ribbon of alternating blue and white stripes. A total of 95 awards was made upon subjects and foreigners (although one such award was cancelled in 1885 and the insignia returned).

*Knights Companion*. The insignia of this class was a smaller variation of that of the Knights Commander and was worn suspended on the left breast by a ribbon of alternating blue and white stripes. A total of 239 awards was made, and the last of this class was conferred on 1st August 1892.

## ROYAL ORDER OF KAPIOLANI

Kapiolani the Great was the daughter of the King of Kau and Hilo and had been an early supporter of Christianity and one of the first Hawaiian converts. In her commemoration King Kalakaua established this Order for recognition of services in the cause of humanity and in the arts and sciences. Instituted on 30 August 1880, it was composed of eight classes.

*Grand Cross*. Only conferred upon 11 subjects and foreigners, the insignia of this class was a silver eight-pointed star on which was mounted a gold eight-pointed cross, enamelled red; between each limb of the cross was a small gold crown, and on the top limb there was a miniature, circular portrait of Kapiolani. In the centre of the cross was a circular shield bearing two letters 'K,' stylized and placed back-to-back mirror-fashion. Around the shield were the words 'KULIA I KA NUU,' meaning 'strive for the summit.' In addition, there was a sash of yellow ribbon fringed with the Hawaiian national colours, white, red and blue; suspended below the bow of this sash was the pendant cross of the Commander. At least one bestowal of the Grand Cross included the star insignia and pendant

**ROYAL ORDER OF KAPIOLAN**
*Badge of the Commander*
*(Shown full size)*

cross with red brilliants in place of the red enamel. Recipients were, with one exception, of the royal blood and included Prince Philip of Saxe-Coburg-Gotha.

*High Grand Officer.* The insignia of this class was the same as that of the Grand Cross, but the pendant cross of the Commander was suspended from the neck rather than from the sash cordon. This was only bestowed three times, all to commoners.

*Grand Officer.* The insignia consisted of the star of the Grand Cross, but not the cordon nor pendant cross. It was conferred only seven times.

*Commander.* The insignia of this class was the central gold eight-pointed cross as mounted on the star of the Grand Cross, but surmounted by a gold crown. It was worn suspended from the neck by a ribbon of alternate red and yellow stripes. There were only 20 recipients.

*Officer.* The insignia was a smaller variation of that of the Grand Officer and was worn on the left breast suspended from the red and yellow ribbon, in the centre of which was fashioned a rosette. This class was conferred 17 times.

*Companion.* Insignia as that of the Officer but in silver and enamel, worn suspended on the left breast. In this class there was a division for ladies who wore the insignia from a bow in the red and yellow ribbon. A total of 60 awards was made (the maximum allowed for in the statute), but one commission was cancelled in 1884 and the insignia returned to the Chancellor.

*Medals.* Awarded in 1st and 2nd classes, the medals were similar to the cross of the Companion but did not include the surmounting crown, nor those between the limbs of the cross. There was no limitation to the number to be awarded, but the number actually given is not known.

## ROYAL ORDER OF THE CROWN OF HAWAII

Instituted by King Kalakaua on 12 September 1882 to commemorate his own coronation, the Order of the Crown of Hawaii was bestowed for distinguished merit and services to the sovereign or state. It was divided into seven classes. (The crosses referred to below appear to have existed in two forms, an eight-pointed Maltese cross (as illustrated) and a convexed cross pattée.)

*Grand Cross.* The insignia was a four-pointed diamond-shaped silver star with the cross superimposed, in the centre of which was a circular shield. On this shield was a gold crown surrounded by the words 'HAWAII KE KALAUNU.' In addition, there was a cordon sash of white ribbon edged with a blue stripe, and from which was suspended the pendant cross of the Commander. This class was conferred upon 37 subjects and foreigners.

*Grand Officer.* The insignia was as that of the Grand Cross but smaller, and without the cordon or sash and pendant cross. There were 51 awards.

*Commander.* The insignia consisted of the central cross emblem of the star but surmounted by a crown and suspended from the neck by a white ribbon edged with a blue stripe. There were 71

**ROYAL ORDER OF THE CROWN OF HAWAII**
*Badge of the Commander*
*(Shown full size)*

awards.

The remaining four classes were *Officer*, *Companion* and *Medals* of two grades.

### ROYAL ORDER OF THE STAR OF OCEANIA

Instituted by King Kalakaua on 16 December 1886 in recognition of his visions to create an empire of Pacific Islands during the 1880s, the Order of the Star of Oceania was created as recognition of services rendered in promoting Hawaiian interests throughout the Pacific and Indian Oceans. There were seven classes.

*Grand Cross*. This was never awarded but consisted of a five-pointed gold star enamelled in green and white. Between the points of the star were silver ornamental rays. In the centre of the star was a shield surrounded by the words 'KA HOKU O OSIANIA' – The Star of Oceania – and in the centre of the shield a beacon and six stars with sea and sky enamelled in green and white. There was also a sash or cordon in pale green ribbon, and below the bow was suspended the pendant star of the Commander. This class was to have been limited to 15.

*Grand Officer*. The insignia was the same as that of the Grand Cross but without the sash or cordon and pendant star. It was also slightly smaller. There were only two awards.

*Commander*. Slightly smaller than that of the Grand Officer, the Commander's insignia was suspended from the neck by a pale green ribbon edged in white. There were only eight awards.

The remaining classes were *Officer*, *Companion* (including a division for ladies) and *Medals* of two grades. The Order was last conferred on 26 July 1890.

## Hungary

### ORDER OF MERIT AND MEDALS OF MERIT

These were established in September 1950 by the Presidential Council of the Hungarian People's Republic, for award to civilian and military personnel alike for meritorious service.

*The Order* is in the usual five classes, and the badges include a star in red enamel.

*The Ribbon* is red for civilians, bordered with narrow stripes, reading outwards, of white, green, white, red, white. The military ribbon has an additional central stripe of white.

*The Medal* is in three classes, gold, silver or bronze, and consists of the red star bearing the coat-of-arms of the Republic, bordered with gold, silver or bronze according to class. The medal ribbons are the same as for the Order.

**ORDER OF THE FLAG OF TH**
**PEOPLE'S REPUBLIC OF HUN**
*Insignia of the First Class (Shown ful*

# Iceland

## ORDER OF THE FALCON

Instituted by King Christian X of Denmark and Iceland in 1921, the Order of the Falcon was subject of new statutes when Iceland became a republic on 11 July 1944. It is conferred in three classes, *Grand Cross*, *Grand Knight* and *Knight*, of which the second is divided into two grades, with and without Star. The *Badge* of the Order is a white-enamelled form of Latin Cross with widened extremities and corners cut. In the centre is a silver falcon on a blue-enamelled oval background, and the *Collar* from which the badge is suspended consists of 25 such ovals interspersed by 25 medallions showing the Icelandic coat of arms.

The *Star* of the Order consists of the badge superimposed on a silver eight-pointed star with faceted rays.

The ribbon is blue with a white stripe close to each edge, and with a narrow red stripe in the centre of each white stripe.

The Order is conferred after nomination by a council of five headed by the President of Iceland for services rendered to the republic and to mankind, and the insignia is returned to the State upon the death of the holder.

## PRESIDENT OF ICELAND'S MEDAL

Instituted in 1954, this medal is awarded to Icelandic subjects and foreigners for services to the President. It is awarded in a single *silver* class and the insignia consists of a medal suspended from a dark blue ribbon, the obverse displaying Ingolfr Arnarson (Iceland's first recorded settler) with the inscription 'HEIDURSPEN-NINGUR FORSETA ISLANDS' – The President of Iceland's Medal, and the reverse the Icelandic coat of arms.

**ORDER OF THE FALCON**
*Original Badge of the First Class*
*(Shown full size)*

# Iraq

## ORDER OF HASHIMI

This Order is in one class and is intended for award to heads of States only. It has a chain worn round the neck with the badge hanging from it, and a green sash ribbon and similar badge.

The badge, which is difficult to describe, has a centre medallion in red enamel bearing a crown in gold. It is edged gold and is surrounded by six rectangular rays in green enamel and gold tracery with pointed ends, each of their inner ends terminating in two triangles of white enamel which form a twelve-pointed star round the centre medallion. Between each of the green rays is a lotus flower in white, gold and green. The links of the chain repeat a somewhat simpler badge of the same design alternating with an elaborate scroll design in gold.

### 502 - ORDER OF KING FEISAL I
Ribbon pale blue with broad chocolate edges.

### 503, 504 - ORDER OF AL RAFIDHAIN (THE TWO RIVERS)
The circular star has seven extending points terminating in small golden globes, the centre of the obverse consisting of a wreath in green enamel surrounding a white circle having an Arabic inscription. In the centre is a gold crown on blue background.

### 505 - KING FEISAL WAR MEDAL
This is a gilt medal upon which the crescent forms the exergue above a semicircular wreath which encloses an Arabic inscription. Crossed rifles form a background. The muzzles at the top are joined by ten rays which form a point from which is mounted a flat loop through which the riband passes.

### 506 - MEDAL FOR BRAVERY
There is believed to be also an Air Force Medal for bravery with a ribbon of pale blue.

### MEDAL OF THE IRAQ RED CRESCENT SOCIETY
This medal was established in three classes, gold, silver, and bronze in 1934. The ribbon is white with a central stripe of red.

### GENERAL SERVICE MEDAL (1939–45)
A large circular gilt medal with a soldier blowing a bugle, and the dates and an Arabic inscription below, and above a small design of a grenade, an anchor, and crossed sword and rifle over two crossed flags. The ribbon has three stripes of scarlet divided by narrower stripes of white with edges of narrow white and black, the black outside.

### VICTORY MEDAL (1945)
A seven-pointed silver star with rays with a circular gilt medallion in the centre with two sprays of laurel surrounding an Arabic inscription and the date. The ribbon has eleven alternate narrow stripes of white and green and red edges.

---

Since the dissolution of the Iraqi monarchy in 1958, awards of some of the above Orders and Medals have been discontinued.


# Israel


### MEDAL FOR HEROISM ('OT HA-GVURA')
This medal is awarded to each person who in action involving

actual conflict with an enemy distinguishes himself or herself conspicuously by gallantry and intrepidity at the risk of his or her life, and above and beyond the call of duty, and by such action directly influences the outcome of battle. The medal, which may be awarded posthumously, corresponds to the British Victoria Cross.

### 507 - FREEDOM STAR ('OT KOMMEMIUT')

This decoration is awarded to every soldier who took part in the War of Liberation and: (a), served in the Israel Defence Forces for a period of at least four months between 1 April 1948 and 10 March 1949, both dates inclusive, or (b), served for a shorter period than that stated above but actively took part in a battle or battles between the dates mentioned. The star may also be awarded posthumously. The blue and white in the ribbon represent the national colours of Israel, and the thin red stripe symbolizes the blood spilt during the war.

### JERUSALEM DEFENCE BADGE ('MAGEN YERUSHALAIM')

This medal was awarded to every soldier who served in one of the units under the command of the O.C. Jerusalem area between 1 April and 10 June 1948, or who served in any other unit which participated in the fighting in or around Jerusalem during the same period. The badge, which is worn on the pocket on the left side consists of a bronze shield with a sword and spray of laurel in white metal, and an inscription below.

### PALMAH BADGE

This badge was awarded to every soldier who was a member of Palmah before 29 November 1947. It is in white metal, and is worn in the same way as the badge just described.

### JEWISH BRIGADE GROUP BADGE

This badge was awarded to every soldier who served in this formation for not less than six months. It is a small metal rectangle striped vertically in light blue, white, and light blue, with a narrow red stripe at the top. The star has a white centre with the rays in yellow. The badge is worn in the same way as the others.

# *Italy*

### THE ORDER OF THE ANNUNZIATA

Until the fall of the monarchy in 1943 this Order, instituted in 1362 as the 'Order of the Collare,' or Collar, was the highest Italian honour and consisted of fifteen knights only. Its holders had the title of 'Cousins of the King,' and took precedence over all other state officials. The statutes were revised several times, and it was Charles III, in 1518, who decreed that it should be known as the 'Annunziata.' On state occasions knights formerly wore a costume of white satin beneath a cloak of purple velvet embroidered in gold; but these fell into disuse, and in later times the insignia consisted of a golden collar worn round the neck from which hung an ornamental openwork gold badge representing the Annunciation, together with a gold and silver star surrounded by eight groups, each of seven golden rays, with, in its centre, the same design as the badge.

Much against his will King Victor Emmanuel III was prevailed upon to confer this high honour upon Ribbentrop, the German Foreign Minister, in May 1939. As Ciano, the Italian Foreign Minister and Mussolini's son-in-law, was to write in his diary – 'Göring . . . had tears in his eyes when he saw the collar of the Annunziata around Ribbentrop's neck. Von Mackensen told me that Göring made a scene, complaining that the collar really belonged to him, since he was the true and only promoter of the Alliance. I promised Mackensen that I would try to get Göring a collar.'

Greatly to the King's displeasure he was forced, as a matter of policy, to award the Annunziata to Göring a year later.

508 - THE ORDER OF ST. MAURICE AND ST. LAZARU

### 508 - THE ORDER OF ST. MAURICE AND ST. LAZARUS (now obsolete)

This Order, founded in 1434, was latterly conferred by the King on persons distinguished in the public service, science, art, letters, trade and charitable works, and also for Military and Naval service. There were five classes: *Knights Grand Cross*, with star on the breast and broad ribbon over the shoulder with the badge on the hip; *Knights Commanders*, with star on the breast and badge round the neck; *Commanders*, with badge round the neck; *Officers* and *Knights*, with badges on the breast. The badge is a Maltese cross placed saltire-wise, green, edged gold with gold knobs on the points, for St. Lazarus; surmounted by a cross 'botoné' enamelled white, edged gold, for St. Maurice. The badge of the first four classes has the Royal Crown above it.

*(Obverse)*

### 509 - MILITARY ORDER OF SAVOY

This Order was founded in 1815, with statutes modified in 1855, 1857, 1861 and 1869. There are five classes, as for the preceding Order. It was primarily intended for rewarding especially distinguished services in war, and for quite exceptional service in peace. The badge is a cross 'Urdé' enamelled white with gold edges resting on a wreath of laurel enamelled green. In the centre, edged with gold, is a circular plaque enamelled crimson with the white cross of Savoy, surrounded by an inscription on a red circular band. The badge of the three superior grades had the Royal Crown above it; that of the *Fourth Class* hangs from a trophy of flags; and the *Fifth Class* from a ring. The stars for the two superior grades are of chased silver with the badge in the centre. The lower grade of this Order could be conferred upon soldiers and sailors. After the fall of the Monarchy the Order was renamed 'The Order of Military Merit of Italy,' and the red cross on a white ground in the centre of the badge was replaced by the letters 'R.I.' ('Republica Italiana') in white on a red ground.

509 - MILITARY ORDER OF SAVOY          *(Reverse)*

## CIVIL ORDER OF SAVOY

This Order was instituted in 1831. There was one class only, that of knights, limited to seventy, who ranked after Knights Commanders of the Order of the Crown of Italy. The badge was worn on the breast, and was a blue-enamelled, square-edged cross, edged gold, worn from a ribbon of white, blue, white. In the centre was the monogram 'C.A.' on a disc of white enamel edged gold.

## 510 - ORDER OF THE CROWN OF ITALY

(now obsolete)

This Order was instituted in 1868 by Victor Emmanuel II to commemorate the union of Italy into a kingdom. There are five classes, as for St. Maurice and St. Lazarus. The badge is a gold cross pattée enamelled white, edged gold, with gold love-knots between the limbs. In the centre, on a blue circular ground edged gold, is a representation of the Iron Crown.

## 511 - ORDER OF MERIT OF THE ITALIAN REPUBLIC

The Order 'Al Merito della Republica Italiana' was established in 1952. Like the older Italian Orders, it has five classes, with a grand cordon awarded in exceptional cases to holders of the grand cross. The design of the badge is the same for all classes, varying only in size. It consists of a cross in white enamel with four Roman eagles in gold between the limbs, surmounted by a crown composed of three battlemented towers in gold. The ribbon is green moiré, with a narrow red stripe near each edge, almost exactly the same as that of the old Turkish Order of the Osmanieh. Ladies are eligible for this Order. There are five classes: *Grand Cross*, with badge on the left hip from a broad ribbon passing over the right shoulder, and on the breast a silver star; *Grand Officer*, with badge round the neck and a star on the breast; *Commander*, with badge round the neck; *Officer*, with badge on the breast and rosette on the ribbon; *Member*, with badge on the breast without rosette.

## 512 - MEDALS FOR MILITARY VALOUR

These were instituted in 1833 in gold, silver, and bronze, for gallantry in action. They are all of the same design, the obverse having the arms of Savoy and two sprays of foliage, surmounted by the crown, and surrounded by the words 'AL VALORE MILITARE.' The reverse has two circular sprays of laurel with room for the name of the recipient in the centre. The gold medals, equivalent to the British Victoria Cross, are very rarely awarded.

Granted to officers and men of the fighting services, these medals can be earned several times over by the same individual. The ribbon is bright blue, moiré, and when worn alone five-pointed stars in gold or silver are worn by possessors of the gold and silver medals.

A silver medal, inscribed on the reverse 'MED. ARGENTO VALOR MILITARE' with an inscription beneath, and on the obverse the shield of the Royal Carabiniere surrounded by the words 'ARMA DEI REALI CARABINIERI NEI SECOLI FEDELE,' was granted to members of that corps for service in Africa in 1936–7. It is worn from the same ribbon as those already described.

**510 - ORDER OF THE CROWN OF ITALY**
*Badge of the Knights Commander*

**511 - ORDER OF MERIT OF THE ITALIAN REPUBLIC**
*Badge of the Grand Officer*

## 513 - MEDALS FOR MARITIME VALOUR

These medals, in gold, silver, and bronze, are awarded for saving life at sea. They are of the same design as the last but with the words 'AL VALORE MARINA' on the obverse.

## 514 - MEDALS FOR AERONAUTICAL VALOUR

These medals are awarded in gold, silver, and bronze. There are two designs. The first has the head of the King on the obverse with the legend 'VITTORIO EMANUELE III RE D'ITALIA,' and on the reverse a wreath with a flying eagle surmounted by a crown, and round the circumference the words 'MEDAGLIA MILITARE AERO-NAUTICA.' The second has on the obverse the shield of Savoy in the claws of a flying eagle with a crown above, and the words 'AL VALORE AERONAUTICA' below. The reverse has fasces on either side with space for the recipient's name in the centre.

## 515 - WAR CROSSES

There are several different War Crosses. The first, instituted during the First World War, is a square-armed bronze cross of normal shape with the words 'MERITO DI GUERRA' surmounted by the crown and Royal monogram on the upper limb, and a Roman sword and spray of oak below. The reverse has a star in the centre with rays reaching to the raised edges. For the Second World War, subsequent to the fall of the Monarchy in 1943, the crown and Royal cypher were replaced by the letters 'R.I.' interlaced. The cross is awarded for war service to those whose conduct has been meri-torious over a period but who have not performed some exception-ally gallant action to merit the award of the Medal for Military Valour. Bars, in the form of small crowns worn on the ribbon, may be awarded for further services. The ribbon is blue with two stripes of white.

Another War Cross, of exactly similar design, but with the in-scription 'CROCE AL VALORE MILITARE,' is worn on the same blue moiré ribbon as the Medal for Military Valour, and appears to be a junior award to the medal.

A fourth specimen is the same shape, but has on the obverse the arms of Spain over the words 'GUERRA POR LA UNIDAD NACIONAL ESPANOLA,' with, below, a sheaf of five arrows. The reverse has the date '17-VII. 1936' over a Roman sword, point up, with stars and sprays of oak and laurel to left and right. The ribbon is in five equal stripes of red, blue, yellow, blue, red. This cross may be of Spanish origin, but was certainly awarded to Italian troops who took part in the Civil War in Spain.

## ITALIAN MEDALS

There is a great profusion of Italian awards, including war medals; medals for long service in the Army, Navy, Air Force, and all the different Government and public departments; besides a further series for service in the Fascist Militia. We cannot hope to mention them all or to reproduce the many ribbons in colour; but the follow-ing, acquired in Rome soon after its occupation by the Allies in June 1944, may be of interest. Practically all Italian medals are in bronze, and have moiré ribbons.

**511 - ORDER OF MERIT OF THE ITALIAN REPUBLIC**
*Insignia of Officer*

**515 - WAR CROSS**          *(Obverse)*

**516 - UNITED ITALY** (1848–70) (reissued with date 1848–1922)

**517 - CAMPAIGN OF 1859**
A silver medal with the effigy of Napoleon III on the obverse awarded to the Italian troops who took part in the campaign.

**GARIBALDI MEDAL**
This silver medal was struck in 1860 and recognized by Royal decree five years later. The Sicilian three-legged badge is worn on the ribbon, which is scarlet with yellow edges.

**518 - WARS OF ITALIAN INDEPENDENCE** (1848–70)
A silver medal with dated laurel bars worn on the ribbon.

**519 - AFRICA CAMPAIGNS** (1891–96)

**520 - CHINA** (1900–01)

**521, 522 - MESSINA EARTHQUAKE** (1908)
A silver medal awarded to those who assisted in succouring the injured after the earthquake at Messina and Reggio in December 1908. The ribbon is in five stripes of white and green, the green being wider than the white. Another medal in gold was awarded for particularly distinguished service on the same occasion. The ribbon is green with white edges.

**523 - LIBYA (War against Turkey)** (1911)

**AVEZZANO EARTHQUAKE** (1915)
Ribbon, red with black edges.

**518 - WAR MEDAL** (1915–18)
Ribbon, eighteen narrow stripes of red, white and green.

**524 - VOLUNTEERS IN WAR OF 1915–18**

**LIBERATION OF FIUME** (1919) (unofficial)
Ribbon, three equal stripes of claret colour, orange and blue. A bronze medal, 39 mm. diameter.

**525 - ETHIOPIAN CAMPAIGN** (1935)

**526 - VOLUNTEERS IN ETHIOPIAN CAMPAIGN**

**527, 528 - WAR IN SPAIN** (1936)
At least four medals of varying designs, appear to have been awarded to Italian troops who participated in the Civil War in Spain. Two are dated 17 July 1936. Two have ribbons of five equal stripes of red and yellow with narrow black edges; another has a ribbon with a broad yellow centre flanked by stripes of red with narrow black edges; while a fourth ribbon has a yellow centre flanked by narrow stripes of black with broad red edges.

**529 - VOLUNTEERS FOR WAR IN SPAIN**
There are two medals, both with claret-coloured ribbons, one with a stripe of yellow, red, yellow in the centre, and the other with a central stripe of red, yellow, red with a thin edging of white.

(*Obverse*)

**521 - MESSINA EARTHQUAKE** (*Reverse*)

(*Obverse*)

**518 - WAR MEDAL** (1915–18)
(*Reverse*)

**530 - ALBANIA** (1939)

**531 - ITALIAN CAMPAIGN AGAINST FRANCE** (1940)
There are two medals, one with the head of Prince Umberto on the obverse, with the legend 'UMBERTO DI SAVOIA. PRINCIPE DI PIEMONTE,' and the other with a representation of an Italian soldier scaling a mountain, and the word 'VINCERE!' above. The reverse of both medals is the same, and shows a flying angel with a shield over the inscription '21.22.23.24 GIVGNO—A—XVIII,' with a mountain range below, and beneath 'BATTAGLIA DEL FRONTE ALPINO OCCIDENTALE.' They were given for the brief campaign over the Alpine passes and along the Riviera coast by Prince Umberto's thirty-two divisions in June 1940. The ribbon for both medals is the same, nineteen narrow alternating stripes of white and red.

*(Obverse)*

**WAR WITH GREECE AND YUGOSLAVIA** (1940–41)
This is a Ninth Army medal, apparently unofficial. The ribbon is half black, half red with borders of narrow green, white and red.

**532 - GREECE** (1940)

**533 - AXIS MEDAL** (1941)
This is a bronze medal, possibly unofficial, with heads of Mussolini and Hitler on the obverse.

**534 - DALMATIA** (1941)

**535 - OCCUPATION OF GREECE** (1941)

**525 - ETHIOPIAN CAMPAIGN** (1935)     *(Reverse)*

**536 - MEDAL FOR AFRICAN CAMPAIGN** (1940–43)
Specimens of a medal intended to commemorate the triumphal occupation of Egypt and the Suez Canal by the Axis forces were found on board a sunken wreck in Bizerta harbour after its occupation by the Allies in May 1943, and were readily obtainable in Italy later. The medal is bronze, 27 mm. in diameter, and on the obverse two knights in armour, Germany and Italy, are standing on the forelegs of a helpless crocodile, the British Empire, and forcibly closing its jaws, the Suez Canal. On the reverse is an archway over a reef knot, with a swastika on one side and the Italian fasces on the other. Round the rim in both languages is the legend – 'GERMAN-ITALIAN CAMPAIGN IN AFRICA.' The symbolism of the design was premature.

**ITALIAN TROOPS IN RUSSIAN CAMPAIGN**
A brooch pin of dull white metal, consisting of the crossed swords on a wreath with the words 'FRONTE RUSSO' was apparently awarded to Italian troops serving against the Russians. Another decoration, which may not be official, was a Maltese cross enamelled white edged silver, with a plain reverse bearing the words 'DNJEPR-DONETZ—BUG—DON—LUGLIO 941 LUGLIO 942' on the four arms, and the letters 'C.S.I.R.' in the centre. The ribbon is half black, half white.

**537 - WAR MEDAL** (1940–43)

## LIBERATION MEDAL (1945)
The ribbon has five equal stripes of green, white, blue, white, red. On the blue centre are two narrow stripes of red.

## VOLUNTEERS FOR LIBERTY
The ribbon is crimson with edges of green, white, red. On the crimson are woven the letters 'V.L.' in gold wire.

## STAR OF ITALIAN SOLIDARITY (1945)
This is in three classes, gold or silver-gilt, silver, and bronze. It consists of a five-pointed star with rays between the points, and in the centre a disc on which is shown in relief a figure succouring a sick man. The *Second* and *Third Classes* have no rays between the points of the star. The ribbon is green with narrow red (outer) and white (inner) edges.

## 538 - LONG SERVICE (ARMY)

## 539 - LONG SERVICE (NAVY)

## LONG SERVICE (COLONIAL TROOPS)
This is a five-pointed star in dull silver with a ribbon of eleven equal stripes of green and white.

## 540, 541, 542 - FASCIST MEDALS
Mussolini instituted a medal for those who took part in the Fascist march on Rome in October 1922. The ribbon is half claret colour, half yellow.

There was a bronze Fascist Medal, bearing the dates 1920–1923. The ribbon is black, with edges of red, white and green. It was apparently awarded for long service in the Militia, and bronze, silver or gold replicas of Roman swords were used on the ribbon for further periods of service when it was worn alone.

There was also a bronze Maltese cross, with four fasces between the limbs, awarded for ten years' service and worn from the same ribbon.

Another Fascist decoration or medal had a black ribbon with a central stripe of red, white and green, and small gilt stars were used on the ribbon when worn alone to denote further periods of service.

# Japan

## ORDER OF THE CHRYSANTHEMUM (KIKKWA DAIJASHO)
This Order was founded in 1876 by the Emperor Mutsu Hito in one class only, and rarely conferred except upon members of the Royal Family or foreign royalties or rulers. The handsome badge is a star of thirty-two rays with double points of different lengths, enamelled white, edged gold, not unlike the points of a compass,

with the longest rays at north, east, south and west, and the shortest midway between them. In the centre is a large cabochon garnet. Between each of the longer rays the circumference is filled in by a small silver chrysanthemum placed between two leaves enamelled green, edged gold. Above the badge and the ring for suspension is a larger embossed chrysanthemum in silver. The broad ribbon, 102 mm. wide, worn over the shoulder with the badge on the hip, is scarlet moiré with violet borders of 22 mm. Another star, similar to the badge, is worn on the breast.

## ORDER OF THE PAULOWNIA SUN (TOKWA DIJASHO)

This Order, founded in 1888, has one class only, and is virtually the highest grade of the Order of the Rising Sun, described below. The badges of both Orders incorporate the red sun with rays of white and gold, and the mauve flowers and green leaves of the paulownia tree, the flower of the Tycoon's arms, embodied in the Imperial Japanese arms. The sash is red moiré with stripes of white towards each edge.

## 543 - ORDER OF THE RISING SUN (KIOKUJITSASHO)

This Order was established in 1876 in eight classes. The decoration has a cabochon garnet in the centre, from which spring thirty-two rays of white enamel edged gold or silver according to class. It hangs from a spray of three paulownia flowers and leaves enamelled in their proper colours. The star consists of the enamelled badge without the paulownia leaves mounted on a similar shaped silver star of eight points. The *Seventh Class* has a decoration formed of the paulownia flowers and leaves alone, in enamel, and the *Eighth Class* the flowers and leaves in silver.

## 544 - ORDER OF THE SACRED TREASURE (ZAIHOSHO)

This Order was instituted in 1888, in eight classes, and frequently bestowed upon Naval and Military officers for war service as well as for distinguished service in peace. The decoration itself is symbolic of the three treasures bequeathed to his successor by the first emperor of Japan – a mirror, a collar and some swords. The central device consists of an eight-pointed silver star (the mirror), on a circular ground of blue enamel. This is encircled by an irregular-shaped collar of sixteen rubies (eight large and eight small), from which spring twenty rays of white enamel (representing the sword blades), edged gold or silver according to class. The two lowest classes have the decoration in plain silver, unenamelled.

## 545 - ORDER OF THE GOLDEN KITE

This Order was instituted in 1891 and awarded solely for bravery in action by officers and men of the Army, Navy and Air Force. The Order has seven classes, and the badge is in the shape of an irregular star in red enamel, edged gold or silver according to class, upon which is a sort of blue saltire with two golden rods or sceptres. Over the saltire is a sword, point down, on the guard of which is a golden kite with wings spread. According to an ancient Japanese legend, it was a kite hovering in the air which helped to win a victory for one of the early Japanese Emperors. The badge of the junior grade is carried out entirely in silver.

## WAR MEDALS, ETC.

**WAR MEDAL** (1874)
Ribbon, white with green edges.

**CHINO-JAPANESE WAR** (1894–95)
Ribbon, three equal stripes of green, white, green.

**CHINA** (1900)
Ribbon, five stripes of white, green, white, green, white with very narrow green edges.

**546 - RUSSO-JAPANESE WAR** (1904–05)

**ANNEXATION OF KOREA** (1912)
Ribbon, yellow with white edges and a central stripe of scarlet.

**VICTORY MEDAL** (1914–18)
The same double rainbow ribbon as for Great Britain and the other Allies.

**547 - WAR WITH GERMANY** (1914–18)

**548 - MANCHURIAN INCIDENT** (1931 and 1934)

**549 - CHINA INCIDENT** (1937)

**CORONATION** (1928)
Ribbon, five equal stripes of violet, white, scarlet, yellow, green.

**2,600th ANNIVERSARY YEAR OF DYNASTY** (1940)
Ribbon, lavender blue with eight very thin stripes in the centre.

**RED CROSS MEDAL**
Ribbon, scarlet with two narrow stripes of saxe blue towards each edge.

# Principality of Liechtenstein

## ORDER OF MERIT OF THE PRINCIPALITY OF LIECHTENSTEIN
Instituted by H.R.H. Prince Franz I on 22 July 1937 for recognition of services to the Principality by its subjects and by foreigners, the Order may be conferred in five classes. The reigning Prince is the Grand Master, and the five classes are:

*Grand Star*, in which the insignia is the Badge suspended from a sash, and the Star of the Order worn on the breast.

*Grand Cross*, as above but with the Star in silver rather than in gold.

*Commander with Star*, in which the insignia is a variation of the Badge is worn suspended from a neck ribbon, and the Star is silver.

*Commander*, as above but without the Star.

*Knight*, in which the Badge is worn suspended from a ribbon on the chest.

The *Badge* is a gold cross pommé, enamelled blue and edged with red, and in the centre a medallion with a stylized, gothic 'L' on a blue ground, surrounded by a red circlet. The *Star* consists of this badge surmounting an 8-pointed gold or silver star (see above) with faceted rays. The ribbon is of red and blue halves, the blue half being worn nearest to the left shoulder.

*Star of the Grand Officer (Shown f*

# Grand Duchy of Luxembourg

### 550 - ORDER OF THE OAK CROWN
This Order was founded in 1841 in five classes, with medals in silver-gilt, silver, and bronze, attached to the Order. The badge is a four-armed cross in white enamel, edged gold, resting on a wreath of oak leaves and acorns in gold. In the centre, on a base of green enamel, is the initial 'W' surmounted by a crown.

### VOLUNTEERS MEDAL (1914–18; 1939–45)
This is a round medal superimposed on a cross and two crossed swords. On the obverse is the seal of John the Blind with the legend 'LUXEMBURGUM VIRTUTI.' The ribbon has narrow horizontal stripes of blue and white with red borders. A silver star is worn on the ribbon by volunteers who were wounded in either war.

### 551 - MILITARY MEDAL
This medal was instituted in 1945, and is the highest purely military decoration of Luxemburg. It is a bronze medal with the effigy and legend of the Grand Duchess on the obverse, and on the reverse the date '1940' and the arms of the Duchy surmounted by a crown.

### 552 - CROIX DE GUERRE (1940–45)
This is a bronze cross, surmounted by a crown and crossed swords. On the obverse, in the centre, the initial 'C' and a crown. On the reverse is a wreath of oak. Palms in silver and in gilt can be awarded to those mentioned in despatches.

### ORDER OF THE RESISTANCE (1940–44)
This Order was instituted in 1946 in two classes; a cross and a medal. The ribbon is the opposite of that for the 'Volunteers' Medal,' viz., narrow red and white horizontal stripes with blue borders.

**550 - ORDER OF THE OAK CR**
*Badge of the Grand Cross*
*(Shown full size)*

## CROSS OF HONOUR AND MILITARY MERIT

This decoration was established in 1951 in three classes, gilt, silver, and bronze. The obverse has the shield of the Grand Duchy with four sword pommels and the words 'HONOR VIRTUS PATRIA,' and the reverse the letters 'CC' beneath a crown. The ribbon is a medium blue with three sets of narrow white, red, white stripes spaced across it. Palms in silver and in gilt may be awarded to holders of the cross mentioned in despatches.

*Campaign ribbons* in three classes were instituted at the same time as the Cross of Honour. They have red edges of varying widths with one, two or three blue stripes on a white background, for one, two or three years' war service.

**550 - ORDER OF THE OAK CROWN** *Fourth Class*

## Principality of Monaco

## ORDER OF CHARLES THE HOLY

This Order was instituted by Prince Charles III on 15 March 1858 for bestowal upon subjects of Monaco and foreigners for services rendered to the Prince and to the Principality. There are five classes:

*Grand Cross*, in which the insignia is the Badge of the Order, worn from a sash, and the Star of the Order, worn on the chest.

*Grand Officer*, in which the Badge of the Order is worn suspended from a ribbon on the chest and the Star is worn on the right side of the chest.

*Commander*, in which the Badge is worn suspended from a neck ribbon.

*Officer*, in which the Badge is worn suspended from a ribbon, with rosette, on the breast.

*Knight*, in which the Badge is worn suspended from a ribbon, without rosette.

The *Badge* is a white-enamelled Maltese Cross, edged in red and tipped with small gold globes; in the centre is a medallion in red with two stylized 'Cs,' mirrored and back-to-back under a small gold crown and surrounded by a circlet bearing the inscription 'PRINCEPS ET PATRIA' (Prince and Country) in gold on a white ground. The obverse of the medallion bears the arms of the Principality with the inscription 'DEO JUVANTE' (With the Help of God). Between the arms of the cross is a wreath of laurel, and the whole medal is suspended by a gold crown. The *Star* of the Order consists of the Badge surmounting an eight-pointed faceted star, but without the suspension crown. The ribbon is red with a broad central white stripe and edged with narrow white stripes.

## ORDER OF THE CROWN

Instituted on 20 July 1960 by H.R.H. Prince Rainier III as a

**ORDER OF CHARLES THE HOLY**
*Badge of the Grand Cross (Shown full size)*

reward for services to the Prince and as a mark of his respect. As Grand Master of the Order, the reigning Prince has the sole right of conferment. There are five classes:

*Grand Officer*, in which the insignia is the Badge worn from a sash, and the Star of the Order.

*Grand Officer*, in which the Badge is worn from a neck ribbon, and the Star worn on the right of the chest.

*Commander*, in which the Badge is worn from a neck ribbon.

*Officer*, in which the Badge is worn suspended from a ribbon on the breast with a rosette.

*Knight*, in which the Badge is worn suspended from a breast ribbon without rosette.

The *Badge* is a form of cross pattée, each arm composed of five fluted bars, the central bar in gold and the others silver. In the centre of the cross is a superimposed white medallion on which is a gold and red crown. Between the arms of the cross are the royal monogram – two 'Rs' placed face-to-face with 'III' between them. The badge is suspended by a wreath of oak and laurel. The *Star* is similar to the Badge but is without the suspension wreath. The ribbon is olive-green with a central red stripe.

### ORDER OF GRIMALDI

Instituted by H.R.H. Prince Rainier III on 18 November 1954, the Order of Grimaldi is named after the parent family line of the Principality and is conferred for services to the reigning Prince by his subjects and by foreigners. The insignia is worn visibly and members of the Order are entitled to a salute by the military. It is conferred in the same five classes as is the Order of the Crown. The Badge is a white-enamelled Mantua Cross, edged in gold and tipped with golden globes; a central medallion in gold bears a figure of a galloping knight, and the badge is suspended by means of a gold crown. The *Star* consists of an enlarged variation of the Badge's central medallion in gold, surrounded by 16 silver rhombs, each faceted and the outer points forming the 16 points of the Star. The ribbon is white with a narrow red stripe near the borders.

**ORDER OF CHARLES THE HOLY**
*Badge of the Grand Cross (Reverse)*
*(Shown full size)*

# Montenegro

### 553 - ORDER OF DANILO

This Order was established in 1852 in five classes: *Grand Cordon, Grand Officer, Commander, Officer* and *Member*. The badge of the *First* to *Fourth Classes* is a blue and red enamel cross lined white. In the centre is the inscription 'DANILO I, PRINCE OF MONTENEGRO.' The reverse bears the date '1852–53.' The whole is surmounted by a gilt crown.

### 554 - MEDALS FOR BRAVERY

Montenegro, like Serbia, also had its Obilitch Medal, which was instituted in 1851, and was awarded solely for bravery in the field. The medal is of gold, and bears on the obverse the head of Miloch Obilitch, the hero of the battle of Kossovo against the Turks in 1389, together with an inscription, and on the reverse the words 'HONOUR, LIBERTY, FOR BRAVERY.' The medal, which is very rare, hangs from a crossover ribbon of the national colours. It could be awarded to officers as well as to men, but not more than one man per company was allowed to receive it. It therefore corresponded to some extent to the Victoria Cross.

Another Montenegrin Medal with the same ribbon is the silver medal 'For Military Valour' instituted by King Nicholas during the wars of 1875–7. It bears on the obverse the national arms, and on the reverse the same wording as the Obilitch Medal. It was reserved exclusively for officers and soldiers of the Army, was granted solely for bravery in battle, and corresponds in some measure to the British D.C.M. and M.M.

# Muscat and Oman

(Obverse)       (Obverse)       (Obverse)

**555 - OMAN GALLANTRY MEDAL** *(Reverse)*   **556 - OMAN BRAVERY MEDAL** *(Reverse)*   **557 - OMAN ACCESSION MEDAL** *(Reverse)*

(*Obverse*)                    (*Reverse*)

**558 - OMAN GENERAL SERVICE MEDAL
WITH KHUNJAR** (*Bar*)

**559 - JABAL AKHDAR
CAMPAIGN MEDAL** (*Reverse*)
(*Note. Obverse as of 555*)

# Netherlands

## 560 - MILITAIRE WILLEMSORDE
## (MILITARY ORDER OF WILLIAM)

This Order was founded by King William I in 1815, and is the highest military decoration. It is awarded to sailors, soldiers and airmen of all ranks, as well as to civilians, for 'most conspicuous acts of bravery, leadership and extreme devotion to duty in the presence of the enemy.' The badge is a white-enamelled Maltese cross with eight points, with a golden pearl on each point. On the arms are the words 'VOOR MOED BELEID TROUW' ('For Courage, Generalship, Loyalty'). The cross is superimposed upon a saltire of green laurels. On the reverse is a medallion of blue enamel, bearing the letter 'W' and a laurel wreath. The badge hangs from the Royal Crown, at the top of which is a ring through which the ribbon passes. There are four classes: *Grand Cross*, with a star on the breast and the badge worn on the left hip from a broad ribbon passing over the right shoulder; *Commander*, with a star on the breast and the badge worn round the neck; *Knight Third Class*, with a badge in gold and enamel on the left breast with a rosette on the ribbon; *Knight Fourth Class*, with a badge in silver and enamel on left breast. The Order corresponds to the British Victoria Cross.

## VERZETSKRUIS (RESISTANCE CROSS) (1946)

This is a bronze four-armed cross surmounted by a crown. In the centre is a knightly figure spearing a dragon underfoot, and between

**562 - ORDER OF THE LION
OF THE NETHERLANDS**
*Badge of the Commander* (*Reverse*)

the arms are short rays. On the arms are the words 'TROUW TOT IN DEN DOOD' ('Faithful unto death'). The ribbon is maroon with an orange stripe near each edge.

## 561 - MEDALS OF HONOUR FOR GALLANTRY IN SAVING LIFE

Medals in gold, silver, and bronze for gallantry in saving life at sea or on land may be awarded to any Netherlander, or to any foreigner saving the life of a Netherlands subject.

## 562 - NEDERLANDSCHE LEEUW (LION OF THE NETHERLANDS)

This Order was also founded by King William I in 1815, for award to the Netherlanders of proven patriotism, outstanding zeal and devotion to their civil duties, and extraordinary ability in science and arts. It can be bestowed on officers of the fighting forces and also upon foreigners. The badge consists of a white-enamelled Maltese cross with a golden 'W' between each of the arms and in the centre a blue-enamelled medallion bearing the motto 'VIRTUS NOBILITAT.' Above the badge is the Royal Crown. The reverse shows the Netherlands lion. There are three classes: *Grand Cross*, with the badge (82 x 61 mm.) worn on a golden star on the left side and a broad ribbon over the right shoulder with the badge on the left hip. *Commander*, with the badge worn round the neck; *Knight*, with the badge worn on the left breast. The ribbon is Nassau blue with an orange stripe near each edge.

*Badge of the Grand Cross (Reverse)*
*(Shown full size)*

Attached to the Order are 'Brothers,' who may be nominated for useful deeds, self-sacrifice or other proofs of philanthropy. They wear a silver medal with the lion on one side and the motto on the other. The ribbon is Nassau blue with a broad centre stripe of orange.

## 563 - ORDE VAN ORANJE NASSAU (ORDER OF ORANGE NASSAU)

This Order was established in 1892 by the Queen Regent, Queen Emma, in the name of her daughter, Queen Wilhelmina, for rewarding Netherlanders or foreigners who have deserved exceedingly well of the state or society. The badge consists of a white-enamelled cross of the same shape as that of the other Netherlands Orders, resting upon a wreath of laurel in gold. In the centre is a blue-enamelled shield with the lion in gold surrounded by a circle of white enamel bearing the words 'JE MAINTIENDRAI.' The reverse, shown in the illustration, has a similar central device with the initial 'W' surmounted by a crown surrounded by the words 'GOD ZIJ MET ONS' on white enamel. For Military or Naval officers the laurel wreath is replaced by silver swords crossed behind the central medallion. There are five classes: *Grand Cross*, with a star on the left side and badge from sash over right shoulder; *Grand Officer*, with star on left side, and badge round neck; *Knight Commander*, with badge round neck; *Officer*, with badge on left breast with rosette on ribbon; *Knight*, with badge in silver on left breast. The ribbon is orange with edges of Nassau blue, the colours being

**563 - ORDER OF ORANGE NASSAU**
*Badge of the Grand Officer (Obverse)*
*(Shown full size)*

divided by a narrow stripe of white. Attached to the Order are medals of gold, silver, and bronze, worn from a narrower ribbon of the same colours. They are circular in shape and surmounted by a crown and bear on one side the representation of the badge, and on the other a 'W' and crown with the words 'GOD ZIJ MET ONS.'

## HUISORDE VAN ORANJE
## (ORDER OF THE HOUSE OF ORANGE)

This Order, established in 1905, is awarded for outstanding services to members of the Royal House and corresponds to the Royal Victorian Order. It has six classes: *Grand Cross*, *Grand Officer*, *Commander*, *Officer* and *Knights*, *First* and *Second Class*, together with Cross of Merit in gold or silver, Medals of Honour in gold, silver or bronze, a silver medal for saving life, and gold and silver medals for science and art.

Ladies can be appointed 'Dames of Honour' of the Order. The ribbon is orange.

## 564 - BRONZEN LEEUW (BRONZE LION)

Both the Bronzen Kruis and the Vliegerkruis, described later, might originally be awarded 'with honourable mention' for acts of a military character of gallantry and leadership in the presence of the enemy which, though not considered to merit the award of the Militaire Willemsorde, were, nevertheless, of a very high standard. The 'honourable mention' was designated by a crown on the ribbon. This emblem, instituted in 1877, was abolished in 1944 and was replaced by a new decoration called the Bronze Lion. It consists of a bronze cross with a circular shield in the centre bearing the crowned lion of the Netherlands. The reverse is plain. The ribbon has nine vertical stripes of alternate Nassau blue and orange, the stripes at each edge being blue. If the cross is given a second time an Arabic figure '2' is worn on the ribbon.

## VERZETSSTER OOST-AZIE (1942–45)
## (EAST ASIA RESISTANCE STAR)

This decoration was awarded for similar reasons as the European Resistance Cross, already mentioned. The ribbon is maroon with two narrow orange stripes in the centre.

## 565 - BRONZEN KRUIS

On 11 June 1940, Queen Wilhelmina established a bronze cross for award to officers, N.C.O.s and men of any of the Netherlands' fighting forces, as well as to those of the Merchant Navy, and to civilians, who distinguish themselves by acts of gallantry or leadership in the presence of the enemy. It may also be awarded to foreigners who, in so doing, further the interests of the Netherlands. The cross, which corresponds to the British D.S.C., M.C., D.S.M., and M.M., can be given for a single outstanding act, as well as for bravery and enterprise in action over a period. The reverse has the sprays of oak and laurel in the centre outside the date '1940,' and on the four arms the inscription 'TROUW – AAN – KONINGEN – EN – VADERLAND.' If awarded a second time an Arabic figure '2' is worn on the ribbon.

*(Obverse)*

563 - ORDER OF ORANGE
NASSAU - GOLD MEDAL
OF HONOUR          *(Reverse)*

## 566 - KRUIS VOOR VERDIENSTE (CROSS FOR MERIT)

This decoration was established by Queen Wilhelmina on 20 February 1941 to honour courageous and resourceful deeds of a non-military character in connection with enemy action. It could be bestowed upon Dutch subjects or foreigners who had 'acted for the benefit of the Netherlands.' It consists of a bronze St. George's Cross with a 'W' surmounted by a crown in the centre and a spray of laurel on either side. The centre of the reverse has the Dutch lion with the two sprays of laurel, and on the top and bottom arms the words 'Voor – Verdienste.' Arabic figures are added to the ribbon for subsequent awards.

## 567 - VLIEGERKRUIS (FLYING CROSS)

This decoration was established by Queen Wilhelmina in August 1941 to honour deeds of courage, initiative and perseverance in aircraft in the air in time of war, either in contact with the enemy or not. It can be bestowed upon officers and men of the Army, Navy or Air Force; on civilians and on foreigners if their action is of exceptional merit to the Netherlands. The cross is of silver. If it is won more than once a 'bar' is added to the ribbon in the shape of Roman numeral in gold – 'II,' 'III,' 'IV,' etc.

## 568 - ERETEKEN VOOR BELANGRIJKE KRIJSVERRIGTINGEN

**566 - CROSS FOR MERIT**
*(Obverse)*

Usually called the 'Expeditiekruis' or 'Expedition Cross,' this decoration was established in 1869 by King William III for award to all ranks taking part in expeditions officially recognized as 'important.' The badge consists of a silver cross with a 'W' on each of the arms and in the centre the effigy of the King encircled by a garter with the words 'Voor Krijgsverrigtingen.' A wreath of oak leaves appears between the arms of the cross which is surmounted by a crown in gold. Bars, with the appropriate name and date, are worn on the ribbon for each expedition, and some thirty bars have been awarded, mostly for operations in the Netherlands East Indies.

The cross really corresponds to the British General Service Medals. The ribbon is green with broad orange edges, and a crown worn upon it denotes an honourable mention. Since 1944 this emblem has presumably been superseded by the specific award of the 'Bronze Lion.'

## 569 - OORLOGSHERINNERINGS KRUIS (COMMEMORATIVE CROSS OF THE WAR)

This decoration was instituted by Queen Wilhelmina in March 1944 for award to everybody in the Armed Forces, the Merchant Navy and Civil Air Lines who had served in the Second World War for at least six months. The cross is in bronze, but with the head of Queen Wilhelmina is an oval garter worded 'Voor Krijgsver-richtingen' surrounded by a wreath. On each arm of the cross is the letter 'W.'

Clasps, or bars, were awarded for general war service and for special operations. A person was not entitled to more than one 'general' bar, but could wear as many 'special' bars as he qualified for. When the ribbon is worn alone bars are indicated by small bronze stars, up to the number of four. The following bars have been authorized:

*General* – 'KRIJG TER ZEE, 1940–45' (War at Sea). 'OORLOGS-VLUCHTEN, 1940–45' (War Flights). 'OORLOGSDIENST-KOOP-VAARDIJ, 1940–45' (War Service, Merchant Navy). OORLOGSDIENST-VISSERIJ, 1940–45' (War Service, Fishing Fleet). KRIJG TE LAND, 1940–45' (War Service on Land).

*Special Operations* – 'NEDERLAND, MEI, 1940.' 'NEDERLANDSCH-INDIE, 1941–42.' 'JAVA-ZEE, 1941–42.' 'MIDDELANDSE ZEE, 1940–45.' 'ARNHEM-NIJMEGEN-WALCHEREN, 1944.' 'NORMANDIE, 1944.' 'OOST-AZIE-ZUID PACIFIC, 1942–45.'

## ERETEKEN VOOR ORDE EN VREDE
## (CROSS FOR ORDER AND PEACE) (1939–45)

This is an eight-pointed bronze star, the top point hidden by a crown. In the centre is a garter with the words 'ORDE-VREDE' encircling the initial 'W,' and between the garter and the crown are crossed swords. The ribbon is in five equal stripes, of red, white, blue, white, red.

## MOBILISATIE OORLOGS KRUIS
## (MOBILIZATION CROSS) (1939–45)

This is a four-armed bronze bross with pointed ends resting on crossed swords and having a wreathed steel helmet in the centre. The ribbon is deep maroon with an orange stripe in the centre.

## 570 - ERETEKEN VOOR LANGDURIGE
## DIENST ALS OFFICIER

This was established in 1844, and consists of a cross with four arms, in the centre of which is a wreath of olive and oak leaves around two crossed swords and the Roman numerals indicating the number of years served. It is awarded to all those who have served for fifteen years or more as officers, and the numeral 'XV' is changed every five years to 'XX,' 'XXV,' 'XXX,' etc. The ribbon is in three equal stripes of orange, white and blue, the orange being worn on the inner side.

## MEDALS FOR HONOURABLE AND
## FAITHFUL SERVICE

These medals were established in 1825 for the Army and 1845 for the Navy, and awarded to N.C.O.s, petty officers and men. They comprise a bronze medal for twelve years' service; silver, for twenty-four years'; gold, for thirty-six years'; and a larger gold medal for fifty years'. Miniatures of the medals are worn on the ribbon in undress uniform, and the ribbon is orange moiré.

## MOBILIZATION CROSS

This decoration was established to commemorate the mobilization of the Netherlands Armed Forces from 1914 to 1919. It is a bronze cross bearing the dates. The ribbon is blue with red, white, and blue edges, divided from the blue in the centre by a narrow white stripe.

A similar cross in German silver, known as the 'White Mobilisation Cross,' was awarded mainly to civilians, and has a white ribbon with similar red, white and blue edges.

## 571 - KRUIS VOOR RECHT EN VRIJHEID (CROSS FOR RIGHT AND FREEDOM)
This decoration was established in July 1951 to reward members of the Netherlands Forces who take part in campaigns undertaken in conjunction with other members of the United Nations. It is a four-armed silver cross with crossed swords between the arms and in the centre an oval shield with a crown and the letter 'J,' for Queen Juliana. The reverse shows the Netherlands lion. A bar bearing the name and date of the campaign is worn with the medal, and in undress an eight-pointed star is carried on the ribbon for each bar awarded.

## DE RUYTER MEDAL
For services to shipping. Ribbon is orange with a gold, silver or bronze disc bearing the letter 'R.'

## GOVERNMENT RED CROSS MEDAL
Ribbon is red.

## ERKENTELIJKHEIDSMEDAILLE (RECOGNITION MEDAL)
Ribbon, orange with white central stripe.

## LOMBOK CROSS (NETHERLANDS EAST INDIES)
Ribbon, orange with four blue stripes.

## MILITARY COAST WATCH LONG SERVICE MEDAL
Ribbon, half blue, half yellow.

## CORONATION MEDAL (QUEEN WILHELMINA) (1898)
Ribbon, orange, blue, orange.

## WEDDING OF QUEEN WILHELMINA AND PRINCE HENRY (1901), AND SILVER WEDDING (1926)
Ribbon, orange, with light blue, yellow and red stripes at each edge, the red outermost.

## 572 - WEDDING OF PRINCESS JULIANA (1937)
Ribbon, orange, with red (outer) and yellow (inner) stripes at each edge, and a stripe of red, yellow and pale blue in the centre.

## 573 - CORONATION MEDAL (QUEEN JULIANA) (1948)
Ribbon, orange with edges of red, white and blue, and two narrow dark blue stripes in the centre.

## 574 - COMMEMORATION MEDAL (AIR-RAID PRECAUTIONS SERVICE) (1940–45)
Ribbon, half dark blue, half grey.

## 'CROSS FOR FIVE CAMPS' (MILITARY FITNESS STANDARD)
Instituted 1931. Ribbon, blue with one vertical silver stripe in the centre.

**575 - ROYAL ORDER OF ST. OLAF**
*Star and Badge of the Grand Cross*
*(Shown full size)*

*Norway*

## 575 - ROYAL ORDER OF ST. OLAF

This, the only Norwegian Order, was founded by King Oscar I in 1847. It has four classes: *Grand Cross*, with star and sash; *Commander*, with badge round the neck; *Knight First Class*, with badge on the breast with rosette on the ribbon; *Knight Second Class*, with badge on the breast with plain ribbon. The Grand Cross has been conferred 'With Chain,' on rare occasions and the Commander's cross may be awarded with a star. When granted to personnel of the Armed Forces there are crossed swords between the crown and the upper limb of the cross. Women are eligible.

## 576 - WAR CROSS

This decoration was instituted in 1941 for award to officers and men of the Norwegian and Allied fighting forces for most conspicuous bravery and leadership before the enemy on land, sea or in the air, as well as to officers and men of the Mercantile Marine, and to Norwegians or Allied subjects who rendered meritorious military or civil activity contributing to the defence of Norway.

The cross is in bronze and the ribbon is in the colours of the Naval and Mercantile ensign. A small bronze sword is worn on the ribbon, each subsequent award being denoted by another sword. The War Cross could be awarded posthumously.

## 577 - WAR MEDAL

This medal was instituted in 1941 for award to officers and men of the Norwegian and Allied fighting forces, as well as to Norwegian and Allied civilians, who had meritoriously taken part in the war for Norway, or had rendered service to the defence of the country.

The medal is in bronze, and the ribbon represents the colours of the national banner – red, with a 4-mm. yellow stripe and a narrower yellow stripe towards each edge. A star could be added to the ribbon for each subsequent award up to three. The medal could also be awarded posthumously.

## 575 - ST. OLAF'S MEDAL

This medal was instituted by the King in March 1939 for contribution to the advancement of Norwegian goodwill abroad, etc. The medal is silver, with the effigy of King Haakon VII and a legend on the obverse, and is surmounted by the monogram 'H.7' and a crown. The medal, 'med ekegren,' or oak leaves, was extended in 1942, for award as a war decoration for personal contribution to the Norwegian cause. In this case a silver spray of oak leaves is worn on the ribbon, with an additional spray for each subsequent award. The ribbon is as for the Order of St. Olaf.

## 578 - KING HAAKON VII FREEDOM CROSS AND FREEDOM MEDAL

These decorations were established in 1945 to commemorate the liberation of Norway, and awarded to military personnel or civilians, including Allies, who had made outstanding contributions to the Norwegian cause during the war.

The cross is of white enamel, narrowly edged gold, with a central plaque enamelled red, edged gold, with the gold monogram 'H.7.' and a crown above. The reverse has the words 'ALT FOR NORGE' across the transverse arms, with '7 JUNI' above and '1945' below. The ribbon is dark blue with a white stripe near each edge, and in service dress is worn with a gilt monogram as used on the obverse of the cross.

The Freedom Medal is of bronze, and has on the obverse the same monogram and crown as used in the cross, with the words 'ALT FOR NORGE' above and '1940–1945' below. The ribbon is plain dark blue, and in service dress is worn with a small bronze monogram and crown.

*(Obverse)*

## PARTICIPATION MEDAL

This medal was instituted for service during the Second World War and awarded to those who took part in the underground movement both at home and abroad. It is a bronze medal with the lion shield and crown of Norway on a circular grille or network, with the dates '9 APRIL 1940' at the top and '8 MAI 1945' below. A small bronze rosette is worn on the ribbon, which has broad red edges and a white centre, with narrow blue stripes towards each edge of the white.

## 579 - HAAKON VII 70th ANNIVERSARY MEDAL

This medal was awarded to personnel serving in the Norwegian forces on 3 August 1942. It is bronze and surmounted by a crown for suspension, with the effigy of the King in military uniform surrounded by the inscription 'HAAKON 7 NORGES KONGE.'

## MEDAL FOR OUTSTANDING SERVICES AS A CITIZEN

This medal was instituted in gold or silver in 1819. The ribbon is scarlet, with a central stripe of blue narrowly edged with white.

**577 - WAR MEDAL** *(Reverse)*

## 580 - MEDAL FOR HEROIC DEEDS

This medal, in gold or silver, was instituted in 1885 for exceptional acts of gallantry in saving life or similar deeds.

## MEDAL FOR CIVIL SERVICES

This medal, in gold and silver, was instituted in 1908 for outstanding merit in art, science or trade or long and faithful public service. The ribbon is scarlet with a central stripe of yellow. This same medal, as the 'Maudheim Medal,' was authorized in 1951 for those who took part in the Norwegian-British-Swedish Expedition in the Antarctic, 1949–52. It was awarded in silver to seven Norwegians, six Englishmen and five Swedes, with a silver bar, 'MAUDHEIM, 1949–52,' on the ribbon.

### SOUTH POLE MEDAL
A gold medal instituted by King Haakon in 1912 for the members of Roald Amundsen's South Polar Expedition, 1910–11. The ribbon is blue with three central stripes of white, red, white.

### CORONATION MEDAL
This medal was issued in commemoration of King Haakon's Coronation in 1906. It was struck in silver and bronze. The ribbon is brownish-red, edged with narrow stripes of white and orange.

### JUBILEE MEDAL
This medal was issued in commemoration of King Haakon's silver jubilee as King, 1930. It is a silver medal on a plain red ribbon, with a bar '1905–1930.'

### KING'S COMMEMORATION MEDAL
This medal was instituted in 1906 for award to Norwegian and foreign court servants. There are three classes: gold, with crown above; silver, with crown; silver. The ribbon is red.

# Philippine Republic

### MEDAL FOR VALOR
This medal consists of a cross of bronze with convex ends with the seal of the Army of the Philippines in the centre in colour. The cross hangs from a bronze bar with the inscription 'FOR VALOR,' and on the reverse of the bar are the words 'THE CONGRESS TO' with space for the recipient's name. The ribbon is crimson moiré with eight white stars arranged as a triangle. When worn alone the ribbon has the stars in two rows, five above and three below.

### DISTINGUISHED CONDUCT STAR
This is a bronze, five-pointed star hung from a bronze bar with the words 'FOR GALLANTRY.' In the centre of the star is the seal of the Army partly surrounded by a circle with eight small discs. The ribbon is red with a central stripe of blue.

### DISTINGUISHED SERVICE STAR
This is another bronze, five-pointed star with a ribbon of blue, red, blue in equal parts.

### THE GOLD CROSS
This decoration has a profile head of President Quezon and hangs from a ribbon of pale blue with three narrow white stripes in the centre.

## MEDAL FOR MILITARY MERIT

The ribbon is jade green with three red stripes in the centre.

## 581 - LEGION OF HONOUR

This has four classes: *Chief Commander, Commander, Officer* and *Legionnaire.* The badge is an eight-pointed gold star on a green-enamelled wreath, having in the centre a lion's head with the tail of a fish. By *Chief Commanders* the badge is worn in the centre of the chest on a sash ribbon over the shoulder. *Commanders* have a smaller badge round the neck, and *Officers* and *Legionnaires* wear it on the breast, the former with a miniature gilt star on the ribbon.

## BRONZE CROSS

The ribbon is blue with a red centre, the colours being divided by white lines, and the blue edges also divided into two by white lines.

## MILITARY COMMENDATION RIBBON

The ribbon is green with three broad white stripes grouped together in the centre.

## WOUNDED SOLDIER'S MEDAL

This is a bronze cross, worn from a ribbon with three equal stripes of white, mauve, white.

## 582 - PHILIPPINE DEFENCE MEDAL

This is a bronze medal. In the centre is a female figure with streaming hair with a sword in her right hand and a shield in the left. The design is encircled by a wreath with three stars at the top. The reverse has the words 'FOR THE DEFENCE OF THE PHILIPPINES.'

## 583 - PHILIPPINE LIBERATION MEDAL

This consists of a bronze shield on a pair of drooping wings, with three stars, the word 'LIBERTY,' and an upright sword. It was issued in 1945 after the liberation of the islands from the Japanese.

## 584 - PHILIPPINE INDEPENDENCE RIBBON

This is a ribbon awarded to personnel of the armed forces of the United States who were on active duty in the Philippines on 4 July 1946.

## PRESIDENTIAL CITATION BADGE

This badge is awarded in much the same way as that for the United States. It consists of a gold frame of palm leaves enclosing a ribbon of three equal stripes of red, white and blue.

## LONG SERVICE MEDAL

This is a bronze cross with shallow limbs with the arms of the Philippines in the centre. The ribbon is crimson.

## DISTINGUISHED AVIATION CROSS

The ribbon is blue, red, blue, with the colours separated by yellow lines, and narrow white outside edges to the blue.

## SILVER WING MEDAL

The ribbon has a broad red centre narrowly edged yellow, with blue edges separated from the yellow by a white stripe.

## THE ANCIENT ORDER OF SIKATUNA

Sikatuna was the Filipino Chieftain who made the blood compact with Legaspi, the first Spanish Governor of the Philippines in the sixteenth century. The Order was instituted in 1951 as an award for diplomatic services. It has four classes: *Commander First Class*, a laureated gold badge worn from a silver-gilt collar; *Commander Second Class*, for war, badge worn round the neck from a ribbon; *Officer*, and *Companion*, the badge worn on the breast, the former with a rosette on the ribbon. The ribbon is red with a blue centre stripe narrowly edged white, and edges of yellow, inside, and white, outside.

## KOREAN CAMPAIGN MEDAL (1951)

This is a bronze medal, with the obverse showing the Temple of Heaven at Seoul, surrounded by a raised border with the words 'KOREAN CAMPAIGN' and three stars. The reverse has the crossed flags of the Philippines and the United Nations, with the seal of Korea above and mountains below. The ribbon is yellow, with a red stripe of 3 mm., white 1.5 mm., and blue 3 mm., in the centre.

## THE QUEZON SERVICE CROSS

This is a large, eight-pointed, ball-tipped cross or star of green and white with rays in the angles. In the centre is the bust of the President and the legend 'SIC FLORET RESPUBLICA.' It hangs by a wreath from a broad yellow ribbon with green edges. In the centre of the yellow are two narrow red stripes, while the green is divided into two by a narrow white line. The outside edges are white.

# *Poland*

## 585 - THE ORDER OF THE WHITE EAGLE

Legend places the establishment of this Order in 1325, but it was officially established in 1705 by King Augustus II, and revived in 1807. In November 1831 it was included among the Russian Orders, but in 1921 was revived as the highest Polish decoration. It has one class only:

*The Badge* is a gold, eight-pointed, red-enamelled, white-bordered Maltese cross having a gold edge, each point being tipped with a small gold ball. From between each arm of the cross sprouts a sheaf of golden rays. In the centre of the cross are the letters 'R.P.' intertwined. It is worn from a sash of light blue moiré ribbon worn over the left shoulder.

*The Star* is a silver eight-pointed star overlaid on a gold centre by a red-enamelled white-edged Maltese cross, on the four arms of which is inscribed the motto of the Order: 'ZA OJCZYZNE I NARÓD' ('For country and nation'). In the centre, on a small white-enamelled medallion, appear the intertwined initials 'R.P.' ('RZECZPOSPOLITA POLSKA' – 'Polish Republic') in gold and encircled by a laurel wreath in a narrow trellised band. It is worn on the left breast.

**586 - THE ORDER OF
MILITARY VIRTUE**
*Insignia of the Fourth Class (Obv*

## 586 - THE ORDER OF MILITARY VIRTUE

This Order was established by King Stanislas Augustus in 1792 and revived in 1919. It has five classes, and is awarded for services in the field.

*The Badge* is an eight-pointed, black-enamelled, gold-edged Maltese cross, the top arm surmounted by an oval with the letters 'R.P.' surrounded by a wreath, each point of the cross being tipped by a small gold ball. On the arms of the cross is inscribed the motto of the Order; on the obverse, 'VIRTUTI MILITARI,' on the reverse, 'HONOR I OJCZYZNA' ('Honour and country'). In the centre of the cross is a small white-enamelled eagle with spread wings on a gold medallion encircled by a laurel wreath on a narrow gold band. The badge of the *First Class* is worn over the right shoulder from a sash of bright blue ribbon with a black stripe at either edge.

*The Star* of the *First Class* consists of a large fluted silver eight-pointed star overlaid by an eight-pointed, black-enamelled, gold-edged Maltese cross, the four arms being inscribed with the motto of the Order. In the centre, on a gold medallion is a small white-enamelled eagle encircled by a black-enamelled band bearing the inscription: 'HONOR I OJCZYZNA,' this in its turn being encircled by a laurel wreath on a narrow gold band. It is worn on the left breast.

The *Second Class* has the cross worn from a ribbon round the neck, and the *Third Class*, a smaller cross, worn on the breast. The badge of the *Fourth Class* is of gold with the motto inscribed on the arms, and the usual enamelled device in the centre, while that of the *Fifth Class* is in silver.

## 587 - THE ORDER OF POLONIA RESTITUTA

This Order was established on 4 February 1921, and awarded for services in the fields of science, art, literature, administration, philanthropy, social work, inventions, the betterment of industry, commerce and agriculture, for acts of bravery and for the averting of catastrophes. It has five classes:

*The Grand Cross.* This is an eight-pointed, white-enamelled, gold-edged Maltese cross, each point being tipped with a small gold ball. In the centre is a small white-enamelled crowned eagle on a red medallion encircled by a dark blue-enamelled band inscribed with the motto of the Order in gold letters. The cross is worn from a sash of red ribbon with a white stripe near each edge worn over the right shoulder, with a star on the right breast. The other classes are:

Cross suspended from the neck. Star on right breast.

Cross suspended from the neck.

Cross on left breast on ribbon with rosette.

Cross worn on left breast on plain ribbon.

### 587 - THE ORDER OF POLONIA RESTITUTA
*Insignia of the Third Class (Obverse)*

## 588 - INDEPENDENCE CROSS AND MEDAL

These were instituted in 1930 to commemorate the independence of Poland after the First World War. The Cross 'with Swords' was awarded to those who performed outstanding deeds for independence before 1914 while armed, and the Cross for important deeds while not armed. For less important deeds the medal was awarded.

### 589, 590 - THE CROSS OF VALOUR

This decoration was established on 11 August 1920, and awarded for services in the field. It is a bronze cross, the obverse bearing the inscription 'NA POLU CHWALY' ('On the field of glory') with the Polish eagle on a shield in the centre. The reverse has the inscription 'WALECZNYM' ('To the brave') and a perpendicular sword transfixing a laurel wreath. On its first institution the badge was worn from a purple moiré ribbon with a broad white stripe towards each edge. For the Second World War the colours were reversed to white with a broad purple stripe towards each edge. When first awarded the badge is worn from a plain ribbon. Each subsequent award, to the number of four, is indicated by a bar on the ribbon.

### 591 - THE CROSS OF MERIT

This decoration was established in 1923 and awarded in recognition of services to the state. It has three classes:

*The Gold Cross*, consisting of an eight-pointed, crimson-enamelled, gold-edged Maltese cross, each point being tipped with a small gold ball. From between each arm of the cross sprouts a sheaf of gold rays. In the centre on a small white-enamelled medallion appear the letters 'R.P.' ('RZECZPOSPOLITA POLSKA' – 'Polish Republic') in gold encircled by a narrow crimson band which is again encircled by a narrow gold band. The cross is worn on the breast from a crimson ribbon having a bright blue stripe near each edge. *The Silver Cross*, carried out in silver and enamel, is worn from the same ribbon; while *The Bronze Cross* is worked entirely in bronze. Each of these crosses may be awarded on four different occasions to one person, each award after the first being indicated by a horizontal bar placed on the ribbon.

### THE CROSS OF MERIT FOR BRAVERY

This decoration was established in 1928 as a supplement to the Cross of Merit and as a special decoration awarded to members of the State Police, to officers and private soldiers of the K.O.P. (the Frontier Defence Corps), to members of the Customs Guards for acts performed under conditions calling for outstanding courage involving risk to life or health in defence of law, of the safety of the frontiers of Poland as well as of the life and property of her citizens.

*The Badge* consists of the Silver Cross of Merit having an inscription on the arms of the cross: 'ZA DZIELNOŚĆ' ('For bravery'). It is worn with the ribbon of the Cross of Merit, bearing a very narrow separate ribbon, half blue, half green, running obliquely from right to left. The cross has only one class, but can be awarded on three separate occasions to the same person, one bar being added for each award after the initial one.

### 592 - MEMORIAL MEDAL FOR WAR OF 1918–21

This medal was authorized in 1928 for the war against Soviet Russia. It is of bronze with the Polish eagle on the obverse and the dates '1918–1921.' The reverse has the inscription 'POLSKA SWEMU OBRONCY' ('Poland to her Defender'), encircled by a wreath of oak. The ribbon has a centre stripe of blue with narrow black edges (the colours of the ribbon of the Order of Military Virtue), and outer stripes of purple with narrow white borders (the colours of the Cross of Valour ribbon), with narrow blue edges.

## THE CROSS OF MERIT OF THE CENTRAL LITHUANIAN ARMIES

This decoration was established on 25 February 1922, and awarded to Polish troops. It is a bronze cross, mounted on a laurel wreath, having in the centre a Polish eagle holding in its talons a shield bearing the Lithuanian coat-of-arms – a horseman riding to the attack. On the obverse side the arms of the cross bear the inscription: 'WILNO, 1920, 9. X.' and '19. XI.' On the reverse the arms of the cross bear two swords with their points inclining towards the corners of the arms of the cross, and the words: 'LITWA SRODKOWA' ('Central Lithuania').

The ribbon is green with seven yellow and red vertical stripes.

## MEDAL COMMEMORATING THE TENTH ANNIVERSARY OF THE RESTORATION OF INDEPENDENCE

This medal was established on 27 September 1928. It is bronze showing on the obverse the effigy of Marshal Pilsudski, and on the reverse a rural figure symbolizing labour, and the date '1918–28.' The ribbon is cornflower-blue, and the medal was awarded to all those who, in the period between 11 November 1918 and 11 November 1928, in the performance of civil, military, state and legal service, carried out their active military duties as professional or non-professional soldiers, or performed actual services in offices and institutions of the state or of the autonomous bodies or other public utility or legal institutions for a period of at least five years.

The following ribbons were issued by the Polish Government in London at the end of the Second World War:

## 593 - MONTE CASSINO (1944)
Diagonally across the ribbon from bottom left to top right (facing) is a silver script bar reading 'MONTE CASSINO.'

## 594 - NAVAL ACTIVE SERVICE MERCHANT NAVY
A ribbon of dark blue with a narrow white stripe towards each edge.

## 595 - ARMY    596 - AIR FORCE

The following medals were issued by the Polish Government in Warsaw:

## CROSS OF GRUNWALD
This is a plain four-armed cross with slightly pointed ends. In the centre is a shield with two swords side by side pointing downwards. The ribbon is red with narrow green edges and a medium light blue centre stripe.

## 597 - WARSAW MEDAL
This medal is for those who took part in the fighting round Warsaw in 1944. It is a bronze ring bearing the dates '1939–1945' and the words 'ZA WARSZAW.' Cut out in the centre is a mermaid bearing

a shield on her left arm and a sword in her upraised right hand.

## 598 - ODER, NEISSE AND BALTIC MEDAL

This medal is for those who participated in the battles in these areas in 1945. It is a circular, bronze medal with, in the centre, a map of the rivers below an eagle. Round the edges are the words 'ZA ODRE, NISSE, BALTYK.'

## VICTORY AND FREEDOM MEDAL

This medal was awarded to all who rendered assistance, whether military or civil, during the war. It is a circular, bronze medal with an eagle in the centre surrounded by a wreath, which is broken at the top by the letters 'KRN.' The ribbon was, at first, half white and half red; it was later changed to three red and two white equal stripes.

## 599 - PARTISANS' CROSS

This is a plain silver cross inscribed 'ZA POLSKE WOLNOSC.'

## NA POLU CHWALY MEDAL (MEDAL 'ON THE FIELD OF GLORY')

This is of silver and bronze, and given for gallantry. The ribbon is black with a broad blue stripe near each edge.

The names only of the following two decorations instituted by the Polish People's Republic are known:

## ORDER SZTANDAR PRACY (ORDER OF THE LABOUR BANNER)

The ribbon is red with narrow black stripe near each edge.

## ORDER BUDONICZY POLSKI LADOWY (ORDER OF BUILDERS OF THE REPUBLIC OF POLAND)

The ribbon is red with narrow blue edges and a white centre stripe of medium width.

# Portugal

**ORDER OF CHRIST**
*Star of the Grand Cross*
*(Shown full size)*

## 600 - MILITARY ORDER OF ST. BENEDICT OF AVIZ

This was introduced into Portugal from Spain in 1162 as a religious military Order; but secularized by Queen Maria in 1789 as an Order for naval and military merit. There are three classes: *Knights Grand Cross*, with sash over the right shoulder, badge on left hip, and star on the breast; *Commanders*, with star on the breast and badge round the neck; *Knights*, with badge on the breast.

The badge is a cross with fleury ornamented ends, enamelled green, edged gold. The star is of chased silver of eight points with the badge in the centre.

## 601 - ORDER OF ST. JAMES OF THE SWORD

This was introduced into Portugal from Spain in 1177, secularized in 1789, and in 1862 designated as an Order of Merit for science, literature and art. There are five classes. The centre cross is in violet enamel, edged gold, resting upon two sprays of palm enamelled green, with the inscription below on a white riband. It hangs from a wreath of laurel enamelled green.

## 602 - THE MILITARY ORDER OF CHRIST

This was established in 1317 in conjunction with Pope John XXII, but became a distinct Portuguese Order in 1522. Like the preceding Orders, it was secularized in 1789, and has three classes. The cross, which has the centre portion of the Portuguese Royal Arms on an oval between each of its limbs, has the limbs enamelled blue with white edges, both colours edged with gold. In the centre, surrounded by a gold circle embellished with stars, is the red cross of the Order of Christ charged with a white cross, on a white ground. The wreath and the balls on the eight points are in gold.

Persons decorated with the Grand Cross of all these three Orders wear a sash combining the three ribbons, green, scarlet and violet, from which hangs a gold oval medallion surmounted by a crown. It contains miniature representations of the three badges in enamel on small white ovals. The star worn on the breast also has a similar design in the centre.

## 603 - MILITARY ORDER OF THE TOWER AND SWORD

This Order was founded in 1459 by Alfonso V, and reinstituted in 1808 by John, Prince Regent of Portugal, afterwards King John VI, to commemorate his safe arrival in Brazil. It was reconstituted again in July 1832 as an Order of Civil and Military Merit. There are five classes, and besides the star and badge Grand Officers receive a collar composed of oak wreaths with a sword in bend across the wreath alternating with towers in gold.

The badge is a five-pointed star in white enamel, edged gold, with a gold ball on each point, resting on a wreath of oak enamelled green, the whole surmounted by a tower in gold. In the centre of the obverse is a dark blue enamel garter with the words 'PELO REI E PELA LEI' enclosing a gold background on which is an open book. The reverse has the words 'VALOR LEALDADE E MERITO' on the blue garter, enclosing a gold background with a sword in bend across a wreath of laurel in green enamel. The star is five-pointed, with the sword and laurel wreath in the centre, and a tower in gold on the uppermost ray of the star.

## CIVIL ORDER OF MERIT

This Order was instituted in 1893 in three classes as a reward for agriculture and industry. The ribbon was white edged green when the Order was awarded for agricultural merit, and white edged red when awarded for industrial merit. It is now obsolete.

## CROSS OF MILITARY MERIT

This is a cross fleury of white enamel suspended from a tower of gold or silver from a ribbon of carmine with narrow white, black, white centre stripes, with three closely spaced blue lines either side on the carmine.

**ORDER OF CHRIST**
*Badge of the Commander*
*(Shown full size)*

## WAR CROSS

This is a bronze cross, the arms being wider at the ends than in the centre and rounded. In the centre is the Republican head surrounded by the words 'REPUBLICA PORTUGUESA 1917' in a garter. The reverse has the Republican shield within a rope border. The decoration was established during the First World War and awarded in much the same way as the French 'Croix de Guerre.' The ribbon is scarlet moiré, with five equally spaced narrow stripes of green.

## MEDALS FOR WAR AND DISTINGUISHED SERVICES, ETC.

### MILITARY VALOUR
Ribbon, nine alternate stripes of dark blue and white.

### DISTINGUISHED SERVICE
Ribbon, nine alternate stripes of red and white.

### GOOD CONDUCT
Ribbon, nine alternate stripes of green and white.

### DISTINGUISHED SERVICE OVERSEAS
Ribbon, half red, half black.

### ASSIDUOUS SERVICES OVERSEAS
Ribbon, nine alternate stripes of red and black.

### PROMOTED FOR BRAVERY
Ribbon, scarlet with central stripe of black.

### CAMPAIGNS OVERSEAS, INCLUDING WAR OF 1914–18
Ribbon, green with red edges.

### MEDAL FOR THOSE WOUNDED (1914–18)
Ribbon, red with two green stripes.

**603 - MILITARY ORDER OF THE TOWER AND SWORD**
*Star of the Grand Officer*
*(Shown full size)*

# Romania

## ORDER OF THE STAR OF THE PEOPLE'S REPUBLIC OF ROMANIA

Conferred on nomination by the State Council of the People's Republic, the Order of the Star has five classes, of which the first two wear the Badge as a star (in gold or silver) on the breast, and of which the third, fourth and fifth wear the Badge as a pendant medal in gold, silver or bronze respectively, suspended from a plain red ribbon, mounted in crossover fashion. The Badge of the first and second classes features a blue-bordered red-enamelled five-pointed star with the date '30 DECEMBRIE 1947' (the date of King Michael I's abdication) inscribed in a central, circular panel. The rays of a five-pointed star appear between the points of the red star. On the Badges of the 3rd, 4th and 5th classes, the monogram 'RPR' (Republica Populare Romine) replace the central date.

## ORDER OF 23RD AUGUST

Originally instituted to recognise the services of men and women in the uprising of 23 August 1944, the Order may now be conferred upon civilians and members of the military, both subjects of Romania and foreigners, for civic, scientific, artistic, philosophical and military services, as recommended by the State Council. Like the Order of the Star, it may be conferred in five classes. The *Badge* is a 10-pointed star (in gold for the first three classes, in silver for the fourth class, and in bronze for the fifth class). The state coat of arms is borne by a central, circular medallion surrounded by a wreath and a garland. The ribbon is red, with edges of blue and yellow (the blue stripe outermost).

## ORDER OF THE DEFENCE OF THE FATHERLAND

Instituted for conferment upon civilians as well as members of the military, both Romanians and foreigners, this Order exists in three classes. In the 1st Class the Badge, in gold with swords in silver, is worn as a star on the breast. In the 2nd Class the Badge, in silver with swords, is worn as a star. In the 3rd Class the Badge is worn as a medal suspended from a ribbon similar to that of the previous Order. The Badge is a five-pointed star mounted upon gold crossed swords (in 1st and 3rd classes) or silver crossed swords (in 2nd class), with the state's coat of arms in silver in the centre of the star.

# *Russia (Prior to 1917)*

## ORDER OF ST. ANDREW

This was the highest Russian Order under the old régime, founded by Peter the Great in 1698, and normally reserved for sovereigns and those of noble birth. It carried with it knighthood in the Orders of St. Alexander Nevsky, the White Eagle, St. Anne and St. Stanislas. It had one class only, and the badge was a double-headed crowned eagle in black and gold with spread wings, upon which was the blue saltire of St. Andrew with the figure of the Saint in natural colours. At the ends of the saltire were the letters 'S-A-P-R' ('Sanctus Andreas Protector Russae'). The badge hung from a gold Imperial Crown filled in with red enamel, and was suspended from a collar on state occasions, otherwise from a sash of pale blue moiré worn over the right shoulder. On the left breast was worn a star of eight faceted rays (88 mm. across the points), in the centre of which was the eagle and the cross surrounded by the motto.

## ORDER OF THE WHITE EAGLE

This Order originated in Poland in 1705; but was given a place

**604 - ORDER OF ST. ANNE**
*Badge of the Commander*

among the Imperial Russian Orders in 1831 on the absorption of Poland into Russia. It had one class only, and the badge is of similar design to that of St. Andrew, having the black, double-headed eagle with outstretched wings, upon which was an eagle in white enamel superimposed upon a cross with V-shaped ends, enamelled red, edged white, resting upon a star with golden rays. The badge hung from an Imperial Crown from a sash of dark blue moiré worn over the right shoulder, with a star on the left breast.

## ORDER OF ST. ALEXANDER NEVSKY

This Order was contemplated by Peter the Great, as an award for military distinction, but was actually instituted by the Empress Catherine in 1725. It had a badge consisting of a cross in red enamel, edged gold, with golden, double-headed eagles between the four limbs. In the centre was a circular plaque in enamel showing the Saint on horseback. It was worn from a sash of scarlet moiré over the right shoulder with a star (82 mm. wide) on the left breast.

## 604- ORDER OF ST. ANNE

This was founded in 1735 in honour of Anna Petrovna, daughter of Peter the Great. There were three classes: *Knights Commanders*, *Commanders* and *Companions*, while members of what is really a *Fourth Class* have enamelled medallions on their sword hilts together with an inscription 'FOR BRAVERY,' and wore the ribbon of the Order as a sword knot. There were also medals of the Order. Like the Order of St. Vladimir, it was originally intended as a civil decoration, but after 1855, 'with swords,' was awarded for war services. The badge is a gold cross pattée (52 mm. wide) enamelled crimson and edged gold. Between each limb is a design in gold scroll work, and, in the centre, an enamelled representation of St. Anne. Recipients of the Order, 'with swords,' had crossed swords between the limbs of the cross, and wore a bow on the ribbon.

## 605- ORDER OF ST. STANISLAS

This Order was founded in 1765. There were three classes: *Knights Grand Cross, Commanders* and *Companions*. The badge is a gold, crimson-enamelled Maltese cross, with double points, each point being tipped with a small gold ball. Between each arm of the cross is the white eagle of Poland in gold. In the centre, on a circular white enamel ground, are two branches of laurel, enamelled green, encircling two intertwined S's in gold. The Order of St. Stanislas when awarded 'with swords' for service in war, had crossed swords between the limbs of the cross. A bow was also worn on the ribbon. There were various medals of the Order which were awarded to N.C.O.s and men.

**605 - ORDER OF
ST. STANISLAS**
*Badge of the Commander*

## 606- THE ORDER OF ST. GEORGE

This Order was founded on the 26 November 1769 by the Empress Catherine. It was awarded only for conspicuous bravery in action against the enemy.

    The four classes into which the Order was divided were as follows:

    *First Class.* A badge of gold in the form of a cross pattée (53 mm. wide), the arms of which are enamelled white. The medallion in the centre bears a coloured representation of St. George slaying the

**606 - ORDER OF ST. GEORGE**
*Insignia of the Third Class*

dragon. The reverse shows the initials of the Saint. This is suspended on the left hip by a sash which is of watered silk, orange with three black stripes.

The star is a diamond-shaped plaque of gold bearing the initials in the centre, surrounded by a riband having gold letters meaning 'For Service and For Bravery.'

*Second Class.* A smaller badge, worn round the neck and a star exactly the same as that of the *First Class.*

*Third Class.* A gold badge (32 mm. wide) worn round the neck.

*Fourth Class.* A silver badge (34 mm. wide) worn on the left breast.

In addition to the Order there were four classes of an insignia under the name of the Cross of St. George:

*First Class.* As for the badge but in gold only, worn from a ribbon with a bow upon it.

*Second Class.* As above, but with no bow.

*Third Class.* The cross in silver, worn with a bow.

*Fourth Class.* As above, but with no bow.

There was a St. George's Medal in gold and silver, with or without bow, worn in a similar manner to the cross.

Over two million Crosses and Medals of St. George were distributed to soldiers, sisters of mercy, and members of Red Cross institutions and hospitals during the First World War and before the abolition of the Monarchy, as awards could be made on the spot by general officers commanding armies in the field. The Crosses of St. George were far more rarely conferred upon officers, however, as in their case each award had to be investigated and approved of by a council composed of the Knights of the Order.

The Order of St. George was essentially military, and could never be conferred upon civilians except for services actually under fire.

The Sword of St. George, which was very rarely bestowed, and then only upon officers of very high rank who had specially distinguished themselves, was a magnificent weapon with a gold hilt emblazoned with the white enamel Cross of the Order and inscribed with the words 'For Bravery.' The possession of the Sword, equally with that of the Cross, gave the possessor the right to wear uniform after retirement from the service.

All the old Russian Orders were abolished in December 1917, but under the Czarist régime various Russian regiments had their colours or bugles decorated with the ribbon of the Order as a distinction for gallantry in the field.

The black and orange ribbon of this Order meant 'through Darkness to Light,' the black representing darkness and the orange light.

## 607 - ORDER OF ST. VLADIMIR

This Order was founded in 1782, and comprised four classes, corresponding to our *Knights Grand Cross, Knights Commanders, Commanders* and *Companions.* There was also a medal of the Order. The Order was originally instituted as a civil decoration, and could be claimed by 'whoever at the peril of his own life saves ten lives from fire or water,' had served the state loyally and faithfully for thirty-five years, who enriched the state, compiled any work of

**607 - ORDER OF ST. VLADIMIR**
*Badge of the Commander*

classical distinction, had rendered assistance in time of famine, or had done anything really notable in his profession. During the Crimean War it was made into a military Order as well as a civil one by the addition of 'swords' and a bow on the ribbon. The badge (43 mm. wide) consists of a gold cross pattée enamelled crimson with black edges, the respective colours edged gold. In the centre, on a circular plaque of black enamel, edged gold, is the Imperial mantle crowned and charged with a cypher. The military badge 'with swords' has two swords placed crosswise between the limbs of the cross.

## ORDER OF ST. CATHERINE

This Order was founded in 1714 by Peter the Great to commemorate the actions of his Empress in 1712 against the Turks. It was for ladies only and sparsely awarded. There were two classes, the *First Class* badge being worn by a scarlet sash with silver edging, and the *Second Class* by a bow of the ribbon. Both the rosette on the sash and the bow of the *Second Class* bore Russian characters in silver embroidery denoting 'For Love and the Fatherland.' The star worn by the *First Class* had eight points with an enamelled centre bearing the motto, a cross and a crown. The badge, similar for both classes, was oval and set upon a cross, all heavily encrusted with diamonds. In the centre was a representation of the Saint, seated and holding a large cross, all in proper colours.

### RUSSIAN CZARIST MEDALS

Russia did not create a new design of ribbon for all war and other medals, but used the ribbons of Orders either alone or in combination. The pale blue ribbon of St. Andrew was used with the highest award for saving life, and the red ribbon of St. Alexander for life-saving medals of a lower category. Among many others the following combination ribbons were used with campaign and other medals:

**608 - PERSIAN WAR** (1826–28)
Half St. Andrew. Half St. George.

**TURKISH WAR** (1877–78)
Half St. Andrew. Half St. Vladimir.

**JAPANESE WAR** (1904–05)
Half St. Alexander Nevsky. Half St. George.

# *Serbia*

### 609 - ORDER OF THE WHITE EAGLE

This Order was instituted in 1883 in five classes: *Knight Grand Cross, Grand Officer, Commander, Officer* and *Companion*. The badge consisted of a double-headed eagle in gold, enamelled white and outlined in gold, with, in the centre, an oval shield with a beaded edge bearing a white cross on a red ground with a cypher in each corner. Above the eagle was a scroll, enamelled blue, surmounted by a crown. The

**609 - ORDER OF THE WHITE EA**
*Star of the Knight Grand Cross*
*(Shown full size)*

badge of the *Fifth Class* is in silver. When awarded for military services there were crossed swords below the crown. The ordinary ribbon was red, watered, with stripes of pale blue near each edge, but it was ordered during the First World War that *all* Serbian Orders or medals which could be awarded in peace, must, if granted for war service, be worn with the plain red moiré ribbon of the Star of Karageorge with swords.

## 610 - ORDER OF ST. SAVA

This Order was instituted in 1883. There were five classes, as for the Order of the White Eagle. The badge was a gold Maltese cross enamelled white with blue edges with, between each limb, a gold, double-headed eagle. In the centre, on a gold oval plaque with a beaded edge was an enamelled figure of St. Sava, surrounded by an inscription in Serbian, 'By his talents he acquired all.' The badge was surmounted by a crown in gold and enamel. The badge of the *Fifth Class* was in silver. The ribbon was normally white with blue stripes towards each edge, though if awarded for war service the ribbon was plain red moiré.

## 611, 612 - STAR OF KARAGEORGE

This was founded in 1904. There were four classes. The design of the obverse and reverse was similar, but had in the centre a heraldic shield on a purple ground, surrounded by a white riband bearing the words in Serbian, 'For Honour and Liberty. 1804.' The arms of the cross were enamelled white, and the rays in between them were gold or silver, according to class. The decoration 'with swords' had crossed swords placed saltire-wise between the lines of the cross, and was awarded solely for war services. In this later case it was worn from the red watered ribbon.

## 612 - MEDALS FOR BRAVERY (OBILITCH MEDALS)

These were in gold and silver. They bore on the obverse the bust of Obilitch, a celebrated warrior who fought in the wars against the Turks in 1389 and was revered as a national hero. Round the circumference, in Serbian characters, was the inscription 'MILOCH OBILITCH.' The reverse bore a cross pattée with crossed swords between its limbs, and, in the centre, a wreath of laurel encircling the Serbian inscription 'For Bravery.' The ribbon is the same as for that of the Star of Karageorge with swords, i.e., plain red.

## MEDALS FOR ZEAL AND DEVOTED SERVICE IN WAR

These medals were awarded in gold and silver and worn with the red moiré ribbon if awarded during the First World War. In ordinary circumstances the ribbon was of dark blue watered silk.

## MEDAL FOR MILITARY VIRTUES

This medal had on one side the Serbian arms, and on the other the inscription 'For Military Virtues' within a laurel wreath. At the top of the medal were two small branches of laurel. The ribbon was ordinarily white, with four blue vertical stripes, but the same rule applied as to the medal being worn with the red moiré ribbon, if awarded for war service.

**610 - ORDER OF ST. SAVA**
*Badge of the Second Class*

**611 - STAR OF KARAGEORGE**
*Badge of the Third Class*

# *Spain*

## 613 - ORDER OF THE GOLDEN FLEECE (TOISON D'OR)

This Order is one of the most knightly and ancient in Europe, and at first consisted of twenty-four knights only. It was instituted on 10 January 1429–30 by Philip the Good, Duke of Burgundy, on the day of his marriage with Isabella of Portugal at Bruges. There seems to be no valid reason for connecting the name of the Order with the Golden Fleece brought from Colchis, according to Greek legend, by Jason and the Argonauts. According to one account, the Duke used the name and devised the badge of the hanging gold fleece because of the fortune he made through wool.

The Order became common to the princes of the house of Austria as descendants of Mary, daughter of Charles the Bold, last Duke of Burgundy, who married Maximilian of Austria in 1477. It came to Spain in 1504 on the accession of Philip, Maximilian's son, to the throne of Castile.

The Order had one class only. On occasions of high ceremony the knights wore a mantle of red, lined with ermine, with the golden fleece badge suspended round the neck from a heavy golden collar of alternate links of double steels interlaced to form the letter 'B' for Burgundy, and 'flints' of blue enamel with white rays emitting golden flames. On less ceremonial occasions the badge was worn round the neck from a ribbon of scarlet moiré.

The Order, essentially aristocratic, was reserved for crowned heads, heads of foreign states, and Spaniards of noble birth.

## 614 - ROYAL ORDER OF CHARLES III

This Order was founded by Charles III in 1771, abolished by Joseph Bonaparte in 1809, but revived five years later by Ferdinand VII. The Order is shown in many of Goya's paintings of the Spanish Royal Family. There are five classes: *Knights with Collar; Knights Grand Cross; Commanders* with star; *Commanders* with badge round the neck; *Knights* with badge on the breast.

## 615 - MILITARY ORDER OF ST. FERDINAND

This Order was founded in August 1811 by the Cortéz in Cadiz, and approved in 1815 by King Ferdinand VII as an exclusive military award for services in action against the enemy. The Order has five classes: *First*, the cross worn from a broad sash over the shoulder and a star on the breast, with laurel wreath; *Second*, cross worn from the buttonhole with star on breast, without laurel garland; *Third*, a smaller cross with laurel wreath at buttonhole and star on the breast; *Fourth*, cross at buttonhole surmounted by a ring without wreath; *Fifth*, cross with wreath at the buttonhole.

The Duke of Wellington was awarded this Order for his services in the Peninsular War.

**613 - ORDER OF THE GOLDEN FLEECE**
(*Shown full size*)

## 616 - ORDER OF ST. HERMENGILDE

This Order was instituted in November 1814 by King Ferdinand VII for military merit. There are three classes: *Grand Cross*; *Commander* with star; *Knight*.

The Duke of Wellington was awarded this decoration.

## 617 - ROYAL AMERICAN ORDER OF ISABELLA THE CATHOLIC

This Order was founded in March 1815 by Ferdinand VII under the patronage of St. Isabella, wife of Diniz of Portugal, and originally intended to reward loyalty in the defence of the Spanish possessions in America. It later became a general Order of Merit. There were originally four classes: *Grand Cross*, with sash and star; *Commander*, with badge round the neck and star; *Commander*, without star; and *Knight*, with badge on the breast.

A *Fifth Class*, in the shape of a silver cross of the Order, was created in 1903, and silver and bronze medals were instituted in 1907.

## ORDER OF MARIA CRISTINA

This Order was instituted in the name of Alfonso XIII by the Queen Regent, Maria Cristina, in July 1890 for rewarding outstanding action and fidelity on the part of officers of the Army and Navy. The design of the present decoration, which differs in slight detail from that previously awarded under the Monarchy, is shown in the illustration. The centre medallion of the Spanish arms is in red and white enamel, with the ribbon and small oval in blue. The lettering and devices on the medallion are in gold.

The Order is in three classes, and is worn on the breast. That for general officers, the *Grand Cross*, has the eight-pointed star in bright gold, with the laurel wreath, swords and superimposed cross in dull gold and the devices thereon in bright silver. Recipients of this highest class also wear a sash over the right shoulder with a smaller badge on the left hip, and the star on the breast. The sash ribbon is white moiré, with a band of red, yellow, red in the centre, and narrow edges of red.

The *Second Class*, awarded to field officers, has a similar star in chipped silver worn on the breast, with the superimposed cross and its emblems, the laurel wreath and swords, all in silver. It has no ribbon.

The *Third Class*, for more junior officers, has no ribbon. The star is again in silver, with the cross, laurel wreath and swords in bronze, and the emblems on the arms in silver.

The service ribbons are of the same colours as the sash ribbon for the Grand Cross.

## 618 - ORDER OF MILITARY MERIT

This Order was instituted by Isabella II in 1864 in four classes, to which a *Fifth Class*, a silver cross, was added in 1868.

The *Grand Cross*, awarded to general officers, is a sash worn over the shoulder with the badge on the opposite hip.

The *Second Class*, for colonels and equivalent ranks, is an eight-

**614 - ROYAL ORDER OF CHARLES III** *Badge of the Commander* (*Shown full size*)

**617 - ROYAL AMERICAN ORDER OF ISABELLA THE CATHOLIC** *Badge of the Grand Cross (Shown full size)*

331

pointed gold star worn on the breast, the star being charged with the badge in enamel.

The *Third Class*, for lieutenant-colonels, is the same with the star in silver.

The *Fourth Class* has the badge in enamel worn from a ribbon on the breast.

The *Fifth Class* the same, but with the badge in silver.

*Badges and Ribbons*. When granted for military service in war the limbs of the cross are enamelled red, and the ribbon is red moiré with a white stripe down the centre. For other service the arms of the cross are white, and the ribbon is white with a central stripe of red.

*Pensions* may be awarded with all classes of the Order. Their recipients are distinguished by white bands on the three lower limbs of the red cross, and red bands on the white cross.

## 619 - ORDER OF NAVAL MERIT
This Order was created in 1866 in four classes, to which a *Fifth Class*, in the shape of a silver cross, was later added. The different grades, and the method of wearing the insignia, are the same as for the Order of Military Merit. The ribbon is in the national colours. The badge is enamelled red, with the anchor in gold, when awarded for war service, and in white, with the anchor in blue, for other service. Pensions can be awarded, and are indicated by gold bands on the arms of the red cross, and blue bands on the white.

## CIVIL ORDER OF ALFONSO XII
This was instituted as an Order of Civil Merit in 1902. It has four classes: *Knights Grand Cross*; *Knights Commanders*, with and without star; *Knights*, with the insignia worn in the usual way. The ribbon is violet.

## 620 - ORDER OF MARIA-LOUISA
This Order was founded in 1792 by Maria Louisa, wife of Charles IV. There is only one class intended for award to ladies of the nobility. The sash from which the decoration is worn passed over the shoulder.

## ORDER OF BENEFICENCE
This Order was instituted in 1856 by Isabella II in three classes for valuable services in welfare or charitable work, the relief of suffering, or distress. There are four different ribbons according to the service performed: mauve, with black stripes towards each edge; mauve, with white stripes near each edge; white, with black stripes towards each edge; plain white.

## ORDER OF CIVIL MERIT
Ribbon, dark blue with a central stripe of white.

All the four awards that follow have been instituted since the régime of General Franco:

## THE YOKE AND ARROWS (YUGO Y FLECHAS)
This has a badge of five arrows passing through a yoke. Photographs of General Franco show him wearing it on the pocket of his service dress. It has been said that the badge is the revival of an ancient one commemorating the wars when the Spanish arrows freed Spain

**619 - ORDER OF NAVAL MERIT**
*Star of the Second Class*
*(Shown full size)*

from the yoke of the Moors. It is now a regular Order in various classes with sash, star, etc., and has a black ribbon with broad red edges.

## ORDER OF ALFONSO X – ORDER OF CISNEROS
Both of these Order have a ribbon of dark red.

## ORDER OF MERIT FOR PUBLIC HEALTH
Ribbon, orange with a black stripe near each edge.

## ORDER OF AERONAUTICAL MERIT
Ribbon, white with red stripe near each edge.

All three African Orders for Spanish Morocco that follow have several classes, including Grand Crosses:

## ORDER OF MEHDANIA
Ribbon, green with white centre stripe.

## ORDER OF HASSANIA
Ribbon, red, green, red.

## ORDER OF AFRICA (1951)
Ribbon, light green with a narrow red stripe near each edge.

## MEDALS
## DEFENCE OF THE CARRACA (1873)
For the defence of the Navy Yard at Cadiz. Ribbon, green with red stripe towards each edge.

## DEFENCE OF BILBAO (1874)
Ribbon, yellow with broad red edges.

## CIVIL WAR (1873–74)
Ribbon, red with central stripe of yellow.

## ALFONSO XII
Created 1875 and awarded for service during the Carlist War 1868–70. Yellow ribbon with red stripes towards each edge.

## CUBA (1868–80)
For combatants – ribbon, red with centre stripe of black. For non-combatants – ribbon, white, with centre stripe of black.

## JOLO (1876) (PHILIPPINE ISLANDS)
Ribbon, five equal stripes; three red, two yellow.

## MINDANAO (1890–91; 1884–85) (PHILIPPINE ISLANDS)
Ribbon, yellow, broad green stripes towards each edge.

## CUBA (1895–98)
Ribbon, nine narrow stripes; five violet, four red. For volunteers; half violet, half red.

**618 - ORDER OF MILITARY MERIT**
*Star of the Third Class*
*(Shown full size)*

**PHILIPPINE CAMPAIGN** (1896–98)
Ribbon, four stripes each of red and yellow.

**LUZON** (1886–97) **(PHILIPPINE ISLANDS)**
Ribbon, half red, half yellow.

**MELILLA (RIFF) CAMPAIGNS (MOROCCO)**
(1909; 1911–12)
Ribbon, yellow, with red stripe near each edge.

**AFRICA SERVICE**
A general service medal instituted in 1912. Ribbon, red, yellow, red, with narrow olive-coloured edges.

**MOROCCO CAMPAIGN** (1916)
Ribbon, green.

**RIFF CAMPAIGN (MOROCCO)** (1925)
Ribbon, orange.
    All the following medals have been issued since the régime of General Franco during the Civil War in Spain and later:

**CAMPAIGN MEDAL** (17 July 1936)
The Vanguard had a ribbon of red, yellow, red, with narrow black edges, and the Rearguard the same with green edges.

**MEDAL FOR WOUNDED**
Ribbon, yellow, green stripe near each edge.

**MEDAL FOR INJURED**
Ribbon, yellow.

**MEDAL FOR PRISONERS**
Ribbon, orange.

**WAR CROSS (OFFICERS)**
Ribbon, white, with a band of red, yellow, red in the centre, and narrow edges of red. (The Maria Cristina ribbon.)

**AIR MEDAL**
Ditto, but with edges of green.

**WAR CROSS (SOLDIERS)**
Ribbon, pale blue with a central strips of white.

**NATIONAL RESURGENCE**
Ribbon, yellow, with red edges.

**VOLUNTEERS OF MAJORCA**
Ribbon, white, with three black stripes.

**VOLUNTEERS OF BILBAO**
Ribbon, white, with red edges.

**VOLUNTEERS AT THE SIEGE OF OVIEDO**
Ribbon, pale blue, with edges of red, yellow, red.

**GOOD SERVICE TO THE FALANGE**
Ribbon, yellow, with two black stripes near each edge.

## SPANISH VOLUNTEERS IN RUSSIA
(1941–42)
Ribbon, white, with one edge of red, yellow, red, and the other of white, red, white, black.

## SPANISH NURSES IN RUSSIA
Ribbon, red, with white edges.

## VOLUNTEERS OF CIUDAD REAL
Ribbon, red, with two yellow and one black stripe grouped in the centre. These volunteers served on the German front in Russia in 1941.

## MEDAL FOR WOUNDED (OFFICERS)
Ribbon, yellow, green edges, with two narrow red stripes in the centre.

## MEDAL FOR WOUNDED (TROOPS)
The same without green edges.

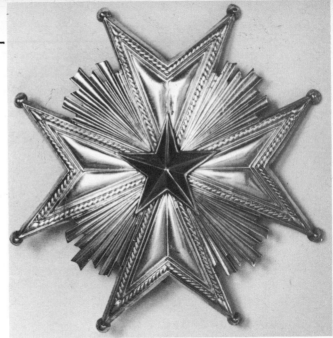

**ORDER OF THE NORTH STAR OR POLE STAR**
*Star of the Commander Grand Cross (Shown full size)*

## ORDER OF THE SERAPHIM
This Order was founded by Frederick I in 1748. Exclusive to the Sovereign and Princes of the blood, it is awarded to a limited number of Swedes who must already be *Commanders* of the *Grand Cross* of the Order of the Sword or the Polar Star, and to Heads of Foreign States.

The Order is in one class only and is known as the 'Blue Ribbon,' the sash being pale blue moiré. The insignia consists of a chain, or collar of alternate seraphims' heads and blue-enamelled patriarchal crosses, and a badge, which, like the star worn on the breast, is an eight-pointed cross in gold and white enamel with golden seraphim between the arms, and in the centre, on a dark blue ground a cross, the letters 'I H S' and three small crowns. The badge is surmounted by a larger crown. There are medals of the Order.

## 621 - ORDER OF THE SWORD
The Order of the Sword is the principal Swedish military Order and, like the Seraphim, and the North or Pole Star, it was founded by Frederick I in 1748. There are five classes, and the badge consists of an eight-pointed cross in white enamel, edged gold, with small golden crowns between the limbs, hung saltire-wise beneath two crossed swords with a crown above. In the centre, on a circular blue ground, are three small crowns and a sword, point up. The badges of the three highest grades have additional crossed swords between the lower limbs of the cross, and single swords between each of the side limbs. The two lowest classes have only the crossed swords beneath the crown at the top. There are medals

**ORDER OF THE NORTH STAR OR POLE STAR** *Badge of the Commander Grand Cross (Shown full size)*

attached to the Order, and the ribbon is yellow moiré with a narrow bright blue stripe towards each edge.

## ORDER OF THE NORTH STAR OR POLE STAR

This is known as the 'Black Ribbon,' and was founded in three classes in 1748 as an award for civil merit. The badge is an eight-pointed cross in white enamel, edged gold, with a crown above, with smaller gold crowns between the limbs, and in the centre, on a circular blue ground, a white star with the motto 'NESCIT OCCASUM.' The ribbon is black moiré.

## ORDER OF VASA

This Order was founded by Gustav III in 1772 for rewarding services rendered to national industries and manufactures. It has the usual three classes and medals, and the badge is an eight-pointed cross in gold and white enamel with the upper and lower arms somewhat longer than the others and crowns between each. It hangs from a crown, and in the centre of the badge, within an oval riband of crimson bearing a motto, is the golden wheatsheaf emblem of the Vasa family. The ribbon is green moiré.

## ORDER OF CHARLES XIII

This Order was founded in 1811 and is awarded only to Freemasons of high degree. It apparently has one class only, and consists of a red cross surmounted by a crown worn round the neck from a scarlet ribbon.

**ORDER OF VASA**
*Badge of the Commander, First C*
*(Shown full size)*

### SWEDISH MEDALS

Swedish medals may be divided into four main categories:

(A) **Royal Jubilee and Commemoration Medals**, which include those awarded for:

   *King Oscar II's Jubilee*, 1897. Ribbon, pale blue.
   *King Oscar II's Golden Wedding*, 1907. Ribbon, pale blue with gold edges.
   *King Gustav V's 70th Birthday*, 1928. Ribbon, pale blue.
   *King Gustav V's 90th Birthday*, 1948. Ribbon, pale blue.
   *King Gustav V's Memorial*, 1951. Ribbon, black.
   *King Gustav VI Adolf's 85th Birthday*, 1967. Ribbon, pale blue.
   **622** - *Crown Prince Gustav's Silver Wedding*, 1906. Ribbon pale blue with yellow edges, and a broader central stripe of yellow with a thin red line.

(B) **Medals awarded by the King in Person**, such as for:
   *Literature and Art*
   *King Oscar II's Jubilee*, to court officials, both with ribbons of dark blue.
   *King Gustav V Olympic Games*, 1912. Ribbon, pale blue with two yellow stripes each side.
   *King Gustav V Postal Congress*, 1924. Ribbon, yellow.
   *King Gustav V Tercentenary of the colonization of 'New Sweden,'* Delaware, U.S.A., 1638–1938. Gold and silver medals with the King's effigy and 'GUSTAVUS—V—REX—SVECIAE' on the obverse,

and on the reverse the inscription 'SUECIAE NOVAE IN MEMORIAM 1638–1938' with a star above and three crowns below. There is a crown above the medal with a ring for suspension and the ribbon is dark blue moiré with yellow edges and a yellow stripe each side.

**(C) Medals for Courage, Fidelity, Long Service, etc.** including those awarded for:

**623** - Bravery in the field or at sea in time of war, with a ribbon, half blue, half yellow, which strictly speaking is the only Swedish war medal, and the following, all of which are worn from ribbons of blue moiré with a yellow stripe near each edge, **No. 624,** and are awarded in gold and silver to those whose labour has merited it with the inscription 'ILLIS QUORUM MERVERE LABORES'; as well as for laudable actions; bravery and merit at sea; merit in the service of the state; civic merit, and long and faithful service. They differ slightly in design and have varying inscriptions.

**(D) Semi-Official Medals.**

These are very numerous and cannot be described in detail, though it is believed that various of them may be worn in uniform and on special occasions. Militia formations and societies; shooting clubs; sea defence corps; volunteer motor-car and motor-boat clubs; aero clubs; military sports societies; air-raid precautions associations; societies for life-saving, ski-running, open air life, gymnastics, fencing, pistol and rifle shooting, hunting, yachting, and for reserve officers of the Army, Navy and Air Force, all have their special medals which may be worn on occasion. Various insurance companies also have their various fire medals.

# Turkey

**625 - THE ORDER OF THE MEDJIDIE** (now obsolete)
This Order was established by the Sultan Abdul Medjid in 1852, and was frequently bestowed upon British subjects for services in Egypt. Over 1,000 British officers received the Order after the Crimean War. The badge is a cut-silver star of seven points, between the arms of which are seven small crescents and stars. In the centre is the Sultan's cypher on a gold or silver ground, and this is surrounded by a crimson riband with a Turkish inscription. A star and a crescent, enamelled crimson, are provided for suspension. There were five classes.

**626 - THE ORDER OF THE OSMANIEH** (now obsolete)
The Order of the Osmanieh was founded in 1861 by the Sultan Abdul Aziz. It was conferred upon many officers of the British Army for services in the various Sudan campaigns, and for their work in Egypt in times of peace, and upon Naval officers. The badge consists of a gold seven-pointed star enamelled green, with a gold ball on each point. Between each of the arms are three silver

**626 - THE ORDER OF THE OSMANIEH**
*Insignia of the Second Class*
*(Shown full size)*

radiations. In the centre, on a ground of crimson enamel, is a Turkish inscription and a gold crescent, and this device is surrounded by a green enamel riband bearing another inscription in gold lettering. The reverse bears a trophy of Turkish flags and drums, and the date. The star hangs from its ribbon by means of a star and crescent and a ring. There were four classes.

### 627 - THE ORDER OF CHASTITY (FOR LADIES)
The Order of Chefakat was instituted in 1880 by the Sultan Abdul Hamid II. It consisted of a five-pointed star in crimson enamel, edged gold and each ray tipped with a small gold ball, and in the centre a gold boss bearing the Sultan's cypher surrounded by a green-enamelled circle bearing an inscription in Turkish. The star rested upon a circular wreath enamelled green with crimson berries, the whole being mounted upon another star with radiating points studded with brilliants protruding between the angles of the enamelled star. The decoration hung from a star and crescent enamelled in crimson. There were three classes. (Now obsolete.)

### 628 - TURKISH STAR FOR GALLIPOLI CAMPAIGN
This decoration consists of a five-pointed, white metal star, each ray tipped with a small white metal ball and edged with white metal, and filled in with common red enamel. The centre is surrounded by a white metal crescent, inside of which, on a red ground, is the Sultan's cypher, and characters representing 'El Ghazi' ('The Victorious'). Below is the date '333' in Turkish figures ('1915'). The reverse is plain, with a brooch pin to which the ribbon is attached. The star itself is tawdry and unfinished, though it is believed that that awarded to officers was better made.

# The Union of Soviet Socialist Republics

### GOLD STAR MEDAL
Awarded to 'Heroes of the Soviet Union,' indivuduals, both civilian and military, who have performed outstanding feats contributing to the honour and material development of the U.S.S.R. The badge is a five-pointed gold star, worn on the left breast above all other decorations, from a red ribbon about 20 mm. wide. The star itself is always worn.

### HAMMER AND SICKLE GOLD MEDAL
This medal is awarded to 'Heroes of Socialist Labour.' It is a civil decoration which differs only from the Gold Star Medal in that a hammer and sickle are superimposed on the centre of the star. It is worn in the same way as its counterpart and is never replaced by a ribbon.

   'Heroes of the Soviet Union' and 'Heroes of Socialist Labour' are automatically awarded the Order of Lenin, described later.

**GOLD STAR MEDAL**

## 629 - ORDER OF VICTORY

This Order was instituted in November 1943 by decree of the Presidium of the Supreme Soviet as the highest military decoration for members of the higher commanding personnel of the Red Army. It is conferred for successful execution of such military operations, on the scale of one or several fronts, which result in a radical change in the situation in favour of the Red Army.

The emblem is of platinum and comprises a five-pointed ruby star, measuring 75 mm. between opposite points and bordered with diamonds. In between the points of the star are diverging rays studded with diamonds. In the centre of the star is a circle covered with blue enamel bordered by a wreath of laurel and oak leaves. In the centre of the circle is a representation of the Kremlin Wall with Lenin's mausoleum and the Spassky Tower, in platinum. The total weight of the diamonds in the emblem is 16 carats.

As a mark of particular distinction a roll of honour inscribed with the names of the recipients of the Order is set up in the Grand Kremlin Palace. The emblem is worn on the left side above the waist, and may be replaced by a ribbon, about 44 mm. wide, worn on the left breast before all others, with a central broad stripe of red, bordered on each side by stripes of green, dark blue, red, light blue, each colour divided by narrow stripes of white, and an edge of three narrow stripes of orange, black, orange.

## 630 - ORDER OF LENIN

This Order was established in 1930 by decree of the Central Executive Committee of the U.S.S.R. It may be awarded to individual citizens, collective bodies, institutions, undertakings and social organizations of the Soviet Union in recognition of special services rendered to the socialist régime through research, technical improvements, or otherwise, in industry, agriculture, trade, transport, or work in State or co-operative enterprises generally.

The badge consists of a circular portrait of Lenin framed in a gold wreath of ears of rye. A red star is set in the wreath on the left side, with the hammer and sickle at the base. Down the right side hangs the Red flag inscribed with the name of Lenin.

## THE MARSHAL'S STAR

This decoration is awarded to marshals of the Soviet Union, and to marshals of artillery, aviation, and tank and mechanized troops. It is a five-pointed gold star with a smaller five-pointed star studded with diamonds in the centre. The star of a marshal of the Soviet Union, in addition, has a large diamond mounted between each of the rays of the star. The decoration is worn round the neck, and the ribbon is red moiré for marshals of the Soviet Union, gold colour for marshals of artillery, pale blue for marshals of the air, and claret colour for marshals of tank and mechanized troops.

**630 - ORDER OF LENIN**

## 631 - ORDER OF THE RED BANNER

Instituted in 1932, this Order may be awarded to officers or men of the Red Army, Navy or Air Force, or any military unit, or any citizen of the U.S.S.R., in recognition of conspicuous bravery or self-sacrifice in time of war, special capacity for leadership, or the performance of some action contributing decisively to the success of Soviet arms.

The badge consists of a laurel wreath, over the upper part of which is spread the Red flag bearing the words 'Workers of all Countries, Unite!' Against a background of white the wreath contains a hammer and a plough, and in the centre a red star, the middle part of which has the hammer and sickle. A red enamel riband round the bottom of the wreath bears the Russian equivalent of the initials 'U.S.S.R.' This Order may be awarded more than once to the same recipient.

### 632- ORDER OF SUVOROV

This Order was created in July 1942 and has three classes with differing insignia. The *First Class* is awarded to commanders of fronts and armies; their deputies, chiefs of staff; heads of operational headquarters and sections; and heads of different fighting categories, artillery, air force, armoured tank, mortar, etc., for excellent organization of front or army operations whereby a numerically superior enemy is defeated. The *Second Class* is awarded to commanders of corps, divisions and brigades, their deputies and chiefs of staff, in similar circumstances, and the *Third Class* to commanders of regiments and battalions and their chiefs of staff.

The insignia of the *First Class* is a platinum five-pointed star, the surface executed in the shape of radiating beams. The centre has a matt gold ground with the Russian inscription 'Alexander Suvorov' round the upper half. In the lower half are sprays of laurel and oak, with the head of Marshal Suvorov in relief in the centre.

The badge of the *Second Class* of the Order is the same, but is of gold with a silver centre, while that of the *Third Class* is carried out entirely in silver. The badges are worn on the right breast without ribbons; and the service ribbons are of green moiré silk, the *First Class* having one orange stripe in the centre, the *Second Class* an orange stripe at each edge, and the *Third Class* three orange stripes, one at the centre and one at each edge.

### 633 - ORDER OF KUTUZOV

This Order is in three classes. The *First Class* is awarded to commanders of fronts and armies, their deputies, heads of staffs, for well-planned and executed front or army operations as a result of which defeat of the enemy is achieved. The *Second Class* is for commanders of corps, divisions, brigades, and heads of staffs; and the *Third Class* for regimental and battalion commanders and their chiefs of staff for similar achievements.

The insignia of the *First Class* is a five-pointed golden star in the shape of radiating beams. The centre is of white enamel, around it a laurel and oak wreath interwoven in the lower half with a red enamel ribbon. In the centre is a gold relief head of Marshal Kutuzov on a background depicting the Kremlin tower culminating in a five-pointed star of ruby-red enamel. Around the centre on a

**631 - ORDER OF
THE RED BANNER**

white enamel band is the inscription 'Michael Kutuzov' in Russian. The spaces between the points of the gold star are covered with five bunches of silver rays emerging from below the white enamel ribbon. The insignia of the *Second Class* is of silver, with the portrait of Kutuzov, a laurel and oak wreath, the inscription and rim of the ribbon being gilt. The badge of the *Third Class* is worked entirely in silver. The badges are worn on the right breast without ribbons. The service ribbons are of dark blue moiré silk; the *First Class* with an orange stripe in the centre, the *Second Class* an orange stripe at each edge, and the *Third Class* three orange stripes, one at the centre and one at each edge.

**633 - ORDER OF KUTUZOV**

### 634 - ORDER OF ALEXANDER NEVSKY

This Order was established in July 1942 and awarded to commanders of regiments, battalions, units and platoons for display of initiative in choosing the right moment for a sudden, bold and headlong attack on the enemy and for infliction of serious defeat with small losses in manpower, also for operational air flights, and the skilful and headlong accomplishment of landing operations with minimum losses, leading up to severe defeat of the enemy, and ensuring the success of a general military undertaking.

The badge is a five-pointed star in red enamel resting on a ten-pointed silver background, with radiating beams. In the centre, on a circular ground, is the head of Prince General Alexander Nevsky with his name in Russian. On each side of the centre portion are sprays of laurel joined at the bottom by a small shield with the hammer and sickle. The heads of two battle-axes or halberds appear above. The Order has only one class and is worn on the right breast. The service ribbon is pale blue with a red central stripe.

**634 - ORDER OF ALEXANDER NEVSKY**

### 635 - ORDER OF GLORY

This Order was instituted in November 1943 for N.C.O.s and the rank and file of the Red Army and for junior lieutenants of the Red Air Force who have distinguished themselves in battle by being first to break into enemy positions or by some act of personal bravery contribute to the success of the operation as a whole, by saving the standard of their unit or capturing an enemy standard, accounting personally for from ten to fifty enemy soldiers, disable not less than two enemy tanks with anti-tank guns or from one to three tanks with hand grenades or save the life of a commander in battle at the risk of their own. There are three classes of the Order, and those decorated receive promotion.

The badge is a five-pointed star, in the centre of which is a circle with a representation of the Kremlin with the Spassky Tower in relief, with two sprays of laurel and the word 'Glory' in Russian below on a red riband. The badge of the *First Class* is in gold; that of the *Second Class* is in silver with gold centre; and that of the *Third Class* in silver. The badges are worn from a ribbon of orange moiré with three black stripes, precisely the same as the old Czarist Order of St. George.

## 636 - ORDER OF THE PATRIOTIC WAR

This Order was instituted during the Second World War for award to those showing great heroism and courage and good results in fighting the Fascist invader. There are two classes.

The *First Class* is awarded to all ranks of the Red Army, Red Navy, Troops of the Peoples Commissiariat of Internal Affairs and Guerilla Detachments who displayed courage, staunchness and gallantry in fighting.

The *Second Class* is awarded to those who by their actions have contributed to the success of war operations.

The insignia of the *First Class* is a red star, bearing the hammer and sickle in gold behind which appear a crossed sword and rifle, surrounded by golden rays.

The insignia of the *Second Class* is the same but in silver instead of gold. Both bear the words 'Patriotic War' in Russian on a white band encircling the sickle-and-hammer emblem. The badges are worn on the right breast without ribbons, but service ribbons are provided – red moiré with a central stripe of lighter red for the *First Class*; red with lighter red edges for the *Second Class*.

**636 - ORDER OF THE PATRIOTIC WAR**
*Insignia of the First Class*

## THE ORDER OF USHAKOV (NAVY)

This consists of a gold (*First Class*) or silver (*Second Class*) five-pointed star on which is a large silver anchor. Over the shank and resting on the arms are chain and rope circles within which, on a light blue ground, is a portrait of Admiral Ushakov in high collared Naval uniform with decorations. In the *First Class* the portrait is silver, in the *Second Class* gold. The star is worn on the right breast, but when ribbons alone are worn they are respectively pale blue with two broad white stripes, and white with two pale blue stripes. The Medal of Ushakov consists of the centre medallion and anchor and hangs from a V-shaped chain from a ribbon of pale blue with dark blue (outer) and white (inner) edge stripes. As well as common usage of the above spelling of this Order's title, reference is also made in Soviet records to the 'Order of Ooshakov.'

**ORDER OF USHAKOV**
*Insignia of the First Class*

## THE ORDER OF NAKIMOV (NAVY)

This is a gold (*First Class*) or silver (*Second Class*) five-pointed star, between the points of which are anchors, crowns and flukes outwards, the shanks split and containing red triangles. The centre consists of a profile of Admiral Nakimov in a peaked cap. The portrait is on a bright blue ground for the *First Class* and all silver for the *Second*. The Medal of Nakhimov is gold and consists of the portrait described above. It hangs from a pale blue ribbon with three white stripes in the centre, while the ribbons of the Order are – *First Class* – black with two broad orange stripes. *Second Class* – orange with two black stripes. As well as common usage of the above spelling of this Order's title, reference is also made in Soviet records to the 'Order of Hakhumov.'

## THE ORDER OF BOGDAN KHMELNITSKY

This Order is in three classes and is awarded by rank to all officers and men of the Soviet armed forces, as well as guerilla leaders and

**ORDER OF NAKIMOV**
*Insignia of the First Class*

guerillas who specially distinguished themselves in battle. The decorations are all ten-pointed stars protruding from a large ornamental ring. The rays are five gold and five silver for the *First Class* and all ten silver for the others. The centres consist of a portrait of Bogdan Khmelnitsky in robes holding a sceptre. It is gold in the first two classes and silver in the third. The ribbons are all pale blue and white, the *First Class* having a white centre stripe, the *Second* white edges, and the *Third* both.

## ORDER OF THE RED BANNER OF LABOUR

This Order was founded in 1928, and is awarded to individual citizens or collective bodies for outstanding services to the Soviet Union in production or scientific research. The decoration is worn on the left breast in the case of individuals, or affixed to the flag or emblem in the case of collectivities. It consists of a hammer and sickle surrounded by a wreath and by the inscription 'Workers of all Countries, Unite!' The Red flag, with the initials 'CCCP' ('U.S.S.R.') covers the top part of the wreath. The ribbon is of blue moiré silk with darker blue stripes at each edge.

## 637 - ORDER OF THE RED STAR

This Order was created in 1930 for officers and men of the Red Army, Navy or Air Force, or units thereof, or institutions, undertakings, or social organizations performing conspicuous services in the defence of the U.S.S.R. either in war or in peace. The badge consists of a red star, in the centre of which is a soldier of the Red Army holding a rifle with fixed bayonet. In a circle round this figure is the inscription 'Workers of all Countries, Unite!' Beneath it are the Russian initials 'CCCP' ('U.S.S.R.') and the sign of the hammer and sickle. The badge is worn alone on the breast, but is represented by a service ribbon of dark red moiré with a central stripe of grey.

## 638 - INSIGNIA OF HONOUR

This decoration, introduced in 1935, may be awarded to individual citizens or collective organizations for outstanding achievements in industry, agriculture, transport, commerce, scientific research, cultural or sporting activities, technical inventions or improvements conferring important economic or military benefits upon the U.S.S.R.

The badge is an oval wreath of oak leaves surrounding the figures of a working man and woman. Behind the two figures is the Red flag, with the inscription 'Workers of all Countries, Unite!' Over their heads is the red star, and beneath their feet the words (in Russian) 'Insignia of Honour.'

## MEDAL FOR VALOUR

This medal is awarded to service personnel of all ranks for personal bravery. Recipients receive a pension of ten roubles a month and have the right of free travel on the tramways. The medal consists of a red- and white-enamelled disc figuring a tank and aeroplanes overhead with the inscription 'For Valour. U.S.S.R.' The ribbon is pale grey moiré with blue stripes at the edges.

**ORDER OF THE
RED BANNER OF LABOUR**

**637 - ORDER OF
THE RED STAR**

## MEDAL FOR DISTINGUISHED SERVICE IN BATTLE

This medal is awarded to military or civilian personnel for distinguished services in a battle area. The award carries a pension of five roubles a month and free travel on the tramways. A red- and white-enamelled disc with crossed rifle and sword and inscription 'For Distinguished Battle Service—U.S.S.R.' The ribbon is pale grey moiré with yellow stripes at the edges.

## MEDAL FOR TWENTY YEARS' SERVICE IN THE RED ARMY

This medal was established in 1938 and awarded for long service. It is a circular silver medal with raised edge and bearing a red-enamelled five-pointed star, edged gold, with the figures 'XX' at the foot, also in gold. The ribbon is grey moiré with narrow red edges.

## MEDAL FOR THIRTY YEARS' SERVICE IN THE RED ARMY

This medal is the same as the twenty-year medal, but with the figures 'XXX.' The ribbon is grey with red centre stripes and red edges.

## MEDAL FOR VALIANT LABOUR

This is primarily a civilian award. It is circular, silver, bearing a red star on which are a silver hammer and sickle; in the upper half are the words 'For valiant labour' in red and the letters 'CCCP' in silver. The ribbon is mauve with narrow red edges.

## MEDAL FOR LABOUR DISTINCTION

This is also primarily a civilian award. It is circular, silver, with raised letters 'CCCP' across the centre. It bears a large hammer and sickle in red, and below are the words 'For labour distinction.' The ribbon is mauve with yellow edges.

## PARTISAN MEDALS

These medals are in two classes, silver and bronze. The obverse bears the profiles of Lenin and Stalin surrounded by the inscription 'To a partisan of the Patriotic War.' The ribbons are: *First Class*, bright green with a narrow red centre stripe; *Second Class*, the same with blue stripe. The medals themselves are worn on the right breast.

## ORDER OF THE OCTOBER REVOLUTION

### LENIN CENTENARY MEDAL (1970)

### 'DEFENCE' MEDALS

Practically all of the medals mentioned below are made in brass, or stainless steel, and have no design on the reverse.

## LENINGRAD

Three soldiers with rifles at the ready position at foot, behind, a tower and surrounding all the words 'For the defence of Leningrad.' Ribbon, olive green with a narrow dark green centre stripe.

**ORDER OF THE OCTOBER REVOLUTION**

### MOSCOW
In centre a tank and the Kremlin. Below, a wreath and above the words 'For the defence of Moscow.' Ribbon, red with three olive green stripes.

### ODESSA
A soldier and a sailor advancing to the left, below, a wreath, above, the words 'For the defence of Odessa.' Ribbon, olive green with a narrow pale blue centre stripe.

### SEVASTOPOL
Profiles of sailor and soldier – arms and flukes of an anchor below, inscription 'For the defence of Sevastopol.' Ribbon, olive green with a narrow deep blue centre stripe.

### 639 - STALINGRAD
Five soldiers facing left with rifles at the ready, in front of a red flag. Inscription 'For the defence of Stalingrad.' Ribbon, olive green with a narrow red centre stripe.

### 640 - CAUCASUS
Within an ornamental border a mountain, aeroplanes, oil wells and tanks. Inscription 'For the defence of the Caucasus.' Ribbon, olive green, with blue edges and in the centre very narrow stripes of blue, white, red, green, red, white, blue.

### ARCTIC
A soldier in winter dress; in front of him a tank; behind, a warship; above, aeroplanes. Inscription 'For the defence of the Soviet Arctic.' Ribbon, three broad stripes of pale blue, pale green, pale blue separated by narrow white stripes, and narrow white edges.

## 'CAPTURE' MEDALS

### BUDAPEST
A star, 'For the capture of Budapest,' hammer and sickle with a branch on either side. Ribbon, orange, pale blue, orange, equal.

**LENIN CENTENARY MEDAL**

### KOENIGSBERG
A radiant star, 'For the capture of Koenigsberg,' a branch with five leaves. Ribbon, green with three black stripes.

### VIENNA
A star, 'For the capture of Vienna,' a branch with twelve leaves. Ribbon, pale blue, dark blue, pale blue, equal.

### 641 - BERLIN
A star with the inscription 'For the capture of Berlin,' and a half wreath of oak leaves. Ribbon, red, with, inset in the centre, the St. George ribbon.

## 'LIBERATION' MEDALS

### PRAGUE
In lower half a sunburst on a half wreath; above 'For the liberation of Prague.' Ribbon, mauve, blue, mauve, equal.

345

## BELGRADE
A wreath encircling 'For the liberation of Belgrade.' Ribbon, green, black, green, equal.

## 642 - WARSAW
At foot a star, rising from this a sunburst, across the centre of which is the word 'Warsaw' on a scroll; above the burst 'For the liberation of Warsaw.' Ribbon, blue, red, blue, equal, with narrow yellow edges.

### GENERAL

## MEDAL FOR WAR IN FINLAND
No description available. Ribbon, blue with two broad white stripes.

## MEDAL FOR THE VICTORY OVER GERMANY (1945)
Profile of Stalin in full dress facing left. Ribbon, that of the Order of St. George – orange with three black stripes. The medal bears two mottos – 'Our cause is just' and 'We are victorious.'

## 643 - MEDAL FOR 'VALIANT LABOUR IN THE GREAT PATRIOTIC WAR OF 1941–45'
Same obverse as above. Ribbon, red, green, red, equal, with narrow yellow edges.

## MEDAL FOR VICTORY OVER JAPAN
Stalin's profile facing right. The ribbon is that of the old Czarist Order of St. Stanislas with yellow edges.

## MEDAL FOR FRONTIER DEFENCE (1951)
Ribbon, green with red edges.

## MEDAL FOR 800 YEARS OF MOSCOW
Instituted in September 1947 for citizens of Moscow. Ribbon, half green, half white, with three red stripes on the white.

## MEDAL FOR DISTINGUISHED SERVICE IN THE PRESERVATION OF PUBLIC ORDER
Established in 1952 for award for bravery and self-denial shown in the liquidation of thieving bandit groups; the prevention of criminal outbreaks; the capture of criminals; the preservation of public order, etc. The ribbon is red, with three central stripes of blue, the centre stripe thinner than the other two.

# *Yugoslavia*

The following Orders and Medals have been instituted since 1945 by President Tito.

**ORDER OF THE YUGOSLAV FL**
*Star of the Second Class (Shown full si*

## ORDER OF NATIONAL HERO
Red, with a narrow white stripe near each edge.

## ORDER FOR BRAVERY
Red, with three narrow yellow stripes rather widely spaced on each side.

## ORDER OF THE YUGOSLAV FLAG

## ORDER OF THE PARTISAN STAR
*First Class*, red. *Second Class*, red, with two broad yellow stripes. *Third Class*, five red and four yellow stripes, equal.

## ORDER OF BROTHERHOOD AND UNITY
*First Class*, red centre and narrow blue edges with broad white stripes between red and blue. *Second Class*, as above, but with a second narrow blue stripe just inside the edge.

## MEDAL FOR BRAVERY
Five blue and four white equal stripes.

## ORDER OF SERVICE TO THE PEOPLE
In three classes and a medal. The ribbon is red with one, two, three or four stripes of blue.

## ORDER FOR LABOUR
In three classes and a medal. The ribbon is blue with one, two, three or four stripes of red.

## ORDER OF THE RED FLAG
Ribbon red with gold thread centre and gold edges.

## ORDER OF FREEDOM
Ribbon red with gold edges.

## ORDER OF HERO OF SOCIALIST LABOUR
Ribbon red with gold centre.

## ORDER OF THE PEOPLE'S ARMY
*Class I* – Ribbon red with broad white borders. *Class II* – Ribbon red with broad white borders and a narrow central stripe of white. *Class III* – Ribbon white with three red stripes in centre.

## ORDER OF ARMY SERVICE
*Class I* – Ribbon red with one white stripe. *Class II* – Ribbon red with two white stripes. *Class III* – Ribbon red with three white stripes. *Medal* – Ribbon red with four white stripes.

## ORDER OF THE YUGOSLAV STAR
Ribbon violet.

## MEDAL FOR DISTINGUISHED SERVICE
Ribbon red with narrow blue edges divided from the red by narrow stripes of white.

**ORDER OF THE YUGOSLAV FLAG**
*Badge of the Second and Third Class*
*(Shown full size)*

# Appendix 1

# Bars to the British Naval General Service Medal (1793-1840)

The following are the 230 known bars awarded to the Naval General Service Medal between 1793 and 1840 for ships' actions and boat service between these dates. In many instances the date on the bar is incorrect for that on which the action occurred, and an historically correct date is therefore shown beside each bar.

| Bar | Correct Date | Bar | Correct Date |
|---|---|---|---|
| 1. NYMPHE 18 JUNE 1793 | (19 June 1793) | 27. MINERVA 19 DEC<sup>R</sup> 1796 | (19 December 1796) |
| 2. CRESCENT 20 OCT<sup>R</sup> 1793 | (20 October 1793) | 28. BLANCHE 19 DEC<sup>R</sup> 1796 | (19 December 1796) |
| 3. ZEBRA 17 MARCH 1794 | (20 March 1794) | 29. INDEFATIGABLE 13 JAN<sup>Y</sup> 1797 | (13 January 1797) |
| 4. CARYSFORT 29 MAY 1794 | (28 May 1794) | 30. AMAZON 13 JAN<sup>Y</sup> 1797 | (13 January 1797) |
| 5. 1 JUNE 1794 | (1 June 1794) | 31. S<sup>T</sup> VINCENT | (14 February 1797) |
| 6. ROMNEY 17 JUNE 1794 | (17 June 1794) | 32. SAN FIORENZO 8 MAR 1797 | (9 March 1797) |
| 7. BLANCHE 4 JAN. 1795 | (5 January 1795) | 33. NYMPHE 8 MARCH 1797 | (9 March 1797) |
| 8. LIVELY 13 MARCH 1795 | (13 March 1795) | 34. CAMPERDOWN | (11 October 1797) |
| 9. 14 MARCH 1795 | (14 March 1795) | 35. PHŒBE 21 DEC<sup>R</sup> 1797 | (21 December 1797) |
| 10. ASTREA 10 APRIL 1795 | (10 April 1795) | 36. MARS 21 APRIL 1798 | (21 April 1798) |
| 11. THETIS 17 MAY 1795 | (16 May 1795) | 37. ISLE S<sup>T</sup> MARCOU 6 MAY 1798 | (7 May 1798) |
| 12. HUSSAR 17 MAY 1795 | (16 May 1795) | 38. LION 15 JULY 1798 | (15 July 1798) |
| 13. MOSQUITO 9 JUNE 1795 | (24 May 1795) | 39. NILE | (1 August 1798) |
| 14. 17 JUNE 1795 | (17 June 1795) | 40. L'ESPOIR 7 AUG. 1798 | (6 August 1798) |
| 15. 23<sup>RD</sup> JUNE 1795 | (23 June 1795) | 41. 12 OCT<sup>R</sup> 1798 | (12 October 1798) |
| 16. LOWESTOFFE 24 JUNE 1795 | (24 June 1795) | 42. FISGARD 20 OCT<sup>R</sup> 1798 | (20 October 1798) |
| 17. DIDO JUNE 24 1795 | (24 June 1795) | 43. SYBILLE 28 FEB<sup>Y</sup> 1799 | (1 March 1799) |
| 18. SPIDER 25 AUG. 1795 | (25 August 1795) | 44. TELEGRAPH 18 MARCH 1799 | (18 March 1799) |
| 19. PORT SPERGUI 17 MARCH 1796¹ | (17 March 1796) | 45. ACRE 30 MAY 1799 | (20 May 1799) |
| 20. INDEFATIGABLE 20 APRIL 1796 | (21 April 1796) | 46. SCHIERMONIKOOG 12 AUG. 1799 | (11 & 13 Aug. 1799) |
| 21. UNICORN 8 JUNE 1796 | (8 June 1796) | 47. ARROW 13 SEP<sup>R</sup> 1799 | (13 September 1799) |
| 22. SANTA MARGARITA 8 JUNE 1796 | (8 June 1796) | 48. WOLVERINE 13 SEP<sup>R</sup> 1799 | (13 September 1799) |
| 23. SOUTHAMPTON 9 JUNE 1796 | (9 June 1796) | 49. SURPRISE W<sup>H</sup> HERMIONE | (25 October 1799) |
| 24. DRYAD 13 JUNE 1796 | (13 June 1796) | 50. SPEEDY 6 NOV<sup>R</sup> 1799 | (6 November 1799) |
| 25. TERPSICHORE 13 OCT<sup>R</sup> 1796 | (13 October 1796) | | |
| 26. LAPWING 3 DEC<sup>R</sup> 1796 | (27 November 1796) | | |

¹ The spelling should be Port Erqui.

| Bar | Correct Date | Bar | Correct Date |
|---|---|---|---|
| 51. COURIER 22 NovR 1799 | (23 November 1799) | 93. EMERALD 13 MARCH 1808 | (13 March 1808) |
| 52. VIPER 26 DECR 1799 | (26 December 1799) | 94. CHILDERS 14 MARCH 1808 | (14 March 1808) |
| 53. HARPY 5 FEBY 1800 | (5 February 1800) | 95. NASSAU 22 MARCH 1808 | (22 March 1808) |
| 54. FAIRY 5 FEBY 1800 | (5 February 1800) | 96. STATELY 22 MARCH 1808 | (22 March 1808) |
| 55. PETEREL 21 MARCH 1800 | (21 March 1800) | 97. OFF ROTA 4 APRIL 1808 | (4 April 1808) |
| 56. PENELOPE 30 March 1800 | (30 March 1800) | 98. GRASSHOPPER 24 APRIL 1808 | (24 April 1808) |
| 57. VINCIEGO 30 MARCH 1800 [2] | (30 March 1800) | 99. RAPID 24 APRIL 1808 | (24 April 1808) |
| 58. CAPTURE OF THE DÉSIRÉE 8 JULY 1800 | (8 July 1800) | 100. REDWING 7 MAY 1808 | (7 May 1808) |
| 59. SEINE 20 AUGT 1800 | (20 August 1800) | 101. VIRGINIE 19 MAY 1808 | (19 May 1808) |
| 60. PHŒBE 19 FEBY 1801 | (19 February 1801) | 102. REDWING 31 MAY 1808 | (1 June 1808) |
| 61. EGYPT | (8 March to 2 September 1801) | 103. SEAHORSE WH BADERE ZAFFER | (5 July 1808) |
| 62. COPENHAGEN 1801 | (2 April 1801) | 104. COMET 11 AUG. 1808 | (11 August 1808) |
| 63. SPEEDY 6 MAY 1801 | (6 May 1801) | 105. CENTAUR 26 AUGT 1808 | (26 August 1808) |
| 64. GUT OF GIBRALTAR 12 JULY 1801 | (12 July 1801) | 106. IMPLACABLE 26 AUGT 1808 | (26 August 1808) |
| 65. SYLPH 28 SEPR 1801 | (28 September 1801) | 107. CRUZIER 1 NOVR 1808 | (1 November 1808) |
| 66. PASLEY 28 OCTR 1801 | (28 October 1801) | 108. AMETHYST WH THETIS | (10 November 1808) |
| 67. SCORPION 31 MARCH 1804 | (31 March 1804) | 109. OFF THE PEARL ROCK 13 DEC 1808 | (13 December 1808) |
| 68. BEAVER 31 MARCH 1804 | (31 March 1804) | 110. ONYX 1 JAN. 1809 | (1 January 1809) |
| 69. CENTURION 18TH SEPT 1804 | (18 September 1804) | 111. CONFIANCE 14 JANY 1809 | (14 January 1809) |
| 70. ARROW 3 FEBY 1805 | (4 February 1805) | 112. MARTINIQUE | (24 February 1809) |
| 71. ACHERON 3RD FEBY 1805 | (4 February 1805) | 113. HORATIO 10 FEBY 1809 | (10 February 1809) |
| 72. SAN FIORENZO 14 FEBY 1805 | (13 February 1805) | 114. SUPÉRIEURE 10 FEBY 1809 | (10 February 1809) |
| 73. PHŒNIX 10 AUGT 1805 | (10 August 1805) | 115. AMETHYST 5 APRIL 1809 | (5 April 1809) |
| 74. TRAFALGAR | (21 October 1805) | 116. BASQUE ROADS 1809 | (11 April 1809) |
| 75. 4 NOVR 1805 | (4 November 1805) | 117. CASTOR 17TH JUNE 1809 | (April 1809) |
| 76. ST DOMINGO | (6 February 1806) | 118. POMPÉE 17 JUNE 1809 | (April 1809) |
| 77. LONDON 13 MARCH 1806 | (13 March 1806) | 119. RECRUIT 17 JUNE 1809 | (April 1809) |
| 78. AMAZON 13 MARCH 1806 | (13 March 1806) | 120. CYANE 25 & 27 JUNE 1809 | (26 & 27 June 1809) |
| 79. PIQUE 26 MARCH 1807 | (26 March 1806) | 121. L'ESPOIR 25 & 27 JUNE 1809 | (26 & 27 June 1809) |
| 80. SIRIUS 17 APRIL 1806 | (17 April 1806) | 122. BONNE CITOYENNE WH FURIEUSE | (6 July 1809) |
| 81. BLANCHE 19 JULY 1806 | (19 July 1806) | 123. DIANA 11 SEPTR 1809 | (11 September 1809) |
| 82. ARETHUSA 23 AUGT 1806 | (23 August 1806) | 124. ANSE LA BARQUE 18 DECR 1809 | (18 December 1809) |
| 83. ANSON 23 AUG. 1806 | (23 August 1806) | 125. CHEROKEE 10 JAN. 1810 | (11 January 1810) |
| 84. CURAÇOA | (1 January 1807) | 126. SCORPION 12 JAN. 1810 | (12 January 1810) |
| 85. PICKLE 3 JAN. 1807 | (3 January 1807) | 127. GUADALOUPE | (5 February 1810) |
| 86. HYDRA 6 AUGT 1807 | (7 August 1807) | 128. THISTLE 10 FEBY 1810 | (10 February 1810) |
| 87. COMUS 15 AUG. 1807 | (15 August 1807) | 129. SURLY 24 APRIL 1810 | (20 April 1810) |
| 88. LOUISA 28 OCTR 1807 | (29 October 1807) | 130. FIRM 24 APRIL 1810 | (20 April 1810) |
| 89. CARRIER 4 NOVR 1807 | (14 November 1807) | 131. SYLVIA 26 APRIL 1810 | (26 April 1810) |
| 90. ANN 24 NOVR 1807 | (24 November 1807) | 132. SPARTAN 3 MAY 1810 | (3 May 1810) |
| 91. SAPPHO 2 MARCH 1808 | (2 March 1808) | | |
| 92. SAN FIORENZO 8 MARCH 1808 | (8 March 1808) | | |

[2] The spelling should be Vincejo.

| Bar | Correct Date | Bar | Correct Date |
|---|---|---|---|
| 133. ROYALIST MAY & JUNE 1810 | (23 February 1810) | 172. ENDYMION WH PRESIDENT | (15 January 1815) |
| 134. AMANTHEA 25 JULY 1810 | (25 July 1810) | 173. GAIETA 24 JULY 1815 | (8 August 1815) |
| 135. BANDA NEIRA | (9 August 1810) | 174. ALGIERS | (27 August 1816) |
| 136. STAUNCH 18 SEPR 1810 | (18 September 1810) | 175. NAVARINO | (20 October 1827) |
| 137. OTTER 18 SEPR 1810 | (18 September 1810) | 176. SYRIA | (4 November 1840) |
| 138. BOADICEA 18 SEPR 1810 | (18 September 1810) | 177. 15 MARCH BOAT SERVICE 1793 | (15 March 1793) |
| 139. BRISEIS 14 OCTR 1810 | (14 October 1810) | 178. 17 MARCH BOAT SERVICE 1794 | (17 March 1794) |
| 140. LISSA | (13 March 1811) | 179. 29 MAY BOAT SERVICE 1797 | (29 May 1797) |
| 141. ANHOLT 27 MARCH 1811 | (27 March 1811) | 180. 9 JUNE BOAT SERVICE 1799 | (9 June 1799) |
| 142. ARROW 6 APRIL 1811 | (30 March 1811) | 181. 20 DECR BOAT SERVICE 1799 | (21 December 1799) |
| 143. OFF TAMATIVE 20 MAY 1811 | (20 May 1811) | 182. 29 JULY BOAT SERVICE 1800 | (29 July 1800) |
| 144. HAWKE 18 AUG. 1811 | (18 August 1811) | 183. 29 AUG. BOAT SERVICE 1800 | (30 August 1800) |
| 145. JAVA | (18 September 1811) | 184. 27 OCTR BOAT SERVICE 1800 | (28 October 1800) |
| 146. LOCUST 11 NOVR 1811 | (10 November 1811) | 185. 21 JULY BOAT SERVICE 1801 | (22 July 1801) |
| 147. SKYLARK 11 NOVR 1811 | (10 November 1811) | 186. 27 JUNE BOAT SERVICE 1803 | (28 June 1803) |
| 148. PELAGOSA 29 NOVR 1811 | (29 November 1811) | 187. 4 NOVR BOAT SERVICE 1803 | (4 November 1803) |
| 149. VICTORIOUS WITH RIVOLI | (22 February 1812) | 188. 4 FEBY BOAT SERVICE 1804 | (4 February 1804) |
| 150. WEAZEL 22 FEBY 1811 | (22 February 1812) | 189. 4 JUNE BOAT SERVICE 1805 | (4 June 1805) |
| 151. ROSARIO 27 MARCH 1812 | (22 April 1812) | 190. 16 JULY BOAT SERVICE 1806 | (16 July 1806) |
| 152. GRIFFON 27 MARCH 1812 | (27 April 1812) | 191. 2 JAN. BOAT SERVICE 1807 | (2 January 1807) |
| 153. MALAGA 29 APRIL 1812 | (22 April 1812) | 192. 21 JAN. BOAT SERVICE 1807 | (21 January 1807) |
| 154. NORTHUMBERLAND 22 MAY 1812 | (22 May 1812) | 193. 19 APRIL BOAT SERVICE 1807 | (20 April 1807) |
| 155. GROWLER 22 MAY 1812 | (22 May 1812) | 194. 13 FEBY BOAT SERVICE 1808 | (13 February 1808) |
| 156. OFF MARDOE 6 JULY 1812 | (6 July 1812) | 195. 10 JULY BOAT SERVICE 1808 | (10 July 1808) |
| 157. SEALARK 21 JULY 1812 | (21 July 1812) | 196. 11 AUG. BOAT SERVICE 1808 | (9 August 1808) |
| 158. ROYALIST 29 DECR 1812 | (29 December 1812) | 197. 28 NOVR BOAT SERVICE 1808 | (29 November 1808) |
| 159. WEAZEL 22 APRIL 1813 | (22 April 1813) | 198. 7 JULY BOAT SERVICE 1809 | (7 July 1809) |
| 160. SHANNON WH CHESAPEAKE | (1 June 1813) | 199. 14th JULY BOAT SERVICE 1809 | (16 July 1809) |
| 161. PELICAN 14 AUG. 1813 | (14 August 1813) | 200. 25 JULY BOAT SERVICE 1809 | (26 July 1809) |
| 162. ST SEBASTIAN | (8 September 1813) | 201. 27 JULY BOAT SERVICE 1809 | (27 July 1809) |
| 163. THUNDER 9 OCTR 1813 | (9 October 1813) | 202. 29 JULY BOAT SERVICE 1809 | (29 July 1809) |
| 164. GLUCKSTADT 5 JANY 1814 | (5 January 1814) | 203. 28 AUG. BOAT SERVICE 1809 | (27 August 1809) |
| 165. VENERABLE 16 JANY 1814 | (16 & 20 January 1814) | | |
| 166. CYANE 16 JAN. 1814 | (16 & 20 January 1814) | | |
| 167. EUROTAS 25 FEBY 1814 | (25 February 1814) | | |
| 168. HEBRUS WITH L'ÉTOILE | (27 March 1814) | | |
| 169. CHERUB 28 MARCH 1814 | (28 March 1814) | | |
| 170. PHŒBE 28 March 1814 | (28 March 1814) | | |
| 171. THE POTOMAC 17 AUG. 1814 | (29 August 1814) | | |

| Bar | Correct Date | Bar | Correct Date |
|---|---|---|---|
| 204. 1 Nov. Boat Service 1809 | (1 November 1809) | 218. 4th April Boat Service 1812 | (4 April 1812) |
| 205. 13 Decr Boat Service 1809 | (12 December 1809) | 219. 1 & 18 Sep. Boat Service 1812 | (1 September 1812) |
| 206. 23 Feb. Boat Service 1810 | (13 February 1810) | 220. 17 Sept. Boat Service 1812 | (17 September 1812) |
| 207. 1 May Boat Service 1810 | (1 May 1810) | 221. 29 Sept. Boat Service 1812 | (29 September 1812) |
| 208. 28 June Boat Service 1810 | (29 June 1810) | 222. 6 Jan. Boat Service 1813 | (6 January 1813) |
| 209. 27 Sep: Boat Service 1810 | (27 September 1810) | 223. 21 March Boat Service 1813 | (21 March 1813) |
| 210. 4 Novr Boat Service 1810 | (4 November 1810) | 224. 29 April Boat Service 1813 | (28 April 1813) |
| 211. 23 Novr Boat Service 1810 | (23 November 1810) | 225. Ap. & May Boat Service 1813 | (29 April & 3 May 1813) |
| 212. 24 Dec. Boat Service 1810 | (24 December 1810) | 226. May 2 Boat Service 1813 | (2 May 1813) |
| 213. 4 May Boat Service 1811 | (5 May 1811) | 227. 8 April Boat Service 1814 | (8 April 1814) |
| 214. 30 July Boat Service 1811 | (30 July 1811) | 228. 24 May Boat Service 1814 | (25 May 1814) |
| 215. 2 Aug. Boat Service 1811 | (3 August 1811) | 229. 3 & 6 Sept. Boat Service 1814 | (3 & 6 September 1814) |
| 216. 20 Sept. Boat Service 1811 | (21 September 1811) | 230. 14 Dec. Boat Service 1814 | (14 December 1814) |
| 217. 4 Dec. Boat Service 1811 | (4 December 1811) | | |

# Index

356